Basic and Clinical Science Course
Section 1

Update on
General Medicine

1998-1999

LEO

LIFELONG

EDUCATION FOR THE

OPHTHALMOLOGIST

American Academy of Ophthalmology

The Basic and Clinical Science Course is one component of the Lifelong Education for the Ophthalmologist (LEO) framework, which assists members in planning their continuing medical education. LEO includes an array of clinical education products that members may select to form individualized, self-directed learning plans for updating their clinical knowledge. Active members or fellows who use LEO components may accumulate sufficient CME credits to earn the LEO Award. Contact the Academy's Clinical Education Division for further information on LEO.

This CME activity was planned and produced in accordance with the ACCME Essentials.

The Academy provides this material for educational purposes only. It is not intended to represent the only or best method or procedure in every case, nor to replace a physician's own judgment or give specific advice for case management. Including all indications, contraindications, side effects, and alternative agents for each drug or treatment is beyond the scope of this material. All information and recommendations should be verified, prior to use, with current information included in the manufacturers' package inserts or other independent sources, and considered in light of the patient's condition and history. Reference to certain drugs, instruments, and other products in this publication is made for illustrative purposes only and is not intended to constitute an endorsement of such. Some material may include information on applications that are not considered community standard, that reflect indications not included in approved FDA labeling, or that are approved for use only in restricted research settings. The FDA has stated that it is the responsibility of the physician to determine the FDA status of each drug or device he or she wishes to use, and to use them with appropriate patient consent in compliance with applicable law. The Academy specifically disclaims any and all liability for injury or other damages of any kind, from negligence or otherwise, for any and all claims that may arise from the use of any recommendations or other information contained herein.

Basic and Clinical Science Course

Thomas A. Weingeist, PhD, MD, Iowa City, Iowa
Senior Secretary for Clinical Education

Thomas J. Liesegang, MD, Jacksonville, Florida
Secretary for Instruction

M. Gilbert Grand, MD, St. Louis, Missouri
BCSC Course Chair

Section 1

Faculty Responsible for This Edition

William G. Tsiaras, MD, *Chair,* Providence, Rhode Island

Emily Y. Chew, MD, Bethesda, Maryland

Andrew W. Danyluk, MD, Pittsfield, Massachusetts

Eric P. Purdy, MD, Fort Wayne, Indiana

Mitchell B. Stein, MD, Mount Kisco, New York

Daniel T. Weaver, MD, Billings, Montana

Marilyn C. Kay, MD, Milwaukee, Wisconsin
Practicing Ophthalmologists Advisory Committee for Education

Each author states that he or she has no significant financial interest or other relationship with the manufacturer of any commercial product discussed in the chapters that he or she contributed to this publication or with the manufacturer of any competing commercial product.

Recent Past Faculty

John D. Bullock, MD

Barry N. Hyman, MD

Edward K. Isbey, Jr, MD

Douglas A. Jabs, MD

Lee M. Jampol, MD

Jeffrey H. Levenson, MD

Travis A. Meredith, MD

James E. Puklin, MD

Brian Younge, MD

In addition, the Academy gratefully acknowledges the contributions of numerous past faculty and advisory committee members who have played an important role in the development of previous editions of the Basic and Clinical Science Course.

American Academy of Ophthalmology Staff

Kathryn A. Hecht, EdD
Vice President, Clinical Education

Hal Straus
Director, Publications Department

Margaret Denny
Managing Editor

Fran Taylor
Medical Editor

Maxine Garrett
Administrative Coordinator

American Academy of Ophthalmology
655 Beach Street
Box 7424
San Francisco, CA 94120-7424

TABLE OF CONTENTS

GENERAL INTRODUCTION

The Basic and Clinical Science Course (BCSC) is designed to provide residents and practitioners with a comprehensive yet concise curriculum of the field of ophthalmology. The BCSC has developed from its original brief outline format, which relied heavily on outside readings, to a more convenient and educationally useful self-contained text. The Academy regularly updates and revises the course, with the goals of integrating the basic science and clinical practice of ophthalmology and of keeping current with new developments in the various subspecialties.

The BCSC incorporates the effort and expertise of more than 70 ophthalmologists, organized into 12 section faculties, working with Academy editorial staff. In addition, the course continues to benefit from many lasting contributions made by the faculties of previous editions. Members of the Academy's Practicing Ophthalmologists Advisory Committee for Education serve on each faculty and, as a group, review every volume before and after major revisions.

Organization of the Course

The 12 sections of the Basic and Clinical Science Course are numbered as follows to reflect a logical order of study, proceeding from fundamental subjects to anatomic subdivisions:

1. Update on General Medicine
2. Fundamentals and Principles of Ophthalmology
3. Optics, Refraction, and Contact Lenses
4. Ophthalmic Pathology and Intraocular Tumors
5. Neuro-Ophthalmology
6. Pediatric Ophthalmology and Strabismus
7. Orbit, Eyelids, and Lacrimal System
8. External Disease and Cornea
9. Intraocular Inflammation and Uveitis
10. Glaucoma
11. Lens and Cataract
12. Retina and Vitreous

In addition, a comprehensive Master Index allows the reader to easily locate subjects throughout the entire series.

References

Readers who wish to explore specific topics in greater detail may consult the journal references cited within each chapter and the Basic Texts listed at the back of the book. These references are intended to be selective rather than exhaustive, chosen by the BCSC faculty as being important, current, and readily available to residents and practitioners.

Related Academy educational materials are also listed in the appropriate sections. They include books, audiovisual materials, self-assessment programs, clinical modules, and interactive programs.

Study Questions and CME Credit

Each volume includes multiple-choice study questions designed to be used as a closed-book exercise. The answers are accompanied by explanations to enhance the learning experience. Completing the study questions allows readers both to test their understanding of the material and to demonstrate section completion for the purpose of CME credit, if desired.

The Academy is accredited by the Accreditation Council for Continuing Medical Education to sponsor continuing medical education for physicians. CME credit hours in Category 1 of the Physician's Recognition Award of the AMA may be earned for completing the study of any section of the BCSC. The Academy designates the number of credit hours for each section based upon the scope and complexity of the material covered (see the Credit Reporting Form in each individual section for the maximum number of hours that may be claimed).

Based upon return of the Credit Reporting Form at the back of each book, the Academy will maintain a record, for up to 3 years, of credits earned by Academy members. Upon request, the Academy will send a transcript of credits earned.

Conclusion

The Basic and Clinical Science Course has expanded greatly over the years, with the addition of much new text and numerous illustrations. Recent editions have sought to place a greater emphasis on clinical applicability, while maintaining a solid foundation in basic science. As with any educational program, it reflects the experience of its authors. As its faculties change and as medicine progresses, new viewpoints are always emerging on controversial subjects and techniques. Not all alternate approaches can be included in this series; as with any educational endeavor, the learner should seek additional sources, including such carefully balanced opinions as the Academy's Preferred Practice Patterns.

The BCSC faculty and staff are continuously striving to improve the educational usefulness of the course; you, the reader, can contribute to this ongoing process. If you have any suggestions or questions about the series, please do not hesitate to contact the faculty or the managing editor.

The authors, editors, and reviewers hope that your study of the BCSC will be of lasting value and that each section will serve as a practical resource for quality patient care.

OBJECTIVES FOR BCSC SECTION 1

Upon completion of BCSC Section 1, the reader should be able to:

- Describe the ophthalmic manifestations of the major systemic diseases covered in this volume

- Summarize the most common human pathogens and their manifestations

- Review the newer antiviral, antifungal, and antibacterial agents and their benefits

- Classify levels of hypertension by blood pressure measurements

- List the major classes of antihypertensive medications and some of their characteristics and side effects

- Describe the various diagnostic procedures used in the evaluation of patients with coronary artery disease

- Review the current treatment options for atrial fibrillation, atrial flutter, and ventricular tachycardia

- Discuss the indications for dietary and pharmacologic treatment of hypercholesterolemia

- Distinguish between obstructive and restrictive, reversible and irreversible, pulmonary diseases and give examples of each type

- Describe the classification, pathophysiology, presentation, and diagnostic criteria for diabetes mellitus

- Review the various therapeutic approaches for diabetes mellitus, including new insulins and oral agents

- List the most prevalent types of cancer for men and for women together with the appropriate screening methods for detecting them

- Review current concepts about the etiologies of most malignancies

- Describe both the traditional and more novel approaches to the treatment of cancers

- Summarize the major behavioral disorders and possible therapeutic modalities for these conditions (including the ocular side effects of psychoactive medications)

- List some of the factors associated with a patient's compliance or noncompliance with medical regimens

- Explain the rationale for and value of screening programs for various systemic diseases

- Summarize the major disease processes affecting most of the adult populations and how preventive measures may reduce the morbidity and mortality they cause

- Identify the different types of epidemiologic studies and the appropriateness of each for a particular research question

- [ ] Assess medical literature more critically in regard to appropriate study design and validity of conclusions

- [ ] Explain the importance of the randomized, controlled clinical study in evaluating the effects of new treatments

- [ ] Differentiate between statistically significant results from observational studies and cause and effect

INTRODUCTION TO SECTION 1

For many patients, the ophthalmologist may be their initial or most frequent contact with a physician. In addition, many systemic diseases—and the drugs used to treat them—have significant ocular manifestations. For these reasons, ophthalmologists must be aware of the general medical concerns of their patients.

Only by keeping current with the larger world of general medicine can ophthalmologists maintain their standing as physicians rather than as focused technicians. Ocular manifestations of systemic diseases, as well as the systemic interactions of ocular therapeutics, form the basis of the ophthalmologist's relationship with fellow physicians.

The authors hope that this book will provide both the resident and the ophthalmologist with current information on the medical conditions that may affect their practice and, most important, their patients.

PART 1

SYSTEMIC DISEASE

CHAPTER I

Infectious Disease

Recent Developments

□ Vancomycin-resistant strains of enterococci have emerged in recent years as a cause of life-threatening infection in hospitalized patients.

□ DNA probes using polymerase chain reaction provide new, more sensitive diagnostic tools for the detection of gonorrhea, syphilis, Lyme disease, and infections caused by *Chlamydia*, mycobacteria, and many viruses.

□ Newer nucleoside analogues and protease inhibitors provide potent drug combinations that are improving survival in HIV-infected patients.

□ Cidofovir and fomivirsen join ganciclovir and foscarnet in the pharmacologic treatment of CMV retinitis.

□ New antibiotics, such as meropenem, cefepime, and sparfloxacin provide expanded antimicrobial coverage.

General Microbiology

Despite formidable immune and mechanical defense systems, we harbor an extensive, well-adapted population of microorganisms on the skin and in the gastrointestinal, vaginal, and upper respiratory tracts. The organisms maintain their foothold on these epithelial surfaces chiefly by adherence, and they indirectly benefit the host by excluding pathogenic bacterial colonization and by priming the immune system. If antimicrobial agents alter this host-microbial interplay by eliminating the normal flora, the host's susceptibility to normally excluded pathogenic microorganisms is increased. When the mechanical defenses of the epithelial layers are breached so as to expose normally sterile areas, or if a critical component of the immune system that normally prevents microbial invasion has a congenital or acquired failure, then severe infections can result from the normal microbial flora.

However, even when both the mechanical and immune defense systems are intact, pathogenic microbes can invade and cause infections by means of specific virulent characteristics, which allow the microbes to invade and multiply. Although these virulent traits vary among different species, several mechanisms of virulence are listed below for illustration.

□ *Attachment. Neisseria gonorrhoeae* and *Neisseria meningitidis* breach epithelial barriers by adhering to host epithelial cell surface receptors by means of a ligand located on the bacteria's pili. The presence of the cell surface receptors is genetically determined.

- *Polysaccharide encapsulation. Diplococcus pneumoniae, Neisseria meningitidis, Haemophilus,* and *Bacteroides* evade phagocytosis in the absence of antibody and complement because of their polysaccharide coating.
- *Blocking lysosomal fusion.* Intracellular existence, as well as protection from humoral immune mechanisms, is a characteristic of *Chlamydia, Toxoplasma, Legionella,* and *Mycobacterium.*
- *Antigenic surface variation.* Antigenic shifts in the cell wall of *Borrelia recurrentis* incapacitate the humoral immune system, which has a lag time in antibody production. Similar antigenic shifts are found in *Chlamydia* and influenza viruses.
- *IgA protease. Haemophilus influenzae, Neisseria gonorrhoeae,* and *Neisseria meningitidis* eliminate the IgA antibody normally found on mucosal surfaces, which would otherwise prevent the microbes' adherence.
- *Endotoxin.* A normal constituent of the gram-negative bacterial cell wall, endotoxin produces dramatic systemic physiologic responses ranging from fever and leukocyte margination to disseminated intravascular coagulation and septic shock.
- *Exotoxin.* This is a diverse set of proteins with specific actions on target tissues, which can cause severe systemic effects in such diseases as cholera or tetanus.

The immune system, which makes possible the host's adaptive response to colonization and infection, is classically divided into the humoral and cellular immune systems. The *humoral immune system,* composed of cells derived from the B-lymphocyte series, is responsible for antibody-mediated opsonization, complement-mediated bacterial killing, antitoxin, and mediation of intracellular infections. The *cellular immune system,* determined by the T lymphocytes, is responsible for interaction and stimulation of the humoral immune system, direct cytotoxicity, release of chemical messengers, and control of chronic infections. The successful interplay between the humoral and cellular immune systems mitigates and usually eradicates the infection, allowing for repair and healing.

Staphylococcus

Staphylococcus aureus colonizes the anterior nares and other skin sites in 15% of community isolates. Ten percent of the tertiary-care hospital isolates are resistant to all beta-lactam antibiotics. Transmission of organisms is usually by direct contact. Resistance of organisms to antimicrobials is usually plasmid determined and is institutionally variable. The increasing prevalence of methicillin-resistant *S aureus* in tertiary referral hospitals appears to be related to their population of high-risk patients. The natural history of staphylococcal infections indicates that immunity is of short duration and incomplete. Delayed hypersensitivity reactions to staphylococcal products may be responsible for chronic staphylococcal disease.

Conditions caused by staphylococcal infections include stye, furuncle, acne, bullous impetigo, paronychia, osteomyelitis, septic arthritis, deep-tissue abscesses, bacteremia, endocarditis, enterocolitis, pneumonia, wound infections, scalded skin syndrome, toxic shock syndrome, and food poisoning.

Acute serious staphylococcal infections require immediate intravenous antibiotic therapy. A penicillinase-resistant penicillin or first-generation cephalosporin would normally be used, pending the results of susceptibility tests. With the emergence of methicillin-resistant staphylococci, vancomycin has become the drug of choice in life-threatening infections, pending susceptibility studies. Because of increasing reports of vancomycin-resistant enterococci, there are concerns about the possibility of future cases of vancomycin-resistant *S aureus* infection, mediated through plasmid transfer.

Staphylococcus epidermidis is an almost universal inhabitant of the skin, present in up to 90% of skin cultures. It can cause infection when local defenses are compromised. Its characteristic adherence to prosthetic devices makes it the most common cause of prosthetic heart valve infections, and it is a common infectious organism of intravenous catheters and cerebrospinal fluid shunts.

Most isolates are resistant to methicillin and cephalosporin; therefore, the drug of choice is vancomycin, occasionally in combination with rifampin or gentamicin. In addition to antibiotic therapy, management often involves removal of the implanted prosthetic device.

Edmond MB, Wenzel RP, Pasculle AW. Vancomycin-resistant *Staphylococcus aureus:* perspectives on measures needed for control. *Ann Intern Med.* 1996;124:329–334.

Hamory BH, Parisi JT, Hutton JP. *Staphylococcus epidermidis:* a significant nosocomial pathogen. *Am J Infect Control.* 1987;15:59–74.

Streptococcus

Group A beta-hemolytic streptococci *(Streptococcus pyogenes)* cause a variety of acute suppurative infections through droplet transmission. The infection is modulated by an opsonizing antibody, which provides a type-specific immunity that lasts for years directed against the protein in the cell wall pili. The range of suppurative streptococcal infections in humans includes pharyngitis, impetigo, pneumonia, erysipelas, wound and burn infections, puerperal infections, and scarlet fever. Genetically mediated humoral and cellular response to certain strains of group A streptococci play a role in the development of the postinfectious syndromes of glomerulonephritis and rheumatic fever, both of which represent delayed, nonsuppurative, noninfectious complications of group A streptococcal infections.

Streptococcus pyogenes remains highly susceptible to penicillin G; however, in the presence of allergy, erythromycin or cephalosporin (if no cross-allergy exists) is substituted. Penicillin prophylaxis against rheumatic fever recurrences is administered for procedures that may result in transient bacteremia; it may not prevent the development of acute glomerulonephritis.

Streptococcus pneumoniae are lancet-shaped diplococci that cause alpha-hemolysis on blood agar. Though 10%–30% of the normal population carries one or more serologic types of pneumococci in their throats, the incidence and mortality of pneumococcal pneumonia increases sharply after age 50, with a fatality rate approaching 25%. Pneumococcal virulence is determined by its complex polysaccharide capsule, of which there are more than 80 distinctive serotypes. The polysaccharide capsule inhibits macrophage engulfment of the organism. Infection is modulated by the development of anticapsular antibodies after 5–7 days; these antibodies allow phagocytosis of the organism by polymorphonuclear leukocytes.

Conditions caused by *S pneumoniae* include pneumonia, sinusitis, meningitis, otitis media, and peritonitis. Pneumococci are usually highly susceptible to penicillin, other beta lactams, or erythromycin. Routine susceptibility testing should be performed on patients with meningitis, bacteremia, or other life-threatening infections. Penicillin-resistant strains of *S pneumoniae* have been reported with increasing frequency in recent years. In many regions, over 25% of isolates are penicillin resistant, and many of these are also resistant to cephalosporins and macrolides. Prophylaxis is available through use of the 23-valent vaccine (see p 223).

Alpha-hemolytic streptococcus and staphylococcus cause the majority of cases of subacute bacterial endocarditis (SBE). Patients with prosthetic cardiac valves and most congenital or acquired cardiac structural or valvular defects should receive SBE prophylaxis whenever they undergo invasive procedures involving the oral, nasopharyngeal, respiratory, gastrointestinal, or genitourinary regions. SBE prophylaxis is usually not considered necessary for routine ocular surgery in an uninfected patient but should be provided for surgery involving the nasolacrimal drainage system or sinuses (see Tables I-1 through I-4).

Dajani AS, Taubert KA, Wilson W, et al. Prevention of bacterial endocarditis. Recommendations by the American Heart Association. *JAMA*. 1997;277:1794–1801.

TABLE I-1

CARDIAC CONDITIONS ASSOCIATED WITH ENDOCARDITIS

Endocarditis Prophylaxis Recommended

High-risk category
    Prosthetic cardiac valves, including bioprosthetic and homograft valves
    Previous bacterial endocarditis
    Complex cyanotic congenital heart disease (eg, single ventricle states, transposition of the great arteries, tetralogy of Fallot)
    Surgically constructed systemic pulmonary shunts or conduits
Moderate-risk category
    Most other congenital cardiac malformations (other than above and below)
    Acquired valvar dysfunction (eg, rheumatic heart disease)
    Hypertrophic cardiomyopathy
    Mitral valve prolapse with valvar regurgitation and/or thickened leaflets

---

Endocarditis Prophylaxis Not Recommended

Negligible-risk category (no greater risk than the general population)
    Isolated secundum atrial septal defect
    Surgical repair of atrial septal defect, ventricular septal defect, or patent ductus arteriosus (without residua beyond 6 mo)
    Previous coronary artery bypass graft surgery
    Mitral valve prolapse without valvar regurgitation
    Physiologic, functional, or innocent heart murmurs
    Previous Kawasaki disease without valvar dysfunction
    Previous rheumatic fever without valvar dysfunction
    Cardiac pacemakers (intravascular and epicardial) and implanted defibrillators

---

(Reprinted from Dajani AS, Taubert KA, Wilson W, et al. Prevention of bacterial endocarditis. Recommendations by the American Heart Association. *JAMA*. 1997;277:1795. ©American Medical Association.)

TABLE I-2

SURGICAL PROCEDURES AND ENDOCARDITIS PROPHYLAXIS

Endocarditis Prophylaxis Recommended

Respiratory tract
> Tonsillectomy and/or adenoidectomy
> Surgical operations that involve respiratory mucosa
> Bronchoscopy with a rigid bronchoscope

*Gastrointestinal tract**
> Sclerotherapy for esophageal varices
> Esophageal stricture dilation
> Endoscopic retrograde cholangiography with biliary obstruction
> Biliary tract surgery
> Surgical operations that involve intestinal mucosa

Genitourinary tract
> Prostatic surgery
> Cystoscopy
> Urethral dilation

Endocarditis Prophylaxis Not Recommended

Respiratory tract
> Endotracheal intubation
> Bronchoscopy with a flexible bronchoscope, with or without biopsy†
> Tympanostomy tube insertion

Gastrointestinal tract
> Transesophageal echocardiography†
> Endoscopy with or without gastrointestinal biopsy†

Genitourinary tract
> Vaginal hysterectomy†
> Vaginal delivery†
> Cesarean section
> In uninfected tissue:
>> Urethral catheterization
>> Uterine dilatation and curettage
>> Therapeutic abortion
>> Sterilization procedures
>> Insertion or removal of intrauterine devices

Other
> Cardiac catheterization, including balloon angioplasty
> Implanted cardiac pacemakers, implanted defibrillators, and coronary stents
> Incision or biopsy of surgically scrubbed skin
> Circumcision

*Prophylaxis is recommended for high-risk patients; optional for medium-risk patients.

†Prophylaxis is optional for high-risk patients.

(Reprinted from Dajani AS, Taubert KA, Wilson W, et al. Prevention of bacterial endocarditis. Recommendations by the American Heart Association. *JAMA*. 1997;277:1797. ©American Medical Association.)

TABLE I-3

PROPHYLACTIC REGIMENS FOR DENTAL, ORAL, RESPIRATORY TRACT, OR ESOPHAGEAL PROCEDURES

SITUATION	AGENT	REGIMEN*
Standard general prophylaxis	Amoxicillin	Adults: 2.0 g; children: 50 mg/kg orally 1 h before procedure
Unable to take oral medications	Ampicillin	Adults: 2.0 g intramuscularly (IM) or intravenously (IV); children: 50 mg/kg IM or IV within 30 min before procedure
Allergic to penicillin	Clindamycin or	Adults: 600 mg; children: 20 mg/kg orally 1 h before procedure
	Cephalexin† or cefadroxil† or	Adults: 2.0 g; children: 50 mg/kg orally 1 h before procedure
	Azithromycin or clarithromycin	Adults: 500 mg; children: 15 mg/kg orally 1 h before procedure
Allergic to penicillin and unable to take oral medications	Clindamycin or	Adults: 600 mg; children: 20 mg/kg IV within 30 min before procedure
	Cefazolin†	Adults: 1.0 g; children: 25 mg/kg IM or IV within 30 min before procedure

* Total children's dose should not exceed adult dose.

† Cephalosporins should not be used in individuals with immediate-type hypersensitivity reaction (urticaria, angioedema, or anaphylaxis) to penicillins.

(Reprinted from Dajani AS, Taubert KA, Wilson W, et al. Prevention of bacterial endocarditis. Recommendations by the American Heart Association. *JAMA*. 1997;277:1798. ©American Medical Association.)

Clostridium Difficile

Clostridium difficile is an endemic anaerobic gram-positive bacillus that is part of the normal gastrointestinal flora. It has acquired importance because of its role in the development of pseudomembranous enterocolitis following the use of antibiotics. Typically, within 1–14 days of starting antibiotic therapy, patients develop fever and diarrhea. The diarrhea occasionally becomes bloody and typically contains a cytopathic toxin that is elaborated by *C difficile*. At present, a tissue-culture assay for the toxin is the best diagnostic test. The most frequently associated antibiotics include clindamycin, ampicillin, chloramphenicol, tetracycline, erythromycin, and the cephalosporins. The treatment of choice has been discontinuing the associated antibiotic and administering oral vancomycin for 7 days. Recently, oral metronidazole has been suggested as an alternative treatment of choice because of its efficacy and its much lower cost compared to vancomycin.

TABLE I-4

PROPHYLACTIC REGIMENS FOR GENITOURINARY AND GASTROINTESTINAL PROCEDURES

SITUATION	AGENTS*	REGIMEN†
High-risk patients	Amoxicillin plus gentamicin	Adults: ampicillin 2.0 g intramuscularly (IM) or intravenously (IV) plus gentamicin 1.5 mg/kg (not to exceed 120 mg) within 30 min of starting the procedure; 6 h later, ampicillin 1 g IM/IV or amoxicillin 1 g orally
		Children: ampicillin 50 mg/kg IM or IV (not to exceed 2.0 g) plus gentamicin 1.5 mg/kg within 30 min of starting the procedure; 6 h later, ampicillin 25 mg/kg IM/IV or amoxicillin 25 mg/kg orally
High-risk patients allergic to ampicillin/amoxicillin	Vancomycin plus gentamicin	Adults: vancomycin 1.0 g IV over 1–2 h plus gentamicin 1.5 mg/kg IV/IM (not to exceed 120 mg); complete injection/ infusion within 30 min of starting the procedure
		Children: vancomycin 20 mg/kg IV over 1–2 h plus gentamicin 1.5 mg/kg IV/IM; complete injection/infusion within 30 min of starting the procedure
Moderate-risk patients	Amoxicillin or ampicillin	Adults: amoxicillin 2.0 g orally 1 h before procedure, or ampicillin 2.0 g IM/IV within 30 min of starting the procedure
		Children: amoxicillin 50 mg/kg orally 1 h before procedure, or ampicillin 50 mg/kg IM/IV within 30 min of starting the procedure
Moderate-risk patients allergic to ampicillin/ amoxicillin	Vancomycin	Adults: vancomycin 1.0 g IV over 1–2 h; complete infusion within 30 min of starting the procedure
		Children: vancomycin 20 mg/kg IV over 1–2 h; complete infusion within 30 min of starting the procedure

*Total children's dose should not exceed adult dose.

†No second dose of vancomycin or gentamicin is recommended.

(Reprinted from Dajani AS, Taubert KA, Wilson W, et al. Prevention of bacterial endocarditis. Recommendations by the American Heart Association. *JAMA.* 1997;277:1799. ©American Medical Association.)

Haemophilus Influenzae

Haemophilus influenzae is a common inhabitant of the upper respiratory tract in 20%–50% of healthy adults and 80% of children. *Haemophilus influenzae* is divided into six serotypes, based on differing capsular polysaccharide antigens. Both encapsulated and unencapsulated species cause disease, but systemic spread is typical of the encapsulated strain, whose capsule protects it against phagocytosis. The exact mechanism of invasion is unknown, but an acute suppurative response results, with eventual humoral immunologic modulation of the infection. Long-term immunity follows with the development of bactericidal antibodies to the type B capsule in the presence of complement. Infants are usually protected for a few months by passively acquired maternal antibodies; thereafter, active antibody levels increase with age, being inversely related to the risk of infection. During their first 5 years, about 0.5% of children become infected, with 60% of the infections as meningitis, which carries less than 5% mortality rate with appropriate management. Of the patients with meningitis, roughly 14% develop significant neurologic damage. Other infections include epiglottitis, orbital cellulitis, arthritis, otitis media, bronchitis, pericarditis, sinusitis, and pneumonia.

Treatment of acute infections has been complicated by the emergence of ampicillin-resistant strains, with an incidence approaching 50% in some geographic areas. Current recommendations are to start empiric therapy with amoxicillin trihydrate–clavulanate potassium (Augmentin), trimethoprim-sulfamethoxazole (Bactrim, TMP-SMZ), or a third-generation cephalosporin, pending susceptibility testing of the organism. Serious or life-threatening infections should be treated with an intravenous third-generation cephalosporin with known activity against *H influenzae,* such as ceftriaxone or cefotaxime, while awaiting results of sensitivity testing. Recent reports note an increase of isolates with reduced sensitivity to cephalosporins, especially in patients with chronic pulmonary disease.

The U.S. Food and Drug Administration has approved two *Haemophilus influenzae* type B (Hib) conjugate vaccines for use in infants. Both have demonstrated their effectiveness in protecting infants and older children against meningitis and other invasive diseases caused by *H influenzae* type B. In studies of fully immunized populations, *H influenzae* infection has been nearly eradicated since introduction of the Hib vaccines.

Vadheim CM, Greenberg DP, Eriksen E, et al. Eradication of *Haemophilus influenzae* type b disease in southern California. Kaiser-UCLA Vaccine Study Group. *Arch Pediatr Adolesc Med.* 1994;148:51–56.

Neisseria

Most of the *Neisseria* are normal inhabitants of the upper respiratory and alimentary tracts; however, the commonly recognized pathogenic species are the meningococci and the gonococci.

Meningococci can be cultured in up to 15% of healthy individuals in nonepidemic periods. Virulence is determined by the polysaccharide capsule and the potent endotoxic activity of the cell wall, which can cause cardiovascular collapse, shock, and disseminated intravascular coagulation. Resolution of the infection is related to circulating group-specific opsonizing antibodies and complement. Complement-deficient or asplenic individuals are at risk for clinical infection. Prolonged immunity is usually acquired through a subclinical or carrier state and becomes more prevalent with increasing age.

The range of infections includes meningitis; mild to severe upper respiratory infections; and less often, endocarditis, arthritis, pericarditis, and endophthalmitis. A less common infection is chronic meningococcemia, characterized by fever, headache, rash, and arthralgia over a period of days to weeks. This occurs sporadically, with the rare development of localized infections. Chronic meningococcemia represents an altered host-organism relationship that is poorly understood. Meningitis with a petechial or puerperal exanthem is the classic presentation, although each may occur in isolation.

The treatment of choice for meningococcal meningitis is high-dose penicillin or, in the case of allergy, chloramphenicol or a third-generation cephalosporin. Rifampin or minocycline is used as chemoprophylaxis for family members or intimate personal contacts of the infected individual. Polysaccharide vaccines for groups A, C, Y, and W-135 strains have been developed and are most effective in older children and adults. The routine administration of meningococcal vaccines is not recommended except in patients who have undergone splenectomy, complement-deficient individuals, military personnel, travelers to endemic regions, and close contacts of infected patients.

Gonococci are not normal inhabitants of the respiratory or genital flora, and their major reservoir is the asymptomatic patient. Among infected women, 50% are asymptomatic, whereas 95% of infected men have symptoms. Asymptomatic patients are infectious for several months, with a transmissibility rate of 20%–50%. Nonsexual transmission is rare. The key to prevention is identification and treatment of asymptomatic carriers and their sexual contacts. Symptomatic infection is characterized by a purulent response, with systemic manifestations of endotoxemia only in the bacteremic phase of the disease. Immunity to gonococcal infection is poorly understood, and repeated infections are common. *Chlamydia trachomatis* coexists with gonorrhea in 25%–50% of women with endocervical gonorrhea and 20%–33% of men with gonococcal urethritis. Diagnosis of gonococcal infections, as well as infections caused by many other bacteria, mycobacteria, viruses, and mycoplasma, has been enhanced with the recent development of highly sensitive DNA probes that utilize DNA amplification through polymerase chain reaction (PCR) techniques.

The range of gonococcal infections includes cervicitis, urethritis, pelvic inflammatory disease, pharyngitis, conjunctivitis, ophthalmia neonatorum, and disseminated gonococcal disease with fever, polyarthralgias, and rash.

Because penicillin- and tetracycline-resistant gonococcal strains have become common in many areas of the United States, treatment should be modified by their local prevalence. Most of the original resistant isolates have been traced abroad, where there is a very high incidence of penicillinase-producing strains. Tetracycline is effective for susceptible strains, penicillin-allergic individuals, or for concurrent chlamydial infections. Ceftriaxone (via intramuscular injection) is a drug of choice for penicillinase-resistant strains. Other alternatives include oral cefixime; cefuroxime; azithromycin (a newer macrolide); and the quinolones ciprofloxacin, ofloxacin, and sparfloxacin. These drugs are so effective against gonococci that single oral dose therapy has become a recommended treatment protocol. The macrolides and quinolones have the added benefit of excellent activity against concomitant *Chlamydia trachomatis* infection. Not surprisingly, the emergence of gonococcal isolates with reduced sensitivity to quinolones has been reported.

Moran JS, Levine WC. Drugs of choice for the treatment of uncomplicated gonococcal infections. *Clin Infect Dis.* 1995;20(suppl1):S47–65.

Pseudomonas Aeruginosa

Pseudomonas aeruginosa is a gram-negative bacillus found free living in moist environments. Together with *Serratia marcescens,* it is one of the two most consistently antimicrobial-resistant pathogenic bacteria. Infection usually requires either a break in the first-line defenses or altered immunity resulting in a local pyogenic response. Its virulence is related to extracellular toxins, endotoxin, and a polysaccharide protection from phagocytosis. Systemic spread can result in disseminated intravascular coagulation, shock, and death. Humoral immune production of antitoxin is correlated with improved survival in bacteremic patients; however, eradication of infection is probably a multifactorial immune process.

Usual sites of infection include the respiratory system, skin, eye, urinary tract, bone, and wounds. Systemic infections caused by a resistant organism carry a high mortality and are usually associated with depressed immunity, often in a hospital setting.

Treatment of serious infections relies on combined antimicrobial coverage with either a semisynthetic penicillin or a third-generation cephalosporin with an aminoglycoside. Ceftazidime has been the most effective cephalosporin for pseudomonal infections. Initial choice of antimicrobials is dependent upon local susceptibility prevalence and should be guided by susceptibility testing. The use of vaccines incorporating multiple *Pseudomonas aeruginosa* serotypes is under investigation for use in patients with severe burns, cystic fibrosis, or immunosuppression. Oral ciprofloxacin has also been useful as a prophylactic agent in patients with cystic fibrosis.

Treponema Pallidum (Syphilis)

The spirochete *Treponema pallidum* is exclusively a human pathogen. It dies rapidly on drying and is readily killed by a wide variety of disinfectant agents and soaps. After a low of 6000 cases in 1956, the number of cases reported annually has risen to about 25,000 per year in the U.S. Infection usually follows direct sexual contact. Less commonly, infection occurs following nongenital contact with an infected lesion or accidental inoculation with infected material. Transplacental transmission from an untreated pregnant woman to her fetus before 16-weeks' gestation results in *congenital syphilis.*

Stages

Initial inoculation occurs through intact mucous membranes or abraded skin and, within 6 weeks, results in a broad, ulcerated, painless papule called a *chancre.* The chancre is infiltrated with lymphocytes, plasma cells, histiocytes, and spirochetes, which readily enter the lymphatic system and bloodstream. The ulcer heals spontaneously, and signs of dissemination appear after a variable quiescent period of several weeks to months.

The secondary stage is heralded by fever, malaise, adenopathy, and patchy loss of hair. Meningitis, uveitis, optic neuritis, and hepatitis occur less frequently. Maculopapular lesions may develop into wartlike condylomata in moist areas, and oral mucosal patches are sometimes seen, all of which are highly infectious. The secondary lesions usually resolve in 2–6 weeks, although up to 25% of individuals may relapse in the first 2–4 years. Without treatment, these individuals enter the latent stage of disease.

Latent syphilis, characterized by positive serologic tests without clinical signs, is divided into two stages. The *early latent stage* is within 1 year of infection. During this time, the disease is potentially transmissible because relapses associated with spirochetemia are possible. The *late latent stage* is associated with immunity to relapse and resistance to infectious lesions.

Tertiary manifestations can occur from 2 to 20 years after infection, and one third of untreated individuals with latent disease will progress to this stage. The remaining two thirds will either have subclinical disease or a spontaneous cure. *Tertiary disease* is characterized by destructive granulomatous lesions with a typical endarteritis that can affect the skin, bone, joints, oral and nasal cavities, parenchymal organs, cardiovascular system, eye, meninges, and central nervous system. Few spirochetes are found in lesions outside the CNS.

Immune mechanisms modulating syphilitic infection can contribute to the manifestations of the later stages of the disease. High titers of treponemal and nontreponemal antibodies are present throughout the secondary stage, conferring immunity to reinfection. The manifestations of the tertiary stage are those of a cellular response; however, the paucity of organisms suggests a delayed hypersensitivity to the spirochete products or an autoimmune-type reaction. Pathologically, obliterative endarteritis with a perivascular infiltrate of lymphocytes, monocytes, and plasma cells is a feature of all active stages of syphilis. Gummas of tertiary syphilis are evidenced by a central area of caseating necrosis with a surrounding granulomatous response.

Diagnosis

Most cases of syphilis are diagnosed serologically. *Nontreponemal tests* such as the VDRL (Venereal Disease Research Laboratory) or RPR (rapid plasma reagin) depend upon the patient's nontreponemal serum antibodies causing immune flocculation of cardiolipin in the presence of lecithin and cholesterol. Nontreponemal tests are usually positive during the early stages of the primary lesion, uniformly positive during the secondary stage, and progressively nonreactive in the later stages. In neurosyphilis, the serum VDRL may be negative while the cerebrospinal fluid VDRL may be positive. These patients require careful evaluation and aggressive treatment with close follow-up. Nontreponemal tests become negative in a predictable fashion after successful therapy and can be used to assess the efficacy of treatment. False-positive results to nontreponemal tests occur in a variety of autoimmune diseases, especially systemic lupus erythematosus. False-positive results can also occur in diseases with a substantial amount of tissue destruction, liver disease, pregnancy, or infections caused by other treponemae.

The *fluorescent treponemal antibody absorption test (FTA-ABS)* involves specific detection of antibody to *Treponema pallidum* after the patient's serum is treated with nonpathogenic treponemal antigens to avoid nonspecific reactions. Hemagglutination tests specific for treponemal antibodies also have high sensitivity and specificity for detecting syphilis. They include the hemagglutination treponemal test for syphilis (HATTS), the *T pallidum* hemagglutination assay (TPHA), and the microhemagglutination test for *T pallidum* (MHA-TP). Treponemal antibody detection tests are more specific than nontreponemal tests, but the titers do not decrease with successful treatment and should thus be considered as confirmatory tests, especially in later stages of disease (see Table I-5).

False-positive results to treponemal tests are found in 15% of patients with systemic lupus erythematosus, in patients with other treponemal infections or Lyme disease, and rarely in patients who have lymphosarcoma or are pregnant, although the fluorescent staining is typically weak.

Newer, more sensitive diagnostic tests for syphilis are under investigation, including direct antigen, enzyme-linked immunosorbent assay (ELISA), and DNA polymerase chain reaction (PCR) techniques. These methods may also improve our ability to diagnose congenital syphilis and neurosyphilis. Laboratory diagnosis of treponemal infection may also involve darkfield microscopy of scrapings from primary

TABLE I-5

PERCENT POSITIVE TESTS IN UNTREATED SYPHILIS

	VDRL	FTA-ABS
Primary	70%	80%
Secondary	100%	100%
Tertiary	70%	98%

and secondary lesions. Scrapings of oral lesions are prone to misinterpretation because spirochetes may be present in normal mouth flora.

Management

Treatment of syphilis is determined by stage and central nervous system involvement. *Treponema pallidum* is exquisitely sensitive to penicillin, which remains the antimicrobial of choice (see Table I-6). Erythromycin, chloramphenicol, tetracycline, and the cephalosporins are acceptable alternatives to penicillin. Lumbar puncture should be performed to determine CSF involvement in latent syphilis of more than 1-year's duration, suspected neurosyphilis, treatment failure, HIV coinfection, high RPR titers (>1:32), or evidence of other late manifestations (cardiac involvement, gumma).

Many reports have described an accelerated clinical course of syphilis in patients infected with HIV; furthermore, incomplete response to standard therapy is also seen in this setting. An HIV-infected patient with syphilis often requires a longer and more intensive treatment regimen, ongoing follow-up to assess for recurrence, and complete neurologic work-up with an aggressive CSF investigation for evidence of neurosyphilis. Patients with any stage of clinical syphilis should also be tested for HIV status.

Brown ST, Zaidi A, Larsen SA, et al. Serological response to syphilis treatment. A new analysis of old data. *JAMA*. 1985;253:1296–1299.

Larsen SA, Steiner BM, Rudolph AH. Laboratory diagnosis and interpretation of tests for syphilis. *Clin Microbiol Rev*. 1995;8:1–21.

TABLE I-6

TREATMENT OF SYPHILIS

SYPHILIS	DRUG OF CHOICE AND DOSAGE
Early <1 yr	Penicillin G 2.4 million U IM × 1
Late >1 yr, no CNS	Penicillin G 2.4 million U IM weekly × 3 wks
Neurosyphilis	Penicillin G 2–4 million U IV q 4 hr × 10 days

Borrelia Burgdorferi (Lyme Disease)

Borrelia burgdorferi is a large, microaerophilic, plasmid-containing spirochete. When transmitted to humans and domestic animals through the bite of the *Ixodes* genus of ticks, it can cause both acute and chronic illness, now known as *Lyme disease*. First recognized in 1975, Lyme disease is the most common vector-borne infection in the United States. Although cases have been reported in 43 states, clusters are apparent in the northeast Atlantic, the upper Midwest, and the Pacific southwest, areas corresponding to the distribution of the *Ixodes* tick population. The range of the disease extends throughout Europe and Asia. In the United States, the number of reported cases has increased fivefold since 1982, partly as a result of the rapid growth in the deer population in rural and suburban areas and partly as a result of increased awareness of the disease.

The life cycle of the spirochete depends upon its horizontal transmission through a mouse. Early in the summer, an infected *Ixodes* tick nymph bites a mouse, which becomes infected; then, in late summer, the infection is transmitted to an immature uninfected larva after it bites the infected mouse. This immature larva then molts to become a nymph and the cycle is repeated. Once a nymph matures to an adult, its favorite host is the white-tailed deer, although it can survive with other hosts.

Stages

Lyme disease usually occurs in three stages following a tick bite: *localized (stage 1), disseminated (stage 2),* and *persistent (stage 3).* Localized disease (stage 1), present in 86% of infected patients, is characterized by skin involvement, initially as a red macule or papule, which later expands in a circular manner, usually with a bright red border and a central clear indurated area, known as *erythema chronicum migrans.*

Hematogenous dissemination (stage 2) can then occur within days to weeks and is manifested as a flu-like illness with headaches, fatigue, and musculoskeletal aching.

More profound symptoms occur as the infection localizes to the nervous, cardiac, and musculoskeletal systems (stage 3). Neurologic complications such as meningitis, encephalitis, cranial neuritis (including Bell's palsy), radiculopathy, and neuropathy occur in 15% of patients. Cardiac manifestations include myopericarditis and variable heart block in 5%. Unilateral asymmetric arthritis occurs in up to 80% of untreated patients.

Late persistent manifestations are usually confined to the nervous system, skin, and joints. Late neurologic signs include encephalomyelitis as well as demyelinating and psychiatric syndromes. Joint involvement includes asymmetric pauciarticular arthritis and skin involvement characterized by localized scleroderma-type lesions or acrodermatitis chronica atrophicans.

Other systemic manifestations during the initial dissemination or the late persistent state include lymphadenopathy, conjunctivitis, keratitis, neuritis, uveitis, hematuria, and orchitis.

Diagnosis

During the early stages of infection, the immune response is minimal, with little cellular reactivity to *Borrelia burgdorferi* antigens and nonspecific elevation of IgM. The spirochete is most easily seen and cultured from the skin lesions during this early stage. During the disseminated phase, cellular antigenic response is markedly increased and specific IgM is followed by a polyclonal B-cell activation, with development of specific IgG antibody within weeks of the initial infection. The infection is immunologically mediated by both serum-mediated complement lysis and cellular phagocytosis. Histopathology demonstrates lymphocytic tissue infiltration, often in a perivascular distribution. Late manifestations may be either HLA-mediated autoimmune damage or prolonged latency followed by persistent infection.

Laboratory diagnosis of *Borrelia burgdorferi* infection depends upon serodiagnosis, as there is a poor recovery rate from blood, cerebrospinal fluid, and synovial fluid during the early stages of infection. The expensive laboratory media needed and the several weeks required for incubation of the organism diminish the practical value of culture-proven infection. Skin-biopsy specimens with monoclonal antibody staining have demonstrated good sensitivity in identifying the organism. Although serodiagnosis remains the practical solution for establishing the diagnosis, laboratory methodology is not standardized. Variations in antigen preparation, adsorption of cross-reacting antibodies, types of assays employed, and intralaboratory quality control have resulted in significant inter- and intralaboratory discrepancies with the same serum sample.

The most commonly used serologic tests are the *immunofluorescence assay (IFA)* or the more sensitive *enzyme-linked immunosorbent assay (ELISA)*. Most laboratories use whole-cell sonicate or whole spirochetes for antigen preparation. The ELISA has been further modified by various investigators with *Treponema reiteri* adsorption or use of the flagellar antigen for detection; however, these methods have not become widely accepted. The ELISA is 50% sensitive during the early stages of the disease, and almost all symptomatic patients are seropositive during the latter disseminated and persistent phases of the infection. Early administration of antibiotics can cause antibody titers to remain below the threshold level; however, cellular reactivity to *Borrelia* antigens remains high. False-positive results can occur in patients with syphilis, Rocky Mountain spotted fever, yaws, pinta, *Borrelia recurrentis,* and various rheumatologic disorders. Western blot analysis has been advocated in identifying false-positive results; however, up to 10% of infected patients may be asymptomatic. Polymerase chain reaction has been used to detect *Borrelia burgdorferi* DNA in serum and cerebrospinal fluid, but its sensitivity in neuroborreliosis is no better than that of the ELISA methods. Although patients with Lyme disease may demonstrate a positive FTA-ABS test for syphilis, the VDRL should be nonreactive.

Management

Treatment of *B burgdorferi* infection depends upon the stage and the severity of the infection. The organism is highly sensitive in vitro to tetracycline, ampicillin, erythromycin, ceftriaxone, and imipenem; it is less sensitive to penicillin. Early Lyme disease is typically treated with oral doxycycline, amoxicillin, or erythromycin. Mild disseminated disease is treated with oral doxycycline or amoxicillin. Serious disease (with cardiac or neurologic manifestations) is typically treated with ceftriaxone or high-dose penicillin G intravenously for up to 6 weeks. Patients who do not respond to the initial regimen may require alternate or combination therapy. Up to 15% of patients may develop a Jarisch-Herxheimer reaction in which symptoms worsen during the first day of treatment.

No vaccine is presently available. Efforts to decrease the incidence of the disease by pesticide spraying have met with limited success. In endemic areas, adults may be able to reduce their risk by applying insect-repellent sprays containing diethyltoluamide (DEET).

Barbour AG. The diagnosis of Lyme disease: rewards and perils. *Ann Intern Med.* 1989;110:501–502.

Duffy J, Mertz LE, Wobig GH, et al. Diagnosing Lyme disease: the contribution of serologic testing. *Mayo Clin Proc.* 1988;63:1116–1121.

Nocton JJ, Bloom BJ, Rutledge BJ, et al. Detection of *Borrelia burgdorferi* DNA by polymerase chain reaction in cerebrospinal fluid in Lyme neuroborreliosis. *J Infect Dis.* 1996;174:623–627.

Steere AC, Levin RE, Molloy PJ, et al. Treatment of Lyme arthritis. *Arthritis Rheum.* 1994;37:878–888.

Chlamydia Trachomatis

Chlamydia is a small, obligate, intracellular parasite that contains DNA and RNA and has a unique biphasic life cycle. This prokaryote uses the host cell's energy-generating capacity for its own reproduction. *Chlamydia trachomatis* can survive only briefly outside the body and is transmitted by close contact. *Chlamydia trachomatis* is the most common sexually transmitted infection, with 4 million new cases per year. Over 15% of infected pregnant women and 10% of infected men are asymptomatic.

Infection is initiated by local inoculation and ingestion of the organism by phagocytes, followed by intracellular reproduction and eventual spread to other cells. The mechanism for immunologic eradication of *Chlamydia* is uncertain but appears to involve cell-mediated immunity. Infections in humans include trachoma, inclusion conjunctivitis, nongonococcal urethritis, epididymitis, mucopurulent cervicitis, proctitis, salpingitis, infant pneumonia syndrome, and lymphogranuloma venereum.

Diagnostic techniques include culture, direct immunofluorescent antibody testing of exudate, and newer DNA probes utilizing polymerase chain reaction.

Chlamydial infections are readily treated with tetracycline, erythromycin, or one of the quinolones or newer macrolides. Single-dose therapy of urethritis and cervicitis with azithromycin or sparfloxacin has recently been proven effective.

Fungal Infections

Candida albicans is a yeast that is normally present in the oral cavity, lower gastrointestinal tract, and female genital tract. Under conditions of disrupted local defenses or depressed immunity, overgrowth and parenchymal invasion occur, with the potential for systemic spread. Increased virulence of *Candida* is related to its mycelial phase, when it is more resistant to the host's cellular immune system, which acts as the primary modulator of infection. Infections include oral lesions (thrush) and vaginal, skin, esophageal, and urinary tract involvement. Chronic mucocutaneous lesions occur in rare individuals with specific T-cell defects. Disseminated disease can involve any organ system, most commonly the kidneys, brain, heart, and eye.

Some other important invasive fungal infections are cryptococcosis, histoplasmosis, blastomycosis, aspergillosis, and coccidioidomycosis. Treatment of serious systemic infections has traditionally involved the use of intravenous amphotericin B, sometimes in combined therapy with either flucytosine or an imidazole such as ketoconazole. Recently, lipid complex and liposome-encapsulated formulations of amphotericin B have been developed to reduce the drug's nephrotoxicity and myelosuppression. Newer imidazoles such as fluconazole and itraconazole are less toxic and better tolerated alternatives, and their use for invasive fungal infections will continue to increase in the future.

Graybill JR. The future of antifungal therapy. *Clin Infect Dis.* 1996;22(suppl2): S166–178.

Hiemenz JW, Walsh TJ. Lipid formulations of amphotericin B: recent progress and future directions. *Clin Infect Dis.* 1996;22(suppl2):S133–144.

Mycobacteria

Mycobacteria include a range of pathogenic and nonpathogenic species distributed widely in the environment. *Mycobacterium tuberculosis* is the most significant human pathogenic species. *M tuberculosis* infects 1.7 billion worldwide and causes 3 million deaths each year. *Nontuberculous mycobacteria* may be responsible for up to 5% of all clinical mycobacterial infections. Atypical mycobacterial infections are more prevalent in immunosuppressed patients and those with AIDS. Infections caused by nontuberculous mycobacteria include lymphadenitis, pulmonary infections, skin granulomas, prosthetic valve infections, and bacteremia. Despite their low virulence, atypical mycobacterial infections are difficult to treat because of resistance to standard antituberculous regimens.

Tuberculosis

Infection usually occurs through inhalation of infective droplets and rarely by way of the skin or gastrointestinal tract. The organism is able to multiply within macrophages with a minor inflammatory response. Cell-mediated hypersensitivity to tuberculoprotein develops 3–9 weeks after infection, with a typical granulomatous response that slows or contains bacterial multiplication. Most organisms die during the fibrotic phase of the response. Reactivation is usually associated with depressed immunity and aging. Systemic spread occurs with reactivation and results in a granulomatous response to the infected foci. Acquired immunity is cell-mediated but incomplete, and the role of delayed hypersensitivity is complex, as high degrees of sensitivity to tuberculoprotein can cause caseous necrosis, which leads to spread of the disease. Infections include pulmonary involvement, which can lead to systemic spread with involvement of any organ system.

Laboratory diagnosis involves culture of infective material on Lowenstein-Jensen medium for 6–8 weeks and use of acid-fast type Ziehl-Neelsen stain or fluorescent antibody staining of infected material. DNA probes using PCR techniques for *M tuberculosis* and other mycobacteria are now available as well.

The tuberculin skin test measures delayed hypersensitivity to tuberculoprotein. Purified protein derivative (PPD) produced from a culture filtrate of M tuberculosis is standardized, and its activity expressed as tuberculin units (TU). Usually, intermediate strength (5 TU) is used; however, if a high degree of sensitivity to tuberculoprotein is suspected, then low strength (1 TU) is used to avoid the risk of excessive reaction locally or at the site of an infected focus. A positive high-strength (250 TU) reaction with doubtful intermediate-strength reaction suggests infection with atypical mycobacteria and resultant cross-sensitization.

A positive PPD reaction is defined as an area of induration 10 mm or greater in the area of intradermal injection of 0.1 cc of PPD read 48–72 hours later. Ninety percent of persons demonstrating 10 mm of induration to 5 TU are infected with M tuberculosis. A positive response indicates that an individual has been infected, although the infection might not be currently active. Induration of 5 mm in persons with HIV infection is sufficient to warrant chemoprophylaxis. For children, the tine test is an easily administered alternative to the PPD.

Among patients who have a positive skin test, the overall risk of reactivation of the disease is 3%–5%. A positive PPD test should be considered in light of the individual patient's radiologic and clinical data as well as age to determine the need for prophylactic treatment. Administration of isoniazid (INH) daily for 1 year reduces the risk of reactivation by 80%; however, the risk of isoniazid hepatotoxicity increases with age and alcohol use. Patients with a positive tuberculin skin test who require long-term high-dose steroids or other immunosuppressive agents should be treated prophylactically with isoniazid for the duration of their immunosuppressive therapy to prevent reactivation of tuberculosis.

Treatment of active infection involves use of two or three drugs because of the emergence of resistance and of delay in culture susceptibility studies. Standard regimens employ multiple drugs for 18–24 months, but with the addition of newer agents, 6–9 months of treatment have been found equally effective. Drugs currently used include isoniazid, rifampin, ethambutol, streptomycin, pyrazinamide, aminosalicylic acid, ethionamide, and cycloserine. All of the agents currently used have toxic side effects, especially hepatic and neurologic, which should be carefully monitored during the course of therapy. Isoniazid and ethambutol can cause optic neuritis in a small percentage of patients, and rifampin may cause pink-tinged tears and blepharoconjunctivitis. In Western countries that have a low incidence of the disease, use of the live attenuated BCG vaccine for prophylaxis against tuberculosis has been restricted to high-risk populations. Its potential value in developing countries has been controversial. The BCG vaccine causes false-positive reactions to the PPD skin test and thus interferes with the efficacy of the PPD skin test as a diagnostic and epidemiologic tool.

Outbreaks of nosocomial and community-acquired tuberculosis resistant to multiple drugs (MDRTB) have been reported recently, particularly in the presence of concurrent HIV infection. MDRTB in patients infected with HIV is associated with widely disseminated disease, poor treatment response, and substantial mortality. Infection has also been documented in health care workers exposed to these patients. MDRTB represents a serious public health threat that will require an aggressive governmental and medical response to limit its spread.

Herpesvirus

As a class, viruses are strictly intracellular parasites, relying on the host cell for their replication. Herpesviruses, which are large-enveloped, double-stranded DNA viruses, are one of the most common human infectious agents, responsible for a wide spectrum of acute and chronic diseases. The major members of the group are herpes simplex viruses (HSV-1 and HSV-2), varicella-zoster virus (VZV), cytomegalovirus (CMV), and Epstein-Barr virus (EBV).

Herpes Simplex

Herpes simplex virus has two antigenic types, each with numerous antigenic strains. Each type has different epidemiologic patterns of infection. Seroepidemiologic studies demonstrate a high prevalence of HSV-1 antibodies with a lower prevalence of HSV-2 antibodies. Many people with HSV antibodies are asymptomatic. Infection is modulated by a predominantly cellular response. The presence of high titers of neutralizing antibodies to HSV does not seem to retard the cell-to-cell transmission of the virus. The virus can spread within nerves and cause a latent infection of sensory and autonomic ganglia. Latent infection does not result in host-cell death, and the exact mechanism of viral genome interaction with the host genome is incompletely understood. Reactivation of HSV from the trigeminal ganglia may be associated with asymptomatic excretion or with the development of mucosal herpetic ulceration.

Herpes simplex type 1 is associated with mucocutaneous superficial infections of the pharynx, skin, oral cavity, vagina, eye, and brain. Herpes encephalitis carries a 30% mortality. *Herpes simplex type 2* is an important sexually transmitted disease that is associated with genital infections, aseptic meningitis, and congenital infection. *Neonatal herpes infection* has multisystem involvement and carries a 70% untreated mortality.

The drug of choice for treating acute systemic infections is acyclovir. Localized disease can be treated with oral acyclovir. Topical treatment of skin or mucocutaneous lesions with acyclovir ointment decreases the healing time. Oral acyclovir can also be used prophylactically for severe and recurrent genital herpes.

Two newer antiviral agents, famciclovir and valacyclovir, are already approved for the treatment of herpes zoster and have been shown to be effective against herpes simplex in recent studies. These agents have better bioavailability and achieve higher blood levels than acyclovir. The virus is also sensitive to vidarabine. Cidofovir (HPMPC), a new antiviral drug used for CMV infections, is also very effective against acyclovir-resistant herpes simplex.

Varicella-Zoster

Varicella-zoster virus produces infection in a manner similar to herpes simplex. After a primary infection, the virus remains latent in dorsal root ganglia, with host cellular immune interaction inhibiting reactivation. Primary infection usually occurs in childhood in the form of chickenpox (varicella), a generalized vesicular rash accompanied by mild constitutional symptoms. Reactivation may be heralded by pain in a sensory nerve distribution, followed by a unilateral vesicular eruption occurring over one to three dermatomic areas. New crops of lesions appear in the same area within a 7-day period. Resolution of the lesions may be followed by postherpetic neuralgia, the mechanism of which is incompletely understood. Other neurologic syndromes following herpes zoster involvement include segmental myelitis, Guillain-Barré syndrome, and Ramsay Hunt syndrome. The incidence of herpes zoster is two to three times higher in patients over age 60. Immunosuppressed individuals have recurrent lesions and may develop disseminated disease with an incidence ten times that of immunocompetent individuals.

Treatment of acute infection in immunocompromised individuals or those with visceral involvement is with acyclovir, famciclovir, or valacyclovir. A new drug, sorivudine, is being studied for treatment of herpes zoster in HIV-infected patients. A live attenuated varicella vaccine (Varivax) is available for prevention of primary disease. Topical capsaicin cream has been helpful in some patients for reducing the pain of postherpetic neuralgia.

Rolan P. Pharmacokinetics of new antiherpetic agents. *Clin Pharmacokinet.* 1995; 29:333–340.

Straus SE, Ostrove JM, Inchauspe G, et al. NIH Conference. Varicella-zoster virus infections. Biology, natural history, treatment, and prevention. *Ann Intern Med.* 1988; 108:221–237.

Cytomegalovirus

Cytomegalovirus (CMV) is a ubiquitous human virus, with 50% of adults in developed countries harboring antibodies, which are usually acquired during the first 5 years of life. The virus can be isolated from all body fluids, even in the presence of circulating neutralizing antibody, for up to several years after infection. Cytopathic effects following infection are similar to HSV.

Clinical syndromes with greatest morbidity include congenital CMV disease, with a 20% incidence of hearing loss or mental retardation and 0.1% incidence of various other congenital disorders including jaundice, hepatosplenomegaly, anemia, microcephaly, and chorioretinitis. Infections in adults include heterophile-negative mononucleosis, pneumonia, hepatitis, and Guillain-Barré syndrome. In immunocompromised patients, CMV interstitial pneumonia carries a 90% mortality. Disseminated spread to the gastrointestinal tract, central nervous system, and eye is common in patients with AIDS. Latent infection within leukocytes accounts for transfusion-associated disease. CMV replication itself can further suppress cell-mediated immunity, with resultant depressed lymphocyte response and development of severe opportunistic infections.

CMV retinitis and colitis have been successfully treated with the nucleoside derivative ganciclovir. This drug is available for intravenous, oral, or intravitreal routes. A slow-release intraocular ganciclovir insert is also available for the treatment of CMV retinitis. It should be noted that the intravitreal and intraocular methods of administration are effective only for CMV retinitis and will not treat colitis or other systemic manifestations. Intravenous foscarnet and cidofovir have also been effective in the treatment of CMV retinitis. Intravitreal cidofovir given at 6-week intervals was highly effective for treating CMV retinitis in a recent study.

Rahhal FM, Arevalo JF, Munguia D, et al. Intravitreal cidofovir for the maintenance treatment of cytomegalovirus retinitis. *Ophthalmology.* 1996;103:1078–1083.

Epstein-Barr Virus

Epstein-Barr virus (EBV) antibodies are found in 90%–95% of all adults. Childhood infections are usually asymptomatic, with symptomatic disease occurring in young adults. Infectious mononucleosis is the usual clinical disease in most symptomatic adults. Transplant patients receiving cyclosporine or patients with AIDS may develop lymphoproliferative disorders. EBV is epidemiologically associated with Burkitt's lymphoma and nasopharyngeal carcinoma. Its host range is restricted to B lymphocytes, nasopharyngeal epithelial, and uterine epithelial cells; however, latent infection appears to be limited to B cells. The virus does not generally produce cytopathic effects in cells, and the viral DNA remains in a circular nonintegrated form within the cell. Lymphoblastoid cell lines infected with EBV can be cultured indefinitely in vitro. The lymphocytosis of mononucleosis is thought to result from a T-cell reaction to infected B cells.

Treatment of acute disease is largely supportive, although the EBV DNA polymerase is sensitive to acyclovir and ganciclovir, which decrease viral replication in tissue culture. No vaccine is presently available against EBV.

Hepatitis

Hepatitis A

Hepatitis A is usually transmitted by the oral route and may be acquired from contaminated water supplies and unwashed or poorly cooked foods. Patients at high risk (travelers to endemic areas, military personnel, drug abusers, family contacts of infected patients, and lab workers exposed to the virus) should be given the hepatitis A vaccine (Havrix). Many adults in the U.S. are already immune, so antibody testing can be done first, followed by vaccination if antibodies are not present.

Hepatitis B

See p 220 of this book for a discussion of hepatitis B.

Hepatitis C

Approximately 20%–40% of acute viral hepatitis reported in the United States is of the non-A, non-B type; of the group, the majority is caused by the hepatitis C virus (HCV). Current estimates suggest that approximately 150,000–170,000 new cases of HCV occur annually in the United States; approximately half of these patients develop evidence of chronic liver disease. Only 6% of reported cases of hepatitis C are transfusion-related. Other recognized risk factors for hepatitis C transmission include parenteral drug use, hemodialysis, and occupational exposure to blood. Although the role of sexual activity in the transmission of hepatitis C virus remains to be fully elucidated, it is clearly not a predominant source of transmission. Treatment of chronic active hepatitis C with interferon has met with limited success, while management of chronic persistent hepatitis C is largely supportive. No vaccine is presently available against HCV.

Hagman HM, Strausbaugh LJ. Vancomycin-resistant enterococci. The "superbug scourge" that's coming your way. *Postgrad Med.* 1996;99:60–65, 69–71.

Ryan KJ. *Sherris Medical Microbiology: An Introduction to Infectious Diseases.* Norwalk, CT: Appleton & Lange; 1994.

Thornsberry C. Emerging resistance in clinically important gram-positive cocci. *West J Med.* 1996;164:28–32.

Treatment of sexually transmitted diseases. *Med Lett Drugs Ther.* 30(757):5–10, 1988.

Acquired Immunodeficiency Syndrome (AIDS)

During the 1980s the acquired immunodeficiency syndrome (AIDS) emerged as a major public health problem. AIDS was originally described in 1981 when *Pneumocystis carinii* pneumonia (PCP) and Kaposi sarcoma were noted to occur in homosexual men and intravenous drug abusers. Since that time, the number of cases has increased exponentially. In 1983, it was discovered that AIDS was caused by a retrovirus, the human immunodeficiency virus (HIV). Subsequently, it became evident that HIV caused a spectrum of disease, including an asymptomatic carrier state, the AIDS-related complex (ARC), and AIDS itself. As of October 1993, 315,390 cases of AIDS had been diagnosed in the United States, of which 194,334 patients had died. It is estimated that approximately 1.0–1.5 million people in the U.S. are infected with HIV. Based on 1990 data, HIV infection is the leading cause of death among young men in 64 of 172 cities with populations greater than 100,000 people. It is also the fourth leading cause of death in young women. In 1994, 59% of cases occurred in nonwhites. Since 1987 the rate of HIV infection in homosexual and bisexual men has been decreasing, while the percentage of cases caused by heterosexual transmission has increased in the last decade from 1.9% to 9.1%.

Etiology and Pathogenesis

AIDS is caused by infection with the human immunodeficiency virus (HIV), previously known as the human T-cell lymphotropic virus type III (HTLV-III), lymphadenopathy-associated virus (LAV), and AIDS-related virus (ARV). HIV is more properly known as HIV-1, as another human T-cell lymphotropic virus known as HIV-2 has been isolated from West Africans and is associated with AIDS as well. Another name for HIV-2 is LAV-2. HIV belongs to a family of viruses known as *retroviruses*. A retrovirus encodes its genetic information in ribonucleic acid (RNA) and uses a unique viral enzyme called *reverse transcriptase* to copy its genome into deoxyribonucleic acid (DNA). Other members of this retrovirus family include the human T-cell lymphotropic retrovirus type I (HTLV-I), which causes adult T-cell leukemia in American, Japanese, and Caribbean patients. Members of this family are exogenous viruses isolated from T cells, especially T-helper (CD4+) lymphocytes. They infect mature T cells in vitro, although other cells can serve as targets. CD4 is the phenotypic marker for this subset and is identified by monoclonal antibodies OKT4 and Leu-3.

The hallmark of the immunodeficiency in AIDS is a depletion of the CD4+ helper/inducer T lymphocytes. HIV selectively infects these lymphocytes, and with HIV replication, the helper T cell is killed. Because of the central role of the helper T lymphocyte in the immune response, loss of this subset results in a profound immune deficiency, leading to the life-threatening opportunistic infections indicative of AIDS. This selective depletion of CD4+ helper T cells leads to the characteristic inverted CD4+/CD8+ ratio (also known as T4/T8 ratio). Years may pass between the initial HIV infection and the development of these immune abnormalities.

In addition to the cellular immune deficiency, patients with AIDS have abnormalities of B-cell function. These patients fail to mount an antibody response to novel T-cell–dependent B-cell challenges, although they have B-cell hyperfunction with polyclonal B-cell activation, hypergammaglobulinemia, and circulating immune complexes. This B-cell hyperfunction may be a direct consequence of HIV infection, as studies have demonstrated that polyclonal activation can be induced in vitro by adding HIV to B cells.

HIV has also been documented to infect the brains of patients with AIDS. It is thought that HIV infection of the brain is responsible for the HIV encephalopathy syndrome. HIV-infected cells in the brain have generally been identified as monocytes or macrophages.

Clinical Syndromes

The clinical syndrome of AIDS consists of recurrent, severe opportunistic infections or unusual neoplasms. In September 1982, the Centers for Disease Control (CDC) published an original case definition of AIDS as the presence of a reliably diagnosed disease at least moderately indicative of an underlying cellular immune deficiency (Kaposi sarcoma in a patient less than 60 years of age, *Pneumocystis carinii* pneumonia, or other opportunistic infection) and the absence of known causes of an underlying immune deficiency or of any other stage of resistance reported to be associated with the disease (immunosuppressive therapy, lymphoreticular malignancy). This original surveillance case definition has been modified by the CDC as new data have become available.

AIDS is now diagnosed when an individual presents with one or more of the indicator diseases outlined in the following list. These diseases are indicative of an underlying cellular immunodeficiency, and the most common presentations are with *Pneumocystis carinii* pneumonia or with Kaposi sarcoma.

These conditions are included in the 1993 AIDS surveillance case definition:

□ Candidiasis of bronchi, trachea, or lungs

□ Candidiasis, esophageal

□ Cervical cancer, invasive

□ Coccidioidomycosis, disseminated or extrapulmonary

□ Cryptococcosis, extrapulmonary

□ Cryptosporidiosis, chronic intestinal (>1 month duration)

□ Cytomegalovirus disease (other than liver, spleen, or nodes)

□ Herpes simplex: chronic ulcer(s) (>1 month duration); or bronchitis, pneumonitis, or esophagitis

□ Histoplasmosis, disseminated or extrapulmonary

□ HIV encephalopathy

□ Isosporiasis, chronic intestinal (>1 month duration)

□ Kaposi sarcoma

□ Lymphoma, Burkitt's (or equivalent term)

□ Lymphoma, immunoblastic (or equivalent term)

□ Lymphoma, primary in brain

□ *Mycobacterium avium* complex or *M kansasii,* disseminated or extrapulmonary

□ *Mycobacterium tuberculosis,* any site (pulmonary or extrapulmonary)

□ *Pneumocystis carinii* pneumonia

□ Pneumonia, recurrent

□ Progressive multifocal leukoencephalopathy

□ *Salmonella* septicemia, recurrent

☐ Toxoplasmosis of brain

☐ Wasting syndrome due to HIV

AIDS represents the most severe end of the spectrum of HIV infection. Acute infection with HIV often manifests as a transient mononucleosis-like syndrome. Patients may then enter a prolonged asymptomatic carrier state (the majority of HIV-infected patients in the United States are in this condition). There is also a syndrome of persistent generalized lymphadenopathy, which is associated with depleted T-helper lymphocytes and HIV infection. Lymphadenopathy with other signs and symptoms has commonly been referred to as the *lymphadenopathy syndrome* or the *AIDS-related complex (ARC)*. Constitutional symptoms in ARC patients include fever, weight loss, chronic diarrhea, oral thrush, and lymphadenopathy. Although these individuals have immunologic defects similar to those found in AIDS patients, they have not developed one of the AIDS-defining opportunistic infections or unusual neoplasms. The CDC has classified HIV infection into the three groups outlined in Table I-7. The shaded boxes illustrate clinical conditions now defined as AIDS.

Seroepidemiology

Antibodies to HIV can be detected in HIV-infected individuals. Such screening is now performed with commercially available kits, all of which are based on an enzyme-linked immunosorbent assay (ELISA) using whole disrupted HIV antigens. The ELISA test for HIV antibodies is sensitive (99%) and specific (99%). However, false-negative tests can occur, especially in the first weeks after HIV infection. Because of the possibility of false-positive ELISA tests, the ELISA test must be posi-

TABLE I-7

1992 REVISED CLASSIFICATION SYSTEM FOR HIV INFECTION AND EXPANDED AIDS SURVEILLANCE CASE DEFINITION FOR ADOLESCENTS AND ADULTS*

	CLINICAL CATEGORIES		
	A	B	C
CD4 + CELL CATEGORIES	Asymptomatic, or PGL**	Symptomatic, not A or C conditions	AIDS-indicator conditions
1. ≥500/mm³	A1	B1	C1
2. 200–499/mm³	A2	B2	C2
3. < 200/mm³	A3	B3	C3

*   The shaded cells illustrate the expansion of the AIDS surveillance case definition. Persons with AIDS-indicator conditions (category C) are currently reportable to the health department in every state and US territory. In addition to persons with clinical category C conditions (categories C1, C2, and C3), persons with CD4 + lymphocyte counts of less than 200/mm³ (categories A3 or B3) are also reportable as AIDS cases in the United States, effective April 1, 1992.

** PGL = persistent generalized lymphadenopathy. Clinical category A includes acute (primary) HIV infection.

tive twice and confirmed by Western blot analysis before a patient is said to have antibodies to HIV. Persons with antibodies to HIV should be considered infectious for HIV.

Seroepidemiologic studies conducted in high-risk populations have shown a steadily increasing prevalence of HIV infection from almost nil prior to 1979 to as high as 70% by 1988. On the basis of these studies, it has been estimated that approximately 1.0–1.5 million people were infected with HIV. Estimates have suggested that up to 100% of patients with HIV infection may ultimately develop AIDS, and the median incubation period between acquisition of HIV infection and the development of AIDS is estimated at 10 years.

Modes of Transmission

Modes of transmission of HIV infection are

- Sexual contact
- Intravenous drug use
- Transfusion
- Perinatal transmission from an infected mother to her child

There have been no documented cases of transmission by casual contact. Furthermore, while HIV infection may be transmitted by blood or blood products, the risk of transmission by accidental needle stick appears quite low (less than 0.5%). Studies of nonsexual household contacts of patients with AIDS have revealed that these people are at minimal or possibly no risk of infection with HIV.

While AIDS has remained relatively confined to high-risk populations in the United States, recent data show that the greatest rate of growth of HIV positivity is in cases acquired through heterosexual contact. Furthermore, in Africa the male-to-female ratio is 1:1, and epidemiologic data have suggested that the disease is transmitted predominantly by heterosexual activity, parenteral exposure to blood transfusion and unsterilized needles, and perinatally from infected mothers to their newborns.

Prognosis and Treatment

Currently, AIDS is an incurable and fatal disease. Nevertheless, infected patients are living longer and have had better quality of life in recent years because of significant improvements in antiviral therapy. Approximately 56% of all AIDS patients have died, and the mortality approaches 100% within 5 years after the diagnosis of AIDS. The risk factors most closely associated with decreased survival in AIDS patients are reduced CD4 levels, length of time since diagnosis, low serum albumin levels (<0.30 gm/L), previous opportunistic infections, high viral load, and new "clinical progression" events.

In 1986, the drug *zidovudine* (also known as azidothymidine, AZT, or Retrovir), a synthetic analogue of thymidine, became available for the treatment of AIDS. Zidovudine is incorporated into DNA by the DNA polymerase (reverse transcriptase) of HIV and prevents further viral DNA synthesis. A controlled trial conducted in 1986 demonstrated significantly decreased mortality during the study period among AIDS and ARC patients treated with zidovudine compared to those taking a placebo. Episodes of opportunistic infections also decreased. The major limiting side effect of this therapy was bone marrow suppression, often requiring chronic transfusions; anemia occurred in 24% of patients and granulocytopenia (<500 granulocytes/mm^3) in 16%.

Over the past several years, significant advances in the treatment of AIDS have been made. Multicenter clinical trials demonstrated that half-dose zidovudine (100 mg orally every 4 hours) was as effective as full-dose zidovudine (200 mg every 4 hours). This lower dose, while equally effective, was associated with a lower incidence of side effects. More recent data revealed that 200 mg every 8 hours is as effective as more frequent dosing schedules.

Data released from these trials also showed that symptomatic HIV-infected individuals with ARC and asymptomatic HIV-infected individuals with CD4 counts less than 500/mm^3 who were treated with zidovudine had delayed progression of the disease to later stages (e.g., AIDS). Furthermore, analysis of survival data showed improved short-term survival for patients with AIDS since 1986, and zidovudine therapy is generally recognized as improving CD4 counts and survival rates in patients with CD4 counts less than 500. Zidovudine was approved for use in HIV-positive adults and children in 1990 and for HIV-positive pregnant women and newborns in 1994. A new timed-release form of the drug, called AZTEC, is being studied for longer dosing intervals.

Some of the newer nucleoside analogues approved for the treatment of HIV infection are *didanosine* (dideoxyinosine, ddI, Videx), *zalcitabine* (dideoxycytidine, ddC, Hivid), *lamivudine* (3TC, Epivir), and *stavudine* (d4T, Zerit). All of these drugs have in vitro activity similar to that of zidovudine against the HIV virus. Their primary benefit over zidovudine is reduced bone marrow toxicity, which makes them more useful in the setting of concurrent leukopenia or use of other marrow-toxic drugs (e.g., ganciclovir). They have been used in combination therapy with zidovudine or in serial therapy when resistance or intolerance to zidovudine is demonstrated. Lamivudine is used primarily in combination therapy with zidovudine, with or without a protease inhibitor. Several nonnucleoside reverse transcriptase inhibitors (nevirapine, delavirdine, and atevirdine) are also available, but they share the disadvantage of rapid emergence of viral resistance. Therefore, they are currently used only in combination therapy.

The major treatment-limiting toxicity of didanosine is acute pancreatitis, and its use is therefore contraindicated in the setting of alcoholism or prior pancreatitis. In addition, it should not be used concurrently with pentamidine. Zalcitabine may cause rapidly progressive, severe peripheral neuropathy, which may not be reversible upon discontinuing therapy. Lamivudine has been associated with neutropenia and peripheral neuropathy in a small percentage of patients. Stavudine causes peripheral neuropathy in 15%–20% of patients.

The *protease inhibitors* are a new class of antiretroviral drugs that prevent the cleavage of precursor proteins into viral elements needed for viral assembly. This results in the production of nonfunctional, noninfectious virions. The protease inhibitors currently approved for the treatment of HIV infection include *saquinavir* (Invirase), *indinavir* (Crixivan), *ritonavir* (Norvir), and *nelfinavir* (Viracept). Many others are currently being developed and studied for their efficacy and safety. The protease inhibitors can be used as monotherapy for patients intolerant of nucleoside analogues but are more often used in double- or triple-drug therapy along with zidovudine and another nucleoside analogue.

Multidrug therapy has been shown to result in dramatic reduction of HIV viral load, increase in CD4 cell counts, and delay of disease progression in infected patients. Researchers are optimistic that this advantage will translate into improved survival and enhanced quality of life for HIV-infected patients. In some studies, triple-drug therapy has achieved what initially appears to be complete eradication of viral antigen. Long-term follow-up of these patients is necessary before these assumptions can be confirmed.

The *immunomodulators* are a diverse group of drugs and immunologic adjuvants being evaluated for their efficacy in enhancing the host immune response to HIV and related opportunistic infections. This long list includes agents that enhance or stimulate T-cell and macrophage response:

- Ditiocarb
- Ampligen
- CD4-IgG
- Human granulocyte colony stimulating factor
- Inosine pranobex
- Lentinan
- Levamisol
- Thymosin alpha-1
- Thymic humoral factor

The following agents induce humoral as well as cellular immune responses:

- Interleukin-2
- PCLUS
- Zinc replacement therapy

Other drugs inhibit viral replication:

- Beta interferon
- Interleukin-10

These immunomodulators are primarily used along with antiretroviral agents in combined therapy study protocols. *Hematopoietic agents,* such as erythropoietin and interleukin-3, enhance the proliferation of blood cells and are useful in the treatment of cytopenias.

A small percentage of the population appears to be naturally immune to HIV infection. These individuals have defective genes for CKR-5, a surface receptor that HIV requires to attach to T cells. This has led to some speculation concerning the possibilities for genetic therapy, in which anti-HIV genes could be "injected" into a patient's chromosomes with a harmless viral vector.

Although no highly successful HIV vaccines have been developed thus far, significant progress has been made toward this goal. Viral components, such as gp 120 and gp 160 envelope glycoproteins, and p17 and p24 viral antigens have been incorporated into vaccines that generate limited immune protection. There is reluctance to study vaccines made up of whole inactivated virions or live attenuated HIV virus because of the possible risk of transmitting the infection through the vaccine. Another obstacle for vaccine development is the need to provide protection for the ten or so known subtypes of HIV now in existence around the world, as well as the new mutations that continue to arise.

Many health care providers who have had occupational exposure to HIV have used zidovudine prophylactically immediately after such exposure. The typical dose has been 200 mg orally every 4 hours for 6 weeks. Treatment with zidovudine may reduce the risk of HIV infection following percutaneous exposure by as much as

80%. Recent recommendations by the Centers for Disease Control also incorporate some of the newer antiviral drugs, such as lamivudine and indinavir, into the prophylactic regimen (see Table I-8).

Opportunistic Infections

Treatment of Pneumocystis carinii *pneumonia* (PCP)   PCP ultimately affects approximately 75% of patients with AIDS and is a major cause of mortality in these patients. However, therapy and prophylaxis of PCP have been improving over the past several years. PCP is generally treated with IV trimethoprim-sulfamethoxazole (Bactrim, Septra, TMP-SMZ) or IV pentamidine. Inhaled pentamidine prevents the recurrence of PCP (secondary prophylaxis) and appears to be efficacious for primary prophylaxis when used in patients with HIV infection and CD4 counts <200/mm^3. The regimen for inhaled pentamidine is generally 300 mg every 4 weeks using a nebulizer. This form of therapy avoids the toxicity of systemically administered pentamidine.

Recent data indicate that oral trimethoprim-sulfamethoxazole prophylaxis is more effective than aerosolized pentamidine for PCP prophylaxis in those patients who can tolerate it, and it may also provide systemic prophylaxis against toxoplasmosis infection. Adverse reactions are, however, frequent in HIV-infected patients. Dapsone, effective for primary and secondary prophylaxis against PCP, is tolerated by most patients who develop rashes with trimethoprim-sulfamethoxazole. Primaquine and clindamycin have been used successfully in treating PCP, but these drugs are reserved for use in patients intolerant of TMP-SMZ or pentamidine. Judicious use of steroids may help reduce morbidity in patients with severe pulmonary inflammation caused by PCP.

Treatment of CMV infections   *Ganciclovir* is the drug of choice for the treatment of CMV retinitis and colitis in immunocompromised patients. Studies of ganciclovir suggest a response in 80%–100% of patients treated with ganciclovir for CMV retinitis, and remissions in 60%–80% of these patients. Treatment generally consists of an initial high-dose induction phase of 5 mg/kg every 12 hours for 2 weeks, followed by long-term, lifetime maintenance at 5 mg/kg daily or 6 mg/kg/day, 5 of 7 days, to prevent relapse. In patients with AIDS, cessation of ganciclovir therapy is universally associated with relapse of the CMV retinitis. Ganciclovir's major toxicity is a reversible bone marrow suppression. One third of patients develop significant granulocytopenia, requiring them to discontinue the drug. Because ganciclovir and zidovudine have similar toxicities, most patients are not able to tolerate systemic therapeutic doses of these drugs simultaneously. Therapy with intravitreal ganciclovir injections has met with increasing popularity in recent years. Unfortunately, in most cases, intravitreal injection of ganciclovir 3–4 times weekly on an indefinite basis is required to prevent progression of CMV retinitis. A slow-release ganciclovir implant (Vitrasert) is also approved for the treatment of CMV retinitis. These implants are surgically inserted within the vitreal cavity and attached at the pars plana.

Foscarnet (Foscavir) was approved by the FDA in 1992 for the treatment of CMV infections. Foscarnet inhibits the DNA polymerase of herpesvirus and HIV, and it demonstrates in vitro activity against CMV, herpes simplex, varicella-zoster, and HIV at concentrations readily achieved with IV therapy. Oral bioavailability is poor, and thus, chronic IV therapy is required for suppression of CMV retinitis in HIV disease.

TABLE I-8

PROVISIONAL PUBLIC HEALTH SERVICE RECOMMENDATIONS FOR CHEMOPROPHYLAXIS
AFTER OCCUPATIONAL EXPOSURE TO HIV

TYPE OF EXPOSURE	SOURCE MATERIAL	ANTIRETROVIRAL PROPHYLAXIS	ANTIVIRAL REGIMEN*
Percutaneous	**Blood**		
	Highest risk[1]	Recommend	AZT plus 3TC plus IDV
	Increased risk[2]	Recommend	AZT plus 3TC±IDV
	No increased risk[3]	Offer	AZT plus 3TC
	Fluid containing visible blood, other potentially infectious fluid,[4] or tissue	Offer	AZT plus 3TC
	Other body fluid (urine)	Not offer	
Mucous Membrane	**Blood**	Offer	AZT plus 3TC±IDV
	Fluid containing visible blood, other potentially infectious fluid,[4] or tissue	Offer	AZT ±3TC
	Other body fluid (urine)	Not offer	
Skin, Increased Risk	**Blood**	Offer	AZT plus 3TC±IDV
	Fluid containing visible blood, other potentially infectious fluid,[4] or tissue	Offer	AZT±3TC
	Other body fluid (urine)	Not offer	

Dosages for Antiviral Regimens

Drug	Dosage
AZT	200 mg PO TID × 4 weeks
3TC	150 mg PO BID × 4 weeks
IDV	800 mg PO TID × 4 weeks
or	
Saquinavir (substituted for IDV)	600 mg PO TID × 4 weeks

* Abbreviations: AZT = zidovudine (Retrovir); 3TC = lamivudine (Epivir); IDV = indinavir (Crixivan) or saquinavir (Invirase) substituted for IDV.

1. Highest risk = **Both** larger volume of blood (e.g., deep injury with a large diameter hollow needle previously in a patient's vein or artery, especially involving an injection of source-patient's blood) **and** blood containing a high titer of HIV (e.g., source with acute retroviral illness or end-stage AIDS; viral load measurement may be considered, but its use in relation to postexposure prophylaxis has not been evaluated).

2. Increased risk = **Either** exposure to larger volume of blood **or** blood with a high titer of HIV.

3. No increased risk = **Neither** exposure to larger volume of blood **nor** blood with a high titer of HIV (e.g., solid suture needle injury from source patient with asymptomatic HIV infection).

4. Includes semen; vaginal secretions; cerebrospinal, synovial, pleural, peritoneal, pericardial, and amniotic fluids.

(Reprinted from Gerberding JL. Prophylaxis for occupational exposure to HIV. *Ann Intern Med.* 1996;125: 497–501.)

Foscarnet's primary value is that it is not generally myelosuppressive and, therefore, may be used without discontinuing zidovudine therapy. Its primary dose-limiting side effect is nephrotoxicity; aggressive pretreatment hydration may reduce this effect significantly.

Cidofovir (HPMPC, Vistide) is a potent antiviral agent with activity against herpes simplex, herpes zoster, CMV, adenovirus, Epstein-Barr virus, and HIV. It blocks DNA synthesis by viral DNA polymerase. Cidofovir provides a prolonged antiviral activity lasting up to several weeks, which allows infrequent dosing. Intravenous (3–5 mg/kg, every other week) and intravitreal cidofovir (20 μg per eye, every 5–6 weeks) have been used successfully in the treatment of CMV retinitis. In one recent study of intravitreal cidofovir, healing of CMV retinitis occurred in all 53 patients. During the follow-up period, none of the patients with no previous anti-CMV therapy had disease progression, and only 14% of the patients with previous anti-CMV therapy had disease progression.

Recently, *fomivirsen,* a new antisense drug that targets CMV mRNA, has been shown to be effective in controlling early or advanced CMV retinitis for up to 1 year when given as an intravitreal dose of 330 mg. In this study, fomivirsen was given weekly for 3 doses, then once every 2 weeks for maintenance therapy.

Treatment of spore-forming intestinal protozoa Spore-forming intestinal protozoa are a frequent cause of gastrointestinal infections in AIDS patients. This group of infections includes cryptosporidiosis (caused by *Cryptosporidium parvum),* microsporidiosis *(Microsporida),* isosporiasis *(Isospora belli),* and cyclosporiasis *(Cyclospora cayatanensis).* Cryptosporidiosis can be treated with clarithromycin, azithromycin, albendazole, or metronidazole. In many patients, symptoms can be successfully controlled, but eradication of the organism can be extremely difficult. Isosporiasis and cyclosporiasis have been treated successfully with trimethoprim-sulfamethoxazole. There are no curative drugs for invasive microsporidiosis, but recent studies have revealed that albendazole or fumagillin may control disease symptoms.

Treatment of tuberculosis and atypical mycobacteria Multidrug resistance has become an increasing problem in AIDS patients with tuberculosis or atypical mycobacterial *(M avium, M kansasii)* infections. Delay in diagnosis and multidrug resistance are strong risk factors for mortality. These factors, along with poor compliance with patient isolation methods, were felt to be responsible for an outbreak of tuberculosis in 1994. This infection was caused by strain W, was resistant to seven antituberculous drugs, and was documented in 367 patients.

Standard drugs used in treating mycobacterial infections include isoniazid, rifampin, ethambutol, streptomycin, para-aminosalicylic acid, ethionamide, pyrazinamide, cycloserine, kanamycin, and amikacin. Some of the newer drugs found to be effective in treating these refractory infections are clofazimine (also used in treating leprosy), capreomycin, rifabutin, azithromycin, clarithromycin, and the quinolones (ciprofloxacin, ofloxacin, and sparfloxacin). The quinolones are very promising because they possess a high level of antimycobacterial activity with few adverse effects. Combined therapy with rifampin or rifabutin, ethambutol, clofazimine, and clarithromycin or ciprofloxacin has been successful in treating atypical mycobacterial infections in AIDS patients in recent studies. Isoniazid prophylaxis has been recommended in HIV-positive patients at high risk for tuberculosis. Prophylactic therapy with azithromycin, clarithromycin, rifabutin, or combined therapy may help prevent disseminated *M avium* complex in AIDS patients.

Treatment of other opportunistic infections   Other opportunistic infections encountered in AIDS patients include CNS toxoplasmosis, disseminated fungal infections, and herpes simplex or herpes zoster infections. Although toxoplasmosis has traditionally been treated with sulfadiazine, pyrimethamine, or clindamycin, more recent data suggest that trimethoprim-sulfamethoxazole (TMP-SMZ) may be equally effective, with far fewer side effects. Also, TMP-SMZ has been used as prophylactic therapy to try to prevent PCP as well as toxoplasmosis. Treatment of disseminated fungal infections is evolving with the availability of the newer imidazoles, fluconazole and itraconazole. Amphotericin B continues to play an important role in treating advanced invasive fungal disease. New formulations of amphotericin B in lipid complexes or liposomes reduce systemic toxicity. The new antiviral agents, valacyclovir and famciclovir, as well as other antiviral agents such as cidofovir, offer alternatives to acyclovir in the treatment of AIDS patients with refractory or disseminated herpes simplex or herpes zoster infections.

Treatment of AIDS-related malignancies   Kaposi sarcoma is usually a localized disease that can be treated with radiotherapy, but metastatic or disseminated disease may require combined chemotherapy such as doxorubicin, bleomycin, and vincristine. In addition, immunotherapy with beta interferon has been used in some patients with Kaposi sarcoma. B-cell lymphomas in AIDS patients often involve the lymph nodes, CNS, and lungs and may require treatment with multidrug chemotherapy, sometimes with regional radiotherapy.

Ophthalmologic Considerations

The ocular manifestations of AIDS are discussed in BCSC Section 9, *Intraocular Inflammation and Uveitis.*

HIV has been demonstrated in tears, conjunctival epithelial cells, corneal epithelial cells, aqueous, retinal vascular endothelium, and retina. While transmission of AIDS or HIV infection by ophthalmic examinations or ophthalmic equipment has not been documented, the following precautions are recommended.

Health care professionals performing eye examinations or other procedures involving contact with tears should wash their hands immediately after the procedure and between patients. Hand washing alone should be sufficient, but when practical and convenient, disposable gloves may be worn. The use of gloves is advisable when there are cuts, scratches, or dermatologic lesions on the hands.

Instruments that come into direct contact with external surfaces of the eyes should be wiped clean and disinfected by a 5–10 minute exposure to (1) a fresh solution of 3% hydrogen peroxide or (2) a fresh solution containing 5000 parts per million free available chlorine—a 1/10 dilution of common household bleach (sodium hypochlorite) or (3) 70% ethanol or (4) 70% isopropanol. The device should be thoroughly rinsed in tap water and dried before use.

Contact lenses used in trial fitting should be disinfected between fittings with a commercially available hydrogen peroxide contact lens disinfecting system or with the standard heat disinfection regimen (78–80°C for 10 minutes).

The demonstration of HIV in corneal epithelium has led to the recommendation that all corneal donors be screened for antibodies to HIV and that all potential donor corneas from HIV antibody-positive individuals be discarded.

For more specific recommendations, see the AAO Information Statement entitled "Updated Recommendations for Ophthalmic Practice in Relation to the Human Immunodeficiency Virus and Other Infectious Agents."

Centers for Disease Control. Classification system for human T-lymphotropic virus type III/lymphadenopathy-associated virus infections. *MMWR.* 1986;35:334–339.

Centers for Disease Control. Guidelines for prophylaxis against *Pneumocystis carinii* pneumonia for persons infected with human immunodeficiency virus. *MMWR.* 1989;38:1S–9S.

Centers for Disease Control. Human immunodeficiency virus infection in the United States: 1988 update. *MMWR.* 1989;38:1S–38S.

Centers for Disease Control. Public health service statement on management of occupational exposure to human immunodeficiency virus, including considerations regarding zidovudine postexposure use. *MMWR.* 1990;39:1S–14S.

Gerberding JL. Prophylaxis for occupational exposure to HIV. *Ann Intern Med.* 1996; 125:497–501.

Henderson DK, Saah AJ, Zak BJ, et al. Risk of nosocomial infection with human T-cell lymphotropic virus type III/lymphadenopathy-associated virus in a large cohort of intensively exposed health care workers. *Ann Intern Med.* 1986;104:644–647.

Rahhal FM, Arevalo JF, Munguia D, et al. Intravitreal cidofovir for the maintenance treatment of cytomegalovirus retinitis. *Ophthalmology.* 1996;103:1078–1083.

Updated recommendations for ophthalmic practice in relation to the human immunodeficiency virus and other infectious agents. Information Statement. San Francisco: American Academy of Ophthalmology; 1992.

Update on Antibiotics

For half a century, the main trend in infectious disease management has been the evolution and refinement of antibiotic therapy. Factors that have stimulated the development of new antibiotics include a spate of resistant bacteria, economics, and the desire to eliminate undesirable side effects. Recently, emphasis has shifted from *aminoglycosides* to *beta-lactams* and the development of new classes of antibiotics such as *carbapenems* and *monobactams.* In addition, *vancomycin, trimethoprim-sulfamethoxazole, erythromycin,* and *rifampin* have enjoyed a popular resurgence and new applications. Newly synthesized *quinolones* offer the possibility of treating serious infections on an outpatient basis. New antiviral drugs such as *acyclovir, ganciclovir, zidovudine,* and *ribavirin* are *nucleoside analogues.* The nucleoside triphosphate inhibits viral DNA polymerase and interrupts the growing DNA chain of the virus. In addition, several new *azole* compounds have been introduced over the past few years for treatment of systemic fungal infections. (For the characteristics of selected antibiotics, see Table I-9 at the end of this chapter.)

Antibacterial Agents

The various antibacterial agents act on bacteria in different ways. For example, unlike humans and other higher animals, most bacteria cannot utilize exogenous folic acid and must, therefore, synthesize their own in order to grow. For instance, sulfonamides and trimethoprim each block a different enzyme in this synthetic pathway. For this reason, bacteria susceptible to both agents are inhibited by lower concentrations of the two drugs acting together than needed with either one alone. Therefore, these two agents often are administered as a fixed-combination drug.

The *quinolones* have a different mechanism of action. In order to function properly, the double-stranded DNA of the bacterial chromosome must be supercoiled by the enzyme DNA gyrase, and quinolones block this enzyme. A number of new *fluoroquinolones,* which have very broad spectra of activity against a wide range of gram-negative and gram-positive bacterial species, have become available.

To make proteins, bacteria begin by copying the code for each protein from its gene on the bacterial chromosome onto a newly synthesized strand of the specialized RNA known as *messenger RNA (mRNA).* The antituberculosis drug rifampin selectively blocks the enzyme that synthesizes this mRNA strand. Once synthesized, the strand of mRNA then threads its way through the bacterial ribosomes to direct each ribosome in the sequence of assembling amino acids into a protein. This process is blocked in different ways by the tetracyclines and by chloramphenicol, erythromycin, and clindamycin; but it resumes again if the drug is discontinued. Because their effect is reversible, these classes of agents are considered to be *bacteriostatic.* In contrast, the aminoglycosides belong to a class of antibiotics that irreversibly derange ribosomal protein synthesis; the process cannot resume even after the drugs are stopped. These drugs, therefore, are *bactericidal.*

The bacterial proteins themselves or their enzymatic products make up the rest of the bacterial cell, including the membrane that encloses the cell. Polymyxin and colistin damage the cell membrane, making it unable to perform essential barrier functions. Surrounding the bacterium and outside of the cell membrane is the bacterial cell wall. The components of the cell wall are synthesized within the bacterial cell, then transported to the outside through the cell membrane before being assembled on its surface. The drugs that block this transport include bacitracin, a topical polypeptide agent derived from a strain of *Bacillus subtilis,* and vancomycin, a glycopeptide.

The final, crucial step in bacterial growth is formation of the bacterial cell wall. The necessary cross-linking of its components is mediated by special enzymes that are unlike anything in the human cell. The antibiotics that selectively inhibit one or more of these enzymes include penicillin and its growing family of related agents. This family includes the semisynthetic penicillins, all of the cephalosporin-like drugs, and newly introduced beta-lactams of novel structure such as imipenem. They are all grouped together under the label of *beta-lactam antibiotics,* because their structural formulas are marked by a distinctive four-atom structure known chemically as a *beta-lactam ring.* When even a small number of one of these beta-lactam molecules tag an infecting bacterium, gaps develop in its cell wall through which the organism ruptures and is destroyed.

Antibacterial agents can thus be separated into groups according to their specific targets on or within bacteria:

☐ Beta-lactams and glycopeptides inhibit cell wall synthesis

☐ Polymyxins distort cytoplasmic membrane function

☐ Quinolones and rifampicins inhibit nucleic acid synthesis

☐ Macrolides, aminoglycosides, and tetracyclines inhibit ribosome function

☐ Trimethoprim and sulfonamides inhibit folate metabolism

All antibiotics facilitate the growth of resistant bacteria consequent to the destruction of susceptible bacteria. Although the wide use of antimicrobial agents for veterinary and agricultural purposes has contributed to the emergence of multiresistant microorganisms, the excessive use of antibiotics, especially in hospitals, has been the most significant catalyst for resistance. Bacteria resist antibiotics by inactivation of the antibiotic, decreased accumulation of the antibiotic within the microorganism, or alteration of the target site on the microbe. For example, resistance to penicillins and cephalosporins is initiated by beta-lactamase enzymes that hydrolyze the beta-lactam ring, thus destroying the antibiotic's effectiveness. Resistance can be mediated by chromosomal mutations or the presence of extrachromosomal DNA, also known as *plasmid resistance.* The latter is more important from an epidemiologic point of view, because it is transmissible, is usually highly stable, confers resistance to many different classes of antibiotics simultaneously, and is often associated with other characteristics that enable a microorganism to colonize and to invade a susceptible host.

Resistance-conferring plasmids have been identified in virtually all bacteria. Moreover, many bacteria contain transposons that can enter plasmids or chromosomes. Plasmids can therefore pick up chromosomal genes for resistance and transfer them to species not currently resistant.

Bacteria that have acquired chromosomal and plasmid-mediated resistance can neutralize or destroy antibiotics in three different ways (they can use one or more of these mechanisms simultaneously):

□ By preventing the antibacterial agent from reaching its receptor site

□ By modifying or duplicating the target enzyme so that it is insensitive to the antibacterial agent

□ By synthesizing enzymes that destroy the antibacterial agent or modify the agent to alter its entry or receptor binding

Antimicrobial susceptibility testing permits a rational choice of antibiotics, although correlation of in vivo and in vitro susceptibility is not always precise. Disk-diffusion susceptibility testing has provided qualitative data about the inhibitory activity of commonly used antimicrobials against an isolated pathogen, and these data are usually sufficient. In serious infections, such as infective endocarditis, it is useful to quantify the drug concentrations that inhibit and kill the pathogen. The lowest drug concentration that prevents the growth of a defined inoculum of the isolated pathogen is the *minimal inhibitory concentration (MIC);* the lowest concentration that kills 99.9% of an inoculum is the *minimal lethal concentration (MLC).* For bactericidal drugs, the MIC and MLC are usually similar.

The antimicrobial activity of a treated patient's serum can be estimated by measuring serum bactericidal titers. Clinical experience suggests that intravascular infections usually are controlled when the peak serum bactericidal titer is 1.8 or greater. Bactericidal therapy is preferred for patients with immunologic compromise or life-threatening infection. Other patients may be treated effectively with either bactericidal or bacteriostatic drugs. Although synergistic combinations are useful in certain clinical situations (e.g., enterococcal endocarditis, gram-negative septicemia in granulocytopenic patients), combined antimicrobial therapy should be used judiciously to avoid potential antagonism and toxicity.

Beta-lactam antibiotics   The beta-lactam group includes the penicillins, cephalosporins, and monobactams, all of which possess a beta-lactam ring that binds to specific microbial binding sites and interferes with cell-wall synthesis. As new beta-lactams emerge, it has become customary to refer to them by generation. The generation is not only a chronological classification but also connotes their antimicrobial spectrum. The majority of new agents have been created by side-chain manipulation of the beta-lactam ring, which has improved resistance to enzymatic degradation. The newer antibiotics, however, show diminished potency against gram-positive cocci, especially staphylococci.

Penicillins. The first *natural penicillins,* types G and V, were degraded by the enzyme penicillinase. The *penicillinase-resistant penicillins,* such as methicillin, nafcillin, oxacillin, and cloxacillin, were developed for treatment of resistant *Staphylococcus* species, and except for a strain of methicillin-resistant *S epidermidis,* they were effective. The next generation of penicillins included the *aminopenicillins,* ampicillin and amoxicillin, created by placement of an amino group on the acyl side chain of the penicillin nucleus. This change broadened their effectiveness to include *Haemophilus influenzae, Escherichia coli,* and *Proteus mirabilis.* The next advance was the *carboxypenicillins,* carbenicillin and ticarcillin, active against aerobic gram-negative rods such as *Pseudomonas aeruginosa, Enterobacter* species, and indole-positive strains of *Proteus.* Therefore, carboxypenicillins are particularly effective for intra-abdominal conditions such as cholangitis, diverticular rupture, and gynecological infections. The fourth-generation penicillins, known as *acylureidopenicillins,* included azlocillin, mezlocillin, and piperacillin. Currently, their usefulness is for the treatment of Enterobacteriaceae, *Pseudomonas aeruginosa,* and febrile neutropenic patients, and for infections secondary to a combination of flora found in skin, soft tissue, intra-abdominal, and pelvic infections. However, because of the possibility of emergence of resistance, the newer penicillins are usually administered with an aminoglycoside. Current data, however, do not indicate that they are superior to the older penicillins in such circumstances.

Allergic reactions are the chief side effects encountered with the use of the penicillins. In fact, among antimicrobial agents, the penicillins are the leading cause of allergy. Allergy to the penicillins may be present in 3%–5% of the general population and in as many as 10% of those who have previously received a penicillin. Furthermore, the reported mortality during penicillin-induced anaphylaxis is approximately 10%. Large doses or prolonged administration seems to be associated with a high frequency of untoward reaction. Allergic reactions to penicillin are less frequent when the drug is administered orally. Reactions are somewhat higher in frequency when aqueous crystalline penicillin G is given by injection, and distinctly higher when procaine penicillin G is given intramuscularly or when a penicillin is applied locally. Cross-allergenicity among the semisynthetic and natural penicillins apparently reflects their common 6-aminopenicillanic acid nucleus and sensitizing derivatives. Cross-allergenicity to cephalosporins may occur in 3%–5% of patients and should be of particular concern when the allergic reaction to either group of antimicrobial agents has been of the immediate type, such as anaphylaxis, angioneurotic edema, or hives.

Cephalosporins. The *first-generation cephalosporins* are active against beta-lactamase-producing gram-positive cocci and gram-negative bacilli, which are responsible for most community-acquired infections. *Bacillus fragilis, Pseudomonas aeruginosa,* and *Enterobacter* species are typically resistant, as are methicillin-resistant staphylococci. None of the first-generation cephalosporins cross the meninges in concentrations sufficient for the treatment of meningitis.

The *second-generation extended-spectrum cephalosporins* have expanded coverage against gram-negative bacilli.

Third-generation cephalosporins have greater activity against gram-negative bacilli than the earlier cephalosporins, specifically inhibiting the majority of Enterobacteriaceae. Unfortunately, none of the third-generation cephalosporins are effective against enterococci. In general, third-generation cephalosporins are less active than their predecessors against gram-positive organisms, especially *Staphylococcus aureus*. Activity against *Bacillus fragilis* is variable. Third-generation cephalosporins penetrate the cerebrospinal fluid and have been used successfully to treat meningitis caused by susceptible microorganisms. It is advisable to limit these expensive antibiotics to situations in which they offer a clear advantage, such as in gram-negative bacillary infections or in place of more toxic agents. With the possible exception of ceftazidime, none of these agents is effective enough to be used by itself against *Pseudomonas aeruginosa* or in a febrile neutropenic patient. Likewise, they should not be used for surgical prophylaxis because of their limited activity against gram-positive organisms.

Parenteral cephalosporins have a direct effect on prothrombin production and on suppression of vitamin K–producing intestinal flora. The risk of hemorrhagic complications is increased in patients who are taking parenteral cephalosporins in conjunction with heparin, possibly the result of an additive or synergistic pharmacological effect. The hypoprothrombinemic effects of oral anticoagulants may be increased by such cephalosporins as cefoxitin, leading to a coagulopathy. Acute intolerance to alcohol may occur in individuals receiving cephalosporins that possess an N-methylthiotetrazole side chain, such as cefamandole or cefoperazone. Patients should avoid alcohol during therapy and for 2–3 days after completion.

Carbapenems. Carbapenems are a new class of antibiotics with a basic ring structure similar to that of penicillins, except that a carbon atom replaces sulfur at the number 1 position. The antibacterial spectrum of the carbapenems is broader than that of any other existing antibiotic and includes *Staphylococcus aureus, Enterobacter* species, and *Pseudomonas aeruginosa*. It also has excellent activity against anaerobic bacteria, including *Bacteroides fragilis*. Cross-resistance with other classes of antibiotics has not been reported, making the carbapenems important for infections involving gram-negative bacilli resistant to cephalosporins and penicillins. Carbapenems produce a postantibiotic killing effect against some organisms, with a delay in regrowth of damaged organisms similar to that seen with aminoglycosides but not with cephalosporins or acylureidopenicillins. This quality can be particularly important for settings in which host defenses are compromised, such as granulocytopenia or sequestered foci of infection.

Imipenem-cilastatin (Primaxin) combines imipenem, a carbapenem, with cilastatin, an inhibitor of renal dehydropeptidase. Cilastatin has no antimicrobial activity and is present solely to prevent degradation of imipenem by dehydropeptidase. Imipenem-cilastatin is an appropriate compound for monotherapy of mixed infections. *Meropenem* and *biapenem* are newer carbapenems that have increased stability against degradation by dehydropeptidases. Several other new carbapenems are currently being developed. *Loracarbef* (Lorabid) is an oral *carbacephem,* a new class of antibiotic that is structurally very similar to cephalosporins. It provides good coverage for most gram-positive and gram-negative aerobic bacteria.

Mention should be made of *clavulanic acid* and *sulbactam*. These beta-lactam molecules possess little intrinsic antibacterial activity, but they are potent inhibitors of many plasmid-mediated beta-lactamases. Currently, four beta-lactam antibiotic plus beta-lactamase inhibitor combinations are available in the United States:

Augmentin (oral amoxicillin and clavulanic acid), *Timentin* (intravenous ticarcillin and clavulanic acid), *Unasyn* (intravenous ampicillin and sulbactam), and *Zosyn* (piperacillin and tazobactam).

Monobactams are a new monocyclic class of antibiotics utilizing only the beta-lactam ring as their core structure. This group possesses excellent activity against aerobic gram-negative bacilli but is ineffective against both gram-positive cocci and anaerobes. The monobactams are similar in antimicrobial spectrum to the aminoglycosides and are generally better tolerated. However, the use of monobactams is limited by their narrow spectrum: many nosocomial infections are polymicrobial, involving gram-positive bacteria or anaerobes in addition to gram-negative aerobic bacilli. Despite the presence of a beta-lactam ring, cross-allergenicity with penicillins and cephalosporins appears to be minimal. *Aztreonam,* the first approved monobactam antibiotic, has an excellent safety profile and good success rate in the therapy of infections caused by aerobic gram-negative bacilli. Aztreonam is generally combined with a semisynthetic antistaphylococcal penicillin or clindamycin in presumptive therapy of known mixed infections.

Aminoglycosides   The aminoglycoside antibiotics inhibit protein synthesis by binding to bacterial ribosomes. Gentamicin, tobramycin, amikacin, kanamycin, streptomycin, and netilmicin can be considered as a group because of their similar activity, pharmacology, and toxicity. Because of poor gastrointestinal absorption, parenteral administration is necessary to produce therapeutic levels.

Aminoglycosides are used for serious infections caused by gram-negative bacilli, including bacteremia in immunocompromised hosts, hospital-acquired pneumonia, and peritonitis. They may be combined with penicillin for the treatment of enterococcal endocarditis. Aminoglycosides are not effective against meningitis because they do not cross the blood-brain barrier. Aminoglycosides are not used for most gram-positive infections because the beta-lactams are less toxic.

The major side effects of the aminoglycosides are nephrotoxicity and ototoxicity. A baseline BUN (blood urea nitrogen) and creatinine should be obtained, as well as serial studies twice a week. Aminoglycoside peak and trough serum levels should be obtained in patients with known renal disease. Combined administration of a loop diuretic such as furosemide with aminoglycosides has a synergistic ototoxic effect, potentially leading to permanent loss of cochlear function.

Penicillins may decrease the antimicrobial effectiveness of parenteral aminoglycosides, particularly in patients with impaired renal function. Aminoglycosides may exacerbate the neuromuscular blocking effects of nondepolarizing muscle relaxants such as tubocurarine. Their combined use during surgery can cause a prolonged respiratory depression accompanied by extended apnea. *Oral* aminoglycosides are used for bowel sterilization prior to gastrointestinal surgery; however, they may cause malabsorption of vitamin K, amplifying the effects of oral anticoagulants.

Once-daily aminoglycoside dosing regimens have been employed in recent years to decrease systemic toxicity, reduce variability in the timing of drug administration, and lower the costs associated with nursing care for intravenous antibiotic administration and drug level monitoring.

Miscellaneous antibacterial agents   *Vancomycin* has regained popularity because of the emergence of methicillin-resistant staphylococci and the recognition that *Clostridium difficile* is a cause of pseudomembranous colitis. Vancomycin has excellent activity against *Clostridium* and against most gram-positive bacteria, including methicillin-resistant staphylococci, diphtheroids, and other *Corynebacterium* species. Vancomycin has been used alone to treat serious infections caused by methicillin-resistant staphylococci. In cases of prosthetic-valve endocarditis caused by methicillin-resistant *Staphylococcus epidermidis*, a combination of vancomycin, rifampin, and gentamicin has been shown to be an effective treatment.

In recent years, several cases of vancomycin-resistant enterococcal infection have been reported. In one study of hospitalized patients, approximately 1% carried vancomycin-resistant enterococci in their gastrointestinal tract. These infections are very difficult or impossible to treat because of multidrug resistance. In vitro studies have shown that plasmid-mediated vancomycin resistance can be transferred to staphylococci, and concern is increasing that vancomycin-resistant staphylococcal infections will soon emerge as a serious clinical problem.

The Centers for Disease Control have issued recommendations regarding appropriate use of vancomycin to help counteract the emergence of bacterial drug resistance. These guidelines include discouraging the use of vancomycin for routine surgical prophylaxis, avoiding its empiric use in febrile neutropenic patients unless there is strong evidence for a beta-lactam resistant gram-positive infection, and avoiding prophylactic therapy for patients with intravascular catheters or vascular grafts. The rationale for these recommendations is that inappropriate use of this drug will only hasten the emergence of new resistant bacterial strains. Similarly, many feel that prophylactic use of vancomycin in routine ophthalmic surgeries is not advisable from an infectious disease and public health standpoint.

Rifampin was originally developed as an antituberculosis agent but is also used to treat a host of intractable bacterial infections. Rifampin is usually employed adjunctively because bacteria develop resistance to the drug when it is used as a single agent. Rifampin often demonstrates higher effectiveness in vivo than in vitro, perhaps because it penetrates directly into leukocytes and kills phagocytosed bacteria. It also penetrates well into bone and abscess cavities. Rifampin in combination with other agents is used successfully in the treatment of *Staphylococcus aureus* and prosthetic-valve endocarditis caused by *Staphylococcus epidermidis*. Rifampin is effective in eradicating the carrier state of nasal *Staphylococcus aureus*. It is also effective prophylactically against *Neisseria meningitidis* and may be useful for treating oropharyngeal carriers of *Haemophilus influenzae* type B.

Another oral antibiotic with potential for the treatment of deep-seated infections is *trimethoprim-sulfamethoxazole (TMP-SMZ)*. After a single oral dose, the mean serum levels of trimethoprim and sulfamethoxazole are about 75% of the concentration that would be achieved through the intravenous route. In addition to its excellent pharmacokinetics, TMP-SMZ has an extremely broad-spectrum; its activity against Enterobacteriaceae is usually comparable to that of a third-generation cephalosporin or even an aminoglycoside. In addition, a number of unusual microorganisms that are resistant to cephalosporins are susceptible to TMP-SMZ. One misconception is that TMP-SMZ has limited activity against gram-positive bacteria; however, most streptococci, staphylococci, and *Listeria monocytogenes* are susceptible to this drug. Beyond the broad-spectrum effect of TMP-SMZ, the concomitant use of *metronidazole* creates an antibiotic combination with activity against microorganisms surpassing that of a third-generation cephalosporin. TMP-SMZ has seen increasing use in the treatment and prophylaxis of *Pneumocystis* and toxoplasmosis in recent years.

Chloramphenicol is a bacteriostatic agent that reversibly inhibits ribosomal protein synthesis. It is active against a wide variety of gram-negative and gram-positive organisms, including anaerobes. The major concern is hematopoietic toxicity, including reversible bone marrow suppression and irreversible aplasia. Aplastic anemia is an idiosyncratic late reaction to the drug and is usually fatal. Reversible leukopenia, thrombocytopenia, and suppression of erythropoiesis are dose-related and can usually be avoided by maintaining peak serum levels of less than 25 micrograms/ml. Other side effects include hemolysis, allergy, and peripheral neuritis.

Macrolides   The macrolide *erythromycin* is often employed for the initial treatment of community-acquired pneumonia. This agent is effective against infections caused by pneumococci, group A streptococci, *Mycoplasma pneumoniae,* and *Chlamydia.* It is also effective against *Legionella* species, which have been recognized as a significant cause of community-acquired pneumonia. Erythromycin is used to treat upper respiratory infections and sexually transmitted diseases in penicillin-allergic patients.

   Clarithromycin (Biaxin), *azithromycin* (Zithromax), and *dirithromycin* (Dynabac) are macrolide antibiotics chemically related to erythromycin. All are well-tolerated alternatives to erythromycin and may offer particular advantages in the treatment of gonococcal and *Chlamydia* infections and in the treatment of *Mycobacterium avium* and other recalcitrant infections associated with AIDS. Azithromycin is subclassified as an *azalide* and it possesses far fewer drug interactions than erythromycin. Many other macrolide antibiotics are available in Europe or being evaluated here in the United States and have similar antimicrobial spectra.

   Clindamycin has a gram-positive spectrum similar to erythromycin and is also active against most anaerobes, including *Bacteroides fragilis.* Except for anaerobic infection, it is rarely the drug of choice. Clindamycin is well absorbed orally, and parenteral formulations are also available. Its major side effect is diarrhea, which may progress to pseudomembranous enterocolitis in some patients.

Tetracyclines   The tetracyclines are bacteriostatic agents that reversibly inhibit ribosomal protein synthesis. Although they have a broad spectrum of activity (including *Rickettsia, Chlamydia, Nocardia,* and *Actinomyces*), resistance is widespread, especially among *Staphylococcus aureus* and gram-negative bacilli. The principal clinical uses of tetracyclines are in treatment of nongonococcal urethritis, Rocky Mountain spotted fever, chronic bronchitis, and sebaceous disorders such as acne rosacea. In addition, they are an alternative for the penicillin-allergic patient with syphilis. Tetracyclines are well absorbed when taken on an empty stomach; however, their absorption is decreased when taken with milk, antacids, calcium, or iron. Tetracyclines are distributed throughout the extracellular fluid, but cerebrospinal fluid penetration is unreliable. Adverse effects include oral or vaginal candidiasis with prolonged use, gastrointestinal upset, photosensitivity, and elevation of the blood urea nitrogen. Tetracyclines should not be administered to pregnant women or to children under 10 years of age because of their effects on developing bone.

Quinolones   In the early 1960s *nalidixic acid* was discovered as an accidental by-product of research on quinolones as antimalarial agents. Nalidixic acid has relatively good activity against aerobic gram-negative bacteria with minimal inhibitory concentrations but only limited activity against gram-positive species; it does not inhibit *Pseudomonas aeruginosa.* Nalidixic acid was adequate therapy for urinary tract infections, but it does not produce sufficient tissue concentrations after oral ingestion to treat systemic infections. When administered intravenously, it produces central nervous system and cardiac toxicity. Consequently, the quinolones were not considered an important class of drugs, particularly in the United States.

Recently, however, the introduction of a fluorine into the basic quinolone nucleus has produced compounds known as *fluoroquinolones*, which have excellent gram-positive activity. The subsequent addition of piperazine created compounds such as *norfloxacin* and *ciprofloxacin* that have a broad spectrum encompassing staphylococci and most of the significant gram-negative bacilli, including *Pseudomonas*. Ciprofloxacin is available in both oral and parenteral forms. It can be used to treat urinary tract infections, gonorrhea, and diarrheal diseases, as well as respiratory, skin, and, particularly, bone infections. Fluoroquinolones introduced more recently into the United States market include *ofloxacin* (Floxin), *temafloxacin* (Omniflox), *lomefloxacin* (Maxaquin), *enoxacin* (Penetrex), and *sparfloxacin* (Zagam); and several others are currently being studied. Oral quinolones offer an alternative form of therapy to beta-lactams and aminoglycosides and have permitted physicians to treat more patients outside the hospital setting.

Antiviral Agents

Acyclovir (Zovirax) is a nucleoside analogue of guanosine that is effective against herpes simplex and varicella-zoster infections. Acyclovir is triphosphorylated in infected cells and then inhibits viral DNA replication. The first phosphorylation step is catalyzed by the enzyme thymidine kinase. The viral-induced thymidine kinase is far more active in phosphorylating acyclovir than the host-cell thymidine kinase. Therefore, acyclovir is very active against virally infected cells and is generally well tolerated.

Acyclovir has proven effective in a variety of herpetic infections. A topical 5% ointment in polyethyleneglycol may be used in localized first episodes of genital herpes. Oral acyclovir at a dose of 200 mg 5 times daily has been effective in acute severe genital herpes. Chronic suppressive oral acyclovir has also demonstrated efficacy in immunocompetent patients with frequently recurring genital herpes. Intravenous acyclovir at a dose of 30 mg/kg every 8 hours is the treatment of choice for herpes simplex encephalitis. Acyclovir at a dose of 500 mg/M^2 every 8 hours has been used successfully for the treatment of herpes zoster infections in immunocompromised patients. This dose is also used in patients with acute retinal necrosis syndrome.

A randomized, double-masked, controlled study of oral acyclovir in patients with herpes zoster ophthalmicus demonstrated that a dose of 600 mg 5 times daily was effective in reducing the incidence of ocular complications of herpes zoster ophthalmicus. However, postherpetic neuralgia was not affected by this therapy. Most clinicians now use higher doses of oral acyclovir to treat herpes zoster, generally 800–1000 mg orally 5 times daily. In addition, studies in Europe have demonstrated that topical ophthalmic acyclovir is superior to topical corticosteroids for herpes zoster keratouveitis; however, topical ophthalmic acyclovir is not available in the United States. Finally, a randomized, controlled study of acyclovir and oral corticosteroids demonstrated that the latter did not help to reduce the incidence of postherpetic neuralgia when added to oral acyclovir.

Famciclovir (Famvir) and *valacyclovir* (Valtrex) are currently approved for the treatment of herpes zoster infections and have also been shown to be effective against herpes simplex in numerous studies. Both of these newer drugs allow less frequent dosing intervals (500 mg every 8 hours for famciclovir, and 1000 mg every 8 hours for valacyclovir).

Ganciclovir (Cytovene), previously known as dihydroxy propoxymethyl guanine, or DHPG, has been approved for the treatment of CMV retinitis in immunocompromised patients. Ganciclovir, a derivative of acyclovir, is now available in intravenous, oral, intravitreal, and intraocular implant forms. Like acyclovir, ganciclovir must be triphosphorylated; however, it does not appear that a viral-specific thymidine kinase is made by cytomegalovirus. Therefore, ganciclovir is somewhat more toxic than acyclovir.

Ganciclovir is generally given in a two-step fashion with an initial induction dose of 5 mg/kg every 12 hours for 14 days, followed by long-term maintenance therapy at a dose of 5 mg/kg once daily. An alternative maintenance dose has been 6 mg/kg/day, 5 out of 7 days. Patients must have a permanent indwelling central venous catheter for long-term outpatient intravenous ganciclovir administration. Studies of ganciclovir have suggested that a response to the drug is seen in 80%–100% of patients with CMV retinitis and that remission occurs in 60%–80%. Similar to other infections in patients with AIDS, CMV retinitis recurs in all patients who discontinue therapy and even in some patients on maintenance therapy. These relapses generally respond to a second induction course.

Ganciclovir's major toxicity is bone marrow suppression, particularly granulocytopenia and thrombocytopenia. Weekly intravitreal ganciclovir injections avoid the problems associated with systemic administration of the drug while providing equally effective maintenance therapy for controlling CMV retinitis. In addition, intraocular ganciclovir implants can be placed surgically at the pars plana for long-term CMV retinitis control.

Studies suggest that intravenous ganciclovir is also of benefit in other cytomegalovirus infections, such as esophagitis and colitis. In transplant patients with cytomegalovirus pneumonia, the use of ganciclovir and gamma globulin has shown promise in reducing mortality.

Foscarnet (Foscavir) inhibits the DNA polymerase of human herpesvirus and the reverse transcriptase of HIV at a different site from the nucleoside analogues. It demonstrates in vitro activity against CMV, herpes simplex, varicella-zoster, and HIV at concentrations readily achieved with IV therapy. Oral bioavailability is poor, and chronic IV therapy is required for suppression of CMV retinitis in HIV disease. Foscarnet's primary value is that it is not generally myelosuppressive and, therefore, may be used without discontinuing zidovudine therapy. Its primary dose-limiting side effect is nephrotoxicity; aggressive pretreatment hydration may reduce this effect significantly.

Cidofovir (Vistide) is a potent antiviral agent with activity against herpes simplex, herpes zoster, CMV, adenovirus, Epstein-Barr virus, and HIV, through its ability to block DNA synthesis by viral DNA polymerase. Cidofovir's prolonged antiviral activity, lasting up to several weeks, allows infrequent dosing. Intravenous (3–5 mg/kg, every other week) and intravitreal cidofovir (20 µg per eye every 5–6 weeks) has been used successfully in the treatment of CMV retinitis. In one recent study of intravitreal cidofovir, CMV retinitis regressed in all 53 patients. Of the patients who had no previous anti-CMV therapy before this study, none had disease progression during the follow-up period, and only 14% of the patients who had previously undergone anti-CMV therapy had disease progression.

Zidovudine (Retrovir), previously known as azidothymidine, or AZT, is a thymidine analogue that inhibits replication of HIV. Zidovudine selectively inhibits HIV reverse transcriptase and viral DNA synthesis. Zidovudine does cross the blood-brain barrier; central nervous system concentrations are 30%–50% of serum concentrations. Randomized, controlled clinical trials have demonstrated that zidovudine prolongs survival and decreases the frequency of opportunistic infections in patients with AIDS. Initially, the standard dosage of zidovudine was 200 mg orally every 4 hours. Subsequently, controlled trials have shown that 100 mg orally every 4 hours is as effective and may be less toxic. Furthermore, studies of patients with the AIDS-related complex (ARC) or with asymptomatic HIV infection have demonstrated that zidovudine decreases the rate of progression to AIDS. The major toxicity of zidovudine is reversible bone marrow suppression, including anemia and granulocytopenia. Zidovudine does not cure HIV infection; patients on zidovudine remain infectious.

Dideoxyinosine (ddI, Videx) has in vitro activity similar to that of zidovudine and has been approved for the treatment of HIV infection. The major treatment-limiting toxicity is acute pancreatitis; the drug is therefore contraindicated in the setting of alcoholism or prior pancreatitis.

Dideoxycytidine (ddC, Hivid) is another nucleoside analogue that inhibits HIV reverse transcriptase. Its use is limited by potentially severe and irreversible peripheral neuropathy. Several other new nucleoside analogue and protease inhibitor drugs for the treatment of HIV infection were discussed on pp 31–32.

Antifungal Agents

Fluconazole (Diflucan) and itraconazole (Sporanox) are newer antifungal imidazoles for treatment of cryptococcal meningitis, candidiasis, and other invasive fungal infections. They are more effective and better tolerated than ketoconazole in the treatment of candidiasis and invasive fungal disease. They function by inhibiting fungal cytochrome p-450-dependent enzymes, thereby blocking synthesis of the fungal cell membrane. The newer imidazoles offer a less toxic alternative to amphotericin B in the treatment of cryptococcal meningitis and may play a role in chronic suppression of Cryptococcus after remission of acute infection in severely immunocompromised patients. Several additional imidazoles are currently being developed and evaluated, including flutrimazole and croconazole.

Terbinafine (Lamisil) is a new allylamine oral antifungal agent that is very effective in controlling onychomycosis due to chronic dermatophyte infections. Treatment must be continued for 6–12 weeks to eradicate the nail infection.

Treatment of Hospital-Acquired Infections

Decisions concerning antibiotic administration in the treatment of serious hospital-acquired infections present important considerations for the prescribing physician. Three distinct stages of therapy tend to occur in such infections; and especially in the latter two stages, cost containment is possible by close monitoring of mode, level, and frequency of antibiotic dosing. The first stage of therapy typically lasts about 3 days, during which time uncertainty exists about the causative organism. Therapy is given empirically, often with the combination of an aminoglycoside and a beta-lactam antibiotic. The second stage begins about the fourth day, at which time definitive microbiological and clinical data are available that should allow for streamlining of antibiotic therapy, usually from combination therapy to less expensive monotherapy. It is at this stage in the patient's hospital stay that routine assessment of antibiotic management offers the first chance to reduce hospital antibiotic costs without compromising the clinical outcome. The *third stage* of therapy typically begins around the seventh day, when the patient is usually clinically stable and afebrile. At this point, often the only reason the patient is kept hospitalized is to continue treatment with parenteral antibiotics. In many patients, however, therapy can be switched to daily intravenous dosing or oral antibiotics, facilitating outpatient therapy. Streamlining antibiotic therapy by changing modes and frequency of administration represents a major step toward effective, responsible cost containment.

Coulton S, Hunt E. Recent advances in the chemistry and biology of carbapenem antibiotics. *Prog Med Chem.* 1996;33:99–145.

Donowitz GR, Mandell GL. Beta-lactam antibiotics. *N Engl J Med.* 1988;318:419–426, 490–500.

Graybill JR. The future of antifungal therapy. *Clin Infect Dis.* 1996;22(suppl2): S166–178.

Hatala R, Dinh T, Cook DJ. Once-daily aminoglycoside dosing in immunocompetent adults: a meta-analysis. *Ann Intern Med.* 1996;124:717–725.

Hodge WG, Lalonde RG, Sampalis J, Deschenes J. Once-weekly intraocular injections of ganciclovir for maintenance therapy of cytomegalovirus retinitis: clinical and ocular outcome. *J Infect Dis.* 1996;174:393–396.

Montecalvo MA, Shay DK, Patel P, et al. Bloodstream infections with vancomycin-resistant enterococci. *Arch Intern Med.* 1996;156:1458–1462.

Neu HC. New antibiotics: areas of appropriate use. *J Infect Dis.* 1987;155:403–417.

TABLE I-9

CHARACTERISTICS OF SELECTED ANTIBIOTICS

ANTIBIOTIC	SPECTRUM*	ROUTE	BACTERIOSTATIC OR BACTERICIDAL	SIDE EFFECTS/ SPECIAL USES
Antibacterial Agents				
Sulfonamides				
Sulfisoxazole (Gantrisin)	Urinary tract infections, +, −, *Nocardia,* lymphogranuloma venereum, trachoma	PO	Bacteriostatic	Crystalluria, allergic reactions (rashes, photosensitivity, and drug fever), kernicterus in newborns, renal damage, Stevens-Johnson syndrome (more likely with long-acting sulfonamides), blood dyscrasia (agranulocytosis), disseminated vasculitis.
Trimethoprim-sulfamethoxazole, TMP-SMZ (Bactrim, Septra)	Urinary tract infections, +, −, shigellosis, *Nocardia, Pneumocystis* pneumonia	PO, IV	Bacteriostatic	Same as above, plus nausea and vomiting, diarrhea, skin rashes, CNS irritability, bone-marrow toxicity. Liver damage and Stevens-Johnson syndrome may be fatal.
Penicillin G				
Aqueous (many brands)	+, *Neisseria,* spirochetes, actinomycosis	IV only	Bactericidal	Penicillin allergy,** CNS toxicity with high blood levels, Coombs-positive hemolytic anemia, rare nephritis.
Procaine (many brands)	Same as above	IM only	Bactericidal	Same as above, plus -*caine* reactions.
Benzathine (Bicillin)	Spirochetes, *Streptococcus* prophylaxis	IM only	Bactericidal	Prolonged penicillin allergy.**

*Symbols: + = gram-positive; − = gram-negative; *Staph* = penicillinase-producers.
**Penicillin allergy includes spectrum from anaphylaxis to serum sickness.

49

Table I-9

Characteristics of Selected Antibiotics (Continued)

ANTIBIOTIC	SPECTRUM*	ROUTE	BACTERIOSTATIC OR BACTERICIDAL	SIDE EFFECTS/ SPECIAL USES
Semisynthetic penicillins				
Penicillin V (Pen-Vee K)	+, Neisseria, spirochetes, actinomycosis	PO	Bactericidal	Much better absorption than penicillin G when given orally in the fasting state.
Methicillin (Staphcillin)	Penicillinase-producing Staph only	IV	Bactericidal	Penicillin allergy,** pain at injection site, rare bone-marrow and renal toxicity, drug fever, Coombs-positive hemolytic anemia, hemorrhagic cystitis.
Cloxacillin (Tegopen)	+, especially Staph	PO	Bactericidal	Penicillin allergy,** GI symptoms. Better absorbed and better tolerated than nafcillin and oxacillin given orally in the fasting state.
Ampicillin (Polycillin)	+, especially enterococcus (except Staph) and some −, especially Haemophilus influenzae, Proteus mirabilis, Salmonella sp, Escherichia coli	IV, PO	Bactericidal	Penicillin allergy,** GI symptoms (from PO administration). Rash common in viral illnesses (maculopapular eruption that is not necessarily allergy).
Ampicillin-sulbactam (Unasyn)	Same as ampicillin plus beta-lactamase producers and some anaerobes	IV	Bactericidal	Penicillin allergy, diarrhea, elevated liver enzymes.
Amoxicillin (Amoxil)	Same as above, except Shigella	PO	Bactericidal	Same as above. Better absorbed than oral ampicillin. Should replace oral ampicillin for everything except bacillary dysentery.

*Symbols: + = gram-positive; − = gram-negative; Staph = penicillinase-producers.
**Penicillin allergy includes spectrum from anaphylaxis to serum sickness.

TABLE 1-9

CHARACTERISTICS OF SELECTED ANTIBIOTICS (Continued)

ANTIBIOTIC	SPECTRUM*	ROUTE	BACTERIOSTATIC OR BACTERICIDAL	SIDE EFFECTS/ SPECIAL USES
Amoxicillin–potassium clavulanate (Augmentin)	Same as amoxicillin plus beta-lactamase producers (Haemophilus influenzae, Branhamella sp, and Staph sp)	PO	Bactericidal	Same as amoxicillin plus more diarrhea.
Ticarcillin (Ticar)	–, especially Pseudomonas aeruginosa and Proteus sp, abdominal anaerobes, and some +, except Staph	IV	Bactericidal	Penicillin allergy,** rare bleeding diathesis, hypokalemia (4.0 mEq Na$^+$/gm), abnormal liver function tests, Candida overgrowth.
Ticarcillin–potassium clavulanate (Timentin)	Same as ticarcillin plus beta-lactamase producers (Klebsiella sp, Bacteroides fragilis, and Serratia sp)	IV	Bactericidal	Same as ticarcillin plus more diarrhea and nausea. Candida overgrowth frequent.
Piperacillin (Pipracil)	–, most active of all semi-synthetic penicillins against Pseudomonas and many other aerobic gram-negative rods including Klebsiella; abdominal anaerobes	IV	Bactericidal	One half as much Na$^+$ as ticarcillin. Similar to ticarcillin, but approximately 25% of patients develop a hypersensitivity reaction and/or diarrhea. Must be used with an amino-glycoside. Rare bleeding diathesis.
Piperacillin-tazobactam (Zosyn)	Same as piperacillin with increased coverage of beta-lactamase producers and anaerobes	IV	Bactericidal	Same as piperacillin

*Symbols: + = gram-positive; – = gram-negative; Staph = penicillinase-producers.
**Penicillin allergy includes spectrum from anaphylaxis to serum sickness.

TABLE I-9
CHARACTERISTICS OF SELECTED ANTIBIOTICS (Continued)

ANTIBIOTIC	SPECTRUM*	ROUTE	BACTERIOSTATIC OR BACTERICIDAL	SIDE EFFECTS/ SPECIAL USES
Cephalosporins				
First-generation cephalosporins				
Cefazolin (Kefzol, Ancef)	+ and some –; not a good *Staph* treatment	IM, IV	Bactericidal	Thrombophlebitis or pain at injection site, skin rash, urticaria, eosinophilia, neutropenia.
Cephalexin (Keflex)	+, *Staph*, and some –	PO	Bactericidal	Same as above plus GI symptoms.
Cefadroxil monohydrate (Duracef)	+, *Staph*, and some –	PO	Bactericidal	Rash, urticaria, GI symptoms.
Second-generation (extended-spectrum) cephalosporins				
Cefamandole (Mandol)	+, especially *Staph*, and some –	IV	Bactericidal	Less thrombophlebitis than above, skin rash, drug fever, eosinophilia, hypoprothrombinemia ± bleeding. Extremely effective prophylaxis for *Staph* including MRSE.
Cefoxitin (Mefoxin)	+, –, abdominal anaerobes (the best of all cephalosporins)	IV	Bactericidal	Thrombophlebitis, fever, skin rash, eosinophilia, nausea, vomiting, diarrhea, bone-marrow and liver toxicity.
Cefonicid (Monocid)	– and some anaerobes	IV	Bactericidal	Often used for prophylaxis with colorectal or gynecologic surgeries; may cause pain at injection site, eosinophilia, GI symptoms, rash.

*Symbols: + = gram-positive; – = gram-negative; *Staph* = penicillinase-producers.

Table 1-9

Characteristics of Selected Antibiotics (Continued)

ANTIBIOTIC	SPECTRUM*	ROUTE	BACTERIOSTATIC OR BACTERICIDAL	SIDE EFFECTS/ SPECIAL USES
Cefaclor (Ceclor, Distaclor)	+ and some –, *Haemophilus* sp	PO	Bactericidal	Toxicity similar to other cephalosporins. Major use will be treating ENT infections in children and respiratory infections in adults with COPD.
Cefuroxime sodium (IV: Zinacef, Kefurox); Cefuroxime axetil (PO: Ceftin)	+ and some –, *Haemophilus* sp	IV, PO	Bactericidal	Rash, GI symptoms.
Cefotetan (Cefotan)	–, anaerobes	IM or IV	Bactericidal	A long half-life cefoxitin. Hypoprothrombinemia, and disulfiram-like reaction.
Third-generation (ultrabroad-spectrum) cephalosporins				
Cefotaxime (Claforan)	–, including many multidrug-resistant organisms	IV	Bactericidal	Cephalosporin hypersensitivity reaction, thrombophlebitis. Good penetration into CSF in meningitis.
Cefoperazone (Cefobid)	–, including *Pseudomonas* sp and many multidrug-resistant organisms, some anaerobes	IM or IV	Bactericidal	Cephalosporin hypersensitivity, hypoprothrombinemia, diarrhea. Can be given q 8–12h.
Ceftriaxone (Rocephin)	Like cefotaxime; gonorrhea, *Borrelia burgdorferi*	IM or IV	Bactericidal	Very long half-life makes it attractive for outpatient therapy. Treatment of choice for gonorrhea. Effective for all forms of Lyme disease.
Ceftazidime (Fortaz, Tazidime, Tazicef)	–, especially *Pseudomonas* sp	IM, IV	Bactericidal	Good anti-pseudomonal cephalosporin, long half-life: q 8–12h administration. The best all-purpose third-generation cephalosporin.

*Symbols: + = gram-positive; – = gram-negative; *Staph* = penicillinase-producers.

TABLE I-9

CHARACTERISTICS OF SELECTED ANTIBIOTICS (Continued)

ANTIBIOTIC	SPECTRUM*	ROUTE	BACTERIOSTATIC OR BACTERICIDAL	SIDE EFFECTS/ SPECIAL USES
Ceftizoxime (Cefizox)	Many – and anaerobes	IV	Bactericidal	Rash, GI symptoms, elevated liver enzymes
Cefixime (Suprax)	+, some – (Haemophilus influenzae, Branhamella catarrhalis)	PO	Bactericidal	Diarrhea, nausea, abdominal pain, flatulence. First oral third-generation cephalosporin.
Cefpodoxime proxetil (Vantin)	+, –, Enterobacter, Pseudomonas, Serratia, Morganella, Enterococcus, generally resistant infections	PO	Bactericidal	Twice daily for ENT, respiratory, urinary, and soft tissue infections. Single dose for uncomplicated gonorrhea.
Cefprozil (Cefzil)	+, –, including Haemophilus	PO	Bactericidal	Rash, GI symptoms.
Ceftibuten (Cedax)	+, –, including Haemophilus, Moraxella	PO	Bactericidal	No real advantages.
Fourth-generation (super-duper broad spectrum) cephalosporins				
Cefepime (Maxipime)	+, –, some anaerobes	IV, IM	Bactericidal	Expensive; slightly better gram-negative coverage than ceftazidime.
Carbacephems				
Loracarbef (Lorabid)	+, –, including Haemophilus	PO	Bactericidal	Rash, GI symptoms.
Cephamycins				
Cefmetazole (Zefazone)	Similar to that of second-generation cephalosporins	IV	Bactericidal	GI symptoms, rash, seizures in patients with renal insufficiency; more side effects than second-generation cephalosporins.

*Symbols: + = gram-positive; – = gram-negative; Staph = penicillinase-producers.

TABLE I-9

CHARACTERISTICS OF SELECTED ANTIBIOTICS (Continued)

ANTIBIOTIC	SPECTRUM*	ROUTE	BACTERIOSTATIC OR BACTERICIDAL	SIDE EFFECTS/ SPECIAL USES
Monobactams				
Aztreonam (Azactam)	Most −; no activity for + or anaerobes	IM, IV	Bactericidal	First of this class of monocyclic beta-lactams. The spectrum of an aminoglycoside without oto- or nephrotoxicity.
Carbapenems				
Imipenem-cilastatin (Primaxin)	+, −, including *Pseudomonas* sp and multidrug-resistant strains, anaerobes	IV	Bactericidal	Nausea, diarrhea, phlebitis, elevated serum glutamic-oxaloacetic transaminase (SGOT), elevated serum glutamic-pyruvic transaminase (SGPT), seizures. Prototype of carbapenems. *Candida* superinfection frequent.
Meropenem (Merrem)	Similar to imipenem, but less active against +, more active against −	IV	Bactericidal	Does not require cilastatin component because more resistant to enzyme degradation; less problem with seizures.
Macrolides				
Erythromycin	+, spirochetes, *Mycoplasma, Legionella, Campylobacter*	PO, IV	Bacteriostatic	GI upset, altered liver function test, hepatic damage, stomatitis, thrombophlebitis (with IV administration). Take with meals or a snack when given orally.

*Symbols: + = gram-positive; − = gram-negative; *Staph* = penicillinase-producers.

Table 1-9

Characteristics of Selected Antibiotics (Continued)

ANTIBIOTIC	SPECTRUM*	ROUTE	BACTERIOSTATIC OR BACTERICIDAL	SIDE EFFECTS/ SPECIAL USES
Clindamycin (Cleocin)	+, anaerobes, actinomycosis	PO, IV	Bacteriostatic	GI toxicity can be severe and even lethal. More completely absorbed than lincomycin and less toxic.
Azalides				
Clarithromycin (Biaxin) Azithromycin (Zithromax) Dirithromycin (Dynabec)	+, *Mycoplasma, Chlamydia, Legionella*	PO	Bacteriostatic	Reversible dose-related hearing loss in high doses. Less GI toxicity than erythromycin.
Tetracyclines†				
In order of bacterial activity:				
Minocycline (Minocin)	+ and –, spirochetes, *Myco-plasma*, lymphogranuloma venereum, psittacosis, *Rickettsia*	PO, IV	Bacteriostatic	Most active. Useful as an alternative to vancomycin for treatment of methicillin-resistant staphylococci, particularly MRSE, and for meningococcal prophylaxis. Vertigo.
Doxycycline (Vibramycin)	Same as above	PO, IV	Bacteriostatic	Hepatic excretion, so may be best in renal failure. Do not use in urinary tract infections. Phototoxic reactions.
Tetracycline	Same as above	PO, IV	Bacteriostatic	Probably best choice for routine use. *Candida* overgrowth.

*Symbols: + = gram-positive; – = gram-negative; *Staph* = penicillinase-producers.
† *Side effects of tetracyclines*: GI disturbance; bone lesions; staining and deformity of teeth in children up to 8 years old and in newborns when given to pregnant women after the fourth month; malabsorption, enterocolitis; photosensitivity reaction (most frequent with demethylchlortetracycline). Parenteral doses may cause serious liver damage, especially in pregnant women and patients with renal disease; allergic reactions, blood dyscrasia, interference with protein metabolism, increased intracranial pressure in infants, Fanconi-like syndrome from deteriorated tetracyclines. Take with meals or a snack, but avoid milk and milk products.

TABLE I-9

CHARACTERISTICS OF SELECTED ANTIBIOTICS (Continued)

ANTIBIOTIC	SPECTRUM*	ROUTE	BACTERIOSTATIC OR BACTERICIDAL	SIDE EFFECTS/ SPECIAL USES
Aminoglycosides (Aminocyclitols)				
Streptomycin	Tuberculosis, −, *Pasteurella* sp, *Franciscella* sp	IM only	Bactericidal	Vestibular damage, drug fever, peripheral neuropathy.
Gentamicin (Garamycin)	Community-acquired −; not effective for + or anaerobes	IM or IV slowly	Bactericidal	Vestibular damage, renal damage, curare-like effect.
Tobramycin (Nebcin)	−, especially *Pseudomonas* and *Aeromonas*	IM or IV slowly	Bactericidal	Less nephrotoxic than gentamicin. Most active against *Pseudomonas*.
Netilmicin (Netromycin)	−, including some gentamicin/ tobramycin-resistant organisms	IM or IV slowly	Bactericidal	May be less toxic than gentamicin or tobramycin.
Amikacin (Amikin)	−, active against many gentamicin/ tobramycin-resistant gram-negatives. Ideal for nosocomial gram-negative infection.	IM or IV slowly	Bactericidal	Nephrotoxic and ototoxic (more deafness than vestibular effects). Curare-like effect.
Quinolones	+, most −, including multidrug-resistant isolates, and MRSA and MRSE. Not good for enterococcus.			Expensive, *Candida* overgrowth, photosensitivity reactions.
Norfloxacin (Noroxin)	Same as above	PO	Bactericidal	Very broad treatment for complicated urinary-tract infections.
Ciprofloxacin (Cipro)	Same as above	PO	Bactericidal	Very broad spectrum makes this a useful oral agent for mixed infections, infectious diarrhea, and multidrug-resistant organisms at any body site except CNS.

*Symbols: + = gram-positive; − = gram-negative; *Staph* = penicillinase-producers.

57

TABLE I-9

CHARACTERISTICS OF SELECTED ANTIBIOTICS (Continued)

ANTIBIOTIC	SPECTRUM*	ROUTE	BACTERIOSTATIC OR BACTERICIDAL	SIDE EFFECTS/ SPECIAL USES
New quinolones				
Ofloxacin (Floxin) Sparfloxacin (Zagam) Enoxacin (Penetrex) Temafloxacin (Omniflox) Lomefloxacin (Maxaquin) Levofloxacin (Levaquin)	Same as above	PO	Bactericidal	Same as above.
Miscellaneous agents				
Vancomycin (Vancocin)	+, especially *Staph* and entero-coccus, *Clostridia*	IV; PO for C *difficile* and *Staph* enterocolitis	Bactericidal	Thrombophlebitis, drug fever, leukopenia. Bad taste with oral administration.
Chloramphenicol (Chloromycetin)	+, −, anaerobes, *Rickettsia*	PO, IV	Bacteriostatic	"Gray baby" syndrome in newborns, bone-marrow toxicity, optic atrophy, and peripheral neuropathy.
Metronidazole (Flagyl, Flagyl IV)	Anaerobes, *Campylobacter*, amoe-bae, *Trichomonas, C difficile*	PO, IV	Bacteriostatic	GI upset, vertigo, ataxia, peripheral neuropathy, phlebitis, carcinogenic (?), Antabuse-like reaction.
Rifampin (Rifadin)	TB, *Staph* (synergy), meningococcal prophylaxis	PO		Hepatotoxicity, flulike syndrome, discoloration of body secretions, drug interactions.
Pentamidine (Pentam300)	*Pneumocystis* pneumonia	IV, aerosol		Hypotension, hypoglycemia, abnor-mal liver function tests, azotemia, bone-marrow toxicity.

*Symbols: + = gram-positive; − = gram-negative; *Staph* = penicillinase-producers.

58

TABLE I-9

CHARACTERISTICS OF SELECTED ANTIBIOTICS (Continued)

ANTIBIOTIC	SPECTRUM*	ROUTE	BACTERIOSTATIC OR BACTERICIDAL	SIDE EFFECTS/ SPECIAL USES
Antifungal Agents				
Nystatin (Mycostatin)	*Candida*	PO tabs or suspension; topical cream, ointment, powder; GU irrigant, vaginal suppository	Fungistatic	Useful for prevention of *Candida* overgrowth or for topical treatment of GI, mucosal, or skin candidiasis.
5-fluorocytosine (Ancobon, Ancotil)	*Candida, Cryptococcus*	PO	Fungistatic	GI distress, leukopenia, hepatotoxicity. Particularly toxic in patients with compromised renal function.
Amphotericin B (Fungizone, Amphotec)	Most invasive fungi, oral candidiasis	IV for systemic use; PO only for oral candidiasis	Fungistatic	Chills, fever, nausea, vomiting, thrombophlebitis, nephrotoxicity, hypokalemia, bone-marrow suppression, shock, cardiotoxicity.
Miconazole (Micatin, Monistat)	*Candida,* dermatophytes	Topical or vaginal cream; IV	Fungistatic	Topical treatment of *Candida* and dermatophytes. When used IV, thrombophlebitis, thrombocytosis, anemia.
Clotrimazole (Lotrimin, Gyne-Lotrimin, Mycelex)	*Candida,* dermatophytes	Topical solution, vaginal suppository; PO	Fungistatic	Same as above.
Ketoconazole (Nizoral)	Many fungi	PO	Fungistatic	Skin rash, pruritis, nausea, gynecomastia, liver toxicity, impaired fertility.
Newer imidazoles				
Fluconazole (Diflucan) Itraconazole (Sporanox) Croconazole	*Candida, Cryptococcus*	PO, IV	Fungistatic	Less toxicity than amphotericin and flucytosine. Better tolerated than ketoconazole.

*Symbols: + = gram-positive; – = gram-negative; *Staph* = penicillinase-producers.

59

TABLE I-9
CHARACTERISTICS OF SELECTED ANTIBIOTICS (Continued)

ANTIBIOTIC	SPECTRUM	ROUTE	BACTERIOSTATIC OR BACTERICIDAL	SIDE EFFECTS/ SPECIAL USES
Allylamines				
Terbinafine (Lamisil)	Dermatophytes causing onychomycosis	PO	Fungistatic	Headache, GI symptoms, rash.
Antiviral Agents				
Acyclovir (Zovirax)	HSV, varicella-zoster	IV, PO, topical		Nephrotoxicity, CNS toxicity, nausea, vomiting.
Famciclovir (Famvir)	HSV, varicella-zoster	PO		Less frequent dosing (q 8 hrs) than acyclovir.
Valacyclovir (Valtrex)	HSV, varicella-zoster	PO		Pro-drug for acyclovir. Less frequent dosing (q 8 hrs).
Ganciclovir (Cytovene)	CMV, EBV, HSV	IV, PO, intraocular		Bone-marrow toxicity, phlebitis, headache, disorientation, nausea, anorexia, myalgia, rash.
Foscarnet (Foscavir)	CMV, EBV, HSV	IV		Nephrotoxicity.
Cidofovir (Vistide)	CMV, EBV, HSV	IV, intraocular		Effective for CMV and acyclovir-resistant HSV; prolonged duration of action allows infrequent dosing (every other week for IV).
Amantadine (Symmetrel, Symadine)	Influenza A	PO		CNS toxicity, anticholinergic reactions.
Zidovudine, AZT (Retrovir)	HIV	PO		Bone-marrow toxicity, headache, myalgia, nausea.
Dideoxyinosine (ddl) Dideoxycytidine (ddC)	HIV	PO		Pancreatitis. Peripheral neuropathy.

CHAPTER II

Hypertension

Hypertension is common in the United States, occurring in approximately 50 million individuals over 18 years of age. Most individuals with hypertension have only mildly elevated pressures, but all are at greater risk for stroke, coronary heart disease, cardiac failure, peripheral vascular disease, and renal insufficiency. Ocular complications of hypertension include retinovascular disease and a greater risk of glaucoma.

Definition

The Joint National Committee on Detection, Evaluation, and Treatment of Hypertension has defined hypertension as a systolic blood pressure greater than 140 and a diastolic blood pressure greater than 90. The readings should reflect resting values after the patient has been seated for at least 5 minutes, with two readings taken at least 2 minutes apart. The patient should not have used caffeine or nicotine within one-half hour before the examination. Initial elevated readings should be confirmed on at least two subsequent visits during the following weeks unless the initial systolic reading is 210 or greater or the diastolic reading is 120 or greater, in which case treatment is initiated. Treatment is also begun if target-organ damage (Table II-1) is evident on initial examination by the presence of bruits, cardiac hypertrophy, absent pulses, or retinopathy.

TABLE II-1

MANIFESTATIONS OF TARGET-ORGAN DISEASE

ORGAN SYSTEM	MANIFESTATIONS
Cardiac	Clinical, electrocardiographic, or radiologic evidence of coronary artery disease; left ventricular hypertrophy or "strain" by electrocardiography or left ventricular hypertrophy by echocardiography; left ventricular dysfunction or cardiac failure
Cerebrovascular	Transient ischemic attack or stroke
Peripheral vascular	Absence of 1 or more major pulses in extremities (except for dorsalis pedis) with or without intermittent claudication; aneurysm
Renal	Serum creatinine $\geq$130 μmol/L (1.5 mg/dL); proteinuria (1+ or greater); microalbuminuria
Retinopathy	Hemorrhages or exudates, with or without papilledema

(Reprinted from: Fifth report of the Joint National Committee on the Prevention, Detection, Evaluation, and Treatment of High Blood Pressure. *Arch Intern Med.* 1993;153:162. ©American Medical Association.)

Classification

Hypertension can be classified on the basis on risk, as seen in Table II-2. The higher the blood pressure, the higher the risk. All stages of hypertension warrant effective therapy. Over 70% of individuals have mild hypertension. Patients in the high normal category represent a susceptible population. Frequent monitoring and modification of lifestyle factors can reduce their risk of developing hypertension. See Table II-3 for recommendations about follow-up based on initial blood pressure measurements.

TABLE II-2

CLASSIFICATION OF BLOOD PRESSURE

CLASSIFICATION	SBP	DBP
Normal	<130	<85
High Normal	130–139	85–89
Mild	140–159	90–99
Moderate	160–179	100–109
Severe	180–209	110–119
Very Severe	>210	>120

TABLE II-3

RECOMMENDATIONS FOR FOLLOW-UP BASED ON
INITIAL SET OF BLOOD PRESSURE MEASUREMENTS FOR ADULTS

INITIAL SCREENING BLOOD PRESSURE, mm Hg*		
SYSTOLIC	DIASTOLIC	FOLLOW-UP RECOMMENDED†
<130	<85	Recheck in 2 y
130–139	85–89	Recheck in 1 y‡
140–159	90–99	Confirm within 2 mo
160–179	100–109	Evaluate or refer to source of care within 1 mo
180–209	110–119	Evaluate or refer to source of care within 1 wk
≥210	≥120	Evaluate or refer to source of care immediately

* If the systolic and diastolic categories are different, follow recommendation for the shorter-time follow-up (eg, 160/85 mm Hg should be evaluated or referred to source of care within 1 month).

† The scheduling of follow-up should be modified by reliable information about past blood pressure measurements, other cardiovascular risk factors, or target-organ disease.

‡ Consider providing advice about lifestyle modifications.

(Reprinted from: Fifth report of the Joint National Committee on Prevention, Detection, Evaluation, and Treatment of High Blood Pressure. *Arch Intern Med.* 1993;153:162. ©American Medical Association.)

White Coat Hypertension

Twenty percent of patients with hypertension have *"white coat" hypertension,* that is, blood pressure that is increased only in a physician's office. These individuals manifest an abnormal physiologic response that warrants further study, as they are at greater risk for cardiovascular disease. Ambulatory blood pressure readings are used in identifying white coat hypertension.

Secondary Hypertension

Although 90% of hypertensive patients have *primary,* or *essential, hypertension* in which the cause remains unknown, the remaining 10% have *secondary hypertension.* Secondary causes of hypertension include renovascular disease, pheochromocytoma, hyperaldosteronism, polycystic kidney disease, aortic coarctation, and Cushing syndrome. In addition to evaluating target organ disease, the initial physical examination should also assess for secondary causes of hypertension. Physical examination signs associated with secondary hypertension include:

- □ *Renovascular:* unilateral abdominal bruits in young females with marked hypertension; new onset hypertension with marked end-organ damage
- □ *Hyperaldosteronism:* persistent hypokalemia
- □ *Pheochromocytoma:* markedly labile blood pressure with tachycardia and headaches
- □ *Polycystic kidney disease:* flank mass
- □ *Aortic coarctation:* delayed or absent femoral pulses
- □ *Cushing syndrome:* truncal obesity and abdominal striae

    Secondary causes of hypertension should be suspected in individuals who have accelerating hypertension, hypertension unresponsive to medications, or a sudden change in previously well-controlled blood pressure.

Epidemiology

More than 22% of adults in the United States have hypertension. The prevalence increases with age and tends to be familial. African Americans have a higher rate of hypertension than whites. Lower socioeconomic groups have a greater incidence of devastating complications not only because of a greater prevalence but also because of a delay in detection.

Therapeutic Approaches

Treatment Value

Morbidity and mortality from cardiovascular disease, renal disease, and stroke increase progressively with higher levels of blood pressure; accordingly, treatment of hypertension will decrease the risk of these conditions. Lowering diastolic blood pressure by 5–6 mm Hg has been shown to result in a 42% reduction in stroke incidence. Treatment of mild and moderate hypertension can decrease the myocardial infarction rate by 20%.

Treatment Goals

Normalizing the blood pressure, making beneficial lifestyle modifications, and controlling cardiovascular risk factors are the goals of successful hypertension management. Although lowering the blood pressure to normal levels is desirable, there is some concern that excessive diastolic pressure reduction in individuals with ischemic heart disease may compromise coronary flow and thereby increase the risk of coronary heart disease. This risk has not been clinically demonstrated, but it remains a theoretical concern.

Lifestyle Factors

Although the effects of lifestyle modification are not as profound as pharmacological approaches, certain modifiable factors can serve as either definitive or adjunctive therapy in the management of hypertension. Modification of lifestyle factors is helpful both for hypertensive patients and for individuals at risk for developing hypertension: it can reduce the risk of hypertensive complications in the first group and prevent the development of hypertension in the second.

Controlling risk factors for atherosclerotic disease is a crucial part of hypertension management. For example, smoking one pack of cigarettes a day increases the risk of coronary disease by five times; the risk increases more than 25-fold in individuals with mild hypertension. Hypertriglyceridemia and hypercholesterolemia play a direct role in the development of atherosclerosis, and their successful normalization plays a key role in reducing morbidity and mortality.

Obesity   Obesity or excess caloric intake is associated with increased blood pressure. Individuals whose weight is in the top third of the population consistently have higher blood pressures than those in the bottom third. Weight loss, independent of sodium intake, consistently results in a drop in the blood pressure among individuals who are more than 10% above their ideal body weight.

Exercise   Regular aerobic exercise involving moderately intense physical activity can effectively lower blood pressure as well as contribute to weight loss and reduced mortality. Sedentary normotensive individuals have a 20%–50% greater risk of developing hypertension than their exercising counterparts.

Sodium   The average American consumes more than 150 mmol (6 g) of salt per day. A 50-mmol per day reduction can lower systemic blood pressure by 7 mm Hg. Individuals vary in their responsiveness to dietary sodium; blacks, older people, and patients with hypertension are more sensitive.

Alcohol   Consumption of alcohol should be limited to less than 1 oz of ethanol (2 oz of 100 proof whiskey, 8 oz of wine, or 24 oz of beer) per day. Higher daily consumption is associated with both an elevation in the blood pressure and resistance to antihypertensive therapy.

Smoking   Cigarette smoking appears to be related to hypertension only as a major risk factor for the development of atherosclerotic vascular disease. However, this relationship is significant in that smoking, therefore, multiplies the risk of coronary disease in hypertensive patients.

Minerals   Maintaining an adequate intake of potassium, calcium, and magnesium contributes to blood pressure normalization.

Pharmacologic Therapy

In considering the appropriate therapy for an individual patient, the physician should weigh multiple factors: hypertension class, end-organ disease, atherosclerotic risk factors, cost, compliance, side effects, and coexisting conditions. In general, the higher the stage, the presence of end-organ damage, and the greater the risk factors for cardiovascular disease, the sooner treatment should be initiated. For example, patients with very severe hypertension and encephalopathy require emergent treatment, while those with mild hypertension may try lifestyle modification before drug therapy is initiated.

Approximately one half of the patients will respond to monotherapy; the individual's treatment response will dictate whether substitution of a similar class drug or the addition of a drug of a different class is indicated. Compliance and drug cost are directly related to treatment success. Successful compliance depends upon minimal dose frequency and side effects. In order to minimize side effects, the physician should take into account any coexisting conditions (Table II-4) and other drugs a patient may be taking (Table II-5).

The major classes of antihypertensive drugs include diuretics, angiotensin-converting enzyme inhibitors, beta blockers, alpha-1 blockers, calcium channel blockers, central sympatholytics, and direct vasodilators (Tables II-6 through II-8).

Diuretics   This group of drugs is divided into the thiazide, loop-acting, and potassium-sparing diuretics. *Thiazide diuretics* increase the sodium load on the kidney's distal tubules and, in the short term, decrease the plasma volume and cardiac output through natriuresis. As the renin-angiotensin-aldosterone system compensates for plasma volume, cardiac output returns to normal and peripheral vascular resistance is decreased, thus reducing blood pressure. Hypokalemia and insulin resistance are the primary side effects of the thiazide diuretics.

The *loop diuretics* act on the ascending loop of Henle and inhibit electrolyte resorption, causing an initial decrease in plasma volume. As with the thiazide diuretics, blood pressure is eventually reduced because of decreased peripheral vascular resistance. Loop diuretics are used primarily in treating patients with renal insufficiency. They are not as useful on a chronic basis in patients with good kidney function.

Potassium-sparing diuretics are competitive antagonists of the mineralocorticoids, thereby preventing potassium loss in the distal tubule. Their mechanism of action is similar to the thiazide diuretics, although less potent. They are often used as adjuncts to the thiazide or loop diuretics to counteract their potassium-depleting effects.

Angiotensin-converting enzyme inhibitors   Angiotensin is a potent vasopressor as well as a mediator of aldosterone release. Therefore, it plays an important role in homeostasis. Angiotensin-converting enzyme inhibitors are vasodilators that decrease vascular resistance while having less effect on plasma volume. Thus, left ventricular hypertrophy may be improved. The efficacy of angiotensin-converting enzyme inhibitors is enhanced when used together with diuretics.

TABLE II-4

ANTIHYPERTENSIVE DRUG THERAPY: INDIVIDUALIZATION BASED ON SPECIAL CONSIDERATIONS (GUIDELINES FOR SELECTING INITIAL THERAPY)*

CLINICAL SITUATION	PREFERRED	REQUIRES SPECIAL MONITORING	RELATIVELY OR ABSOLUTELY CONTRAINDICATED
Cardiovascular			
Angina pectoris	β-blockers, calcium antagonists	…	Direct vasodilators
Bradycardia/heart block, sick sinus syndrome	…	…	β-blockers, labetalol, verapamil, diltiazem
Cardiac failure	Diuretics, ACE inhibitors	…	β-blockers, calcium antagonists, labetalol
Hypertrophic cardiomyopathy with severe diastolic dysfunction	β-blockers, diltiazem, verapamil	…	Diuretics, ACE inhibitors, $α_1$-blockers, hydralazine, minoxidil
Hyperdynamic circulation	β-blockers	…	Direct vasodilators
Peripheral vascular occlusive disease	…	β-blockers	…
After myocardial infarction	Non-ISA β-blockers	…	Direct vasodilators
Renal			
Bilateral renal arterial disease or severe stenosis in artery to solitary kidney	…	…	ACE inhibitors
Renal insufficiency			
Early (serum creatinine 130–221 μmol/L [1.5–2.5 mg/dL])	…	…	Potassium-sparing agents, potassium supplements
Advanced (serum creatinine ≥221 μmol/L [≥2.5 mg/dL])	Loop diuretics	ACE inhibitors	Potassium-sparing agents, potassium supplements
Other			
Asthma/COPD	…	…	β-blockers, labetalol
Cyclosporine-associated hypertension	Nifedipine, labetalol	Verapamil,† nicardipine,† diltiazem†	…
Depression	…	$α_2$-agonists	Reserpine
Diabetes mellitus			
Type I (insulin dependent)	…	β-blockers	…
Type II	…	β-blockers, diuretics	…
Dyslipidemia	…	Diuretics, β-blockers	…
Liver disease	…	Labetalol	Methyldopa
Vascular headache	β-blockers	…	…
Pregnancy			
Preeclampsia	Methyldopa, hydralazine	…	Diuretics, ACE inhibitors
Chronic hypertension	Methyldopa	…	ACE inhibitors

*ACE indicates angiotensin-converting enzyme; ISA, intrinsic sympathomimetic activity; and COPD, chronic obstructive pulmonary disease.
†Can increase serum levels of cyclosporine.
(Reprinted from: Fifth report of the Joint National Committee on the Prevention, Detection, Evaluation, and Treatment of High Blood Pressure. *Arch Intern Med.* 1993;153:167.
©American Medical Association.)

TABLE II-5

SELECTED DRUG INTERACTIONS WITH ANTIHYPERTENSIVE THERAPY*

Diuretics

Possible situations for decreased antihypertensive effects

>   Cholestyramine and colestipol decrease absorption

>   NSAIDs (including aspirin and over-the-counter ibuprofen) may antagonize diuretic effectiveness

Possible situations for increased antihypertensive effects

>   Combinations of thiazides (especially metolazone) with furosemide can produce profound diuresis, natriuresis, and kaliuresis in renal impairment

Effects of diuretics on other drugs

>   Diuretics can raise serum lithium levels and increase toxic effects by enhancing proximal tubular resorption of lithium

>   Diuretics may make it more difficult to control dyslipidemia and diabetes

β-Blockers

Possible situations for decreased antihypertensive effects

>   NSAIDs may decrease effects of β-blockers

>   Rifampin, smoking, and phenobarbital decrease serum levels of agents primarily metabolized by liver due to enzyme induction

Possible situations for increased antihypertensive effects

>   Cimetidine may increase serum levels of β-blockers that are primarily metabolized by liver due to enzyme inhibition

>   Quinidine may increase risk of hypotension

Effects of β-blockers on other drugs

>   Combinations of diltiazem or verapamil with β-blockers may have additive sinoatrial and atrioventricular node depressant effects and may also promote negative inotropic effects on failing myocardium

>   Combination of β-blockers and reserpine may cause marked bradycardia and syncope

>   β-blockers may increase serum levels of theophylline, lidocaine, and chlorpromazine due to reduced hepatic clearance

>   Nonselective β-blockers prolong insulin-induced hypoglycemia and promote rebound hypertension due to unopposed α stimulation; all β-blockers mask adrenergically mediated symptoms of hypoglycemia and have potential to aggravate diabetes

>   β-blockers may make it more difficult to control dyslipidemia

>   Phenylpropanolamine (which can be obtained over the counter in cold and diet preparations), pseudoephedrine, ephedrine, and epinephrine can cause elevations in blood pressure due to unopposed α-receptor–induced vasoconstriction

ACE Inhibitors

Possible situations for decreased antihypertensive effects

>   NSAIDs (including aspirin and over-the-counter ibuprofen) may decrease blood pressure control

>   Antacids may decrease the bioavailability of ACE inhibitors

Possible situations for increased antihypertensive effects

>   Diuretics may lead to excessive hypotensive effects (hypovolemia)

---

* This table does not include all potential drug interactions with antihypertensive drugs. NSAID indicates nonsteroidal anti-inflammatory drug; ACE, angiotensin-converting enzyme.

TABLE II-5

Effect of ACE inhibitors on other drugs

Hyperkalemia may occur with potassium supplements, potassium-sparing agents, and NSAIDs

ACE inhibitors may increase serum lithium levels

Calcium Channel Blockers

Possible situations for decreased antihypertensive effects

Serum levels and antihypertensive effects of calcium antagonists may be diminished by these interactions: rifampin-verapamil; carbamazepine-diltiazem and verapamil; phenobarbital and phenytoin-verapamil

Possible situations for increased antihypertensive effects

Cimetidine may increase pharmacologic effects of all calcium antagonists due to inhibition of hepatic metabolizing enzymes resulting in increased serum levels

Effects of calcium channel blockers on other drugs

Digoxin and carbamazepine serum levels and toxic effects may be increased by verapamil and possibly by diltiazem

Serum levels of prazosin, quinidine, and theophylline may be increased by verapamil

Serum levels of cyclosporine may be increased by diltiazem, nicardipine, and verapamil; cyclosporine dose may need to be decreased

α-Blockers

Possible situations for increased antihypertensive effects

Concomitant antihypertensive drug therapy (especially diuretics) may increase chance of postural hypotension

Sympatholytics

Possible situations for decreased antihypertensive effects

Tricyclic antidepressants may decrease effects of centrally acting and peripheral norepinephrine depleters

Sympathomimetics, including over-the-counter cold and diet preparations, amphetamines, phenothiazines, and cocaine, may interfere with antihypertensive effects of guanethidine and guanadrel

Severity of clonidine withdrawal reaction can be increased by β-blockers

Monoamine oxidase inhibitors may prevent degradation and metabolism of norepinephrine released by tyramine-containing foods and may cause hypertension; they may also cause hypertensive reactions when combined with reserpine or guanethidine

Effects of sympatholytics on other drugs

Methyldopa may increase serum lithium levels

---

* This table does not include all potential drug interactions with antihypertensive drugs. NSAID indicates nonsteroidal anti-inflammatory drug; ACE, angiotensin-converting enzyme.

(Adapted from: Fifth report of the Joint National Committee on the Prevention, Detection, Evaluation, and Treatment of High Blood Pressure. *Arch Intern Med.* 1993;153:168. ©American Medical Association.)

Beta blockers   Circulating or locally released catecholamines stimulate beta adrenergic receptors sites, resulting in vasoconstriction, bronchodilation, tachycardia, and increased myocardial contractility. Beta blockers reverse these effects. There are two types of beta sites: beta-1 is present on vascular and cardiac tissue, and beta-2 is in the bronchial tree. In addition, beta blockers inhibit the release of renin, which is part of the angiotensin pathway.

The beta blockers can be divided into several groups: *nonselective* (beta-1 and -2), *cardioselective* (greater beta-1 than -2), and those with *intrinsic sympathomimetic activity*. Cardioselective agents cause the fewest asthmatic reactions and are less likely to delay recovery from hypoglycemia in diabetics. Beta blockers with intrinsic sympathomimetic activity minimize the bradycardiac response of the other types of beta blockers.

Alpha-1 blockers   When the postsynaptic alpha-1 receptors for catecholamines are blocked, both arterial and venous dilation occur, lowering peripheral vascular resistance. Although alpha-1 blockers cause less tachycardia than direct vasodilators, they produce more postural hypotension.

Direct vasodilators   These drugs lower peripheral vascular resistance. They frequently produce reflex tachycardia and, less often, cause orthostatic hypotension. These drugs are usually combined with a beta blocker or a central sympatholytic agent to minimize their effect on heart rate or cardiac output.

Calcium channel blockers   These agents inhibit the entry of calcium into smooth muscle cells. This effect reduces vascular contractility and decreases peripheral vascular resistance. However, they can partially block the SA and AV node as well as causing a negative inotropic effect in the heart. The three types of calcium channel blockers are phenylalkylamines (verapamil), dihydropyridines (nifedipine, felodipine, etc.), and benzothiazepines (diltiazem).

Phenylalkamines decrease cardiac output more than systemic vascular resistance. *Dihydropyridines* decrease vascular resistance more than cardiac output, and *benzothiazepines* reduce cardiac output and systemic vascular resistance equally. All types reduce renal afferent tone and cause an increase in salt and water excretion, lowering plasma volume.

Sympatholytics   The central sympatholytics affect the brain's vasomotor center, decreasing sympathetic output. This, in turn, reduces peripheral vascular resistance, cardiac output, and blood pressure.

The following tables list the proprietary and generic drugs in each class, frequent side effects, and a breakdown of the combination drugs.

The fifth report of the Joint National Committee on Detection, Evaluation, and Treatment of High Blood Pressure. *Arch Intern Med.* 1993;153:154–183.

Hyman BN, Moser M. Hypertension update. *Surv Ophthalmol.* 1996;41:79–89.

The sixth report of the Joint National Committee on Prevention, Detection, Evaluation, and Treatment of High Blood Pressure. *Arch Intern Med.* 1997;157:2413–2446.

TABLE II-6

ANTIHYPERTENSIVE DRUGS (BY TYPE)

Diuretics

    Thiazide types

        Bendroflumethiazide (Naturetin)
        Benzthiazide (Exna)
        Chlorothiazide (Diuril)
        Chlorthalidone (Hygroton)
        Hydrochlorothiazide (Esidrix)
        Hydroflumethiazide (Saluron, Diucardin)
        Indapamide (Lozol)
        Methyclothiazide (Enduron)
        Metolazone (Zaroxolyn, Mykrox)
        Polythiazide (Minizide)
        Trichlormethiazide (Naqua, Metahydrin)

    Loop

        Bumetanide (Bumex)
        Furosemide (Lasix)
        Torsemide (Demadex)

    Potassium-sparing

        Amiloride (Midamor)
        Spironolactone (Aldactone)
        Triamterene (Dyrenium)

    Diuretic combinations

        HCTZ/spironolactone (Aldactazide)
        HCTZ/triamterene (Dyazide, Maxzide)
        HCTZ/amiloride (Moduretic)

Angiotensin-Converting Enzyme (ACE) Inhibitors

        Benazepril (Lotensin)
        Captopril (Capoten)
        Enalapril (Vasotec)
        Fosinopril (Monopril)
        Lisinopril (Prinivil, Zestril)
        Moexipril (Univasc)
        Quinapril (Accupril)
        Ramipril (Altace)
        Trandolapril (Mavic, Tarka)

Angiotensin II Receptor Antagonists

        Losartan (Cozaar)
        Valsartan (Diovan)

Beta-Adrenergic Blockers

        Atenolol (Tenormin)
        Betaxolol (Kerlone)
        Bisoprolol (Zebeta)
        Metoprolol (Lopressor, Toprol)
        Nadolol (Corgard)
        Propranolol (Inderal)
        Timolol (Blocadren)

Beta-Adrenergic Blockers With Intrinsic Sympathomimetic Activity

        Acebutolol (Sectral)
        Carteolol (Cartrol)
        Labetalol (Normodyne, Trandate)
        Penbutolol (Levatol)
        Pindolol (Visken)

HCTZ = hydrochlorothiazide

TABLE II-6

Alpha-Adrenergic Blockers

        Doxazosin (Cardura)
        Prazosin (Minipress)
        Terazosin (Hytrin)

Direct Vasodilators

        Hydralazine (Apresoline)
        Minoxidil (Loniten)

Calcium Channel Blockers

        Amlodipine (Norvasc)
        Diltiazem (Cardizem, Dilacor)
        Felodipine (Plendil)
        Isradipine (DynaCirc)
        Nicardipine (Cardene)
        Nifedipine (Adalat, Procardia)
        Nisoldipine (Sular)
        Verapamil (Calan, Isoptin, Verelan)

Central Sympatholytics

        Clonidine (Catapres)
        Guanabenz (Wytensin)
        Guanfacine (Tenex)
        Methyldopa (Aldomet)

Peripheral Adrenergic Neuron Antagonists

        Guanadrel (Hylorel)
        Guanethidine (Ismelin)
        Reserpine

Combination Drugs

    Beta blockers and diuretics
        Atenolol/chlorthalidone (Tenoretic)
        Bisoprolol/HCTZ (Ziac)
        Metoprolol/HCTZ (Lopressor HCT)
        Nadolol/bendroflumethiazide (Corzide)
        Propranolol/HCTZ (Inderide)
        Timolol/HCTZ (Timolide)

    ACE inhibitors and diuretics
        Benazepril/HCTZ (Lotensin HCT)
        Captopril/HCTZ (Capozide)
        Enalapril/HCTZ (Vaseretic)
        Lisinopril/HCTZ (Prinizide, Zestoretic)

    Angiotensin II receptor antagonist and diuretic
        Losartan/HCTZ (Hyzaar)

    Other combinations
        Guanethidine/HCTZ (Esimil)
        Hydralazine/HCTZ (Apresazide)
        Methyldopa/HCTZ (Aldoril)
        Reserpine/HCTZ (Hydropres)

HCTZ = hydrochlorothiazide

TABLE II-7

ANTIHYPERTENSIVE DRUGS (BY BRAND NAME)

Accupril— Quinapril (ACE)
Adalat—Nifedipine (Ca^{+2})
Aldactazide—HCTZ/Spironolactone (Dcomb)
Aldactone—Spironolactone (K$^+$)
Aldomet—Methyldopa (Symp)
Aldoril—Methyldopa/HCTZ (Other)
Altace—Ramipril (ACE)
Apresazide—Hydralazine/HCTZ (Other)
Apresoline—Hydralazine (Vaso)
Blocadren—Timolol (Beta)
Bumex—Bumetanide (Loop)
Calan—Verapamil (Ca^{+2})
Capoten—Captopril (ACE)
Capozide—Captopril/HCTZ (ACE+D)
Cardene—Nicardipine (Ca^{+2})
Cardizem—Diltiazem (Ca^{+2})
Cardura—Doxazosin (Alpha)
Cartrol—Carteolol (Beta+)
Catapres—Clonidine (Symp)
Corgard—Nadolol (Beta)
Corzide—Nadolol/Bendroflumethiazide (B+D)
Cozaar—Losartan (AT-2)
Demadex—Torsemide (Loop)
Dilacor—Diltiazem (Ca^{+2})
Diucardin—Hydroflumethiazide (TZ)
Diuril—Chlorothiazide (TZ)
Dyazide—HCTZ/Triamterene (Dcomb)
DynaCirc—Isradipine (Ca^{+2})
Dyrenium—Triamterene (K$^+$)
Enduron—Methyclothiazide (TZ)
Esidrix—Hydrochlorothiazide (TZ)
Esimil—Guanethidine/HCTZ (Other)
Exna—Benzthiazide (TZ)
Hydropres—Reserpine/HCTZ (Other)
Hygroton—Chlorthalidone (TZ)
Hylorel—Guanadrel (Periph)
Hytrin—Terazosin (Alpha)
Hyzaar—Losartan/HCTZ (AT-2+D)
Inderal—Propranolol (Beta)
Inderide—Propranolol/HCTZ (B+D)
Ismelin—Guanethidine (Periph)
Isoptin—Verapamil (Ca^{+2})
Kerlone—Betaxolol (Beta)

Lasix—Furosemide (Loop)
Levatol—Penbutolol (Beta+)
Loniten—Minoxidil (Vaso)
Lopressor—Metoprolol (Beta)
Lopressor HCT—Metoprolol/HCTZ (B+D)
Lotensin—Benazepril (ACE)
Lotensin HCT—Benazepril/HCTZ (ACE+D)
Lozol—Indapamide (TZ)
Maxzide—HCTZ/Triamterene (Dcomb)
Metahydrin—Trichlormethiazide (TZ)
Midamor—Amiloride (K$^+$)
Minipress—Prazosin (Alpha)
Minizide—Polythiazide (TZ)
Moduretic—HCTZ/Amiloride (Dcomb)
Monopril—Fosinopril (ACE)
Mykrox—Metolazone (TZ)
Naqua—Trichlormethiazide (TZ)
Naturetin—Bendroflumethiazide (TZ)
Normodyne—Labetalol (Beta+)
Norvasc—Amlodipine (Ca^{+2})
Plendil—Felodipine (Ca^{+2})
Prinivil—Lisinopril (ACE)
Prinizide—Lisinopril/HCTZ (ACE+D)
Procardia—Nifedipine (Ca^{+2})
Saluron—Hydroflumethiazide (TZ)
Sectral—Acebutolol (Beta+)
Tenex—Guanfacine (Symp)
Tenoretic—Atenolol/Chlorthalidone (B+D)
Tenormin—Atenolol (Beta)
Timolide—Timolol/HCTZ (B+D)
Toprol—Metoprolol (Beta)
Trandate—Labetalol (Beta+)
Vaseretic—Enalapril/HCTZ (ACE+D)
Vasotec—Enalapril (ACE)
Verelan—Verapamil (Ca^{+2})
Visken—Pindolol (Beta+)
Wytensin—Guanabenz (Symp)
Zaroxolyn—Metolazone (TZ)
Zebeta—Bisoprolol (Beta)
Zestoretic—Lisinopril/HCTZ (ACE+D)
Zestril—Lisinopril (ACE)
Ziac—Bisoprolol/HCTZ (B+D)

KEY

ACE = Angiotensin-converting enzyme inhibitor
ACE+D = ACE inhibitor and diuretic
Alpha = Alpha-adrenergic blocker
AT-2 = Angiotensin II receptor antagonist
AT-2+D = Angiotensin II receptor antagonist and diuretic
B+D = Beta-adrenergic blocker and diuretic
Beta = Beta-adrenergic blocker
Beta+ = Beta-adrenergic blocker with intrinsic sympathomimetic activity
Ca^{+2} = Calcium channel blocker
Dcomb = Diuretic combination
K+ = Potassium-sparing diuretic
Loop = Loop diuretic
Other = Miscellaneous combination
Periph = Peripheral adrenergic neuron antagonist
Symp = Central sympatholytic
TZ = Thiazide-type diuretic
Vaso = Direct vasodilator

TABLE II-8

ANTIHYPERTENSIVE DRUGS: ADVERSE EFFECTS

DRUGS	SELECTED SIDE EFFECTS*	PRECAUTIONS AND SPECIAL CONSIDERATIONS
Diuretics†		
Thiazides and related diuretics	Hypokalemia, hypomagnesemia, hypo-natremia, hyperuricemia, hypercalcemia, hyperglycemia, hypercholesterolemia, hyper-triglyceridemia, sexual dysfunction, weakness	Except for metolazone and indapamide, ineffective in renal failure (serum creatinine ≥221 μmol/L [≥2.5 mg/dL]); hypokalemia increases digitalis toxic effect; may precipitate acute gout
Loop diuretics	Same as for thiazides except loop diuretics do not cause hypercalcemia	Effective in chronic renal failure
Potassium-sparing agents	Hyperkalemia	Danger of hyperkalemia in patients with renal failure, in patients treated with ACE inhibitor or with NSAIDs
Amiloride	...	...
Spironolactone	Gynecomastia, mastodynia, menstrual irregularities, diminished libido in males	...
Triamterene	...	Danger of renal calculi
Adrenergic inhibitors		
β-blockers†	Bronchospasm, may aggravate peripheral arterial insufficiency, fatigue, insomnia, exacerbation of CHF, masking of symptoms of hypoglycemia; also, hypertriglyceridemia, decreased high-density lipoprotein cholesterol (except for drugs with ISA); reduces exercise tolerance	Should not be used in patients with asthma, COPD, CHF with systolic dysfunction, heart block (greater than 1st degree), and sick sinus syndrome; use with caution in insulin-treated diabetics and patients with peripheral vascular disease; should not be discontinued abruptly in patients with ischemic heart disease
β-blockers with ISA		
Labetalol	Bronchospasm; may aggravate peripheral vascular insufficiency; orthostatic hypotension	Should not be used in patients with asthma, COPD, CHF, heart block (greater than 1st degree), and sick sinus syndrome; use with caution in insulin-treated diabetics and patients with peripheral vascular disease
α-adrenergic blockers	Orthostatic hypotension, syncope, weakness, palpitations, headache	Use cautiously in older patients because of orthostatic hypotension

* The listing of side effects is not all-inclusive, and clinicians are urged to refer to the package insert for a more detailed listing. Sexual dysfunction, particularly impotence in men, has been reported with the use of all antihypertensive agents. Few data are available on the effect of antihypertensive agents on sexual function in women.

† Some of the metabolic side effects of diuretics and β-blockers can be minimized by appropriate dietary counseling.

TABLE II-8

ANTIHYPERTENSIVE DRUGS: ADVERSE EFFECTS (Continued)

DRUGS	SELECTED SIDE EFFECTS*	PRECAUTIONS AND SPECIAL CONSIDERATIONS
ACE inhibitors	Cough, rash, angioneurotic edema, hyperkalemia, dysgeusia	Hyperkalemia can develop, particularly in patients with renal insufficiency; hypotension has been observed with initiation of ACE inhibitors, especially in patients with high plasma renin activity or receiving diuretic therapy; can cause reversible, acute renal failure in patients with bilateral renal arterial stenosis or unilateral stenosis in solitary kidney and in patients with cardiac failure and with volume depletion; rarely can induce neutropenia or proteinuria; absolutely contraindicated in 2nd and 3rd trimesters of pregnancy
Calcium channel blockers		
Dihydropyridines Amlodipine Felodipine Isradipine Nicardipine Nifedipine	Headache, dizziness, peripheral edema, tachycardia, gingival hyperplasia	Use with caution in patients with CHF; may aggravate angina and myocardial ischemia
Diltiazem Verapamil	Headache, dizziness, peripheral edema (less common than with dihydropyridines), gingival hyperplasia, constipation (especially verapamil), atrioventricular block, bradycardia	Use with caution in patients with cardiac failure; contraindicated in patients with 2nd- or 3rd-degree heart block or sick sinus syndrome
Central sympatholytics		
Clonidine Guanabenz Guanfacine hydrochloride	Drowsiness, sedation, dry mouth, fatigue, orthostatic dizziness	Rebound hypertension may occur with abrupt discontinuance, particularly with previous administration of high doses or with continuation of concomitant β-blocker therapy
Clonidine patch	Same as for clonidine; localized skin reaction to patch	...

*The listing of side effects is not all-inclusive, and clinicians are urged to refer to the package insert for a more detailed listing. Sexual dysfunction, particularly impotence in men, has been reported with the use of all antihypertensive agents. Few data are available on the effect of antihypertensive agents on sexual function in women.

TABLE II-8

ANTIHYPERTENSIVE DRUGS: ADVERSE EFFECTS (Continued)

DRUGS	SELECTED SIDE EFFECTS*	PRECAUTIONS AND SPECIAL CONSIDERATIONS
Methyldopa	...	May cause liver damage, fever, and Coombs-positive hemolytic anemia
Peripheral adrenergic neuron antagonists		
Guanadrel sulfate Guanethidine monosulfate	Diarrhea, orthostatic and exercise hypotension	Use cautiously because of orthostatic hypotension
Rauwolfia alkaloids Reserpine	Lethargy, nasal congestion, depression	Contraindicated in patients with history of mental depression or with active peptic ulcer
Direct vasodilators	Headache, tachycardia, fluid retention	May precipitate angina pectoris in patients with coronary artery disease; generally, use with diuretic and β-blocker
Hydralazine	Positive antinuclear antibody test	Lupus syndrome may occur (rare at recommended doses)
Minoxidil	Hypertrichosis	May cause or aggravate pleural and pericardial effusions

*The listing of side effects is not all-inclusive, and clinicians are urged to refer to the package insert for a more detailed listing. Sexual dysfunction, particularly impotence in men, has been reported with the use of all antihypertensive agents. Few data are available on the effect of antihypertensive agents on sexual function in women.

(Adapted from: Fifth report of the Joint National Committee on Prevention, Detection, Evaluation and Treatment of High Blood Pressure. *Arch Intern Med.* 1993;153:154–183.)

CHAPTER III

Cerebrovascular Diseases

Vascular stroke is the third leading cause of death in developed countries, ranking behind heart disease and cancer. Among white populations in the United States and Canada, the annual incidence rate is between 1 and 2 per 1000, while the incidence rate is higher among blacks. The incidence of stroke is declining at a rate approaching 5% per year, probably because of improved control of hypertension and other risk factors. Vascular stroke occurs as a result of two major causes: cerebral ischemia and intracranial hemorrhage.

Cerebral Ischemia and Infarction

Cerebral ischemia occurs as a result of interference with the circulation to the brain. The reduction in blood flow may be generalized or localized. Ischemia must be distinguished from hypoxemia from such causes as carbon monoxide poisoning, chronic obstructive pulmonary disease (COPD), and pulmonary emboli.

Clinical manifestations of cerebral ischemia are paresis, paresthesia, amaurosis fugax, and facial paresthesias. Vertebrobasilar symptoms include but are not limited to vertigo, diplopia, binocular visual loss, ataxia, paresis, paresthesia, dysarthria, headache, nausea, and vomiting. Cardiac emboli can produce symptoms similar to insufficiency of the internal carotid or vertebrobasilar arteries; thus, the occurrence of transient symptoms does not give definitive evidence of an arterial abnormality in the carotid or vertebrobasilar territory. There are varying degrees of ischemia, which may be classified by severity and duration.

Transient ischemic attacks (TIAs) are a loss of neurologic function caused by ischemia. They are abrupt in onset, persist for less than 24 hours, and clear without residual signs. Most TIAs last only a few minutes. *Reversible ischemic neurologic disability (RIND)* is a loss of neurologic function persisting for more than 24 hours but less than 7 days that leaves no lasting symptoms or signs. A *partial nonprogressive stroke (PNS)* is an ischemic event that leaves a persistent disability but is short of a calamitous stroke. A *completed stroke* is an ischemic event that produces a major degree of permanent neurologic disability.

Medium- and small-artery disease caused by hypertension, diabetes, and atherosclerosis accounts for the majority of strokes. The most common site for obstructive disease of the carotid artery is in the region of the carotid sinus, followed by the portion within the cavernous sinus. Strokes caused by emboli of cardiac origin account for 20% of the total. Mural thrombi forming on the endocardium in conjunction with myocardial infarction account for 8%–10%. Atrial fibrillation, mitral stenosis, mitral valve prolapse, and atrial myxoma are other cardiac conditions associated with intracranial embolism.

Nonarteriosclerotic angiopathies capable of causing TIA and stroke include aortic dissection and inflammatory arteritis, for example, collagen vascular disease, giant cell arteritis, meningovascular syphilis, and moyamoya disease. *Moyamoya disease* is a rare vaso-occlusive disease of the carotid and cerebral arteries that causes TIA symptoms or hemorrhagic strokes in children and young adults. It was originally described in Japanese patients in the 1960s but has been reported more recently in the United States and Europe as well.

Other conditions with potential for altering blood coagulation and leading to cerebral ischemia include pregnancy and the postpartum period, use of oral contraceptives, postoperative and posttraumatic states, hyperviscosity syndromes, polycythemia, and sickle cell disease.

Diagnostic Studies

Investigation of the systemic arteries and the heart is essential in determining the cause of cerebral ischemia. Differences in upper limb pulses and blood pressure may indicate serious subclavian disease. Multiple bruits may suggest widespread arterial disease but may be present without significant occlusion. Evidence for a cardiac embolic source should be pursued aggressively, especially in younger normotensive individuals with cerebral ischemia. *Electrocardiography* should be routine to exclude cardiac dysrhythmia and occult myocardial infarction.

Echocardiography is often helpful in excluding intracardiac emboli. *Transesophageal Doppler echocardiography* is most sensitive in this regard. *Lumbar puncture* is required in rare cases of stroke or TIA, particularly if meningovascular syphilis is a serious consideration. *Duplex ultrasonography* is a noninvasive technique to detect obstructive or stenotic carotid artery disease.

Ideally, all suspected cases of stroke and threatened stroke should receive a *computerized tomogram (CT)* of the brain. *Magnetic resonance imaging (MRI)* is often more sensitive in detecting early cerebral infarction, while CT scanning is very sensitive to the presence of intracranial hemorrhage. These techniques can distinguish between cerebral hemorrhage, old and recent infarction, and hemorrhagic infarction; they can also exclude unsuspected space-occupying lesions. *Magnetic resonance cerebral angiography* may be needed if the neurologic event cannot be differentiated by clinical criteria from an arteriovenous malformation, cerebrovascular malformation, or giant aneurysm. *Diffusion-weighted* and *hemodynamically weighted echo-planar MR imaging* are new techniques that are useful in the evaluation of hyperacute cerebral ischemia. They may help to open an early window of opportunity during which treatment is beneficial in salvaging tissue at risk.

Treatment

Treatment of threatened stroke includes reduction of risk factors when possible, although these factors are not always amenable to successful manipulation. For example, a hereditary predilection cannot be altered. Hypertension should be controlled. Control of both hyperlipidemia and diabetes is indicated, although there are no data to demonstrate that these measures reduce the incidence of stroke. Cigarette smoking should be eliminated. The use of anticoagulant drugs, such as heparin and warfarin sodium, is widely accepted in threatened stroke from emboli arising in mural thrombi following myocardial infarction and in nonvalvular atrial fibrillation.

Controlled studies have not demonstrated the effectiveness of anticoagulants in the treatment of TIAs in the carotid and vertebrobasilar territory. Anticoagulants are not helpful for patients with completed stroke, but they may be useful in an evolving stroke.

Antiplatelet therapy with *aspirin* is beneficial in patients with cardiac cerebral emboli who cannot tolerate long-term use of anticoagulant drugs. The benefit of aspirin in patients with TIA is less certain. The optimal dosage of aspirin has not yet been determined. Low doses of aspirin (75–300 mg daily) cause less gastrointestinal discomfort than higher doses and reduce the incidence of stroke in patients with unstable angina or acute myocardial infarction. *Ticlopidine* is the only other platelet-inhibiting drug proven beneficial in clinical trials. It alters platelet membrane fibrinogen interaction but does not affect the cyclooxygenase pathway. Side effects include bone marrow suppression, rash, and, very commonly (22%), diarrhea. The benefit of antiplatelet agents in patients with noncardiac cerebral ischemia appears modest at best.

Recent studies have further investigated the role of thrombolytic agents for acute ischemic stroke. A modest improvement in function may result when patients are given *tissue plasminogen activator (tPA)* within 3 hours of symptom onset. However, use of this agent incurs a 5%–10% risk of symptomatic intracerebral hemorrhage, about 50% of which will be fatal. In 11 studies recently completed or in progress, fewer than 3000 stroke patients will have been studied. By comparison, in the trials of thrombolytics for acute myocardial infarction, more than 50,000 patients were randomized before this treatment intervention was judged safe and effective. The role of thrombolytic agents in the treatment of acute ischemic stroke remains controversial: further studies are necessary before firm conclusions can be drawn.

Intracranial Hemorrhage

Intracranial hemorrhage constitutes approximately 15% of acute cerebrovascular disorders. Bleeding from aneurysms of arteries comprising the circle of Willis, bleeding from arterioles damaged by hypertension or arteriosclerosis, and trauma are the most common causes of intracranial hemorrhage. Although there are many causes of intracranial hemorrhage, the anatomic location of the bleeding greatly influences the clinical picture. By location, hemorrhages can be grouped into the following general categories:

□ Subarachnoid hemorrhage

□ Intracerebral hemorrhage

□ Surface bleeding that extends into the brain

□ Intraventricular hemorrhage

Aneurysms that rupture entirely into the subarachnoid space present with features of meningeal irritation or a transient increase in intracranial pressure. The most common symptom of subarachnoid hemorrhage is the sudden development of a violent, usually localized, headache. This headache is at first frontal or temporal, later becoming occipital and then spreading to involve the entire head and neck. In an adult not prone to headaches, a moderately intense headache (with or without associated neck stiffness) that disappears in 2–3 days may be a sign of a warning leak. Brief loss of consciousness or a seizure preceded by an awareness of dizziness or vertigo and by vomiting are common at the onset. Common physical signs include neck rigidity, fundus or preretinal hemorrhages, and cranial nerve palsies.

Vascular malformations within and on the surface of the brain parenchyma commonly present with seizures and headaches, less often with hemorrhage. Arteriovenous malformations produce symptoms more commonly than other types of cerebrovascular malformations.

Hypertensive-arteriosclerotic intracerebral hemorrhages are often catastrophic events. Headache is a predominant feature at the onset in at least one half of hemorrhages and, by contrast, in less than one fourth of thromboembolisms. Vomiting is prominent as an early symptom. Restlessness and vomiting are more common with hemorrhage than with infarction. Generalized seizures are common with intracerebral hemorrhage, are less frequent with subarachnoid hemorrhage, and are uncommon (less than 10%) with cerebral infarction.

Arterial "berry" aneurysms are round or saccular dilatations characteristically found at arteriole bifurcations on the circle of Willis and its major branches or connections. Intracranial aneurysms occur in all age groups but most commonly rupture in the fifth, sixth, and seventh decades. Approximately 85% of congenital berry aneurysms develop in the anterior part of the circle of Willis derived from the internal carotid artery in its major branches. The most common site is at the origin of the posterior communicating artery from the internal carotid artery. Such an aneurysm typically presents with headache and third nerve palsy involving the pupil. Vascular malformations within and on the surface of the brain parenchyma constitute about 7% of cases with subarachnoid hemorrhage. Four varieties are recognized:

☐ Capillary telangiectasia

☐ Cavernous angioma

☐ Venous angioma

☐ Arteriovenous malformation (AVM)

Capillary telangiectasias are most commonly discovered as incidental postmortem findings in the brain stem. Venous angiomas are cerebrovascular abnormalities often associated with the Sturge-Weber syndrome. These lesions are best identified by MRI.

The most important clues in the diagnosis of hypertensive intracranial hemorrhage are explosive onset, history of high blood pressure, early decline of the level of consciousness, and detection of meningeal irritation and blood in the spinal fluid (preferably by CT scanning) with evidence of a focal lesion. Little other than the past history clinically distinguishes the symptoms of subarachnoid hemorrhage resulting from the rupture of an AVM from those caused by a ruptured aneurysm. Focal neurologic signs and evidence of the sudden development of a mass lesion are frequent accompaniments of a rupture.

Findings that suggest an AVM as the cause of subarachnoid hemorrhage include a history of previous focal seizures, slowly stepwise progressing focal neurologic signs, and occasionally, recurrent unilateral throbbing headache resembling migraine. In addition to meningeal irritation and focal neurologic signs reflecting bleeding, a bruit is present over the orbit or skull in approximately 40% of patients.

Immediate CT examination demonstrates blood in the subarachnoid space in about 95% of the cases of ruptured aneurysm or AVM. CT will identify the size and location of intracerebral hemorrhages, as well as the degree of surrounding edema and the amount and location of any distortion of the brain. CT scan can identify blood in the subarachnoid space and/or brain and ventricles in 95% of patients with subarachnoid hemorrhage.

If subarachnoid hemorrhage is suspected and CT scanning is negative, lumbar puncture is indicated. A CT scan should always be carried out first to rule out a mass lesion. Arteriography remains the definitive procedure to identify an aneurysm or AVM. Angiography is essential to identify areas of local or general vasospasm and should be performed in all cases of subarachnoid hemorrhage that are considered reasonable operative risks or when diagnostic doubt exists.

Initial restoration of normal blood pressure and its maintenance at normal levels is mandatory in the treatment of ruptured aneurysms. Surgical intervention is best accomplished by placing a small clip or ligature across the neck of the sac. If the aneurysm cannot be directly obliterated, surgical ligation of a proximal vessel may be necessary. Symptomatic AVMs can sometimes be dissected and removed, depending on location. Proton-beam irradiation remains controversial. Ligation of the feeding vessels coupled with balloon catheter embolization may be carried out. Treatment of intracerebral hemorrhage is mostly unsatisfactory.

Carotid Artery Disease

Asymptomatic carotid bruits occur in 4% of the population over 40 years of age. The annual stroke rate in patients with an asymptomatic bruit is approximately 2%. This same population has an annual mortality rate of 4%, primarily from complications of heart disease. Bruit is more a marker for the presence of arteriosclerotic disease than a predictor of stroke. Patients with asymptomatic carotid bruits should be screened for risk factors related to atherosclerosis: hypertension, smoking, and hypercholesterolemia. The degree and severity of stenosis should be determined by noninvasive studies.

In the recently completed Asymptomatic Carotid Atherosclerosis Study (ACAS 1995) 1662 patients with asymptomatic stenosis of >60% were randomized to either carotid endarterectomy (CEA) or medical treatment. Although the estimated 5-year risk of stroke was 53% lower (5.1% versus 11.0%) for the CEA group, the only significant difference was in the frequency of TIA or minor stroke ipsilateral to the CEA. This benefit was demonstrated only for men under age 68 years. No significant differences were discerned between the medical and surgical groups with regard to major ipsilateral stroke or death, and the benefits disappear with surgical major morbidity and mortality of greater than 3%. Therefore, patients with asymptomatic carotid stenosis of greater than 60% may be considered for elective CEA; patients with less than 60% stenosis should be retested at 6–12 month intervals and followed for disease progression. Aspirin (325 mg daily) and risk factor reduction are also employed in this patient group.

Ocular and cerebral conditions associated with carotid stenosis include amaurosis fugax, ocular ischemic syndromes, TIAs, and stroke. The ophthalmologist is often the first physician to see a patient with amaurosis fugax or ocular ischemia. Amaurosis is usually embolic, having either a carotid or cardiac source. The annual stroke rate among patients with isolated amaurosis fugax is thought to be approximately 2%. A cardiac source of embolization should be excluded for all patients presenting with isolated amaurosis fugax or transient visual loss. The best procedure for this is transesophageal cardiac ultrasonography. It should be noted that untreated patients with amaurosis fugax, retinal plaques, and/or retinal infarcts share with monocular TIA patients not only an equal prevalence of carotid atherostenosis but also a 30% 5-year expectancy for myocardial infarction and an 18% death rate during the same interval.

If evidence suggests that a carotid lesion is the cause of the amaurosis fugax, or if venous stasis retinopathy is present, then duplex scanning should be performed to determine the presence of vessel wall disease or carotid stenosis. The lesion found by arteriography should explain the symptoms.

No hard data are currently available from which to make a clear recommendation about an appropriate course of therapy. It appears that a trial of aspirin (325 mg/day) should be the initial approach for all patients. Ticlopidine therapy may be considered for patients unable to take aspirin. Carotid endarterectomy with electroencephalogram (EEG) monitoring should be considered only if the surgeon has a perioperative morbidity rate of less than 3% and if any of the following conditions exist:

□ Antiplatelet therapy proves to be ineffective

□ Stenosis appears to be progressive

□ The patient has no operative risk factors

Patients with TIA or previous stroke in the territory of carotid stenosis are judged to be symptomatic. The risk of stroke within a year of symptom onset is 10% in patients with TIA; the risk thereafter is about 6% per year with a 5-year risk of 35%–50%.

In the North American Symptomatic Carotid Endarterectomy Trial (NASCET) reported in 1991, carotid endarterectomy was evaluated in 659 patients with a recent (within 120 days) hemispheric or retinal TIA or a recent nondisabling stroke, who had high-grade (70%–99%) stenosis in the symptomatic carotid artery. All of the patients received optimal medical care, including antiplatelet therapy with aspirin, as well as treatment for hypertension, hyperlipidemia, or diabetes, when appropriate. The patients were randomized, and 331 received medical therapy alone, while 328 also underwent carotid endarterectomy. The surgical group had lower rates of ipsilateral stroke (9.0% versus 26.0%), any stroke (12.6% versus 27.6%), major or fatal stroke (3.7% versus 13.1%), and death from all causes (4.6% versus 6.3%). The perioperative fatality rate was only 0.6%, and the perioperative rate of major stroke or death was 2.1%. The benefit of surgery for reducing the risk of ipsilateral stroke increased with higher degrees of stenosis: 12% risk reduction for 70%–79% stenosis; 18% risk reduction for 80%–89% stenosis; and 26% risk reduction for 90%–99% stenosis.

The authors of the study emphasized that there is still continuing uncertainty regarding carotid endarterectomy for symptomatic stenosis in the range of 30%–69%. The European Carotid Surgery Trial (ECST 1991, 1996) and the Veterans Administrative Cooperative Study (VACS 1991) used different methods and end points but also demonstrated a statistically significant benefit for CEA in selected patients with greater than 70% stenosis.

A meta-analysis of these studies was published recently. The major end points were death and nonfatal stroke or myocardial infarction. For the first month after randomization, the greatest risk (2.7x) was in the CEA group. Rates for perioperative (30 days) major morbidity and mortality were 5.5% and 7.5%. After the first 30 days, the risk of stroke or death was 33% lower in the group treated surgically. The 2-year risk of major or fatal stroke on the side of the symptomatic carotid was 13.1% for the medical group versus 2.5% for the CEA group. The risks of major morbidity and mortality with CEA are proportional to the severity of neurologic illness and comorbid factors, such as ischemic heart disease. The risks for patients with symptomatic unilateral high-grade stenosis and favorable comorbidity are 1%–3% in the hands of capable surgeons. The long-term restenosis rate following CEA is about 10% at 5 years.

It is feasible to reopen the internal carotid artery after acute (<8 hours) occlusion. The risks are high with emergency CEA, however, and the success rate is less than 50%. Patients with carotid occlusion are usually placed on warfarin therapy for several months in the hope of decreasing distal thrombus progression and subsequent embolic stroke.

In summary, patients with symptomatic carotid stenosis >70% should be considered for CEA unless there is acute stroke, maximal neurologic defect, or other medical contraindication to surgery. The major perioperative morbidity and mortality for the surgical team should not exceed 5% for patients with TIA, 7% for patients with minor stroke, or 10% for patients with recurrent stenosis.

The following approach to a patient presenting with a cerebral or retinal TIA should be considered.

□ The patient should be evaluated for the presence of risk factors associated with atherogenesis: hypertension, obesity, hyperlipidemia, and smoking.

□ Appropriate medical therapy should be instituted.

□ The presence of coronary artery disease and a cardiac source of emboli should be excluded by appropriate testing.

□ The patency of the extracranial carotid artery system should be determined using duplex ultrasonography.

If ipsilateral carotid stenosis exceeds 70%, if bilateral carotid stenosis greater than 50% is present, or if long-term evidence indicates progressive disease, carotid endarterectomy should be considered—but only if the surgeon's perioperative stroke and death rate is less than 3%. Otherwise, antiplatelet therapy with aspirin (325 mg/day) or ticlopidine should be initiated. A patient presenting with TIA symptoms who has previously undergone CEA should be evaluated and treated in similar fashion. Special attention should be paid to the evaluation of early restenosis and thrombosis.

As an additional note, elevated plasma homocysteine levels have been linked to extracranial carotid stenosis and directly to an increased risk of stroke and occlusive vascular disease. Folic acid reduces this risk by lowering plasma homocysteine levels. Folates naturally occur in green vegetables and are supplemented in bread and breakfast cereals in the US. Increasing dietary folic acid intake can, therefore, be recommended to all patients with carotid stenosis and generalized cardiovascular disease.

Barnett HJ, Eliasziw M, Meldrum HE, et al. Drugs and surgery in the prevention of ischemic stroke. N Engl J Med. 1995;332:238–248.

Becker WL, Burde RM. Carotid artery disease. A therapeutic enigma. Arch Ophthalmol. 1988;106:34–39.

Beneficial effect of carotid endarterectomy in symptomatic patients with high grade carotid stenosis. North American Symptomatic Carotid Endarterectomy Trial Collaborators. N Engl J Med. 1991;325:445–453.

Carotid endarterectomy for patients with asymptomatic internal carotid artery stenosis. Executive Committee of the Asymptomatic Carotid Atherosclerosis Study Group. JAMA. 1995;273:1421–1428.

Endarterectomy for moderate symptomatic carotid stenosis: interim results from the MRC European Carotid Surgery Trial. *Lancet.* 1996;347:1591–1593.

Goldstein LB, Hasselblad V, Matchar DB, et al. Comparison and meta-analysis of randomized trials of endarterectomy for symptomatic carotid artery stenosis. *Neurology.* 1995;45:1965–1970.

Hacke W, Kaste M, Fieschi C, et al. Intravenous thrombolysis with recombinant tissue plasminogen activator for acute hemispheric stroke. The European Cooperative Acute Stroke Study. *JAMA.* 1995;274:1017–1025.

Moore WS, Barnett HJ, Beebe HG, et al. Guidelines for carotid endarterectomy: a multidisciplinary consensus statement from the ad hoc Committee, American Heart Association. *Stroke.* 1995;26:188–201.

Perry IJ, Refsum H, Morris RW, et al. Prospective study of serum total homocysteine concentration and the risk of stroke in middle-aged British men. *Lancet.* 1995;346:1395–1398.

Randomised controlled trial of streptokinase, aspirin, and combination of both in treatment of acute ischaemic stroke. Multicenter Acute Stroke Trial—Italy (MAST-I) Group. *Lancet.* 1995;346(8989):1509–1514.

Sandercock P. Thrombolytic therapy for acute ischaemic stroke: promising, perilous, or unproven? [Editorial] *Lancet.* 1995;346:1504–1505.

Selhub J, Jacques PF, Bostrom AG, et al. Association between plasma homocysteine concentration and extracranial carotid artery stenosis. *N Engl J Med.* 1995;332:286–291.

Tissue plasminogen activator for acute ischemic stroke. The National Institute of Neurological Disorders and Stroke rt-PA Stroke Study Group. *N Engl J Med.* 1995;333:1581–1587.

CHAPTER IV

Acquired Heart Disease

Recent Developments

□ Coronary stents are placed after angioplasty to maintain artery patency and improve long-term survival.

□ Stress echocardiography detects regional ventricular wall-motion abnormalities and is a sensitive diagnostic tool for detecting myocardial ischemia.

□ In addition to creatinine kinase, other biochemical markers of myocardial ischemia are myoglobin, troponin T, and troponin I.

□ New antiarrhythmics: *adenosine* for supraventricular tachycardia, *ibutilide* for atrial flutter or fibrillation, and new class III drugs *(sotalol, almokalant, dofetilide, and clofilium)* for ventricular dysrhythmias.

Ischemic Heart Disease

Ischemia is defined as a local, temporary oxygen deprivation associated with inadequate removal of metabolites, caused by reduced tissue perfusion. *Ischemic heart disease (IHD)* is caused by decreased perfusion of the myocardium, usually secondary to stenotic or obstructed coronary arteries. Coronary artery atherosclerosis is by far the most common cause of cardiac ischemia, but other diseases and disorders may also result in regional or generalized ischemia, such as coronary artery spasm, coronary arteritis, superimposed coronary thrombosis, intercoronary shunting, severe anemia, hypoxemia, or reduced arterial perfusion pressure.

The cardinal symptom in patients with IHD is *angina pectoris,* usually manifested as a substernal pressure-like pain or tightness that is often triggered by physical exertion, emotional distress, or eating. Angina typically lasts 5–10 minutes and is usually relieved by rest and/or nitroglycerin. Patients may present with pain radiating into other areas, including the jaw, arm, neck, shoulder, back, chest wall, or abdomen. Occasionally, angina may be misinterpreted as indigestion or musculoskeletal pain. Myocardial ischemia may be painless in diabetic patients, often delaying the diagnosis until the disease is more advanced.

The level of physical activity that results in angina pectoris is clinically significant, and it is useful in determining the severity of coronary artery disease, the treatment recommended, and the prognosis. The Canadian Cardiovascular Society functional classification for anginal symptoms is useful for describing the severity of symptoms and the degree of disability in IHD (Table IV-1).

TABLE IV-1

CANADIAN CARDIOVASCULAR SOCIETY FUNCTIONAL CLASSIFICATION
FOR ANGINAL SYMPTOMS

SYMPTOM CLASS	SYMPTOM
0	Asymptomatic
1	Ordinary physical activity, such as walking, does not cause angina. Angina with strenuous, rapid, or prolonged exertion.
2	Slight limitation of ordinary activity. Angina with rapid walking or rapid stair climbing, walking uphill, stair climbing after meals, in cold, when under stress; walking more than two blocks on the level, climbing more than one flight of ordinary stairs.
3	Marked limitation of ordinary physical activity. Angina with walking fewer than two blocks, climbing fewer than one flight of stairs.
4	Inability to carry on any physical activity without discomfort, or rest angina.

Clinical Syndromes

Patients with IHD may be categorized into several discrete clinical syndromes:

□ Stable angina pectoris

□ Unstable angina

□ Variant (Prinzmetal) angina

□ Myocardial infarction

□ Congestive heart failure

□ Sudden cardiac death

□ Asymptomatic patient with IHD

Stable angina pectoris   Angina is considered stable if it responds to rest or nitroglycerin and the patterns of frequency, ease of onset, duration, and response to medication have not changed substantially over a 3-month interval.

Unstable angina   This pattern of angina is characterized by a significant increase in the frequency or duration of chest pain, with or without a decrease in the level of physical activity required to provoke angina. This term is also used to describe patients with rest angina or prolonged anginal episodes. Unstable angina is often associated with an ulcerated plaque or thrombus within the coronary arteries. Coronary artery spasm may be superimposed on the underlying atherosclerotic disease. Patients with unstable angina are hospitalized and monitored for the following reasons: the symptoms are similar to those of a myocardial infarction; cardiac arrhythmias may occur; and unstable angina may progress to myocardial infarction.

Variant (Prinzmetal) angina In this syndrome, angina occurs at rest and is not related to physical exertion. Elevation of the ST segment is seen on electrocardiography (ECG) during the anginal episodes, which are caused by coronary artery spasm. Underlying atherosclerosis is present in 60%–80% of cases, and thrombosis and occlusion may result during the episodes of coronary spasm.

Myocardial infarction Myocardial infarction (MI) results when ischemia becomes severe or prolonged enough to cause irreversible myocardial injury and necrosis, usually due to thrombotic occlusion of a coronary artery. MI may occur suddenly, without warning, in a previously asymptomatic patient or in a patient with stable or variant angina; it may also follow a period of unstable angina. The pain is similar to angina but is usually more severe and more prolonged. Patients commonly experience nausea, vomiting, diaphoresis, weakness, anxiety, dyspnea, light-headedness, and palpitations. Symptoms may begin during or after exertion or at rest. Nearly 25% of myocardial infarcts are painless; painless MI is more common in diabetics and with increasing age. These patients may present with congestive heart failure, hypotension, or syncope. Subendocardial (nontransmural, non–Q wave) infarcts usually result in a smaller region of myocardial injury, cause less ventricular dysfunction and heart failure, and have a lower mortality than transmural (Q wave) infarcts. However, these patients have a greater incidence of post-MI angina. Approximately 20% go on to develop an acute Q wave infarction within 3 months.

Congestive heart failure secondary to IHD Congestive heart failure is discussed later in this chapter. See pages 96–103.

Sudden cardiac death Sudden cardiac death is usually caused by a severe arrhythmia, such as ventricular tachycardia, ventricular fibrillation, profound bradycardia, or asystole. It may occur as the result of MI, during an episode of angina, or without warning in a patient with frequent arrhythmias secondary to underlying IHD or ventricular dysfunction. Other causes for sudden cardiac death are Wolff-Parkinson-White syndrome, hereditary QT interval prolongation syndrome, torsades de pointes, atrioventricular block, aortic stenosis, myocarditis, cardiomyopathy, ruptured or dissecting aortic aneurysm, and pulmonary embolism.

Asymptomatic patients with IHD Asymptomatic patients with IHD are at particular risk for unexpected myocardial infarction, life-threatening arrhythmias, and sudden cardiac death. They may develop advanced coronary artery disease and have multiple infarcts before the correct diagnosis is made and appropriate treatment is initiated. Diabetics and elderly patients are more likely to have painless ischemia. Approximately 25% of MIs may be asymptomatic and detected on a subsequent ECG. A patient who has unexplained dyspnea, weakness, arrhythmias, or poor exercise tolerance requires further diagnostic testing, including noninvasive procedures or coronary arteriography.

Clinical Signs

The clinical findings in IHD are variable and depend upon the severity of myocardial ischemia or injury, the left ventricular dysfunction, and the presence of arrhythmias. Examination and ECG findings may be normal between episodes of angina. However, during an attack, increased heart rate, an S_3 or S_4 gallop, an apical systolic murmur caused by papillary muscle dysfunction, markedly elevated blood pressure, or arrhythmias may be detected. A significant fall in blood pressure during angina is an ominous sign, indicating myocardial dysfunction. Patients with IHD may also have evidence of peripheral or carotid artery atherosclerosis, with decreased pulsations or bruits.

The examination findings during MI include those mentioned above for angina. Other common findings are arterial hypotension, diaphoresis, pallor, coolness of the extremities, low-grade fever, and signs of pulmonary congestion and increased central venous pressure caused by left ventricular dysfunction.

Noninvasive Cardiac Diagnostic Procedures

Noninvasive diagnostic testing in IHD includes electrocardiography, serum enzyme measurements, echocardiography, various types of stress testing, and newer imaging studies, such as positron emission tomography and magnetic resonance cardiac imaging.

The *electrocardiograph (ECG)* may be normal between episodes of ischemia in patients with angina. During angina, the ST segments often become elevated or depressed by up to 4–5 mm. T waves may be inverted; they may become tall and peaked; or inverted T waves may normalize. These ECG findings, when associated with characteristic anginal pain, are virtually diagnostic of IHD. However, absence of ECG changes does not exclude myocardial ischemia with certainty.

During MI, QT interval prolongation and peaked T waves may be seen, followed by ST segment elevation. ST segments remain elevated for several days to weeks, then return to normal. T wave inversion appears in the leads corresponding to the site of the infarct. Q waves or a reduction in the QRS amplitude appear with the onset of myocardial necrosis. Q waves may be absent in a subendocardial (nontransmural) infarction. ST segment elevation, T wave inversion, and Q waves usually occur in the ECG leads related to the site of the infarct and may be accompanied by reciprocal ST depression in the opposite leads. Approximately one half of all infarctions involve the inferior myocardial wall, and most of the remaining half involve the anteroseptal regions. Tachycardia and ventricular arrhythmias are most common within the first few hours after the onset of infarction. Bradyarrhythmias such as heart block are more common with inferior infarction, while ventricular tachycardia and fibrillation are observed more frequently with anteroseptal infarction.

Cardiac enzyme testing is valuable in differentiating MI from unstable angina or noncardiac causes of chest pain. Angina typically does not cause myocardial necrosis, and therefore, cardiac enzyme elevation is not usually observed. Following MI, however, cellular enzymes are released from the infarcted myocardium and are detectable in the blood.

Of the cardiac enzymes that are clinically useful, *creatinine kinase (CK or CPK)* is the most indicative of the size of the infarction. Serial plasma samples should be drawn for CK and CK isoenzymes after the onset of chest pain. CK levels begin to rise approximately 4 hours after MI, peaking between 12 and 24 hours after the event. CK is nonspecific and can also be elevated following injury to skeletal muscles or the brain. Three isoenzymes of CK can be identified. The MB isoenzyme is relatively specific for myocardium, although it constitutes only about 15% of the total CK released after infarction, the remainder being MM or skeletal muscle isoenzyme. The third isoenzyme is BB and is found primarily in the brain and kidneys. An abnormally elevated CK-MB isoenzyme is the hallmark for diagnosis of MI.

Five isoenzymes exist for the ubiquitous enzyme *lactate dehydrogenase (LDH)*. An increase in the ratio of LDH-1 to LDH-2 is suggestive of acute MI, and this ratio peaks at approximately 48–72 hours after onset. LDH remains elevated longer than CK and is more useful in patients presenting several days after the suspected onset of infarction.

Other myocardial biochemical markers useful for detecting infarction are *serum myoglobin, cardiac troponin T,* and *cardiac troponin I.* Serum myoglobin is the first marker to rise following myocardial damage and can be elevated between 1 and 20 hours after infarction. Troponin T elevation also detects low levels of myocardial injury in patients with unstable angina.

Echocardiography employs one- and two-dimensional ultrasound and color flow Doppler techniques to image the ventricles and atria, the heart valves, left ventricular contraction and wall-motion abnormalities, left ventricular ejection fraction, and the pericardium. Patients with IHD, particularly following infarction, commonly have regional wall-motion abnormalities that correspond to the areas of myocardial injury. Echocardiography can be used to estimate the ejection fraction of the left ventricle. A very low ejection fraction represents poor systolic ventricular function and is associated with higher mortality following infarction. Other less frequent complications of infarction, such as mitral regurgitation from papillary muscle injury, ventricular septal defect, ventricular aneurysm, ventricular thrombus, and pericardial effusion, can also be detected with echocardiography. Color flow Doppler produces tomographic images of the heart chambers and provides information on the flow of blood across abnormal valves, pressure differences within the chambers, intracardiac shunts, and cardiac output.

Patients with angina may have normal findings on clinical examination, ECG, and echocardiography between episodes of ischemia. Various *exercise tests* have been developed to induce myocardial ischemia under controlled conditions. The treadmill exercise test is standardized according to the Bruce Protocol or other similar regimens, to provide an incremental rise in the cardiovascular workload according to sex- and age-related norms. (A stationary bicycle may also be used in exercise testing.) A 12-lead electrocardiogram, the heart rate, and the general physical status of the patient are continuously monitored during the procedure, while blood pressure is recorded at 3-minute intervals. The end point in angina patients is a symptom or sign of cardiac ischemia, such as angina, dyspnea, ST segment depression, arrhythmia, or hypotension. The level of exercise required to induce ischemia is inversely correlated with the likelihood of significant coronary artery disease. False positives and false negatives occur, and the sensitivity increases with the number of coronary arteries involved. This test is often performed with a lower workload following MI to help determine functional status and prognosis. However, the end point is a predetermined workload, usually 70% of the predicted maximal heart rate, rather than ischemic symptoms in a patient with a recent MI.

Exercise echocardiography (stress echocardiography) is useful for imaging cardiac valve and wall-motion abnormalities and ventricular dysfunction induced by ischemia during exercise. Predischarge exercise stress echocardiography provides useful prognostic information following acute myocardial infarction.

The sensitivity of exercise testing can be increased by using radionuclide techniques, such as *thallium-201 myocardial scintigraphy,* or *blood-pool isotope (MUGA) scans.* Thallium accumulates in normal myocardium and reveals a perfusion defect in areas of myocardial ischemia. Thallium scans have a high sensitivity and specificity for coronary artery disease. Patients with stable angina will have normal thallium-201 perfusion at rest. During exercise, the thallium scan may reveal areas of decreased myocardial perfusion ("cold spots") that may not be detected by ST segment changes. These areas normalize 4 hours later on the resting or reperfusion scan if they represent areas of ischemia rather than areas of previous infarction or scar. Intravenous dipyridamole can be substituted for exercise to simulate stress-induced changes in coronary artery blood flow during thallium-201 imaging. Blood-pool isotope scans suggest IHD if the ejection fraction fails to increase or decreases with exercise, or if regional wall-motion abnormalities develop during exercise.

Thallium-201 imaging is also helpful in the diagnosis of an acute MI, if performed within the first 6–24 hours after onset. *Tomographic imaging* of myocardial perfusion is possible with thallium-201, using a technique called *single-photon emission computed tomography (SPECT)*. This technique provides better imaging of infarcts and improved detection of multivessel disease. While an infarct is displayed as a cold spot on thallium-201 imaging, it is displayed as a hot spot on *technetium-99 pyrophosphate imaging*. Technetium-99 pyrophosphate is used for infarct-avid imaging, because it accumulates in necrotic myocardial cells rather than normal myocardium. A new infarct is visualized best between 24 and 48 hours after onset with Tc-99 scintigraphy. Other imaging tests that are being evaluated in the detection and management of IHD are *positron emission tomography, ultrafast computed tomography, cardiac magnetic resonance imaging,* and *magnetic resonance fluoroscopy.*

Invasive Cardiac Diagnostic Procedures

Coronary arteriography and *ventriculography* provide valuable information about the presence and severity of coronary artery disease and about ventricular function. These techniques can indicate the specific areas of coronary artery stenosis or occlusion, the number of involved vessels, the ventricular systolic and diastolic volumes, the ejection fraction, and regional wall-motion abnormalities. This information assists the cardiologist and cardiac surgeon in planning appropriate management of the patient.

Coronary artery stenosis is hemodynamically significant when the arterial lumen diameter is narrowed by more than 50% or the cross-sectional area is reduced by more than 75%. Common indications for coronary arteriography are

□ Intractable angina unresponsive to medical therapy

□ A markedly positive exercise stress test

□ Atypical chest pain

□ Recent MI in a patient under age 40

□ Suspected left ventricular aneurysm

□ Postinfarction ventricular septal defect or papillary muscle dysfunction

□ Cardiomyopathy

□ Recurrent life-threatening arrhythmias unresponsive to medical treatment

□ Preoperative or postoperative assessment of patients undergoing coronary bypass or heart valve surgery

Ergonovine can be administered to patients with a normal arteriogram to attempt to induce coronary artery spasm during arteriography. A positive ergonovine response is suggestive of Prinzmetal angina.

Epidemiology

The most widely accepted risk factors for atherosclerosis and ischemic heart disease are cigarette smoking, elevated serum cholesterol, hypertension, a positive family history for IHD, and diabetes mellitus. Obesity, sedentary lifestyle, stress, personality type, use of oral contraceptive drugs, and menopause are of less clear significance. Lipids other than cholesterol are important in assessing the risk of coronary artery disease. (Hypercholesterolemia and hyperlipoproteinemia are discussed in chapter V of this book.)

Pathophysiology and Clinical Course

Atherosclerosis involves primarily the vessels on the epicardial surface of the heart and does not usually involve arterioles within the myocardium itself. An exception is diffuse coronary small-vessel disease, in which wall thickening and lumen narrowing occur in the small intramyocardial arteries and arterioles. This process appears to be distinct from atherosclerosis and is more common in patients with diabetes, hypertension, collagen vascular diseases, amyloidosis, and cardiomyopathies.

Atherosclerosis is characterized by focal accumulation of lipids, fibrous tissue, and blood products in the intima of medium-sized arteries, including the coronary, carotid, vertebral, iliac, femoral, and popliteal arteries, and the aorta. Therefore, patients with IHD are at increased risk for peripheral vascular disease or cerebrovascular disease, and vice versa. All of these diseases have essentially the same risk factors. Lipids pass into the intima from the bloodstream, and platelets accumulate at sites of endothelial injury. Cigarette smoking and hypertension promote endothelial injury, and hypercholesterolemia can increase the insudation of lipids into the intima. Progressive changes in the arteries are characterized by development of intimal fatty streaks, followed by fibrous plaques, then atherosclerotic plaques. Complications include ulceration of a plaque with release of its contents as cholesterol emboli, hemorrhage from a plaque, and thrombosis near a plaque.

The balance between arterial supply and myocardial demand for oxygen determines whether ischemia occurs. Significant coronary stenosis, thrombosis, or occlusion, reduced arterial pressure, hypoxemia, or severe anemia can impede the supply of oxygen to the myocardium. On the demand side, an increase in heart rate, ventricular contractility, or wall tension (which is determined by systolic arterial pressure, ventricular volume, and ventricular wall thickness) may each cause increased utilization of oxygen. When the demand for oxygen exceeds the supply, ischemia occurs. If this ischemia becomes prolonged, infarction and myocardial necrosis result. Transmural infarcts are usually caused by complete occlusion of the responsible artery, while non–Q wave infarcts are more likely to be caused by a stenotic but patent artery at the time of presentation. It has been hypothesized that spontaneous recanalization of a transiently occluded coronary artery occurs in patients with a nontransmural infarct. This spontaneous reperfusion lessens the amount of myocardial damage and the clinical consequences. Therefore, the initial hospital course is often uncomplicated in patients with nontransmural infarcts.

The patient with a non–Q wave infarction may be considered to have an incomplete infarction, with potential for reocclusion of the infarcted artery and extension of the myocardial damage. The increased incidence of reinfarction in such patients becomes manifest in many instances during the initial hospitalization, and certainly within the first 6 months following the infarction. Although the in-hospital prognosis for patients with non–Q wave infarction is better than that for patients with Q wave infarction, the prognosis at 6–12 months tends to equalize. As such, patients with non–Q wave infarction represent a specific subgroup for whom aggressive diagnostic evaluation and treatment are needed. The detection and dilation or bypass of a high-grade coronary stenosis may prevent subsequent reinfarction.

The complications of MI depend upon its severity. If infarction occurs, regional and global ventricular contractile dysfunction may result in congestive heart failure or pulmonary edema. Mild to moderate heart failure occurs in nearly 50% of patients following MI, and severe heart failure in about 15%. Cardiogenic shock, which results in a dramatic fall in systemic blood pressure, is observed in 10% of patients with MI and has a mortality rate of over 75%. Rupture of the ventricular septum or a papillary muscle is uncommon, with each occurring in about 5% of patients. Rupture of the left ventricular wall, which may occur at any time within 2 weeks, has been found to be the cause of sudden death in about 9% of autopsies after acute MI. In some patients, post-MI pericarditis develops, characterized by a pericardial friction rub 2–3 days after infarction. When accompanied by fever, arthralgia, and pleuropericardial pain, the diagnosis is most likely *post-MI, or Dressler, syndrome*. This condition can be treated with aspirin, other nonsteroidal anti-inflammatory agents, or corticosteroids. Injury along the conduction pathways of the atria or ventricles may result in bradycardia, heart block, supraventricular tachycardias, or ventricular arrhythmias. Arrhythmias often exacerbate ischemic injury by reducing the perfusion pressure in the coronary arteries. Most acute deaths from MI are a result of these arrhythmias.

Treatment of Ischemic Heart Disease

The goals of management for the patient with coronary artery disease are to reduce or eliminate angina, prevent myocardial damage, and prolong life. The first line of attack should include eliminating risk factors for atherosclerosis through cessation of cigarette smoking; control of blood pressure, serum cholesterol, and weight; and establishment of a regular exercise program. Recent studies have reported actual regression of atherosclerotic lesions following intensive lipid-lowering therapy. Antiplatelet therapy with daily aspirin has also been advocated for all patients with coronary artery disease because of the significant reduction in risk of MI.

Medical management   Medical management of angina pectoris is designed to deliver as much oxygen as possible to the potentially ischemic myocardium and/or to reduce the oxygen demand to a level compatible with an active, comfortable life. Oxygen supply may be maximized through the coronary arteries by the use of coronary vasodilators. *Nitroglycerin* or other *nitrates* may be given sublingually for acute episodes of angina. Long-acting orally administered nitrates or topically applied nitroglycerin ointments or transdermal patches may be administered for prevention and long-term control of angina. Unstable angina is often managed with intensive-care monitoring and intravenous nitroglycerin, which can be carefully titrated to control the angina without causing excessive hypotension. The systemic effects of nitrates include venous dilation and a decline in arterial pressure; these physiologic effects contribute to the therapeutic effects. The *slow-channel calcium-blocking* *agents* (such as *diltiazem, nifedipine, verapamil, nicardipine,* and *amlodipine*) are effective in chronic angina and may be useful in preventing episodes of coronary spasm. Improving the oxygen-carrying capacity of the blood by treating anemia or coexisting pulmonary disease or by eliminating cigarette smoking to prevent carboxyhemoglobinemia will provide some additional beneficial effect.

To reduce oxygen utilization, the heart rate and contractility may be diminished pharmacologically. Ventricular wall tension can also be decreased, particularly by controlling systemic hypertension and by reducing the ventricular volume with venous dilators such as the nitrates. The best agents for reducing heart rate and contractility are the *beta-adrenergic blockers.* The resting rate may be reduced to 50 beats per minute and the exercise heart rate to about 100–110 with a program of light to moderate exercise. Beta blockers are useful in the management of stable and unstable angina. The beta-adrenergic blockers and calcium channel blockers (particularly verapamil) must be used with caution when left ventricular dysfunction is present.

Surgical management   Mechanical dilation of coronary plaques by *percutaneous transluminal coronary angioplasty (PTCA)* is performed with an intra-arterial balloon-tipped catheter. This procedure is especially effective in patients with single-vessel disease but is also commonly used for multivessel disease. Patients are considered for PTCA if they have severe angina that is unresponsive to medication and show a significant stenosis (at least 75% narrowing) on coronary arteriography. It is usually not recommended for disease involving the left main coronary artery. Following the angioplasty, calcium-channel blockers and aspirin are often administered to help prevent thrombosis and spasm of the treated artery.

Approximately 50% of carefully selected patients have initial symptomatic improvement following PTCA. However, recurrent stenosis occurs in 30%–40%, usually within 3 months. Up to 6%–8% of patients develop severe angina during or immediately after PTCA and require emergency bypass grafting for impending MI. About 3% of patients develop acute infarction, and aortic dissection may rarely occur following PTCA.

Newer devices for the removal of atheromatous lesions are being investigated, including *excimer* and *argon lasers, atheroma-cutting blades,* and *high-speed rotary devices. Mechanical stents* are used to maintain patency in a dilated atheromatous coronary artery. Stenting has reduced the frequency of complications, such as acute infarction, following angioplasty and is now considered a standard therapeutic technique in interventional cardiology. It is also being used successfully to treat diseased coronary bypass graft vessels.

The antiplatelet glycoprotein (GP) IIb/IIIa receptor antagonists, *tirofiban* (Aggrastat), *abciximab* (ReoPro), and *integrilin,* have been studied extensively and were found to be very effective in improving postangioplasty clinical outcomes. These new drugs are currently being evaluated following coronary stenting and atherectomy.

When angioplasty is inappropriate or ineffective and medical therapy has failed to control symptoms in severe multivessel disease, *coronary artery bypass surgery* may be considered. The bypass graft provides a shunt from the aorta to the diseased coronary artery beyond the area of obstruction in order to increase blood flow, thereby eliminating angina and often preventing or reducing the risk of infarction and cardiac death. Coronary artery bypass grafting has also been shown to increase left ventricular function, improve quality of life, and increase life expectancy as compared to medical treatment in patients with significant left main coronary artery and multi-vessel CAD with left ventricular dysfunction. Saphenous veins are most commonly used as the bypass material, but the internal mammary artery has become standard for the left anterior descending artery because of its improved long-term patency rate.

Surgical decisions are based on the clinical status of the patient as well as on the anatomic and physiologic factors identified during testing. Bypass grafting is recommended in patients with obstruction or high-grade stenosis of the left main coronary artery or significant stenoses of all three major arteries with reduced left ventricular function. In patients with three-vessel disease and good ventricular function or significant stenoses in only one or two arteries, surgery is indicated primarily for the relief of angina. Patients with the lowest risk for surgery are those with the following findings:

□ Proximal disease in a major coronary artery with a large patent arterial lumen beyond the stenosis

□ Good runoff of blood from the distal branches of the obstructed areas on arteriography

□ Good or only moderately reduced ventricular function

The overall operative mortality rate should be only 1%–2% in these patients. Some cardiac surgeons believe that severe left ventricular dysfunction with an ejection fraction of 20% or lower may be a contraindication to bypass grafting because of the increased operative mortality. Anginal symptoms may progress or recur in approximately 5% of patients per year following bypass grafting.

Treatment of Acute Myocardial Infarction

Patients with acute MI require a coordinated treatment program that can simultaneously manage myocardial ischemia, prevent further injury and necrosis, detect and treat arrhythmias, manage heart failure and other complications of infarction, and initiate a rehabilitation program.

Patients seen in the first 6 hours after the onset of symptoms may benefit from early restoration of coronary blood flow by thrombolytic therapy. Currently, several intravenous thrombolytic agents are available, which effectively lyse coronary thrombi and restore coronary blood flow in most patients. The most frequently used agents are *streptokinase* (1.5 million units over 30–60 minutes), *tissue plasminogen activator*, or *tPA* (100 mg over 1.5–3.0 hours), and *anisoylated plasminogen streptokinase activator complex*, or *APSAC* (30 units given as a bolus). Large-scale clinical trials of these agents have shown a reduction in mortality associated with MI, particularly when administered within the first 3 hours after onset. At the present time, none of these three agents has shown clear superiority in reducing mortality, but streptokinase is much less expensive than the other two agents. The most serious potential complication of thrombolytic therapy is CNS hemorrhage, and streptokinase causes fewer strokes and cerebral hemorrhages than either tPA or APSAC. *Reteplase* (Retavase) is a newer thrombolytic agent that appears to be similar to APSAC.

The use of an intravenous thrombolytic agent is indicated for a patient who presents with chest pain of at least 30-minutes' duration and whose electrocardiogram shows ST segment elevation of at least 1 mm in two or more contiguous ECG leads. Although most studies have restricted the use of these drugs to patients 75 years of age or younger, older patients have a distinctly higher infarction mortality and may very well benefit from thrombolytic therapy. Contraindications include known sites of potential bleeding, a history of prior cerebrovascular accident, recent surgery, or prolonged cardiopulmonary resuscitation efforts.

Angioplasty has been evaluated extensively as an adjunct in the management of MI. Recent information from the Thrombolysis in Myocardial Infarction (TIMI) trial suggests that angioplasty should perhaps be reserved for patients who exhibit recurrent ischemic events following an acute infarction or for those who manifest ischemia on exercise stress testing prior to discharge or in the follow-up period. If immediately available, PTCA may be useful for patients in whom thrombolytic therapy is contraindicated and for those who develop cardiogenic shock. Some patients can be best managed by coronary bypass grafting shortly after infarction if arteriography identifies high-risk coronary artery lesions that are not amenable to angioplasty or medical treatment.

Patients with acute MI should be monitored in an intensive care or coronary care unit as soon as possible after onset. Pain is relieved with intravenous morphine or other opiates. Ischemia is treated with nitrates, oxygen, and beta blockers or calcium channel blockers. Congestive heart failure or pulmonary edema is managed with vasodilators, diuretics, digoxin, and/or other inotropic agents. Continuous cardiac monitoring is performed to detect significant arrhythmias. If thrombolytic therapy is administered, anticoagulation with intravenous heparin is given for 3–5 days. *Aspirin* 162–325 mg has been demonstrated to be as effective as thrombolytic therapy in reducing mortality from MI and should be started as soon as MI is diagnosed.

If long periods of bed rest are required, prophylaxis against deep-vein thrombosis with the use of elastic stockings or subcutaneous low-dose heparin is recommended. Early mobilization is encouraged in patients without complications, often by the third day after the onset of infarction.

Major early complications of MI include the many types of arrhythmias. Ventricular arrhythmias consisting of ventricular ectopic beats or premature depolarizations are present in almost all patients with acute MI. If these are seen in significant numbers or progress into runs of ventricular tachycardia, they are usually treated with intravenous lidocaine. If ventricular tachycardia is unresponsive to medications or produces significant hypotension, emergency DC cardioversion is carried out.

Ventricular fibrillation requires immediate electrical defibrillation. Because of the risk of worsening the arrhythmias, the use of oral antiarrhythmic agents to control ventricular ectopy in the post-MI period is generally contraindicated. The Cardiac Arrhythmias Suppression Trial (CAST study) demonstrated up to a threefold increase in mortality with the routine use of oral antiarrhythmic medication in non–life-threatening PVCs after MI.

Beta blockers play an important role in the management of patients following acute MI. Several randomized and controlled trials have shown that beta blockers (*atenolol, propranolol, metoprolol,* and *timolol*) initiated within several days of infarction and continued after discharge can reduce subsequent mortality. Consequently, beta blockers should be used in the routine management of acute MI in those patients without contraindications, such as bronchospastic lung disease, severe left ventricular dysfunction, heart block, and other bradyarrhythmias.

Prognosis

About 60% of patients who die of cardiac disease expire suddenly before reaching the hospital. The prognosis for those hospitalized with MI, on the other hand, has become remarkably good. In some recent studies using thrombolytic therapy, mortality has been in the range of 5%. Mortality is affected by a wide variety of factors, such as the degree of heart failure, myocardial damage, severity of the underlying atherosclerotic process, heart size, and previous ischemia.

An important aim of a good cardiac program is to enable patients to return to their usual jobs after discharge from the hospital. About 80%–90% of patients with uncomplicated MI can return to work within 2–3 months. Patients should be advised to modify or eliminate their risk factors for atherosclerosis. Dietary programs, reduction of physiological and psychological stress, and a cardiac rehabilitation program may be of benefit to many patients.

Bashore TM. *Invasive Cardiology: Principles and Techniques.* Toronto: Decker; 1990.

Brown G, Albers JJ, Fisher LD, et al. Regression of coronary artery disease as a result of intensive lipid-lowering therapy in men with high levels of apolipoprotein B. *N Engl J Med.* 1990;323:1289–1298.

Eeckhout E, Kappenberger L, Goy JL. Stents for intracoronary placement: current status and future directions. *J Am Coll Cardiol.* 1996;27:757–765.

Giuliani ER, Fuster V, Gersh B, et al, eds. *Cardiology: Fundamentals and Practice.* 2nd ed. St Louis: Mosby; 1991:318–348, 415–447, 459–600, 1129–1502.

Goldberger E. *Essentials of Clinical Cardiology.* Philadelphia: Lippincott; 1990:1–8, 88–155, 201–232.

Gore JM, Dalen JE. Cardiovascular disease. *JAMA.* 1997;277:1845–1846.

Hamm CW, Katus HA. New biochemical markers for myocardial cell injury. *Curr Opin Cardiol.* 1995;10:355–360.

Hennekens CH, O'Donnell CJ, Ridker PM, et al. Current issues concerning thrombolytic therapy for acute myocardial infarction. *J Am Coll Cardiol.* 1995;25 (suppl7):18S–22S.

Pasternack RC, Braunwald E, Sobel BE. Acute myocardial infarction. In: Braunwald E, ed. *Heart Disease: A Textbook of Cardiovascular Medicine.* 3rd ed. Philadelphia: Saunders; 1988:1222–1313.

Preliminary report: Effect of encainide and flecainide on mortality in a randomized trial of arrhythmia suppression after myocardial infarction. The Cardiac Arrhythmias Suppression Trial Investigators. *N Eng J Med.* 1989;321:406–410.

Rutherford JD, Braunwald E, Cohn PF. Chronic ischemic heart disease. In: Braunwald E, ed. *Heart Disease: A Textbook of Cardiovascular Medicine.* 3rd ed. Philadelphia: Saunders; 1988:1311–1378.

Congestive Heart Failure

Congestive heart failure (CHF) is a general term that applies to a clinical state in which a patient manifests subjective or objective features indicative of impaired function of the left or right ventricle or both. Symptoms and signs of CHF may occur when the heart is not able to pump a sufficient amount of blood for a prolonged period of time to meet the body's requirements. *Compensated CHF* refers to patients whose clinical manifestations of CHF have been controlled by treatment. *Decompensated CHF* represents heart failure with symptoms that are not under control. *Refractory CHF* exists when previous therapeutic measures have failed to control the clinical manifestations of the syndrome. Pulmonary edema usually results from severe left ventricular failure, with increased pulmonary capillary pressure, causing parenchymal and intra-alveolar fluid accumulation in the lung. Table IV-2 shows the New York Heart Association classification scheme for heart failure symptoms.

Symptoms

Heart failure causes a variety of symptoms, depending upon the severity of ventricular dysfunction. Symptoms may result from inadequate tissue perfusion caused by pump failure or from the failing heart's inability to empty adequately, leading to edema and fluid accumulation in the lungs, extremities, and other sites. The most frequent symptoms of left ventricular failure are dyspnea with exertion or at rest, orthopnea, paroxysmal nocturnal dyspnea, diaphoresis, generalized weakness, fatigue, anxiety, and light-headedness. With more severe CHF, the patient may also experience a productive cough, copious pink, frothy sputum, and mental confusion. Angina may also occur if the CHF results from ischemic heart disease. Right heart failure may occur separately from or secondary to chronic left heart failure. Patients with right heart failure typically develop peripheral edema.

Clinical Signs

Examination findings in acute left ventricular failure may include respiratory distress, use of the respiratory accessory muscles, pinkish sputum or frank hemoptysis, coarse rales on pulmonary auscultation, expiratory wheezes, a rapid heart rate, an S_3 gallop, diaphoresis, and deterioration in mental status. Blood pressure is often markedly elevated but may be reduced during MI. Long-standing cases of CHF show signs of right ventricular failure, especially elevated central venous pressure, pedal edema, hepatomegaly, and cyanosis. In some patients, pleural effusion or ascites may be detected.

TABLE IV-2

NEW YORK HEART ASSOCIATION CLASSIFICATION
FOR HEART FAILURE SYMPTOMS

SYMPTOM CLASS	SYMPTOM
I	No symptoms
II	Comfortable at rest; symptoms with ordinary activity
III	Comfortable at rest; symptoms with less than ordinary activity
IV	Symptoms at rest

Diagnostic Evaluation

The history and clinical examination of the patient are the most important components in the diagnostic assessment of CHF. Helpful diagnostic studies in the evaluation of CHF and its underlying etiologies include chest x-ray, ECG, blood gases, hemoglobin level, serum electrolytes, and urinalysis. If the primary mechanism of heart failure is unclear, additional tests may prove useful in selected patients. Such tests may include echocardiography, exercise stress testing, cardiac nuclear-imaging studies, coronary arteriography, right and left heart catheterization, Holter monitoring, pulmonary function tests, and thyroid function tests.

The ECG may reveal acute ischemic changes, acute or old myocardial infarction, ventricular hypertrophy, chamber enlargement, atrial fibrillation, or other arrhythmias. Typical chest x-ray findings are prominent pulmonary vessels, interstitial or alveolar pulmonary edema, cardiomegaly, and pleural effusions. Patients with severe pump failure may have abnormal serum electrolytes owing to poor renal perfusion. Abnormalities in the blood or urine may help detect severe anemia or renal failure as a precipitating factor in CHF. Abnormal liver enzymes are common if venous congestion is present as a result of right ventricular failure. Echocardiography and other cardiac studies can help differentiate the many cardiac causes of CHF, including ischemic heart disease, valvular heart disease, cardiomyopathies, and cardiac arrhythmias. Pure right ventricular failure may result from chronic pulmonary disease, pulmonary hypertension, tricuspid or pulmonary valve disease, right ventricular infarction, or constrictive pericarditis.

Ejection fraction (EF) is the calculated percentage of blood ejected by the ventricle during a single or average contraction. In normal patients, the EF is over 50%. An EF of 40%–50% indicates mild impairment; 25%–40%, moderate impairment; and below 25%, severe impairment. EF can be measured using echocardiography, radionuclide ventriculography, and contrast ventriculography. The first of these is the most useful and least invasive method of determining and sequentially following EF and the systolic state of the ventricles.

Epidemiology

The epidemiology of a large percentage of patients with CHF parallels that of IHD, because IHD is currently the primary cause of heart failure. Accordingly, the same risk factors for atherosclerosis apply to ischemic CHF. Patients with CHF are more sensitive to a high intake of sodium and should receive dietary instructions to achieve a low-sodium diet. When CHF is not the result of IHD, other causes must be investigated. A history of rheumatic fever, atrial fibrillation, pernicious anemia, hyperthyroidism, or other disorders may suggest one of the less common etiologies of CHF. Although CHF is most commonly found in adults, it can also occur in children with congenital heart or valve defects, cardiomyopathy, myocarditis, or, in rare instances, following infarction from Kawasaki disease.

The prognosis for patients with CHF depends directly upon the degree of ventricular impairment. The New York Heart Association classification system of CHF by symptoms (Table IV-2) correlates well with survival. In a study from Duke University, patients with class IV CHF had 1- and 3-year mortality rates of 55% and 82%, respectively. In the Framingham study, the overall 5-year mortality rate was 62% in men with CHF and 42% in women.

Etiology

As noted above, ischemic heart disease is presently the most common cause of CHF. Cumulative injury to the ventricular myocardium from ischemia and infarction can lead to impaired ventricular systolic and diastolic function, and, ultimately, pump failure. Additional causes of systolic dysfunction are

- Valvular heart disease (primarily aortic stenosis and aortic or mitral regurgitation)
- Cardiomyopathies (which may have metabolic, infectious, toxic, connective tissue, or idiopathic etiologies)
- Myocarditis (from viral or inflammatory diseases)

Diseases that impair the relaxation and filling properties of the left ventricle can result in diastolic dysfunction. Such disorders include:

- Infiltrative diseases (amyloidosis, sarcoidosis, metastatic disease, and others)
- Causes of chronic constrictive pericarditis, coronary artery disease, cardiomyopathy
- Left ventricular hypertrophy (which can be caused by arterial hypertension, idiopathic hypertrophic subaortic stenosis, and coarctation of the aorta)

Actually, both systolic and diastolic dysfunction often occur simultaneously in the common causes of CHF, namely ischemic heart disease, valvular disease, and the congestive cardiomyopathies. Some of the causes of high–cardiac output heart failure are

- Severe anemia
- Hyperthyroidism
- Arteriovenous fistulas
- Beriberi
- Paget disease

In high-output failure, the demand for oxygen is so great that the heart eventually fails because it cannot maintain the excessive cardiac output indefinitely. Some patients may have more than one mechanism for heart failure, such as a patient with ischemic heart disease who develops CHF after becoming severely anemic. The specific causes for right ventricular failure have been mentioned earlier.

Pathophysiology and Clinical Course

The left and right ventricles function as pumping chambers, and their action can be subdivided into a *systolic*, or contraction, phase and a *diastolic*, or relaxation, phase. During *systole,* the ventricular muscle actively contracts, developing pressure and ejecting blood into the aorta or pulmonary artery for forward perfusion. During *diastole,* the ventricular muscle actively and passively relaxes and allows a refilling of the ventricle from the corresponding atrium. Either or both of these phases may become impaired, leading to systolic and/or diastolic dysfunction. Some of the symptoms and clinical signs of CHF can be distinguished as being attributable to systolic or diastolic impairment. Treatment varies, depending upon which type of dysfunction predominates.

Systolic dysfunction   The ability of the heart to contract and eject blood is determined by preload, afterload, and contractility. *Preload* refers to the amount of stretch to which muscle fibers are subjected at the end of diastole, or refilling. Preload is determined by blood volume and venous return. Excessive preload is often referred to as *volume overload*. Up to a point, as the preload increases, the force of contraction also increases, allowing adequate emptying of the ventricle.

Afterload is the amount of tension or force in the ventricular muscle mass just after onset of contraction, as the ventricle begins emptying. Clinically, afterload represents the pressure that the ventricle must withstand during contraction. Thus, the aortic pressure determines afterload for the left ventricle, while the pulmonary artery pressure determines afterload for the right. Even a normal ventricle may fail with extremely high preload or afterload.

Contractility refers to the intrinsic ability of the myocardial fibers to contract, independent of the preload or afterload conditions. Contractility can be adversely affected by metabolic, ischemic, or other structural derangement of the myocardial cells. Abnormal intracellular modulation of calcium ions is a key component in the development of heart failure. Clinical disorders that affect preload, afterload, or contractility will result in systolic dysfunction. Likewise, therapy directed toward improvements in these parameters can be used to treat systolic dysfunction.

Diastolic dysfunction   Several of the disorders that impair the diastolic, or relaxation, properties of the ventricle have been listed above among the etiologies of CHF. Diastolic dysfunction causes elevated filling pressures in the ventricles and atria. In the left ventricle, diastolic dysfunction causes pulmonary venous hypertension and its clinical manifestations, such as dyspnea on exertion, orthopnea, and paroxysmal nocturnal dyspnea. Clinical signs of diastolic dysfunction are pulmonary edema with rales, lung congestion visible on chest x-ray, and hypoxemia.

The clinical course of CHF may follow a downward spiral of left ventricular systolic and diastolic dysfunction, ventricular dilation, and a decline in the ejection fraction, followed by right heart failure. A continuous reduction in cardiac output and tissue perfusion may be accompanied by increasing pulmonary and systemic venous congestion. This progression may be slowed, or even halted in some patients, with appropriate treatment.

Medical and Nonsurgical Management

In the management of heart failure, treatment strategies can be directed at the systolic or diastolic ventricular dysfunction. Specific treatment for some causes of right heart failure is also available.

Systolic dysfunction   If the preload is reduced, systolic function can occasionally be improved by carefully increasing preload by volume infusion. This increase in preload dilates the ventricle and is one of the mechanisms by which the heart intrinsically attempts to compensate for poor systolic function. However, this mechanism fails and systolic function is impaired when the ventricle becomes overly dilated.

Reducing afterload is the most effective way to manage systolic dysfunction in most clinical situations. Reducing vascular resistance and lowering arterial blood pressure decreases the burden on the left ventricle and enhances contraction and ejection. Regardless of the baseline values, lowering blood pressure (while maintaining adequate tissue perfusion) is the mainstay of treatment of systolic dysfunction. The most effective drugs for reducing afterload in current clinical practice are the *angiotensin-converting enzyme (ACE) inhibitors*, which include *captopril, enalapril, lisinopril,* and several new agents. These drugs are effective in decreasing the clinical manifestations of CHF and have been demonstrated in clinical trials to lower mortality. Other drugs that reduce afterload by lowering blood pressure and peripheral vascular resistance are *hydralazine, clonidine, calcium channel blockers,* and the *alpha-adrenergic blockers* such as *prazosin* or *doxazosin.* These alternative drugs can be considered for patients who cannot tolerate ACE inhibitors because of renal dysfunction or other relative contraindications. Additional benefits of alpha-adrenergic blockers are reduction of serum cholesterol and triglycerides and increase in HDL levels. Hospitalized patients with more severe CHF, particularly pulmonary edema, may require more aggressive afterload reduction with intravenous agents such as *nitroprusside, nitroglycerin,* or *enalapril.*

The contractility of the left ventricle can be enhanced with inotropic agents. *Digitalis,* the time-honored drug for increasing contractility, is a mainstay of treatment, especially for long-term outpatient maintenance therapy. The intravenous sympathomimetic amines *dopamine* and *dobutamine* are more potent inotropic agents, useful in managing severe CHF in hospitalized patients. In addition to enhancing contractility, dobutamine reduces afterload by peripheral vasodilation. A patient on these potent drugs requires close monitoring of blood pressure, heart rate, cardiac output, and urine production. The phosphodiesterase III inhibitors *amrinone* and *milrinone* are newer inotropic drugs available in oral and intravenous forms. However, up to 20% of patients taking amrinone develop thrombocytopenia, and oral milrinone has been associated with increased mortality. Intermittent or continuous infusion intravenous milrinone is effective for providing hemodynamic support in patients with acute decompensated congestive heart failure.

Diastolic dysfunction   Diastolic function can be improved by reducing preload, which in turn lowers filling pressures in the ventricle. This can be achieved by reducing circulating blood volume, by increasing the capacitance of the venous bed, and by improving systolic function to more effectively empty the ventricle. *Diuretics* are the most effective agents for reducing blood volume. *Oral thiazide* or *loop diuretics* are effective for long-term diuresis, but *intravenous loop diuretics* such as *furosemide* or *bumetanide* are more potent for severe CHF or pulmonary edema. Venous capacitance can be increased by administering venous dilators, particularly the *nitrates.* Intravenous *furosemide* and *morphine* also have some venodilation effects, partially explaining their effectiveness in treating pulmonary edema. Any of the measures previously discussed that improve systolic function will also indirectly enhance diastolic function by reducing the residual blood volume in the ventricle following contraction.

Other approaches to CHF   Other strategies for managing CHF include seeking the underlying causes or contributing factors responsible for the failure and correcting them, if possible. Precipitating factors can include excessive salt or fluid intake, poor medication compliance, excessive activity, obesity, pulmonary infection or embolism, MI, renal disease, anemia, thyrotoxicosis, or arrhythmias.

Intermittent arrhythmias may seriously compromise the ventricular pumping function. Tachyarrhythmias may aggravate ischemia by increasing cardiac oxygen consumption, while bradyarrhythmias may decrease cardiac output and blood pressure further and exacerbate the manifestations of heart failure. Because many antiarrhythmic drugs have a depressant effect on contractility, they should be used judiciously in patients with heart failure. Cardiac pacing may be needed for heart block and other severe bradyarrhythmias.

Other measures that can assist in the management of CHF are restricting dietary sodium, avoiding fluid overload by carefully monitoring oral and intravenous fluid intake, controlling pain and anxiety, treating concomitant metabolic or pulmonary diseases, and providing supplemental oxygen to hypoxemic patients.

Patients with acute pulmonary edema should be managed in an intensive care setting with continuous ECG monitoring. Unstable patients often benefit from hemodynamic monitoring with Swan-Ganz catheterization to follow pulmonary capillary wedge pressures, cardiac index, and cardiac output. These parameters are particularly helpful in managing patients with severe CHF or cardiogenic shock.

Invasive or Surgical Management

Patients with isolated mitral or aortic valve stenosis may be treated with *percutaneous balloon valvuloplasty*. This procedure has been shown to be effective in reducing the pressure gradient across the valve and providing clinical improvement in symptomatic patients. The long-term benefits and effectiveness of mitral valvuloplasty appear to be encouraging, but aortic valvuloplasty has a high rate of restenosis and recurrence of symptoms. Consequently, aortic valve balloon dilation is recommended only for patients who are not considered surgical candidates or for those needing only a palliative rather than a curative procedure.

Surgical mitral commissurotomy and *valve replacement* are the mainstays of surgical therapy for heart failure caused by severe valvular or multivalvular disease. When the surgeon is experienced in this procedure and the case is uncomplicated, the in-hospital mortality rate is usually below 5%.

Depending upon the underlying etiologies, other surgical procedures required in patients with CHF may include coronary angioplasty, coronary artery bypass grafting, left ventricular aneurysmectomy, or pericardectomy. *Cardiac transplantation* has become an effective surgical treatment for patients with refractory CHF. Many transplant centers have achieved a 5-year survival rate above 75%. The use of corticosteroids and immunosuppressive agents, such as cyclosporine or the newer investigational drug FK-506, has reduced transplant rejection and mortality.

Braunwald E. Clinical manifestations of heart failure. In: Braunwald E, ed. *Heart Disease: A Textbook of Cardiovascular Medicine.* 3rd ed. Philadelphia: Saunders; 1988:471–543.

Effect of enalapril on survival in patients with reduced left ventricular ejection fractions and congestive heart failure. The SOLVD Investigators. *N Engl J Med.* 1991;325:293–302.

Giuliani ER, Fuster V, Gersh B, et al, eds. *Cardiology: Fundamentals and Practice.* 2nd ed. St Louis: Mosby; 1991:651–687, 791–858.

Goldberger E. *Essentials of Clinical Cardiology.* Philadelphia: Lippincott; 1990: 148–160, 180–200.

Hurst JW. *The Heart, Arteries, and Veins.* 6th ed. New York: McGraw-Hill; 1986: 345–369.

Morgan JP. Abnormal intracellular modulation of calcium as a major cause of cardiac contractile dysfunction. *N Engl J Med.* 1991;325:625–632.

Shipley JB, Tolman D, Hastillo A, et al. Milrinone: basic and clinical pharmacology and acute and chronic management. *Am J Med Sci.* 1996;311:286–291.

Disorders of Cardiac Rhythm

Abnormalities of cardiac rhythm can vary widely from asymptomatic premature atrial complexes or mild sinus bradycardia to life-threatening ventricular tachycardia or fibrillation. Disorders of cardiac rhythm can be categorized into several groups:

□ Bradyarrhythmias and conduction disturbances

□ Ectopic or premature contractions

□ Tachyarrhythmias

Although many rhythm and conduction disturbances are caused by underlying IHD, other etiologies include valvular heart disease, myocarditis, cardiomyopathy, congenital aberrant conduction pathways, pulmonary disease, toxic or metabolic disorders, neurogenic causes, and cardiac trauma.

The electrical impulse that initiates each heartbeat normally begins in the *sinoatrial (SA) node* and is conducted down through the atria and ventricles, resulting in a coordinated series of contractions of these chambers. The SA node is the primary pacemaker of the heart. It controls the heart rate and is influenced by neural, biochemical, and pharmacological factors. If the SA node function is depressed or absent, secondary pacemakers in the *atrioventricular (AV) junction, the bundle of His,* or the *ventricular muscle* can generate stimuli and maintain the heartbeat. Normally, stimulus formation in these other secondary pacemaker sites is slower than that of the SA node. However, abnormal stimuli can also be generated at any of these sites at a very rapid pace, resulting in a tachycardia.

Bradyarrhythmias and Conduction Disturbances

Sinus bradycardia A sinus rhythm (initiated by the SA node) slower than 60 beats per minute is referred to as *sinus bradycardia.* It is usually innocuous and can occur in normal or athletic individuals, but it can also be caused by increased vagal tone, intracranial lesions, acute rheumatic fever, hypothyroidism, semistarvation, pregnancy, or infections such as typhoid. Sinus bradycardia can also be caused by drugs such as beta blockers, calcium channel blockers, digitalis, or quinidine. Although sinus bradycardia is usually asymptomatic, light-headedness or syncope may occur if the rate becomes extremely slow. Treatment is almost never indicated.

Sinus arrest Also called *sinus block* or *SA block,* this disorder involves an absence of the entire complex for one or more beats. Single or multiple beats may be dropped. If the period of sinus arrest is prolonged, an AV nodal or ventricular escape beat may occur. Sinus arrest may be caused by increased vagal tone, sick sinus syndrome, carotid artery sinus hypersensitivity, hypokalemia, or the same medications that can cause sinus bradycardia. Patients may be asymptomatic if the pause is brief, or they may experience light-headedness or syncope if the period of sinus arrest is more than 5–6 seconds. If the cause is a medication, it should be stopped; and if the agent is digoxin or quinidine, the drug level should be checked. If the patient is unstable or develops syncope from a long pause, emergency treatment with intravenous atropine will usually increase the heart rate temporarily while definitive treatment is planned. If the patient is symptomatic and the episodes are frequent, a pacemaker may be necessary.

Atrioventricular junctional rhythm   When the sinus node is depressed or non-functional due to vagal stimulation or underlying heart disease, the AV node may take over the pacemaking function. Other causes include rheumatic fever, MI, general anesthesia, carotid sinus pressure, digitalis, or quinidine. During AV nodal pacing, the atria and ventricles contract independently. This may cause a throbbing sensation in the neck. The heart rate in an AV junctional rhythm is usually about 30–60 beats per minute. Periodic prominent pulsations in the neck veins, occurring during systole, are noted. On the ECG, the QRS complex appears normal; however, the P waves are abnormal in shape and may follow the QRS in some leads. No treatment is usually necessary, but evaluating the patient for underlying cardiac disease may be appropriate.

Atrioventricular block   Atrioventricular block is caused by a delay or block in conduction through the AV junction. In first-degree AV block, the PR interval seen on ECG may only be prolonged; in second- or third-degree AV block, ventricular beats may be dropped. AV block may be caused by vagal stimulation, as observed with carotid sinus pressure, postural changes, hyperthyroidism, rheumatic fever, or measles. Other possible etiologies are digitalis, quinidine, morphine, uremia, cardiac tertiary syphilis, infectious endocarditis, MI, valvular disease, congenital heart block, and atrial or ventricular septal defects.

First-degree AV block is asymptomatic and is diagnosed by the prolongation of the PR interval beyond 0.2 seconds on ECG. There are two types of *second-degree AV block.* In the *Wenckebach type,* the PR interval progressively becomes longer until a QRS (ventricular beat) is dropped; then the cycle repeats itself. In *Mobitz type II* AV block, the QRS complex is dropped at regular intervals, typically 1 out of every 2, 3, or 4 beats; and the QRS complex is usually widened. Patients with second-degree AV block may experience palpitations. The pulse rate is irregular in Wenckebach block and slow and regular in Mobitz type II block. The prognosis is usually worse with Mobitz type II block, because it more often heralds underlying cardiac disease.

Complete, or *third-degree, AV block* is more ominous and usually causes more symptoms. All of the atrial stimuli are blocked at the AV node, so the P waves from the atria and the QRS complexes are completely asynchronous. The rate and width of the QRS complexes depend upon whether they originate in the AV node, the bundle of His, or the ventricles. When the stimuli arise in the ventricles, the QRS complex is very wide and aberrant; this is called an *idioventricular escape rhythm.* Patients may be asymptomatic or may become light-headed if the rate is very slow. If the ventricular rate is profoundly slow or if the beats cease for an interval, syncope may occur. This is known as *Stokes-Adams syndrome.* Cyanosis and seizures may follow rapidly if the attack persists. Atropine or isoproterenol can be given intravenously for immediate management of profound bradycardia or symptomatic heart block. A temporary transvenous pacemaker may be inserted to pace the heart until a permanent programmable pacemaker is implanted.

Intraventricular or fascicular blocks   Of the two main branches of the bundle of His, the right has a single fascicle while the left has at least two. *Left anterior hemiblock (fascicular block)* is characterized by marked left axis deviation on ECG and may result from MI, pulmonary embolism, cardiac surgery, or cardiac catheterization. It is insignificant unless it occurs concomitantly with right bundle branch block. *Left posterior hemiblock (fascicular block)* results in right axis deviation on ECG and may be caused by ischemic heart disease, myocarditis, or valvular heart disease. It is nearly always associated with right bundle branch block, resulting in a *bifascicular block*. No treatment is required for fascicular blocks. Historically, the left bundle branch has been thought to consist of two fascicles, anterior and posterior. However, recent anatomic and ECG evidence suggests the existence of three left fascicles.

Complete left bundle branch block (LBBB) results in a delay in conduction to the left ventricle, causing some asynchrony between the contraction of the two ventricles. This condition may be transient or permanent. Common etiologies are hypertensive or ischemic cardiac disease, cardiac surgery, myocarditis, cardiomyopathy, and quinidine. It is occasionally also seen in normal hearts. LBBB is asymptomatic and causes widened QRS complexes (0.12 second or more) and secondary ST segment and T wave changes. It may obscure the Q wave and interfere with the electrocardiographic diagnosis of MI. Most clinicians feel that young patients with LBBB have an excellent prognosis; but in the Framingham study, older patients with LBBB had a higher risk of developing cardiac disease and a fourfold higher 10-year mortality compared to patients without LBBB. Treatment is not necessary, but an evaluation for underlying heart disease is advised.

Right bundle branch block (RBBB) delays conduction to the right ventricle but does not cause symptoms. It is observed in normal persons, but it can also be associated with pulmonary embolism, MI, rheumatic heart disease, cardiac surgery, chest trauma, myocarditis, cor pulmonale, cardiomyopathy, and congenital heart defects. Wide QRS complexes are observed on ECG. When RBBB is not associated with pulmonary embolism or MI, prognosis is good. However, significant coronary artery disease has been reported in as many as 20% of asymptomatic patients with RBBB.

Premature Contractions

The principal types of premature contractions are

□ Premature atrial contraction (PAC)

□ Atrioventricular junctional premature contraction (JPC)

□ Premature ventricular contraction (PVC)

These premature complexes arise from ectopic foci in the atria, AV node, or ventricles. They may appear sporadically, frequently, in continuous runs of several beats, or in a regular pattern such as *bigeminy* (every other beat) or *trigeminy* (every third beat).

Premature contractions often occur in normal hearts as a result of physiological, pharmacological, or toxic stimuli, such as emotional excitation, caffeine, cigarette smoking, or alcohol. Other causes include IHD, pulmonary diseases, cardiac surgery, and digoxin. Premature contractions may result from increased automaticity in the atria or ventricles. Supraventricular tachycardia or atrial fibrillation may arise from PACs, and ventricular tachyarrhythmias may follow frequent PVCs, usually through a reentry mechanism. Premature beats are sometimes asymptomatic, but frequently the patient will experience palpitations and a feeling of fullness in the neck. The pulse may be irregular. On ECG, PACs are detected by their premature P wave, followed by a normal, widened, or dropped QRS complex. PVCs always have a widened, irregular QRS that looks very different from the normal narrow QRS complexes on ECG. Multiple PVCs will have the same appearance if they arise from the same focus *(uniform* or *unifocal)*. PVCs may have two or more different shapes if they originate in different foci *(multiform* or *multifocal)*. In most instances, PACs and unifocal PVCs are insignificant. However, multifocal PVCs or runs of several consecutive PVCs may indicate serious underlying heart disease or digitalis toxicity and are associated with an increased risk of ventricular tachycardia and fibrillation.

If premature contractions occur in an otherwise healthy patient, treatment is usually not necessary, but any precipitating factors should be eliminated or reduced. If the palpitations trouble the patient, low-dose beta blockers are occasionally used to reduce the premature contractions. Treatment should also be considered if a patient has documented organic heart disease with previous episodes of ventricular arrhythmia or is felt to be at high risk for severe arrhythmia. Other indications for considering medical treatment are 5 or more PVCs per minute, multifocal PVCs, and PVCs that fall on the preceding T wave (R-on-T phenomenon). Paradoxically, most of the antiarrhythmic agents can be proarrhythmic in some patients, so cautious monitoring of the heart rate and rhythm are necessary. If a beta blocker is not effective or is contraindicated, quinidine, procainamide, disopyramide, or the newer antiarrhythmic agents should be tried. Emergency treatment of multiple PVCs or runs of PVCs *(ventricular tachycardia)* in the setting of acute MI or severe ischemia is usually initiated with intravenous lidocaine.

Tachyarrhythmias

Supraventricular tachycardias   This category includes paroxysmal atrial tachycardia, AV junctional tachycardia, atrial flutter, and atrial fibrillation. The exact site of the pacing focus may be difficult to determine when the heart rate is very rapid. The prognosis for supraventricular tachycardias is usually better than that associated with ventricular tachycardia. These tachycardias may be paroxysmal, with a sudden onset and an intermittent pattern, or chronic, as with chronic atrial fibrillation. There are many etiologies for supraventricular tachycardia, including emotional stress, caffeine, theophylline, alcohol, stimulants, digitalis toxicity, thyrotoxicosis, pheochromocytoma, hypokalemia, any organic cardiac disease, congenital heart defects, pericarditis, pulmonary diseases, chest trauma, and malignancies.

Paroxysmal atrial tachycardia (PAT) may originate from a single focus or from many different foci. The latter situation is termed *multifocal atrial tachycardia* and is often associated with chronic pulmonary disease. The heart rate in PAT is often higher than 140 beats per minute. *AV junctional tachycardia* is very similar and has the same etiologies as PAT. AV junctional tachycardia can only be differentiated from PAT if junctional P waves are present. If AV block and PAT are observed together, digitalis toxicity should be suspected. Clinical manifestations of PAT include palpitations, sensation of a rapid heart rate, lightheadedness, and rarely, syncope. Patients with ischemic heart disease may experience angina or dyspnea.

Usually, the QRS complex is narrow on ECG. If the QRS is widened, with an initial up-sloping delta wave, then the *Wolff-Parkinson-White (WPW) syndrome* should be considered. In this syndrome, the ventricles are stimulated early by preexcitation through accessory fibers. PAT, atrial flutter, or atrial fibrillation may occur with a very rapid rate in WPW syndrome because of a circus movement involving the accessory conduction pathways. Because of the wide QRS complex seen in PAT with the WPW syndrome, this rhythm can resemble ventricular tachycardia.

For most patients with PAT, the prognosis is excellent. However, if the rate remains over 200 beats per minute for a prolonged period of time or if underlying ischemia or heart failure is present, PAT can be fatal. Currently, the treatment of choice for PAT is *intravenous adenosine*. It has a very short half-life and has approximately a 90% success rate in converting the rhythm to normal sinus rhythm. Other therapeutic measures include Valsalva maneuvers, carotid sinus pressure or massage, intravenous verapamil (except in WPW syndrome), digitalis, beta blockers, or quinidine. Patients with hemodynamic instability may require DC cardioversion. Precipitating factors should be reduced or eliminated, and any underlying disease should be treated.

Atrial flutter is associated with a rapid atrial rate of 200–380 beats per minute. The ventricular rate is slower, usually with 2:1, 3:1, or 4:1 conduction. Atrial flutter is caused by rapid formation of ectopic atrial stimuli. When the atrial rate increases to 400–600 beats per minute, the contractions are less organized and atrial fibrillation is present. Atrial flutter occurs in some normal patients, but it is also associated with MI, hyperthyroidism, mitral stenosis, and pneumonia. It is occasionally caused by digitalis toxicity. If the ventricular rate is slow, atrial flutter may occur without symptoms. If the rate is very rapid (over 200 beats per minute), the symptoms are similar to those of PAT. The regular, rapid P waves of atrial flutter are called *F (flutter) waves* and have a sawtooth appearance. Some degree of AV block is usually present, resulting in QRS complexes at regular intervals. Atrial flutter may be paroxysmal or permanent. This arrhythmia can be fatal if the ventricular rate is very rapid in the setting of ischemia or heart failure. An attempt should be made to convert atrial flutter to sinus rhythm or stable atrial fibrillation. Treatment measures include digitalis, quinidine, procainamide, or overdrive atrial pacing. *Ibutilide (Corvert)* is a new agent that is effective for the rapid conversion of recent onset atrial flutter or fibrillation. Adenosine should not be used if the rhythm can be confirmed as atrial flutter, because it is usually ineffective and may cause increased ventricular response or bradyarrhythmias.

Atrial fibrillation is similar to atrial flutter except that the atrial rate is so fast that the contractions are chaotic and asynchronous, with ineffective atrial emptying. The etiologies and symptoms are similar to those of atrial flutter. The pulse rate is usually irregular, and characteristic changes are usually seen on ECG, with irregular (fibrillation) waves and an irregular ventricular rate. Occasionally, aberrantly conducted beats will result in a wide QRS that can resemble a PVC.

Because atrial contractions are ineffective in atrial fibrillation, cardiac output can be reduced markedly when the ventricular rate is very rapid. This may result in CHF. Atrial thrombi may accumulate from stagnation of blood in the atrial appendages. These thrombi may embolize to the lungs, brain, or other organs. Anticoagulation is indicated in patients with chronic atrial fibrillation associated with valvular disease, cardiomyopathy, or cardiomegaly, and before attempting conversion to sinus rhythm.

Conversion of atrial fibrillation can be attempted with quinidine, procainamide, ibutilide, or DC cardioversion. In many patients with chronic atrial fibrillation, maintenance therapy is often directed toward controlling the ventricular rate. This can usually be accomplished with digitalis, verapamil, or beta blockers.

Cox et al have developed a new surgical treatment for atrial flutter or fibrillation, called the *Maze procedure.* It interrupts all of the possible reentry circuits to the atrium with multiple incisions. A single uninterrupted pathway is left intact for normal conduction to occur from the sinus node to the AV node. Of the 178 patients who underwent the Maze procedure, 93% were free of arrhythmia, and the rest were converted to sinus rhythm with medical therapy.

Ventricular Tachyarrhythmias

Ventricular tachycardia (VT) usually follows a series of PVCs, which may be unifocal or multifocal. It may also occur in patients with complete AV block, atrial flutter, or atrial fibrillation. Underlying etiologies include coronary artery disease, hypokalemia, hypomagnesemia, digitalis, quinidine, and other drugs that are potentially proarrhythmic. A recent study suggests that hearts with low ejection fractions receive markedly increased reflex cardiac sympathetic stimulation, and this may play a role in initiating and sustaining ventricular arrhythmias.

VT is only infrequently observed in young patients with no organic heart disease. Brief episodes of VT cause palpitations, while prolonged attacks in patients with organic cardiac disease can lead to heart failure or cardiac shock. If the rate is not very high and there is no significant underlying heart disease, VT may be well tolerated. The heart rate may be between 100 and 300 beats per minute but is usually above 140. Wide aberrant QRS complexes and secondary ST and T changes are seen on ECG.

In the setting of acute MI or significant myocardial ischemia, VT is treated aggressively, because of the high risk of degeneration into ventricular fibrillation with its increased mortality. Emergency treatment of unstable patients with VT includes the use of intravenous lidocaine, procainamide, the newer antiarrhythmic agents, or immediate DC cardioversion. Asymptomatic patients with normal hearts may not need any treatment. Stable patients with cardiac disease who have recurrent episodes of VT should have an evaluation for precipitating factors such as hypokalemia, hypomagnesemia, drug toxicity, or severe coronary artery stenosis. Intravenous magnesium supplementation administered to patients following cardiac surgery has been shown to significantly reduce the incidence of postoperative ventricular arrhythmias and to improve left ventricular function. Patients with VT and active cardiac disease are at increased risk for heart failure and sudden cardiac death and should be treated aggressively. Any patient who has experienced significant hypotension, syncope, or presyncope during VT also requires treatment.

Treatment is often begun with medical therapy, using standard antiarrhythmic agents such as quinidine, procainamide, or disopyramide (Table IV-3). If these agents are ineffective, the newer antiarrhythmic drugs may be considered. These include tocainide, encainide, flecainide, mexiletine, amiodarone, sotalol, and propafenone, as well as other investigational drugs. Nearly all of these agents have the potential for worsening ventricular arrhythmias, so they should be initiated with careful monitoring. With a decline in use of class I agents in recent years, interest in sotalol has increased because of its relative safety, its efficacy in controlling ventricular tachycardia, and its combined class II and class III antiarrhythmic effects. Newer class III agents, such as almokalant, dofetilide, and clofilium are currently being evaluated for the treatment of ventricular tachyarrhythmias.

Electrophysiological testing is often performed on patients with refractory ventricular arrhythmias. In this procedure, direct transcatheter electrical stimulation of various sites in the ventricle induces arrhythmias, while several antiarrhythmic agents are injected. This allows a rapid comparison of the efficacy of different drugs in a controlled, monitored setting. If medical therapy is not successful in controlling

VT, surgical options include ventricular aneurysmectomy, ventricular electrical mapping and resection of the arrhythmogenic focus, or an automatic implantable cardioverter-defibrillator (AICD).

Torsades de pointes is a variant of VT in which the wide QRS complexes resemble ventricular fibrillation but undergo constant cyclic changes in morphology. Torsades de pointes is often associated with a prolonged QT interval and may be caused by antiarrhythmic drugs, phenothiazines, tricyclic antidepressants, nonsedating antihistamines (terfenadine or astemizole), hypokalemia, hypocalcemia, or hypomagnesemia. Treatment involves replacement of potassium or magnesium and overdrive pacing, if necessary. Quinidine and similar drugs should not be used, as they may increase the abnormal QT interval and worsen the arrhythmia.

Ventricular fibrillation (VF) is the most ominous of all the cardiac arrhythmias because it is fatal when untreated or when refractory to treatment. It is a major cause of out-of-hospital sudden cardiac death. The ventricular contractions are rapid and uncoordinated, resulting in absence of effective ventricular pumping that soon leads to syncope, convulsions, then death, if the VF is not interrupted. Ventricular fibrillation often occurs as a terminal rhythm in a dying patient, during or after MI, in patients with complete heart block, or as a result of electrocution, anesthesia, or drug toxicity from digitalis, quinidine, or other antiarrhythmic agents. It rarely occurs spontaneously in an otherwise healthy individual. The prognosis is generally poor in patients with VF because each episode can be fatal. However, some patients with complete heart block have recurrent self-limiting episodes of VF for years.

The patient loses consciousness within several seconds of onset of ventricular fibrillation. A bizarre, chaotic rhythm is noted on ECG, and there is no blood pressure or effective pulse. Emergency cardiopulmonary resuscitation efforts must be initiated immediately, while attempting to convert the VF to a more stable rhythm, to prevent permanent cerebral anoxic injury and death (see material on CPR, part 2, chapter XIV). Additional resuscitation measures include intravenous lidocaine or bretylium, electrical defibrillation, and intubation with airway management. Patients who have been resuscitated from VF require close monitoring and are candidates for prophylactic therapy with antiarrhythmic drugs or an implantable defibrillator.

Cox JL, Schuessler RB, Lappas DG, et al. An 8$^{1}/_{2}$-year clinical experience with surgery for atrial fibrillation. *Ann Surg.* 1996;224:267–273.

England MR, Gordon G, Salem M, et al. Magnesium administration and dysrhythmias after cardiac surgery. *JAMA.* 1992;268:2395–2402.

Giuliani ER, Fuster V, Gersh B, et al, eds. *Cardiology: Fundamentals and Practice.* 2nd ed. St Louis: Mosby; 1991:694–729, 859–1126.

Goldberger E. *Essentials of Clinical Cardiology.* Philadelphia: Lippincott; 1990: 325–364.

Meredith IT, Broughton A, Jennings GL, et al. Evidence of a selective increase in cardiac sympathetic activity in patients with sustained ventricular arrhythmias. *N Engl J Med.* 1991;325:618–624.

O'Callaghan PA, McGovern BA. Evolving role of sotalol in the management of ventricular tachyarrhythmias. *Am J Cardiol.* 1996;78:54–60.

Singh BN. The coming of age of the class III antiarrhythmic principle: retrospective and future trends. *Am J Cardiol.* 1996;78:17–27.

TABLE IV-3

SIDE EFFECTS OF ANTIARRHYTHMIC DRUGS*

CLASS	DRUG	COMMENTS
I. Membrane-stabilizing Group A	Quinidine	Proarrhythmic effects, GI side effects
	Procainamide	Lupuslike syndrome
	Disopyramide	Negative inotropic action; can worsen CHF; anticholinergic side effects (e.g., dry mouth, urinary retention)
Group B	Lidocaine	CNS toxicity, seizures; may worsen bradycardia
	Phenytoin	Bradycardia, cardiac arrest, hypotension; increases effects of group A drugs
	Tocainide	Hematologic, CNS, GI side effects
	Mexiletine	Proarrhythmic effects, GI and CNS side effects
Group C	Propafenone	Mild hypotension or bradycardia, GI side effects
	Flecainide	Proarrhythmic effects
	Aprindine	Proarrhythmic effects
	Encainide	Proarrhythmic effects, bradycardia, hypotension
II. Beta-adrenergic blockers	Propranolol	Bradycardia, may worsen CHF; CNS and GI side effects
	Metoprolol	Bradycardia, may worsen CHF
	Esmolol	Hypotension, may worsen CHF
	Atenolol	Bradycardia, may worsen CHF
III. Action-potential prolonging	Bretylium	Hypotension, GI side effects
	Amiodarone	Thyroid disorders, corneal deposits, pulmonary fibrosis; increases digoxin levels
	Sotalol	May worsen CHF, possible proarrhythmic effects
IV. Calcium channel blockers	Verapamil	Hypotension, bradycardia, AV block, may worsen CHF; constipation, increases digoxin levels
	Diltiazem	Hypotension, bradycardia, AV block, may worsen CHF

*Doses must be reduced in patients with reduced renal or hepatic function. Monitor blood levels.

Ophthalmologic Considerations

Many of the adult patients seen and treated by ophthalmologists are in the age group at risk for IHD and its many complications. These patients often undergo stressful eye surgery under local or general anesthesia. Ophthalmologists need to be cognizant of the risks of myocardial ischemia, infarction, CHF, and arrhythmias in these patients. All surgical patients should have a preoperative history and physical examination, and those in the age group most at risk for heart disease (over age 40) should also have a preoperative ECG. Chest x-rays are of less clear value in assessing patients for cardiac disease but should be requested in smokers and in any patient with dyspnea, COPD, or a history of CHF. A patient with active heart disease that is unstable or not optimally controlled should receive clearance for surgery from the family physician, internist, or cardiologist. Cardiovascular contraindications to elective surgery include MI within the last 6 months, unstable angina, symptoms or clinical findings of severe CHF, and frequent or poorly controlled arrhythmias.

Care should be taken to avoid using beta-blocker eyedrops in patients with asthma, COPD, severe heart failure, heart block, and other significant bradyarrhythmias. It is also important to be aware of the additive effects of topical and oral beta blockers and some calcium channel blockers, particularly verapamil. One of the newer antiarrhythmic drugs, amiodarone, can cause whorl-like corneal deposits, and rarely, optic neuropathy, but the corneal deposits are not usually clinically significant.

CHAPTER V

Hypercholesterolemia

Highlights

☐ Dietary therapy should be the first line of treatment in reducing serum cholesterol.

☐ Regular aerobic exercise and small amounts of alcohol intake have a beneficial effect on serum cholesterol by increasing HDL cholesterol.

☐ The HMG-CoA reductase inhibitors lovastatin, pravastatin, simvastatin, fluvastatin, and atorvastatin significantly reduce serum LDL cholesterol and total cholesterol.

Epidemiology

Coronary heart disease (CHD) is the leading cause of death in the United States, accounting for more deaths than all forms of cancer combined. Several major studies have confirmed earlier reports that lowering of serum cholesterol reduces the risk of CHD and mortality and that hypercholesterolemia is one of the most important risk factors for CHD. Extensive epidemiologic evidence has shown prospectively that elevated serum cholesterol in healthy people predicts the future development of CHD.

Serum total cholesterol and high-density-lipoprotein (HDL) cholesterol levels should be measured in all adults 20 years of age and older at least once every 5 years; this measurement may be made in the nonfasting state. Levels below 200 mg/dL are classified as *desirable blood cholesterol,* those 200–239 mg/dL as *borderline high blood cholesterol,* and those 240 mg/dL and above as *high blood cholesterol.* The cutoff point that defines high blood cholesterol (240 mg/dL) is a value above which risk of CHD rises steeply and corresponds approximately to the 80th percentile for the adult United States population. The cutoff points recommended are uniform for adult men and women of all ages. An HDL cholesterol level <35 mg/dL is classified as low and considered a major risk factor; a level ≥60 is considered a "negative" (that is, a protective) risk factor, which offsets one "positive" (that is, deleterious) risk factor in assessing total risk of CHD.

Interestingly, recent meta-analyses of cholesterol-lowering trials reveal an *increase* in mortality from nonatherosclerotic causes (cancer, suicide, accidental and violent death) associated with *low* levels of cholesterol (especially <160 mg/dL). Therefore, treatment to further reduce cholesterol levels may not be advisable for patients with already normal or low cholesterol levels.

Along with cholesterol testing, all adults should also be evaluated for the presence of other CHD risk factors, including hypertension, cigarette smoking, diabetes mellitus, severe obesity, and a history of CHD in the patient or of premature CHD in family members. Patients with other risk factors should be given other forms of preventive care, as appropriate.

Diagnosis

Patients with desirable blood cholesterol levels (<200 mg/dL) should be given general dietary and risk-reduction educational materials. Serum cholesterol levels of 200 mg/dL or greater should be confirmed by repeating the test; the average of the two test results is then used to guide subsequent decisions. All patients with CHD (regardless of total cholesterol levels), patients with high blood cholesterol (>240 mg/dL), and those with borderline high cholesterol (200–239 mg/dL) and two or more other risk factors should undergo lipoprotein analysis; age (men ≥45 years old and women ≥55 years old) is now considered a risk factor for the purpose of estimating risk status. Patients with confirmed borderline high blood cholesterol levels who do not have CHD or two other risk factors do not need further evaluation and active medical therapy; they should be given the dietary information designed for the general population and reevaluated at 1 year (see Table V-1).

Once someone is identified as requiring lipoprotein analysis, the focus of attention should shift from total cholesterol to low-density-lipoprotein (LDL) cholesterol. The ultimate objective of screening is to identify individuals with elevated LDL-cholesterol levels. Similarly, the specific goal of treatment is to lower LDL-cholesterol levels. Hence, the level of LDL cholesterol will serve as the key index for clinical decision-making about cholesterol-lowering therapy.

Young adults (men <35 years old and premenopausal women) with moderately high LDL cholesterol levels (160–220 mg/dL) are at low risk for CHD unless they have multiple other risk factors. In the absence of multiple risk factors, dietary therapy and increased physical activity are indicated, with drug therapy reserved for those with very high LDL cholesterol (≥220 mg/dL).

TABLE V-1

CHOLESTEROL CLASSIFICATION AND TREATMENT RECOMMENDATIONS FOR
PATIENT WITHOUT CHD

TOTAL CHOLESTEROL (mg/dL)	CLASSIFICATION	ACTION
<200	Desirable	If HDL cholesterol ≥35 mg/dL, provide educational materials and retest in 5 years
		If HDL cholesterol <35 mg/dL, perform lipoprotein analysis (fasting total cholesterol, total triglycerides, and HDL cholesterol)
200–239	Borderline	If HDL cholesterol ≥35 mg/dL with fewer than two other risk factors, provide dietary information, increase physical activity, and repeat testing in 1–2 years
		If HDL cholesterol <35 mg/dL or two or more other risk factors, perform lipoprotein analysis
≥240	High	Perform lipoprotein analysis

Levels of LDL cholesterol of 160 mg/dL or greater are classified as *high-risk LDL cholesterol,* and those 130–159 mg/dL as *borderline high-risk LDL cholesterol.* Patients with high-risk LDL-cholesterol levels and those with borderline high-risk LDL-cholesterol levels who have two or more risk factors should have a complete clinical evaluation and then begin cholesterol-lowering treatment. A basic principle is that the presence of other risk factors or definite CHD warrants initiating treatment at lower LDL-cholesterol levels and setting lower LDL-cholesterol treatment goals. A low level of HDL cholesterol (<35 mg/dL) is now considered to be a major risk factor (like hypertension). The presence of CHD places an individual in a separate risk category with lower LDL cholesterol goals than previously recommended (see Table V-2).

The clinical evaluation should include a complete history, physical examination, and basic laboratory tests. This workup will attempt to determine whether the high LDL-cholesterol level is secondary to another disease or to a drug and whether a familial lipid disorder is present. The patient's total coronary risk and clinical status, as well as age and sex, should be considered in developing a cholesterol-lowering treatment program.

Treatment

Dietary Therapy

Treatment begins with dietary therapy and increased physical activity. The minimal goal of therapy is to lower LDL cholesterol to levels below the cutoff points for initiating therapy (see Table V-2). Ideally, even lower levels of LDL cholesterol should be attained, if possible, to further reduce risk.

Even though the goal of therapy is to lower the LDL-cholesterol level, monitoring the *total* cholesterol level is adequate for following most patients during dietary therapy. Using total cholesterol levels has the advantages of avoiding the additional costs and the inconvenience of obtaining a fasting blood specimen, as required for the measurement of LDL-cholesterol levels. Serum total cholesterol levels of 240 and

TABLE V-2

TREATMENT DECISIONS BASED ON LDL CHOLESTEROL

	INITIATION LEVEL	LDL GOAL
Dietary therapy		
No CHD and with < two risk factors	≥ 160 mg/dL	< 160 mg/dL
No CHD and with ≥ two risk factors	≥ 130 mg/dL	< 130 mg/dL
With CHD	> 100 mg/dL	≤ 100 mg/dL
	CONSIDERATION LEVEL	LDL GOAL
Drug therapy		
No CHD and with < two risk factors	≥ 190 mg/dL	< 160 mg/dL
No CHD and with ≥ two risk factors	≥ 160 mg/dL	< 130 mg/dL
With CHD	≥ 130 mg/dL	≤ 100 mg/dL

200 mg/dL correspond roughly to LDL-cholesterol levels of 160 and 130 mg/dL, respectively. Thus, the monitoring goals during dietary therapy are to lower the serum total cholesterol level to <240 mg/dL for patients with an LDL-cholesterol goal of <160 mg/dL, or to <200 mg/dL for patients with an LDL-cholesterol goal of <130 mg/dL.

The general aim of dietary therapy is to reduce elevated cholesterol levels while maintaining a nutritionally adequate eating pattern. Dietary therapy should follow the step-one and step-two diets as appropriate. These regimens are designed to progressively reduce intake of saturated fatty acids and cholesterol and to promote weight loss in patients who are overweight by eliminating excess total calories. The *step-one diet* should be prescribed and explained by the physician and staff. This diet calls for total fat intake of less than 30% of calories, saturated fatty acids less than 10% of calories, and cholesterol less than 300 mg/day. If the response to the step-one diet is insufficient, the *step-two diet* requires a further reduction in saturated fatty acid intake to less than 7% of calories and in cholesterol to less than 200 mg/day.

The step-one diet calls for the reduction of the major and obvious sources of saturated fatty acids and cholesterol in the diet; many patients can achieve this goal without a radical alteration in dietary habits. However, the step-two diet is a rigorous regimen requiring careful planning and attention to ensure that an acceptable and nutritious total diet is maintained while the intake of saturated fatty acids and cholesterol is severely reduced. Involvement of a registered dietitian is very useful. Increasing dietary sources of fiber, particularly oat bran, has been shown to provide additional modest reductions in serum cholesterol.

After a patient starts on the step-one diet, the serum total cholesterol level should be measured and adherence to the diet assessed at 4–6 weeks and at 3 months. If the total cholesterol-monitoring goal is met, then the LDL-cholesterol level should be measured to confirm that the LDL goal has been achieved. If this is the case, the patient enters a long-term monitoring program and is seen quarterly for the first year and twice yearly thereafter. At these visits, total cholesterol levels should be measured and dietary and behavior modifications reinforced.

If the cholesterol goal has not been achieved with the step-one diet, the patient should generally be referred to a registered dietitian. With the aid of the dietitian, the patient should progress to the step-two diet or to another trial on the step-one diet (with progression to the step-two diet if the response is still not satisfactory). On the step-two diet, total cholesterol levels should be measured again and adherence to the diet assessed after 4–6 weeks and at 3 months of therapy. If the desired goal for lowering total cholesterol (and LDL cholesterol) has been attained, long-term monitoring can begin. If not, drug therapy should be considered. A minimum of 6 months of intensive dietary therapy and counseling should usually be carried out before initiating drug therapy; shorter periods can be considered in patients with severe elevations of LDL cholesterol (>220 mg/dL) or with definite CHD. Drug therapy should be *added* to dietary therapy and not substituted for it.

Pharmacologic Therapy

Drug therapy should be considered for an adult patient who has an LDL-cholesterol level of 190 mg/dL or higher despite dietary therapy but does not have two or more risk factors. If two or more risk factors are present, then drug therapy should be considered at LDL-cholesterol levels of 160 mg/dL or higher. The goals of drug therapy are the same as those of dietary therapy. These are minimal goals; if possible, considerably lower levels of LDL cholesterol should be attained.

Individualized clinical judgment is needed for patients who do not meet these criteria for drug therapy but have not attained their minimal goals on dietary therapy. In general, maximal efforts should be made in this group to reduce cholesterol levels and CHD risk by means of nonpharmacological approaches. Consideration should also be given to the use of low doses of bile acid sequestrants in these patients, especially in males. Drug therapy is generally indicated in patients with established CHD if LDL cholesterol levels are ≥130 mg/dL after maximal dietary therapy; clinical judgment should determine the use of drug therapy with LDL cholesterol levels of 100–129 mg/dL.

Historically, the drugs of first choice were the *bile acid sequestrants (cholestyramine, colestipol)* and *nicotinic acid* (see Table V-3). Both cholestyramine and nicotinic acid have been shown to lower CHD risk in clinical trials, and their long-term safety has been established. However, these drugs require considerable patient education to achieve compliance because they are associated with poor patient tolerance. Nicotinic acid is preferred in patients with concurrent hypertriglyceridemia (triglyceride levels >250 mg/dL), because bile acid sequestrants tend to increase triglyceride levels.

The newer drugs that have begun to replace older medications as first-line therapy are the *3-hydroxy-3-methyl glutaryl coenzyme-A (HMG-CoA) reductase inhibitors* (such as *lovastatin, pravastatin,* and *simvastatin*). These drugs are very effective in lowering LDL-cholesterol levels and have been shown to reduce mortality from ischemic heart disease. In a study of 8245 patients with moderate hypercholesterolemia, lovastatin was found to be very well tolerated. Adverse drug effects requiring discontinuation ranged from 1.2% at 40 mg/day to 1.9% at 80 mg/day. The most common adverse reactions with this class of drugs are liver transaminase elevations and diarrhea. Newer agents in this class include *fluvastatin* (Lescol) and *atorvastatin*.

Other available drugs include the *fibric acid derivatives gemfibrozil* and *clofibrate*. They are primarily used for lowering elevated triglyceride levels but also are effective in reducing total cholesterol and LDL-cholesterol levels. Gemfibrozil also increases HDL-cholesterol levels and may have beneficial effects on atherogenesis. In postmenopausal women with high serum cholesterol, *estrogen replacement therapy*, which lowers LDL-cholesterol and raises HDL-cholesterol levels, can be considered. In hypertensive patients, *alpha-adrenergic blockers* provide modest reduction in cholesterol and triglyceride levels, while thiazide diuretics and beta blockers may have an adverse effect.

The LDL-cholesterol level should be measured at 4–6 weeks and then again at 3 months after drug therapy is initiated. If the LDL-cholesterol goal has been achieved, the patient should be seen every 4 months (or more frequently if drugs requiring closer follow-up are used) in order to monitor the cholesterol response and possible side effects of therapy. For long-term monitoring, serum total cholesterol alone can be measured at most follow-up visits, with lipoprotein analysis (and LDL-cholesterol estimation) once a year.

If the response to initial drug therapy is not adequate, the patient should be given another drug or a combination of two drugs. The combination of a bile acid sequestrant with either nicotinic acid or an HMG-CoA reductase inhibitor has the potential of lowering LDL-cholesterol levels by 40%–50% or more. The combination of colestipol and nicotinic acid has been shown to have a beneficial effect on coronary atherosclerotic lesions. The judicious use of one or two drugs should enable most patients to meet cholesterol-reduction goals.

TABLE V-3

AGENTS THAT LOWER SERUM LIPIDS

DRUGS	INDICATIONS	MAJOR ADVERSE EFFECTS
Cholestyramine (Questran)	Adjunctive therapy in primary hypercholester-olemia (elevated LDL)	Constipation, bloating, heartburn, abdominal pain, gas, nausea, belching; can cause vitamin A and D deficiency
Colestipol HCl (Colestid)	Same as cholestyramine	Same as cholestyramine
Clofibrate (Atromid-S)	Lowers VLDL and triglycerides	Cholelithiasis, pancreatitis; contraindi-cated with significant hepatic or renal insufficiency
Niacin (Nicotinic acid)	Adjunctive therapy in elevated total choles-terol, elevated LDL, or elevated triglycerides	Gastric irritation, flushing, pruritus; start with low dose and work up; low-dose aspirin (75 mg) 30 minutes before niacin may reduce flushing
Lovastatin (Mevacor)	Adjunctive therapy in elevated total choles-terol, elevated LDL, or elevated triglycerides	Mild and transient flatulence, diarrhea, myositis, liver test alterations
Gemfibrozil (Lopid)	Elevated triglycerides; also lowers LDL and may elevate HDL cholesterol	Abdominal pain, diarrhea, fatigue, dysgeusia, nausea, dizziness, blurred vision, hepatotoxicity, cholelithiasis
Probucol (Lorelco)	Adjunctive therapy in primary hypercholes-terolemia	Diarrhea, flatulence, abdominal pain, dizziness, palpitation; may produce QT interval prolongation on ECG
Pravastatin (Pravachol)	Same as lovastatin	Liver enzyme elevations, diarrhea
Simvastatin (Zocor)	Same as lovastatin	Liver enzyme elevations, lupuslike syndrome

Since the completion of the Adult Treatment Panel report, a new development has occurred that might have modified the panel's thinking about the benefit of specific therapy, namely, the report of the Helsinki Heart Study. This study demonstrated that treatment of hyperlipidemic patients with gemfibrozil significantly reduced the risk for CHD. In addition to inducing a significant (albeit moderate) reduction in LDL-cholesterol concentrations, gemfibrozil also decreased triglyceride levels and moderately increased the levels of HDL cholesterol. Within-group analyses of the factors contributing to the reduction in CHD rates in this study led the authors to conclude that both the reduction in LDL-cholesterol levels and the increase in HDL-cholesterol levels played a role. Furthermore, in another study, the Cholesterol-Lowering Atherosclerosis Study (CLAS), the combination of diet, bile acid seques-trants, and nicotinic acid was shown to retard the progression of atherosclerosis in native coronary arteries and in coronary bypass grafts, and in some cases it might even have caused regression of coronary plaques. This diet and drug combination markedly lowered LDL-cholesterol levels and also caused a striking rise in HDL-cholesterol concentrations and a decrease in triglyceride levels. The findings of these two trials are intriguing with regard to the possibility that a therapeutic increment in HDL-cholesterol levels may help reduce risk for CHD.

A recent randomized double-masked crossover study compared gemfibrozil and lovastatin in patients with elevated LDL cholesterol (over 160 mg/dL) and low HDL cholesterol (below 40 mg/dL) levels. The patients received gemfibrozil 600 mg twice daily and lovastatin 20 mg twice daily, each for 6 weeks at a time. Lovastatin and gemfibrozil reduced LDL-cholesterol levels by 34% and 9%, respectively, and increased HDL-cholesterol levels by 15% and 18%, respectively. In this study, lovastatin was superior to gemfibrozil in lowering LDL cholesterol and equal to gemfibrozil in increasing HDL-cholesterol levels.

In general, the patient's HDL-cholesterol level can be useful in helping the clinician select the most appropriate drug or drugs for cholesterol-lowering therapy. For example, if a patient has high LDL levels together with low HDL levels, it is reasonable to choose a drug (or drug combination) that both markedly reduces LDL and raises HDL levels. In addition, the HDL-cholesterol level can be of clinical use in helping to modulate the intensiveness of cholesterol-lowering therapy. As discussed earlier, an HDL cholesterol level of ≥60 mg/dL is now thought to offset one deleterious risk factor for CHD.

The basic framework of the Adult Treatment Panel guidelines (cutoff points for initiation of therapy and minimal goals of therapy) should generally be adhered to in a patient with high LDL levels and unremarkable HDL levels. In contrast, the clinician could reasonably be more aggressive in treating a patient with high LDL- and low HDL-cholesterol levels in order to reduce LDL cholesterol to a level substantially below the minimal target goals.

Other Therapeutic Factors

Regular aerobic exercise has been shown to provide a supplemental benefit in the management of hypercholesterolemia by increasing HDL-cholesterol levels. Moderate alcohol consumption has also been shown to increase HDL-cholesterol levels. In patients with elevated LDL-cholesterol levels, alcohol consumption was inversely related to risk of ischemic heart disease. This association was not observed in patients without elevated LDL-cholesterol levels.

Ophthalmologic Considerations

Hypercholesterolemia is a significant risk factor in the development of ischemic heart disease, cerebrovascular disease, and peripheral vascular disease. The ophthalmologist may be the first physician to detect or recognize manifestations of atherosclerosis, particularly amaurosis fugax, retinal vascular emboli or occlusions, ischemic optic neuropathy, or cortical visual field deficits from a previous cerebral infarction. Detection of atherosclerosis may initiate a diagnostic evaluation that reveals significant carotid artery stenosis or coronary artery disease. The reduction or elimination of risk factors for atherosclerosis, including hypercholesterolemia, is an important component in the management of these patients.

Because of early high-dose animal studies, cataract development was thought to be a possible adverse effect from lovastatin. However, clinical experience has revealed that lovastatin and other HMG-CoA reductase inhibitors do not significantly increase the risk of cataracts.

Bradford RH, Shear CL, Chremos AN, et al. Expanded Clinical Evaluation of Lovastatin (EXCEL) study results. I. Efficacy in modifying plasma lipoproteins and adverse event profile in 8245 patients with moderate hypercholesterolemia. *Arch Intern Med.* 1991;151:43–49.

Bradford RH, Shear CL, Chremos AN, et al. Expanded Clinical Evaluation of Lovastatin (EXCEL) study results: two-year efficacy and safety follow-up. *Am J Cardiol.* 1994; 74:667–673.

Eaton CB, Lapane KL, Garber CE, et al. Physical activity, physical fitness, and coronary heart disease risk factors. *Med Sci Sports Exerc.* 1995;27:340–346.

Frick MH, Elo O, Haapa K, et al. Helsinki Heart Study: Primary prevention trial with gemfibrozil in middle-aged men with dyslipidemia. *N Engl J Med.* 1987;317: 1237–1245.

Geurian KL. The cholesterol controversy. *Ann Pharmacother.* 1996;30:495–500.

Grundy SM, Goodman DW, Rifkind BM, et al: The place of HDL in cholesterol management. *Arch Intern Med.* 1989;149:505–510.

Hamilton VH, Racicot FG, Zowall H, et al. The cost-effectiveness of HMG-CoA reductase inhibitors to prevent coronary heart disease. Estimating the benefits of increasing HDL-C. *JAMA.* 1995;273:1032–1038.

Hein HO, Suadicani P, Gyntelberg F. Alcohol consumption, serum low density lipoprotein cholesterol concentration, and risk of ischaemic heart disease: six year follow up in the Copenhagen male study. *BMJ.* 1996;312:736–741.

McKenney JM, Barnett MD, Wright JT Jr, et al. Comparison of gemfibrozil and lovastatin in patients with high low-density lipoprotein and low high-density lipoprotein cholesterol levels. *Arch Intern Med.* 1992;152:1781–1787.

Rubenfire M, Maciejko JJ, Blevins RD, et al. The effect of pravastatin on plasma lipoprotein and apolipoprotein levels in primary hypercholesterolemia. The Southeastern Michigan Collaborative Group. *Arch Intern Med.* 1991;151:2234–2240.

CHAPTER VI

Pulmonary Diseases

The lungs can be affected by numerous pathological processes including inflammation (allergic, infectious, autoimmune, occupational exposure, toxic), vascular insults, fibrosis, carcinoma, and changes secondary to cardiac or musculoskeletal problems. The functional consequences of the pathological changes can be divided into *obstructive* and *restrictive* limitations on gas exchange.

Symptoms of lung disease include dyspnea, cough, and wheezing. *Dyspnea* develops when the demand for gas exchange exceeds the capacity of the respiratory response, as in hypoxemia or hypercapnia. *Cough* develops when mucus, inflammatory debris, or irritants affect the bronchi, causing a reflex clearing expectoration. *Wheezing* occurs when bronchospasm narrows the large airways, and exhaled air is forced through the narrowed passages.

Obstructive Lung Diseases

Chronic obstructive lung disease is the fourth leading cause of death in the United States. In obstructive lung diseases, the rate of exhalation is slowed, which prolongs the respiratory cycle. Changes in the bronchi and bronchioles and in the lung parenchyma can all cause airway obstruction. Obstructive diseases can be separated into reversible and irreversible conditions, although a component of each is present in all obstructive diseases.

Reversible obstructive diseases are grouped under the term *asthma,* which denotes airway obstruction secondary to bronchospasm. In asthma, the airways are hyperresponsive and develop an inflammatory response to various stimuli, although the specific cause and duration of the bronchospasm are variable. In some individuals, allergic IgE-mediated reactions to defined antigens cause bronchospasm. In many other patients the cause is unknown. Precipitating factors may include exercise, aspirin, sulfites, tartrazine dye, emotional stress, cold air, environmental pollutants, or viral infection. Bronchial smooth muscle constriction, mucosal edema, excess mucus accumulation, and epithelial cell shedding all contribute to airway obstruction. This obstruction may be reversible spontaneously or with treatment.

Irreversible obstructive disease (sometimes known as chronic obstructive pulmonary disease, or COPD) comprises a group of conditions in which forced expiratory flow is reduced in either a constant or slowly progressive manner over months or years. Some conditions, such as *cystic fibrosis,* an inherited defect in exocrine gland function, or *bronchiectasis,* either secondary to recurrent necrotizing bacterial infections or as part of Kartagener syndrome, have an identifiable causality. However, most irreversible obstructive diseases, such as *emphysema, chronic bronchitis,* or *peripheral airway disease,* cannot be ascribed to specific conditions; rather, they represent an individual response to cigarette smoking and other airborne pollutants. For example, such responses occur in the setting of either alpha-1 antitrypsin deficiency (in certain forms of emphysema) or airway hyperactivity and mucus hypersecretion (as in bronchitis). The pathologic consequences of the abnormal response result in specific damage to lung tissue. Emphysema is characterized by pathological enlargement of the terminal bronchiole air spaces by destruction of the alveolar connective tissue septa. Bronchitis is characterized by hypertrophied mucous glands in the bronchi; while in peripheral airway disease, only the small airways demonstrate fibrosis, inflammation, and tortuosity.

Two clinical types of patients are seen in the advanced stages of chronic airway obstruction. The first type, known as *pink puffers,* tend to be thin, have hyperinflated lung fields, exhibit dyspnea without significant hypoxemia, and are free of the signs of right heart failure. The second type, known as *blue bloaters,* demonstrate cyanosis, marked hypoxemia, and peripheral edema with right heart failure *(cor pulmonale).*

Restrictive Lung Diseases

The restrictive lung diseases encompass a diverse group of conditions that cause diffuse parenchymal damage. The physiologic consequences of this damage include a reduction in total lung volume, diffusing capacity, and vital capacity. Occasionally, patients without parenchymal involvement who have diseases of the chest wall, respiratory muscles, pleura, or spine may have similarly restricted lung volumes. A *fibrotic* parenchymal response can occur as a result of occupational exposure to various substances including asbestos, silica dust, graphite, talc, coal, and tungsten. A *granulomatous* hypersensitivity reaction can develop in response to moldy hay, grains, birds, humidifiers and cooling systems, sawdust and wood pulp, or isocyanates and other noxious gases. Nonoccupational pulmonary disease can result from collagen vascular diseases, sarcoidosis, eosinophilic granuloma, Wegener granulomatosis, Goodpasture syndrome, alveolar proteinosis, idiopathic pulmonary hemosiderosis, idiopathic pulmonary fibrosis, and other idiopathic parenchymal diseases. Therapeutic agents such as dilantin, penicillin, gold, methotrexate, or radiation can also cause pulmonary disease.

Evaluation

Although all patients with respiratory problems should be under the care of a capable internist or pulmonologist, ophthalmologists and other physicians should also be aware of the methods used in the diagnosis and evaluation of patients with breathing disorders. The following should be considered:

□ *Symptoms:* dyspnea, orthopnea, chronic cough, chronic sputum production.

□ *History:* occupational exposure, family history, cigarette use.

□ *Signs:* audible wheezing, cyanosis, finger clubbing, forced expiratory time greater than 4 seconds, increased anteroposterior diameter of the chest.

□ *Laboratory studies:* elevated hematocrit, hypoxia or hypercapnia on arterial blood gas measurement.

□ *Chest roentgenography:* parenchymal disease, hyperinflation, diaphragmatic flattening, increased retrosternal lucency, pleural abnormalities.

□ *Computerized tomography of the chest* can detect minimal degrees of emphysema, obviating the need for tissue diagnosis.

□ *Pulmonary function tests* measure the volume of air forcefully expelled over time. The forced expiratory volume over 1 second (FEV$_1$) represents the first second of exhalation, while the total lung capacity (TLC) represents the total volume exhaled. Both parameters and their serial rate of decline in a patient represent objective measures of lung function as well as prognostic indicators of comorbidity and mortality from lung cancer and cardiovascular disease. FEV$_1$ <80% of predicted suggests obstructive disease, while TLC <70% of predicted suggests restrictive disease.

□ *Bronchoscopy, transbronchial biopsy,* and *bronchial lavage* are used to obtain culture material, cytologic material, and pathologic specimens for analysis.

Treatment

Treatment of pulmonary disease has two major goals: first, to favorably alter the natural history of the disease; and, second, to improve the individual's symptoms and functional status and minimize associated problems.

Nonpharmacological Approaches

In the case of chronic bronchitis and emphysema, *cessation of smoking* can favorably alter the course of the disease. Similarly, *avoidance of precipitants* of airway obstruction is important in ameliorating asthmatic conditions. In patients with severe pulmonary hypertension and cor pulmonale, use of *supplemental oxygen* to maintain an arterial oxygen pressure above 60 mm Hg has demonstrated a modest reduction in pulmonary hypertension and improved survival. However, a patient receiving supplemental oxygen must be carefully monitored, as its use may decrease the respiratory drive to eliminate carbon dioxide, aggravating the respiratory acidosis that may lead to carbon dioxide narcosis. *Breathing exercises* and *postoperative chest physiotherapy* have demonstrable short-term effects in improving respiratory function.

Pharmacologic Therapy

Pharmacologic approaches include medications that are specific for the particular pulmonary condition and medications that improve the patient's symptoms and functional status (Table VI-1). *Specific medications* directly alter the pathophysiologic mechanisms underlying the patient's pulmonary disease. Some examples include cyclophosphamide for Wegener granulomatosis, steroids for sarcoidosis, and plasmapheresis with immunosuppressive drugs in Goodpasture syndrome.

Symptomatic medications are designed to reduce the obstructive or restrictive components affecting the patient's lung function. Medications used to treat symptomatic bronchospastic airway obstruction include bronchodilators, inhibitors of inflammation, and antibiotics during infection-precipitated airway closure.

Bronchodilators, which include theophylline, beta-adrenergic agonists, and anticholinergics, act primarily by relaxing the tracheobronchial smooth muscle. Although *theophylline* produces bronchodilation in a manner that varies directly with the serum level, it is a weak phosphodiesterase inhibitor whose mechanism of action is unclear. Theophylline has a narrow therapeutic index: thus, serum levels should be measured (normally 10–20 mg/l) in order to avoid toxic effects such as

TABLE VI-1

DRUGS FOR THE TREATMENT OF CHRONIC OBSTRUCTIVE PULMONARY DISEASE

Beta-2 selective adrenergic agents
  Albuterol (Proventil, Ventolin)
  Bitolterol mesylate (Tornalate)
  Pirbuterol acetate (Maxair)
  Salmeterol xinofoate (Serevent)
  Terbutaline sulfate (Brethaire, Brethine, Bricanyl)

Anticholinergics
  Ipratropium bromide (Atrovent)

Xanthine derivatives and combinations
  Theophylline (Aerolate, Marax, Quibron, Respbid, Slo-Phyllin, Theo-Dur,
  Uniphyl)

Leukotriene inhibitors
  Zafirlukast (Zyflo)
  Zileuton (Accolate)

Mast-cell stabilizers
  Cromolyn sodium (Intal)
  Nedocromil sodium (Tilade)

Corticosteroids
  Beclomethasone dipropionate (Beclovent, Vanceril)
  Bedesonide (Pulmicort)
  Flunisolide (AeroBid)
  Triamcinolone acetonide (Azmacort)

nausea, tachycardia, headache, seizures, and ventricular arrhythmias while maintaining efficacy. Theophylline and its derivatives are administered either parenterally or orally.

Beta-adrenergic agonists activate smooth muscle adenyl cyclase and cause a rise in intracellular cAMP, resulting in bronchodilation. The selective beta-2 adrenergics, which have greater bronchodilatory and less cardiostimulatory effects, are commonly used, often in metered-dose inhalers (they can also be administered orally or parenterally). They have replaced the nonselective beta-adrenergic agents such as isoproterenol. The selective beta-2 agonists include *albuterol, bitolterol, isoetharine, metaproterenol,* and *terbutaline.* These drugs differ in onset and duration of action. For example, isoetharine's onset is within 1–3 minutes and lasts for 60–90 minutes, whereas bitolterol's duration is 6–8 hours. *Salmeterol,* a particularly long-acting beta-2 adrenergic, is helpful in maintenance treatment of asthma; it should not be used for acute exacerbations. Although *epinephrine* causes predominantly beta-adrenergic stimulation in the lungs, it also causes peripheral alpha-adrenergic stimulation resulting in vasoconstrictive hypertension and tachycardia. It is most often administered subcutaneously to help control an acute asthma attack.

Anticholinergic agents directly relax smooth muscle by competing for acetylcholine at muscarinic nerve-ending receptors. *Atropine* and similar agents have been replaced by poorly absorbing atropinic congeners such as *ipratropium bromide* and *atropine methonitrate.* These newer inhalation agents have few systemic and minimal cardiac effects. They have an additive bronchodilator effect when combined with submaximal doses of beta-adrenergic agonists.

Inhibitors of inflammation include corticosteroids, leukotriene inhibitors, and cromolyn sodium. *Corticosteroids* not only suppress inflammation of the bronchioles but also potentiate the bronchodilator response to beta-adrenergic agonists by suppressing the release of arachidonic acid from cell membranes and up-regulating the beta-adrenergic receptors. *Inhaled steroids* can be used chronically to reduce bronchial hyperreactivity; they are not used to manage acute attacks. *Systemic steroids,* however, are highly effective in managing acute episodes. They should be reserved for serious flare-ups to avoid adverse side effects. *Leukotriene inhibitors* suppress the effects of inflammatory mediators. They are especially useful for prophylaxis and chronic maintenance therapy in asthma. *Cromolyn sodium* prevents the release of chemical mediators from mast cells in the presence of IgE antibody and the specific antigen. *Immunotherapy* has been shown to be helpful for asthmatic patients when a defined triggering antigen is present.

As mentioned above, patients with cor pulmonale have increased survival when treated appropriately with supplemental oxygen. In addition, *diuretics* and *vasodilators* can improve the symptoms in cor pulmonale patients, but they have not proved to increase survival.

Preoperative and Postoperative Considerations

Before operating on a patient with pulmonary disease, the surgeon should consult with an internist or pulmonologist to carefully define the patient's functional respiratory status, especially with respect to a supine position. The patient's respiratory function should be maximized with medications and nonpharmacologic means as appropriate. During surgery, supplemental oxygen (if necessary) should be monitored and adjusted based on the patient's arterial oxygen and carbon dioxide tensions. The patient should be sedated only if necessary and, in that case, should be carefully monitored for arterial gas values.

Niklas RA. National and international guidelines for the diagnosis and treatment of asthma. *Curr Opin Pulm Med.* 1997;3:51–55.

Petty TL, Weinmann GG. Building a national strategy for the prevention and management of and research in chronic obstructive pulmonary disease. National Heart, Lung, and Blood Institute Workshop Summary. *JAMA.* 1997;277:246–253.

Standards for the diagnosis and care of patients with chronic obstructive lung disease (COPD) and asthma. American Thoracic Society. *Am Rev Respir Dis.* 1987;136: 225–244.

Weiss ST. Atopy and airway responsiveness in chronic obstructive pulmonary disease. *N Engl J Med.* 1987;317:1345–1347.

West JB. Assessing pulmonary gas exchange. *N Engl J Med.* 1987;316:1336–1338.

CHAPTER VII

Hematologic Disorders

Composition of Blood

Formed elements—erythrocytes (red blood cells, or RBCs), white blood cells, and platelets—compose approximately 45% of the total blood volume. The fluid portion, *plasma,* is about 90% water. The remaining 10% of the plasma consists of proteins (albumin, globulin, fibrinogen, and enzymes), lipids, carbohydrates, hormones, vitamins, and salts. If a blood specimen is allowed to clot, the fibrinogen is consumed and the resultant fluid portion is called *serum.*

Erythropoiesis

It is believed that all blood cells originate from an uncommitted pluripotential stem cell, designated the *colony-forming unit-spleen (CFU-S).* This in turn gives rise to (1) the *lymphoid stem cell (CFU-L)* and (2) the *myeloid,* or *hematopoietic stem cell (CFU-C,* or *colony-forming unit-culture).* The hematopoietic stem cell is thought to be the common precursor of RBCs, granulocytes, monocytes, and platelets. Stem cells are not morphologically recognizable, but their existence has been shown by various culture techniques.

RBCs are formed in the bone marrow in a series of steps. The CFU-C gives rise to a *burst-forming unit-erythroid (BFU-E),* which, in response to erythropoietin (see below) becomes a *colony-forming unit-erythroid (CFU-E).* This differentiates through morphologically identifiable stages during which the nucleus condenses and the cell gradually shrinks: pronormoblast, basophilic normoblast, polychromatophilic normoblast, and orthochromic normoblast. This phase takes approximately 3 days. The nucleus is then extruded, forming the reticulocyte, which is slightly larger than the normal mature RBC. The reticulocyte remains in the bone marrow 2–3 more days and is then released into the peripheral blood. The mature erythrocyte is round, biconcave, and about 7 μm in diameter. Circulating RBCs have a life span of about 120 days.

Erythropoiesis is initiated by *erythropoietin,* a hormone that is found in the plasma and is produced mainly in the kidney. (It is believed that some erythropoietin is also produced by the liver.) Any reduction in oxygen tension in the kidney (for example, from hypoxemia, low hemoglobin level, arterial insufficiency, and so on) stimulates production of erythropoietin, which causes stem cells to differentiate into pronormoblasts, leading to increased production of RBCs. In addition, immature reticulocytes are prematurely released into the peripheral blood. A number of tumors are associated with inappropriate production of erythropoietin, leading to erythrocytosis. These include benign and malignant kidney tumors, cerebellar hemangioblastoma, pheochromocytoma, and adrenal adenoma.

The production of RBCs and hemoglobin requires many substances. Iron is needed for proliferation and maturation of erythrocytes. Folic acid and B_{12} are necessary for DNA replication and cell division. Also required are manganese; cobalt; copper; vitamins C, E, B_6, thiamine, riboflavin, and pantothenic acid; and the hormones erythropoietin, thyroxine, and androgens.

Anemia

The *anemias* are a diverse group of disorders that have in common a reduction in the amount of circulating hemoglobin or erythrocytes, resulting in a decrease in the amount of oxygen reaching the tissues of the body. Normal hemoglobin levels are different for men (14–18 g/dL) and women (12–16 g/dL). Likewise, normal hematocrit values differ (men: 40%–54%, women: 37%–47%).

Diagnosis and Clinical Evaluation

The anemias may be classified by etiology, pathophysiological mechanism, or morphology; none of these methods is ideal as a diagnostic approach. From a clinical standpoint, morphological classification may be the most useful, as it differentiates the various etiologies according to RBC size, information that is usually available on a complete blood count (CBC) report at the time of presentation. Thus, the mean corpuscular volume (MCV) is used to create three general categories of anemia: *microcytic* (MCV <83), *normocytic* (MCV 84–95), and *macrocytic* (MCV >95). The amount of hemoglobin (chromicity) has been used in the past as a second criterion, but in general microcytic anemias are hypochromic while normocytic and macrocytic anemias are normochromic.

The evaluation of the anemic patient is then guided by the morphology of the individual's erythrocytes. The causes of *microcytic anemia* include iron deficiency, thalassemia, and sideroblastic anemia. *Normocytic anemia* may be caused by defective formation of RBCs or the presence of tumor cells in the bone marrow in such conditions as aplastic anemia, myeloproliferative diseases, metastatic cancer, renal and inflammatory diseases, and chronic infection. Normocytic anemia may also be caused by abnormal hemoglobin or increased destruction of RBCs, as in sickle cell anemia, acquired hemolytic anemias, hemolytic disease of the newborn, and hypersplenism. *Macrocytic anemia* may result from deficiency of vitamin B_{12} or folic acid in cases of pernicious anemia, sprue, poor diet, alcoholism, and pregnancy, and after gastrectomy. It is also caused by accelerated erythropoiesis associated with hemolysis, acute blood loss, marrow replacement, or liver disease.

Clinical Consequences of Anemia

Mild anemia is often asymptomatic. As the disease worsens, however, physiological adaptation to the blood's diminished oxygen-carrying capacity becomes clinically apparent. Blood flow is redistributed, shifting from skin and kidney to more oxygen-dependent tissues such as the brain, heart, and muscles. This produces the pallor and cool skin typical of anemic patients. With exercise or increasingly severe anemia, cardiac output is increased to provide more oxygen to the body. Exercise intolerance or fatigue at rest reflect the inability of the blood to provide adequate oxygen to major organs. High-output cardiac failure may develop in susceptible individuals. Infarction of major organs can result, especially in patients with preexisting vascular insufficiency.

Anemia of Chronic Disorders

Usually presenting as a mild normocytic or microcytic anemia, *anemia of chronic disorders* is the most common form of anemia seen in hospitalized patients. It develops in association with malignancy, chronic infections (infectious endocarditis, tuberculosis, osteomyelitis), and chronic inflammation, such as in connective tissue and inflammatory bowel diseases. A hemoglobin level of less than 9 g/dL and a hematocrit value of less than 27% are unusual in this condition and should prompt an investigation into other possible causes, such as occult blood loss or iron deficiency. Anemia of chronic disorders results from a combination of shortened RBC survival, impaired iron metabolism, and failure of the bone marrow to adequately increase RBC production.

Anemia in Elderly Patients

Studies have shown that the incidence of anemia increases each decade over 60 years of age, especially in men. It has been suggested that the hematologic standards used for older men be age-adjusted. Evaluation of mild anemia (hemoglobin 12–14 g/dL) in this population fails to find a cause in most cases. These cases have sometimes been called *physiologic anemia* and attributed to the aging process. Below 12 g/dL, however, treatable causes—especially iron deficiency and hypothyroidism—are often discovered. Regardless of the hemoglobin level, however, all cases of iron-deficiency anemia in this age group *must* be worked up.

Sickle Cell Disease

Affecting 0.2%–0.4% of the black population in the United States, sickle cell disease is a chronic anemia caused by an abnormal beta chain in the hemoglobin molecule. The resulting abnormal hemoglobin S, constituting 90%–100% of the hemoglobin in homozygous individuals, causes intravascular hemolysis (*sickling*) that presents as painful episodes of vascular occlusion. Joint, bone, and abdominal pain are common, as are pulmonary and cerebral infarction. Heterozygotes have up to 50% hemoglobin S and are generally asymptomatic; they are said to have *sickle cell trait.*

Treatment of Anemia

Treatment is directed at the underlying cause whenever possible. Iron deficiency can be corrected with oral iron supplementation, provided there is adequate absorption and no source of chronic blood loss, such as gastrointestinal bleeding.

A recombinant form of the protein erythropoietin is available and approved for use in the treatment of anemic patients with end-stage renal failure who are undergoing or awaiting hemodialysis. It is extremely effective under these circumstances. Erythropoietin is also being studied for use in anemia of chronic disorders and myelodysplastic diseases and in boosting hemoglobin levels prior to autologous blood donation. Erythropoietin appears to be effective in each of these situations, although higher doses are necessary than in renal failure.

Ophthalmologic Considerations

Ocular manifestations of anemia include distended, tortuous retinal veins, hemorrhages, and cotton-wool spots. Retrobulbar neuritis may occur as part of the demyelinating disorder seen in pernicious anemia (vitamin B_{12} deficiency).

The eye is frequently affected by sickle cell disease. Comma-shaped capillary segments are seen on the bulbar conjunctiva. Hyphemas, even small ones, frequently cause marked elevation of intraocular pressure due to trabecular obstruction by cells that sickle in the hypoxic environment of the anterior chamber. Carbonic anhydrase inhibitors cause metabolic acidosis, which may exacerbate sickling; they should probably not be used in these patients. Fundus abnormalities include choroidal vascular occlusion, angioid streaks, and venous tortuosity. Arteriolar occlusions, usually in the equatorial region, lead to hemorrhage (*salmon patches*), retinal pigment disruption (hyperpigmented *black sunbursts*), and neovascular tufts (*sea fans*). See BCSC Section 12, *Retina and Vitreous,* for illustrations and further discussion of the ocular manifestations of sickle cell disease.

The use of general anesthesia in sickle cell patients carries a risk of precipitating a sickling crisis. Although the exact mechanism is not known, hypotension, hypovolemia, and hypoxemia are all believed to add to the likelihood of a crisis. The patient must therefore be meticulously monitored to avoid these conditions. Recently, *hydroxyurea* has been proven effective in reducing the frequency and intensity of sickle cell crises and improving hematologic parameters.

Disorders of Hemostasis

Hemorrhage is the cardinal symptom of disorders of the blood-clotting mechanisms. A basic understanding of the hemostatic process and the manifestations associated with specific abnormalities will help the ophthalmologist manage patients both medically and surgically. (See Figure VII-1 for a diagram of blood-clotting pathways.)

Hemostasis is initiated by damage to a blood-vessel wall. This event triggers constriction of the vessel, followed by accumulation and adherence of platelets at the site of injury. Coagulation factors in the blood are activated, leading to formation of a fibrin clot, which will stop the bleeding if the injury is not too large. Slow fibrinolysis ensues, dissolving the clot while the damage is repaired. Circulating inhibitors are also present, modulating the process by inactivating coagulation factors to prevent widespread clotting.

Laboratory Evaluation of Hemostasis and Blood Coagulation

Various techniques are used to assess the status of a patient's hemostatic mechanisms. Following are some of the most common tests:

- *Platelet count.* Minor bleeding may be seen at platelet counts below 50,000/μl. Abnormal bleeding at higher platelet counts suggests abnormal platelet function. Below 20,000/μl, serious spontaneous bleeding may occur.

- *Bleeding time.* A small dermal wound is created and the duration of bleeding is recorded. This is a screening test of the vascular and platelet components of hemostasis. Since disorders of blood vessels are rare, the results essentially reflect platelet number and function. Bleeding time is prolonged when platelet counts drop below 50,000–100,000/μl.

- *Partial thromboplastin time (PTT).* The PTT requires all of the coagulation factors involved in the intrinsic and common pathways. It is most commonly used to measure the effect of heparin therapy. Platelet abnormalities do not affect the result of this test.

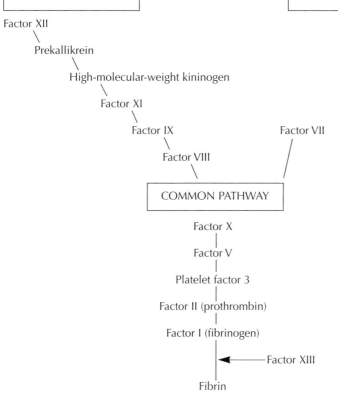

FIG VII-1—Blood-clotting pathways.

□ *Prothrombin time (PT).* The PT measures the integrity of the extrinsic and common pathways. It requires a 30% concentration of the vitamin K–dependent factors II, VII, and X (though not factor IX, a part of the intrinsic pathway) and will therefore be prolonged in conditions affecting these factors (see below). The PT is most commonly used to monitor anticoagulant therapy. It may be slightly prolonged by the action of heparin.

In recent years, efforts have been made to tailor anticoagulation therapy according to the nature of the problem being treated. For example, treatment or prevention of deep venous thrombosis is thought to require less oral anticoagulation therapy than endocardial mural thrombi or cardiac replacement valves. However, because of intra- and interlaboratory variation in test results, it has been difficult to standardize therapeutic dosages. To solve this problem, the International Normalized Ratio (INR) has been developed. The INR modifies the standard PT ratio (patient PT/control PT) to reflect the particular thromboplastin reagent used by a laboratory. The resulting reported INR value is an expression of the ratio of the patient's PT to the laboratory's mean normal PT. Thus, for prevention or treatment of deep vein thrombosis, the recommended INR value (comparable to subsequent values measured over time or across different laboratories) is 2.0–3.0; for tissue replacement valves, 2.0–3.0; for mechanical replacement valves, 2.5–3.5.

Clinical Manifestations of Hemostatic Abnormalities

Hemorrhage resulting from hemostatic derangement must be differentiated from hemorrhage caused by localized processes. The presence of generalized or recurrent bleeding suggests abnormal hemostasis. *Petechiae* (small capillary hemorrhages of the skin and mucous membranes) and *purpura* (ecchymoses) are typical of platelet disorders and vasculitis. Subcutaneous hematomas and hemarthroses characterize coagulation abnormalities. Bleeding following trauma may be massive and life threatening in coagulation disorders, whereas it is more likely to be slow and prolonged when platelet function is impaired.

Vascular Disorders

A number of inherited and acquired disorders of blood vessels and their supporting connective tissues result in pathological bleeding. *Hereditary hemorrhagic telangiectasia* (Osler-Weber-Rendu disease) is an autosomal dominant condition characterized by localized dilation of capillaries and venules of the skin and mucous membranes. The lesions increase over a period of decades, often leading to profuse bleeding.

Several inherited connective tissue disorders are associated with hemorrhage. *Ehlers-Danlos syndrome* is characterized by hyperplastic, fragile skin and hyperextensible joints; it is dominantly inherited. In *osteogenesis imperfecta,* also a dominant trait, bone fractures and otosclerosis (leading to deafness) are common. In both of these conditions, easy bruising and hematomas are frequently seen. *Pseudoxanthoma elasticum,* a recessive disorder, is much rarer but is often complicated by gastrointestinal hemorrhage. *Marfan syndrome* is sometimes associated with mild bleeding as well as with dissecting aortic aneurysms.

Scurvy, the result of severe ascorbic acid deficiency, is associated with marked vascular fragility and hemorrhagic manifestations resulting from abnormal synthesis of collagen. In addition to the classic findings of perifollicular petechiae and gingival bleeding, intradermal, intramuscular, and subperiosteal hemorrhages are common. *Amyloidosis* is another acquired disorder in which petechiae and purpura are common.

Ophthalmologic considerations   All of the inherited vascular disorders have associated ocular findings. Conjunctival telangiectasias are seen in hereditary hemorrhagic telangiectasia. Blue sclerae are typical of osteogenesis imperfecta. Blue sclerae are also seen in Ehlers-Danlos syndrome, which may also manifest microcornea, myopia, and angioid streaks; retinal detachment and ectopia lentis have also been reported. Angioid streaks also occur in about 30% of patients with pseudoxanthoma elasticum. Almost all patients with Marfan syndrome have some degree of ectopia lentis; severe myopia and retinal detachment are common.

Platelet Disorders

By far the most common cause of abnormal bleeding, platelet disorders may result from an insufficient number of platelets, inadequate function, or both. Mild derangement of platelet function may be asymptomatic or may cause minor bruising, menorrhagia, and bleeding after surgery. More severe dysfunction leads to petechiae, purpura, gastrointestinal bleeding, and other types of serious bleeding.

Thrombocytopenia A reduction in the number of platelets may result from decreased production, increased destruction, or abnormal distribution. Production may be suppressed by many factors, including radiation, chemotherapy, alcohol use, malignant invasion of the bone marrow, aplastic anemia, and B_{12} or folic acid deficiency.

Accelerated destruction may occur through immunologic or nonimmunologic causes. *Idiopathic thrombocytopenic purpura (ITP)* is the result of platelet injury by antiplatelet antibodies. The acute form of ITP is usually seen in children and young adults, often following a viral illness, and commonly undergoes spontaneous remission. Chronic ITP is more common in adults and is characterized by mild manifestations; spontaneous remission is uncommon. Treatment consists of corticosteroid therapy or splenectomy. Danazol is also effective in treating ITP, and when combined therapy is necessary, it allows the use of lower doses of corticosteroids. A neonatal form is seen in babies born to women with ITP as a result of transplacental passage of antiplatelet antibodies. Recovery follows physiologic clearance of the antibodies from the child's circulation.

Many drugs have been implicated as causes of immunologic platelet destruction; readers are referred to the source textbooks for details. Another important cause is *posttransfusion isoantibody production,* which occurs predictably after transfusions containing platelets, unless HLA typing is undertaken, and leads to decreasing efficacy of later platelet transfusions.

Nonimmune causes of thrombocytopenia include *thrombotic thrombocytopenic purpura (TTP)* and the syndromes of intravascular coagulation and fibrinolysis (discussed below). In addition to the symptoms of thrombocytopenia, TTP is characterized by thrombotic occlusions of the microcirculation and hemolytic anemia. Fever, neurologic symptoms, anemia, and renal dysfunction occur with abrupt onset, with death occurring in days to weeks in the majority of untreated cases. Early treatment with exchange plasmapheresis has improved the survival rate to over 80%. Additional treatment includes antiplatelet drugs, corticosteroids, and splenectomy.

Abnormal distribution of platelets is most commonly caused by splenic sequestration. The usual clinical setting is hepatic cirrhosis, and the level of thrombocytopenia is mild. Patients with severely depressed platelet counts probably also have accelerated platelet destruction in the spleen.

Platelet dysfunction Patients in this category usually come to the physician's attention because of easy bruising, epistaxis, menorrhagia, or excessive bleeding after surgery and dental work. Unlike patients with marked thrombocytopenia, patients with platelet dysfunction rarely have petechiae.

Hereditary disorders of platelet function are rare. Much more important clinically are the acquired forms, of which drug ingestion is the most common cause. As with drugs causing antiplatelet antibodies, the list of causative agents is very long. A single aspirin tablet taken orally irreversibly inhibits platelet aggregation for the life span of the circulating platelets present, causing a modest prolongation of the bleeding time for at least 48–72 hours following ingestion. This reaction has remarkably little effect in normal individuals, although intraoperative blood loss may be slightly increased. However, in patients with hemophilia, severe thrombocytopenia, uremia, and those on warfarin or heparin therapy, significant bleeding may result.

Nonsteroidal anti-inflammatory drugs cause reversible inhibition of platelet function in the presence of the drug; the effect disappears as the drug is cleared from the blood. Other commonly used drugs that may affect platelet function include ethanol, tricyclic antidepressants, and antihistamines.

In addition to uremia, clinical conditions associated with abnormal platelet function include liver disease, multiple myeloma, systemic lupus erythematosus, chronic lymphocytic leukemia, and Hermansky-Pudlak syndrome (an autosomal recessive form of oculocutaneous albinism).

Disorders of Blood Coagulation

Hereditary coagulation disorders Inherited abnormalities involving all of the coagulation factors except factors III and IV have been reported. The most common and most severe is factor VIII deficiency, called *hemophilia A,* or *classic hemophilia.* Typical manifestations of this X-linked disease include severe and protracted bleeding, after even minor trauma, and spontaneous bleeding into joints (hemarthroses), the central nervous system, and the abdominal cavity.

Treatment involves infusion of coagulation factor VIII. Transfusion of pooled human factor VIII in the past had always carried a significant risk of transmission of hepatitis B virus; in the 1980s transmission of the human immunodeficiency virus became a major problem as well. Those risks have now been eliminated with the availability of recombinant factor VIII.

Von Willebrand disease, another relatively common hereditary disorder, is caused by deficiency or abnormality of a portion of the factor VIII molecule called von Willebrand's factor. This deficiency causes platelet adhesion abnormalities, leading to bleeding symptoms that are mild in most cases and may escape detection until adult years.

Acquired Coagulation Disorders

Vitamin K deficiency Vitamin K is required for the production of factors II (prothrombin), VII, IX, and X in the liver. Normal diets contain large amounts of vitamin K, and it is also synthesized by gut flora. Causes of vitamin K deficiency include biliary obstruction and various malabsorption syndromes (including sprue, cystic fibrosis, and celiac disease), in which intestinal absorption of vitamin K is reduced. Suppression of endogenous gastrointestinal flora, seen commonly in hospitalized patients on prolonged broad-spectrum antibiotic therapy, will decrease intestinal production of vitamin K. However, clinical deficiency will occur only if there is also diminished dietary intake. Nutritional deficiency is unusual but may be seen with prolonged parenteral nutrition. Laboratory evaluation will reveal prolongation of both the PT and PTT. Most forms of vitamin K deficiency will respond to subcutaneous or intramuscular administration of 20 mg of vitamin K_1, with normalization of coagulation defects within 24 hours. Vitamin K_1 should not be given intravenously because of risk of sudden death from an anaphylactoid reaction.

One special form of vitamin K deficiency is *hemorrhagic disease of the new-born,* which is the result of a normal, mild deficiency of vitamin K–dependent factors during the first 5 days of life and the absence of the vitamin in maternal milk. It is now rarely seen in developed countries because of the routine administration of vitamin K_1 to newborns.

Liver disease   Hemostatic abnormalities of all types may be associated with disease of the liver, the site of production of all the coagulation factors except factor VIII. As liver dysfunction develops, decreased levels of the vitamin K–dependent factors are seen first, followed by factors V, XI, and XII; both the PT and PTT are prolonged. Thrombocytopenia, primarily the result of hypersplenism, and a prolonged bleeding time due to platelet dysfunction are common. In addition, intravascular coagulation and fibrinolysis (see below) are common, further complicating the clinical picture.

Mild hemorrhagic symptoms are common in patients with significant liver disease. Severe bleeding is usually gastrointestinal in origin, arising from peptic ulcers, gastritis, and esophageal varices. Treatment is difficult at best and consists of blood and coagulation factor replacement. Local measures, such as vasopressin infusion or balloon tamponade of bleeding varices, can sometimes control potentially catastrophic bleeding.

Intravascular coagulation and fibrinolysis (ICF)   Also known as *disseminated intravascular coagulation (DIC)* or *consumption coagulopathy,* ICF is a complex syndrome involving widespread activation of the coagulation and fibrinolytic systems within the general circulation. Utilization and consumption of coagulation factors and platelets produces bleeding; formation of fibrin and fibrin degradation products (fibrin split products) leads to occlusion of the microcirculation, various forms of organ failure, and occasionally thrombosis of larger vessels. Laboratory findings may vary but usually include thrombocytopenia, hypofibrinogenemia, and elevated levels of fibrin split products. The PT and PTT are usually, though not invariably, prolonged.

Clinically, two forms of ICF are recognized. The acute form is characterized by the abrupt onset of severe, generalized bleeding. The most common causes are obstetrical complications (most notably abruptio placentae and amniotic fluid embolism), septicemia, shock, massive trauma, and major surgical procedures. Treatment, other than specific measures aimed at the underlying disease, is controversial. Among the modalities used are heparinization and replacement of blood, platelets, and fibrinogen.

Chronic ICF is associated with disseminated neoplasms, some acute leukemias, and autoimmune diseases. Laboratory values range from normal to moderately abnormal; levels of coagulation factors may even be elevated. Bleeding and thrombosis (especially leg-vein thrombosis and pulmonary embolism) may occur, but in most patients the syndrome remains undiagnosed unless renal failure occurs as a result of intravascular coagulation in the kidney. In these patients, the disease has been demonstrated by the presence of fibrin in renal tissue obtained by biopsy. On occasion, chronic ICF may convert to the acute form.

Circulating anticoagulants   Two types of endogenous inhibitors of the hemostatic mechanism are known: antibodies that affect specific coagulation factors and those that nonspecifically affect lipid-dependent coagulation reactions.

Although inhibitors of most of the coagulation factors have been reported, most are rare. The exceptions are antibodies to factors VIII and IX. Up to 10% of patients with hemophilia A develop antibodies, presumably due to sensitization following administration of factor VIII. Development of these anticoagulants can also be seen in normal elderly patients, in nonhemophiliac patients following drug reactions, and in those with collagen vascular diseases. Clinical manifestations range from mild bleeding to full-blown hemophilia. The PTT is prolonged and the PT is normal. Treatment involves various regimens of coagulation factor replacement and immunosuppression to try to eliminate the inhibitor.

In recent years, the importance of nonspecific circulating anticoagulants has gained greater recognition. Termed *antiphospholipid antibodies,* this group includes the so-called *lupus anticoagulant* and *anticardiolipin antibodies.* These substances have an affinity for negatively charged phospholipids, which are important in the conversion of prothrombin to thrombin. Although this process leads to anticoagulation in vitro, with resultant prolongation of the PTT, clinical bleeding is rare. Paradoxically, 30%–50% of these patients have significant arterial and venous thrombotic complications; recurrent fetal loss is a particular problem. The practicing ophthalmologist should be aware of the reported association of these antibodies with retinal vein and artery occlusions, retinal vasculitis, choroidal infarction, and arteritic anterior ischemic optic neuropathy.

Approximately 10% of patients with systemic lupus erythematosus have antiphospholipid antibodies. Interestingly, one of the antigens used in VDRL testing is the negatively charged phospholipid cardiolipin, which probably explains the occurrence of false-positive VDRL reactions in patients with lupus. Antiphospholipid antibodies can also be found in other autoimmune diseases, in AIDS, and in association with phenothiazine and procainamide use.

Therapeutic anticoagulation Many clinical situations require intentional disruption of the hemostatic process. The effect of aspirin on platelet function has already been discussed.

Heparin is a mucopolysaccharide that binds antithrombin III, inhibiting the formation of thrombin. It is given intravenously, and therapy is assessed by measuring the PTT. Aspirin should not be given to heparinized patients, because the resultant platelet dysfunction may provoke bleeding.

The orally administered warfarin derivatives, of which warfarin sodium (Coumadin) is the most widely used, inhibit the production of normal vitamin K–dependent coagulation factors (II, VII, IX, and X). Therapeutic effect is assessed by measuring the patient's PT. One critical issue is the long list of commonly used drugs that interact with warfarin. These interactions may cause an unintended increase or decrease in the PT, depending on the drug.

Heparin and the warfarin derivatives are used to prevent the formation of new thrombi and the propagation of existing thrombi, but neither affects the original clot. Thrombolytic agents such as *streptokinase, urokinase,* and *tissue plasminogen activator (tPA)* are used to dissolve existing thrombi, most notably in the very early stages of myocardial infarction resulting from coronary artery thrombosis. They are also currently being used for early treatment of thrombotic stroke; this controversial treatment may increase the risk of converting a thrombotic stroke into a hemorrhagic stroke.

Ahn YS. Efficacy of danazol in hematologic disorders. *Acta Haematol.* 1990;84: 122–129.

Asherson RA, Merry P, Acheson JF, et al. Antiphospholipid antibodies: a risk factor for occlusive ocular vascular disease in systemic lupus erythematosus and the "primary" antiphospholipid syndrome. *Ann Rheumatol Dis.* 1989;48:358–361.

Bowles CA. Vasculopathy associated with the antiphospholipid antibody syndrome. *Rheum Dis Clin North Am.* 1990;16:471–490.

Brown BA. *Hematology: Principles and Procedures.* 5th ed. Philadelphia: Lea & Febiger; 1988.

Doig RG, O'Malley CJ, Dauer R, et al. An evaluation of 200 consecutive patients with spontaneous or recurrent thrombosis for primary hypercoagulable states. *Am J Clin Pathol.* 1994;102:797–801.

el-Hazmi MA, al-Momen A, Kandaswamy S, et al. On the use of hydroxyurea/erethropoietin combination therapy for sickle cell disease. *Acta Haematol.* 1995;128–134.

el-Hazmi MA, Warsy AS, al-Momen A, et al: Hydroxyurea for the treatment of sickle cell disease. *Acta Haematol.* 1992;88:170–174.

Pignon JM, Poirson E, Rochant H. Danazol in autoimmune haemolytic anaemia. *Br J Haematol.* 1993;83:343–345.

Rafuse PE, Canny CL. Initial identification of antinuclear-antibody-negative systemic lupus erythematosus on ophthalmic examination: a case report, with a discussion of the ocular significance of anticardiolipin (antiphospholipid) antibodies. *Can J Ophthalmol.* 1992;27:189–193.

Stephens CJ. The antiphospholipid syndrome. Clinical correlations, cutaneous features, mechanism of thrombosis and treatment of patients with the lupus anticoagulant and anticardiolipin antibodies. *Br J Dermatol.* 1991;125:199–210.

Thorup OA, ed. *Fundamentals of Clinical Hematology.* Philadelphia: Saunders; 1987.

Watts MT, Greaves M, Rennie IG, et al. Antiphospholipid antibodies in the aetiology of ischaemic optic neuropathy. *Eye.* 1991;5:75–79.

CHAPTER VIII

Rheumatic Disorders

The rheumatic disorders are a heterogeneous collection of diseases that include rheumatoid arthritis, the seronegative spondyloarthropathies, juvenile rheumatoid arthritis, systemic lupus erythematosus, scleroderma, polymyositis and dermato-myositis, Sjögren syndrome, relapsing polychondritis, Behçet syndrome, and the vasculitides, including polyarteritis nodosa, allergic granulomatosis, Wegener gran-ulomatosis, giant cell arteritis, and Takayasu arteritis. Ocular involvement is common in the rheumatic diseases but varies among the different disorders. Two classes of drugs commonly used to treat rheumatic disorders—corticosteroids and nonste-roidal anti-inflammatory drugs—are discussed at the end of the chapter.

Rheumatoid Arthritis

Rheumatoid arthritis is the most common rheumatic disorder, affecting approxi-mately 1% of adults. Rheumatoid arthritis is classically an additive, symmetrical, deforming, peripheral polyarthritis. All joints may be involved, but it affects primar-ily the small joints of the hands and feet. Like all inflammatory arthritides, it is asso-ciated with the *gel phenomenon,* a stiffness at rest that improves with use; patients often complain of morning stiffness. Approximately 80% of patients with rheumatoid arthritis are positive for a rheumatoid factor, which is an autoantibody directed against immunoglobulin G (IgG).

Extra-articular disease in rheumatoid arthritis may affect a wide variety of non-articular tissues. Rheumatoid nodules, located subcutaneously on extensor surfaces, occur in approximately 25% of patients with rheumatoid arthritis. The lungs may be affected with rheumatoid pleural effusions, pleural nodules, pulmonary nodules, and occasionally interstitial fibrosis. Cardiac disease includes pericarditis and rheuma-toid nodules involving the conducting system and/or heart valves.

Rheumatoid vasculitis affects fewer than 1% of patients with rheumatoid arthri-tis. It generally presents either as a peripheral polyneuropathy or as refractory skin ulcers. Patients may develop digital gangrene or occasionally visceral ischemia. *Felty syndrome* is a triad of rheumatoid arthritis, splenomegaly, and leukopenia. Patients with Felty syndrome often have hyperpigmentation, chronic leg ulcers, and recurrent infections.

Therapy

Treatment of rheumatoid arthritis is approached in a stepwise additive fashion, with the initial therapy being a nonsteroidal anti-inflammatory drug (NSAID). All of the different NSAIDs (for example, aspirin, indomethacin, naproxen, sulindac) appear to be about equally effective, although the response of the individual patient may vary from one drug to another.

The second phase of treatment is to add a *remittive agent,* also known as a *slow-acting antirheumatic drug (SAARD).* While these second-line agents are sometimes referred to as *disease-modifying antirheumatic drugs (DMARDs),* true disease modification is difficult to document. Many feel that these agents may have a favorable impact on the natural disease course. These agents are classified by toxicity as follows.

- *Least toxic:* hydroxychloroquine, oral gold, and sulfasalazine

- *More toxic:* methotrexate, parenteral gold, azathioprine, cyclosporine, and penicillamine

- *Most toxic:* chlorambucil, cyclophosphamide

These drugs often take several months to have an effect but can induce a remission of the active arthritis and are believed to retard development of joint destruction. *Methotrexate* is often used very early in the disease course; it is the SAARD agent preferred by many rheumatologists because it is more effective and better tolerated than some of the other agents listed. Because of their toxicity, the most potent immunosuppressive drugs are reserved only for very severe and unresponsive cases. Low-dose *prednisone* (5–10 mg orally per day) is sometimes added to the treatment regimen in order to increase the patient's mobility and functional capacity. Therefore, if an NSAID alone fails to treat the patient adequately, most rheumatologists add an SAARD, with or without low-dose corticosteroids, very early in the disease course.

Ophthalmologic Considerations

Ocular manifestations of rheumatoid arthritis include Sjögren syndrome, scleritis, and marginal corneal ulcers. Baseline ophthalmic evaluation of patients with rheumatoid arthritis is suggested to monitor for the development of retinal toxicity from hydroxychloroquine therapy. Most reported retinal complications of this drug have occurred in patients who have taken a cumulative dosage of more than 800 g. The ocular manifestations of rheumatoid arthritis are discussed in BCSC Section 6, *Pediatric Ophthalmology and Strabismus*; and Section 9, *Intraocular Inflammation and Uveitis.* Retinal complications from hydroxychloroquine are discussed in Section 12, *Retina and Vitreous.*

Seronegative Spondyloarthropathies

The seronegative spondyloarthropathies include ankylosing spondylitis, Reiter syndrome, arthritis with inflammatory bowel disease, and psoriatic spondylitis. They are linked by their statistical association with the antigen type HLA-B27 and by their overlapping features, but they are distinguished by their somewhat different clinical patterns. The most common ophthalmic manifestation of these diseases is nongranulomatous acute anterior uveitis (AAU). Indeed, AAU shares with the seronegative spondyloarthropathies a statistical association with HLA-B27, as approximately 50% of patients with nongranulomatous AAU are HLA-B27 positive. See BCSC Section 9, *Intraocular Inflammation and Uveitis,* for illustrations and further discussion of these conditions.

Ankylosing Spondylitis

Ankylosing spondylitis is characterized by involvement of the axial skeleton and bony fusion (ankylosis). The etiology is unknown, but the strong association with HLA-B27 suggests a genetic predisposition. While more than 90% of Caucasian patients with ankylosing spondylitis possess the HLA antigen B27, only 6%–8% of the general population is HLA-B27 positive. The prevalence of ankylosing spondylitis is approximately 0.1%–0.2% of the population. Men are affected three times more commonly than women; moreover, the radiographic features seem to evolve more slowly in women.

The classic features of ankylosing spondylitis are chronic low back pain, fusion of the axial skeleton (spinal ankylosis), and sacroiliitis. The demonstration of sacroiliitis on x-ray examination of the sacroiliac joints is the sine qua non for the diagnosis of spondylitis. The end stage of this process is a completely fused and immobilized spine, also known as a *bamboo* or *poker* spine. In addition to the spinal arthritis that is the hallmark of the disease, patients may develop an arthritis of the shoulders and hips, limited chest expansion, and restrictive lung disease. Other extra-articular features include apical pulmonary fibrosis, ascending aortitis, aortic valvular incompetence, and heart block. The primary ocular manifestation of ankylosing spondylitis is recurrent, acute, nongranulomatous iridocyclitis, which occurs in approximately 25% of these patients.

Reiter Syndrome

Reiter syndrome is characterized by the classic triad of arthritis, urethritis, and conjunctivitis. Like ankylosing spondylitis, Reiter syndrome has a clear genetic predisposition in that 63%–95% of patients are HLA-B27 positive. It has become clear that Reiter syndrome develops in a genetically susceptible host following an infection by bacteria such as *Chlamydia trachomatis* in the genitourinary tract or by *Salmonella, Shigella, Yersinia,* or *Campylobacter* in the gastrointestinal tract. Fragments of *Yersinia, Salmonella,* and *Chlamydia* have been identified in the synovial tissues of patients with Reiter syndrome, but intact organisms have not been cultured. The male-to-female ratio is at least 5:1.

The arthritis of Reiter syndrome typically appears within 1–3 weeks of the inciting urethritis or diarrhea. It is an asymmetric, episodic oligoarthritis affecting primarily the lower extremities, in particular the large joints such as the knees or ankles. Other articular features include periostitis, particularly heel pain, interphalangeal arthritis of the toes and fingers producing "sausage digits," and sacroiliitis. Mucocutaneous lesions include urethritis in men and cervicitis in women, circinate balanitis, painless oral ulcers, nail lesions, and keratoderma blenorrhagicum. Patients may also have systemic symptoms including fever and weight loss. The disease tends to follow an episodic and relapsing course. Systemic treatment includes NSAIDs and sulfasalazine in addition to appropriate antibiotic therapy. Patients should undergo HIV testing prior to consideration of immunosuppressive therapy.

Ophthalmologic considerations   Conjunctivitis is one of the hallmarks of the disease and is part of the original triad described by Reiter. The more serious ocular manifestation is uveitis, which, as in ankylosing spondylitis, is an acute, nongranulomatous, recurrent iridocyclitis that occurs in 15%–25% of patients with Reiter syndrome.

Inflammatory Bowel Disease

Inflammatory bowel disease consists of two distinct diseases: ulcerative colitis and Crohn disease. *Ulcerative colitis* is an inflammatory disorder of the gastrointestinal mucosa with diffuse involvement of the colon. *Crohn disease* is a focal granulomatous disease involving all areas of the bowel and affecting both the large and small intestine. Crohn disease is also known as *regional enteritis, granulomatous ileocolitis,* and *granulomatous colitis.* Symptoms of inflammatory bowel disease include diarrhea, bloody diarrhea, and cramping abdominal pain.

Extraintestinal manifestations of inflammatory bowel disease include dermatitis, mucous membrane disease, ocular inflammation, and arthritis. Skin disorders occur in approximately 15% of patients with inflammatory bowel disease and include erythema nodosum and pyoderma gangrenosum. Arthritis occurs in up to 22% of patients and is seen in two distinct variants. *Enteropathic (colitic) arthritis* is a predominantly lower-extremity, nondeforming oligoarthritis. The activity of enteropathic arthritis parallels the activity of the bowel disease. The second type is *ankylosing spondylitis,* which is present in at least 7%–12% of patients with inflammatory bowel disease. The activity of the spondylitis is unrelated to the activity of the bowel disease. Multiple series have shown that 50% of patients with spondylitis and inflammatory bowel disease are HLA-B27 positive. Those who are HLA-B27 positive are more likely to develop spondylitis and iridocyclitis. Ocular inflammation, including iridocyclitis, scleritis, and less commonly, retinal vasculitis, occurs in approximately 3%–11% of patients with inflammatory bowel disease.

Juvenile Rheumatoid Arthritis

Juvenile rheumatoid arthritis (JRA) is defined as an arthritis of greater than 6 consecutive weeks' duration with an onset before 16 years of age. JRA is commonly classified by the pattern of presentation of the arthritis: polyarticular arthritis (polyarthritis), pauciarticular arthritis (pauciarthritis), and systemic disease. *Polyarthritis* is defined as presentation with more than five joints involved, while *pauciarthritis* involves four or fewer. *Systemic disease,* the disorder originally described by Still, has prominent systemic features with a variable arthritis.

More recently, specific subgroups of JRA have been defined. Some children with pauciarticular arthritis appear to have a juvenile-onset ankylosing spondylitis. These children have a mean age of onset of 12 years old and a male-to-female ratio of 5:1. The arthritis is pauciarticular and affects the large joints and lower extremities. Sacroiliitis is common, and many of these children progress to classic ankylosing spondylitis with time. More than half of these children are HLA-B27 positive, and about one quarter will develop an acute recurrent iridocyclitis. The disease appears to share the clinical and immunogenetic features of the seronegative spondyloarthropathies in adults, including the same types of arthritis and uveitis.

Older children (over 10 years of age) may develop a seropositive (rheumatoid-factor positive), rheumatoid-like polyarthritis. Among this subgroup, girls are more commonly affected than boys. The arthritis is an additive, symmetrical, deforming polyarticular arthritis identical to adult rheumatoid arthritis, tends to be persistent, and results in severe morbidity. Ocular disease is uncommon in this subgroup.

The systemic variant of JRA is also known as *Still disease.* The male-to-female ratio is approximately 1:1, and it affects young children, generally under 5 years of age. The arthritis has a variable relation to the onset of disease but generally presents as a polyarthritis. The systemic features predominate and include fever, a salmon-colored evanescent maculopapular rash, lymphadenopathy, hepatitis, splenomegaly, serositis, an elevated erythrocyte sedimentation rate, and leukocytosis. Ocular disease is generally not associated with this variant.

Antinuclear antibody (ANA) positive pauciarticular disease is generally seen in children under 5 years of age, and girls are affected more often than boys. Over 80% of these patients have a positive ANA. The arthritis is an oligoarticular, large-joint, lower-extremity arthritis, which tends to spontaneously remit without leaving significant articular deformities. The most severe manifestation of this disease is *chronic iridocyclitis,* which often responds poorly to treatment and may cause serious visual disability. Because these children are usually asymptomatic, early detection can occur only with regular ophthalmologic slit-lamp examination. (See BCSC Section 6, *Pediatric Ophthalmology and Strabismus;* and Section 9, *Intraocular Inflammation and Uveitis.*)

Systemic Lupus Erythematosus

Systemic lupus erythematosus (SLE) is generally regarded as the prototypical autoimmune disease. The etiology of SLE is unknown, but familial aggregation of autoimmune diseases and the association with the HLA types HLA-DR2 and DR3 suggest a genetic predisposition. Pathogenetically, SLE is characterized by B-cell hyperreactivity, polyclonal B-cell activation, hypergammaglobulinemia, and a plethora of autoantibodies. These autoantibodies include antinuclear antibodies (ANA), antibodies to DNA (both single-stranded DNA [anti-ssDNA] and double-stranded or native DNA [anti-dsDNA or anti-nDNA]), and antibodies to cytoplasmic components. SLE classically has been considered an immune complex disease, in which immune complexes incite an inflammatory response and lead to tissue damage.

SLE affects women five times as often as men, and the disease may affect almost any organ system. Cutaneous disease, which occurs in approximately 70%–80% of patients, is most often manifested by the characteristic butterfly rash across the nose and cheeks, also known as a *malar flush.* Other cutaneous manifestations include discoid lesions, vasculitic skin lesions such as cutaneous ulcers or splinter hemorrhages, purpuric skin lesions, and alopecia. Less common skin lesions include a maculopapular eruption, lupus profundus, bullous skin lesions, and urticarial skin lesions. Mucosal lesions, characteristically painless oral ulcers, occur in 30%–40% of patients. Photosensitivity occurs in many patients with SLE.

About 80%–85% of patients with SLE will have articular disease at some point, either polyarthralgias or a nondeforming, migratory polyarthritis. Cutaneous nodules, myalgias, and myositis are far less common. Systemic features, including fatigue, fever, and weight loss, occur in over 80% of patients with lupus. Renal disease is present in approximately 50%–75% of patients with SLE. Clinically, it presents as either proteinuria with nephrotic characteristics or glomerulonephritis with an active urinary sediment. Lupus nephritis is a major cause of the morbidity and mortality of SLE.

Raynaud's phenomenon occurs in 30%–50% of patients. Cardiac disease includes pericarditis, occasionally myocarditis, and Libman-Sacks endocarditis. Pleuropulmonary lesions include pleuritic chest pain and, less commonly, pneumonitis. Hepatosplenomegaly and adenopathy can be seen in over 50% of patients with SLE. Central nervous system (CNS) involvement occurs in more than 35% of patients with SLE. Peripheral neuropathy and cranial nerve palsies are less common.

The most common manifestations of CNS lupus are headache, seizures, an organic brain syndrome, and psychosis. Transverse myelitis is an uncommon manifestation in patients with SLE but is often seen in association with optic neuritis.

The hematologic system is frequently affected by SLE. Patients often have an anemia of chronic disease but may also develop an autoimmune hemolytic anemia. Leukopenia, in particular lymphopenia, is a characteristic feature. Thrombocytopenia occurs in approximately one third of patients.

Because of the diffuse manifestations of SLE, the following diagnostic criteria have been established:

□ Malar rash

□ Discoid lupus

□ Photosensitivity

□ Oral ulcers

□ Arthritis

□ Serositis (pleuritis, pericarditis)

□ Renal disorder (proteinuria, nephritis)

□ Neurologic disorder (seizures, psychosis)

□ Hematologic disorder (hemolytic anemia, leukopenia, lymphopenia, thrombocytopenia)

□ Immunologic disorder (positive LE cell preparation, anti-DNA test, anti-Sm, false-positive test for syphilis)

□ Antinuclear antibody

Four or more of these criteria are needed in order to establish a diagnosis of SLE. It should be emphasized that these criteria are used in clinical investigation and not for patient management.

Ophthalmologic Considerations

The major ocular manifestations of SLE are

□ Involvement of the skin of the eyelids with cutaneous disease, most often discoid lesions

□ Secondary Sjögren syndrome

□ Retinal vascular lesions

□ Neuro-ophthalmic lesions

Retinal vascular manifestations are the most common form of ophthalmic involvement in patients with SLE. They consist of cotton-wool spots with or without intraretinal hemorrhages. The prevalence varies from 3% of outpatients to 28%–29% of hospitalized patients. Neuro-ophthalmic involvement in SLE includes cranial nerve palsies, lupus optic neuropathy, and central retrochiasmal disorders of vision. The cerebral disorders of vision include hallucinations, visual field defects, and cortical blindness.

Scleroderma

Scleroderma, also known as *progressive systemic sclerosis,* is a systemic connective tissue disease of unknown etiology characterized by fibrous and degenerative changes in the skin and viscera. It is much more common in women and rare in childhood. In addition to the thickening and fibrous replacement of the dermis, the disease is characterized by vascular insufficiency and vasospasm. The hallmark of scleroderma is the skin change, which consists of thickening, tightening, and induration, with subsequent loss of mobility and contracture. The disease most characteristically begins peripherally and involves the fingers and hands, with a subsequent centripetal spread up the arms to involve the face and body. Telangiectasia and calcinosis are common. More than 95% of scleroderma patients will have Raynaud's phenomenon, and some will develop digital ulcers.

Organ involvement is common and includes esophageal dysmotility with gastroesophageal reflux in over 90% of patients. The small and large intestines may be involved with decreased motility, malabsorption, and diverticulosis. Cardiopulmonary disease is manifested primarily by pulmonary fibrosis, which results in restrictive lung disease with a decreased diffusing capacity. The consequences of the interstitial fibrosis include pulmonary hypertension and right heart failure. Conduction abnormalities and arrhythmias occur as a consequence of cardiac fibrosis. Musculoskeletal features include polyarthralgias, tendon friction rubs, and occasionally myositis.

Renal disease is a major cause of mortality and is often associated with the onset of malignant hypertension and a rapid progression to renal failure. This process is sometimes known as *scleroderma renal crisis* or *scleroderma kidney.* This complication was uniformly fatal until the late 1970s; however, aggressive antihypertensive therapy may sometimes reverse the scleroderma renal crisis. ACE inhibitors are very effective in treating the hypertension associated with scleroderma renal disease and in delaying the progression to renal failure.

A spectrum of disease is associated with scleroderma. The *CREST syndrome* is named for its features of *C*alcinosis, *R*aynaud's phenomenon, *E*sophageal dysmotility, *S*clerodactyly, and *T*elangiectasia. This syndrome appears to have a more benign and more slowly progressive course than systemic sclerosis. *Diffuse systemic sclerosis* is a more rapidly progressive skin disease with more severe visceral involvement. *Overlap syndromes* occur between scleroderma and other diseases. The best-known overlap syndrome is *mixed connective tissue disease (MCTD),* which has features of systemic lupus erythematosus, systemic sclerosis, and myositis. It is characterized by antibodies to ribonuclear protein (RNP), and it has been suggested that some of its clinical features respond to steroids.

Ophthalmologic Considerations

Ocular manifestations of scleroderma include eyelid involvement resulting in tightness and blepharophimosis (but only rarely corneal exposure); conjunctival vascular abnormalities, including telangiectasia and vascular sludging; and keratoconjunctivitis sicca. Occasionally, a patient develops retinopathy of malignant hypertension, with cotton-wool spots, intraretinal hemorrhages, and optic disc edema, as a result of scleroderma renal crisis.

Polymyositis and Dermatomyositis

Polymyositis and dermatomyositis are inflammatory diseases of skeletal muscle characterized by pain and weakness in the involved muscular groups. Typically, weakness begins insidiously and involves the proximal muscle groups, particularly those of the shoulders and hips. *Dermatomyositis* is distinguished from *polymyositis* by the presence of cutaneous lesions. These skin lesions are an erythematous to violaceous rash variably affecting the eyelids (heliotrope rash), cheeks, nose, chest, and extensor surfaces. The knuckles of the fingers may develop plaques known as *Gottron's papules*. The diagnosis of myositis is based upon the characteristic clinical features and abnormal laboratory tests. Laboratory abnormalities include elevated serum levels of skeletal muscle enzymes, abnormal electromyography, and a muscle biopsy revealing muscle damage and inflammation.

Polymyositis and dermatomyositis have been classified into seven groups:

- Primary idiopathic polymyositis
- Primary idiopathic dermatomyositis
- Dermatomyositis (or polymyositis) associated with malignancy
- Childhood dermatomyositis (or polymyositis)
- Polymyositis or dermatomyositis associated with collagen vascular disease (overlap group)
- Inclusion body myositis
- Miscellaneous: eosinophilic myositis, localized nodular myositis, and others

Dermatomyositis with malignancy is seen most often in patients over 50 years of age and rarely in young patients. Vasculitis is common in patients with childhood dermatomyositis. Inflammatory myositis with a defined connective tissue disease is seen most often in association with systemic lupus erythematosus or scleroderma.

Ophthalmologic Considerations

Other than the heliotrope rash of dermatomyositis, ocular involvement is relatively uncommon in inflammatory myositis. Occasionally, ophthalmoplegia due to involvement of the extraocular muscles by the myositis may occur.

Sjögren Syndrome

Sjögren syndrome was originally described as a triad of dry eyes, dry mouth, and rheumatoid arthritis. Subsequently, it became apparent that Sjögren syndrome could coexist with a variety of other connective tissue diseases, including systemic lupus erythematosus and scleroderma (secondary Sjögren syndrome) or without a definable connective tissue disease (primary Sjögren syndrome).

The cause of the dry eyes and dry mouth in patients with Sjögren syndrome is a mononuclear inflammatory infiltrate into the lacrimal and salivary glands, resulting in glandular destruction and dysfunction. Several studies have demonstrated that the minor salivary gland biopsy is a useful tool for documenting the presence of such an inflammatory infiltrate. Patients with Sjögren syndrome often have autoantibodies to the Ro and La antigens; these antigens are also known as SSA (Sjögren syndrome-A) and SSB (Sjögren syndrome-B) respectively. Preliminary criteria for the diagnosis of Sjögren syndrome have recently been published, including parameters referring to oral and ocular symptoms, ocular signs, salivary gland involvement, histopathologic features, and the presence of autoantibodies anti-Ro/SSA and anti-La/SSA. The presence of four out of six items exhibited a high sensitivity and specificity (Table VIII-1). There appears to be a subset of primary Sjögren syndrome patients who have vasculitis, hyperglobulinemia, CNS lesions, and an increased risk of malignancy, particularly lymphoma. Treatment is aimed at symptomatic relief and substitution of the missing secretions. (See also BCSC Section 8, *External Disease and Cornea.*)

Relapsing Polychondritis

Relapsing polychondritis is an episodic disorder characterized by recurrent, widespread, potentially destructive inflammation of cartilage, the cardiovascular system, and the organs of special sense. The most common clinical features are auricular inflammation, arthropathy, and nasal cartilage inflammation. Auricular chondritis

TABLE VIII-1

PRELIMINARY CRITERIA FOR THE CLASSIFICATION OF SJÖGREN SYNDROME

1. Ocular symptoms
   A positive response to at least 1 of the following 3 questions:
      (a) Have you had daily, persistent, troublesome dry eyes for more than 3 months?
      (b) Do you have recurrent sandy or gravelly feeling in the eyes?
      (c) Do you use tear substitutes more than 3 times a day?

2. Oral symptoms
   A positive response to at least 1 of the following 3 questions:
      (a) Have you had a daily feeling of dry mouth for more than 3 months?
      (b) Have you had recurrent or persistently swollen salivary glands as an adult?
      (c) Do you frequently drink liquids to aid in swallowing dry foods?

3. Ocular signs
   Objective evidence of ocular involvement determined on the basis of a positive result on at least 1 of the following 2 tests:
      (a) Schirmer-1 test (≤5 mm in 5 minutes)
      (b) Rose bengal score (≥4, according to the van Bijsterveld scoring system)

4. Salivary gland involvement
   Objective evidence of salivary gland involvement, determined on the basis of a positive result on at least 1 of the following 3 tests:
      (a) Salivary scintigraphy
      (b) Parotid sialography
      (c) Unstimulated salivary flow (≤1.5 ml in 15 minutes)

5. Histopathologic findings
   Focus score ≥1 on minor salivary gland biopsy
   (focus defined as an agglomeration of at least 50 mononuclear cells, focus score defined as the number of foci/4mm^2 of glandular tissue)

6. Autoantibodies
   Presence of at least 1 of the following autoantibodies in the serum: Antibodies to Ro (SS-A) or La (SS-B) antigens or antinuclear antibodies or rheumatoid factor

A patient is considered as having probable Sjögren syndrome if 3 of 6 criteria are present, and as definite if 4 of 6 criteria are present.

and nasal chondritis are the features that most often suggest the diagnosis. Laryngotracheobronchial disease may lead to a fatal complication from laryngeal collapse. Involvement of the internal ear, cardiovascular system, and skin are less common. Cardiovascular lesions include aortic insufficiency due to progressive dilation of the aortic root, and vasculitis. Skin lesions are most often due to cutaneous vasculitis. Over 30% of patients will have an associated autoimmune disease such as systemic vasculitis, SLE, or rheumatoid arthritis; Sjögren syndrome; and even Hodgkin disease or diabetes mellitus.

The pathogenesis of relapsing polychondritis appears to be due to autoantibodies to collagen types II, IX, and XI. This appears to be mediated by CD4+ lymphocytes. In some of the reported cases, the autoantibody titer has correlated with the clinical course and severity of the disease. Ocular manifestations occur in about 50% of patients with relapsing polychondritis. The most common ocular conditions are conjunctivitis, scleritis, uveitis, and retinal vasculitis.

Vasculitis

The spectrum of vasculitis is outlined in Table VIII-2. The *polyarteritis group of systemic necrotizing vasculitis* is characterized by necrotizing vasculitis of the medium- and small-sized muscular arteries. *Hypersensitivity vasculitis,* also known as *allergic vasculitis* or *leukocytoclastic vasculitis,* is characterized by involvement of the post-capillary venules with infiltration of polymorphonuclear leukocytes and leukocytoclasis. *Wegener granulomatosis* is characterized by granuloma formation and vasculitis. *Temporal,* or *giant cell, arteritis* is characterized by involvement of large- and medium-sized arteries with a chronic inflammation, giant cells, and internal elastic lamina damage.

Systemic Necrotizing Vasculitis

Polyarteritis nodosa   The polyarteritis group of systemic necrotizing vasculitis is subdivided into classic *polyarteritis nodosa (PAN)* and *allergic granulomatosis (Churg-Strauss angiitis)*. Both types are characterized by necrotizing vasculitis of the

TABLE VIII-2

OUTLINE OF THE VASCULITIDES

Systemic necrotizing vasculitis
   Classic polyarteritis nodosa
   Allergic granulomatosis (Churg-Strauss angiitis)
   Overlap syndrome
Hypersensitivity vasculitis
   Serum sickness
   Henoch-Schonlein purpura
   Vasculitis with connective tissue disease
   Vasculitis with malignancy
Wegener granulomatosis
Lymphomatoid granulomatosis
Giant cell (temporal) arteritis
Takayasu arteritis

medium- and small-sized muscular arteries. The lesions are segmental, and lesions in different stages of development are present simultaneously. Medium-sized arteries often develop aneurysms, which can be detected by angiography. In classic polyarteritis nodosa, eosinophilia, granulomas, and an allergic history are not present. Renal involvement is common, related to either vasculitis or glomerulonephritis. Hypertension develops as a consequence of the renal disease, and gastrointestinal disease with infarction of the viscera can occur. Neurologic disease can present as a mononeuritis multiplex or as CNS lesions.

The mean age of onset of PAN is in the 40–50 year age group, and men are affected more often than women. Survival in patients with untreated PAN is poor. However, most patients are now treated with a combination of corticosteroids and an immunosuppressive drug such as cyclophosphamide, and this therapy appears to improve disease control and long-term outcome.

Ocular manifestations occur in approximately 10%–20% of patients with PAN and include hypertensive retinopathy in patients with renal disease, ischemic retinopathy from the vasculitis, CNS lesions resulting in visual loss (e.g., homonymous hemianopia), cranial nerve palsies, scleritis, and marginal corneal ulceration. *Cogan syndrome,* manifested by interstitial keratitis, hearing loss, tinnitus, and vertigo, is associated with PAN in up to 50% of cases (see also BCSC Section 8, *External Disease and Cornea*).

Allergic granulomatosis (Churg-Strauss angiitis) An allergic diathesis, particularly asthma, is present in allergic granulomatosis. Lung disease is the sine qua non for making the diagnosis. Eosinophilia is generally present, and pathological examination often shows granulomas with eosinophilic tissue infiltration. In addition to the arteriole fibrinoid necrosis seen in classic PAN, the small vessels, capillaries, and venules are often involved. The vasculitis-related ocular complications seen in classic PAN also occur in allergic granulomatosis. Additionally, conjunctival granulomas have been reported in patients with allergic granulomatosis.

Wegener Granulomatosis

Wegener granulomatosis was originally described as the classic triad of necrotizing granulomatous vasculitis of the upper respiratory tract, lower respiratory tract, and focal segmental glomerulonephritis. The clinical features of Wegener granulomatosis include granulomatous inflammation of the paranasal sinuses in 90% of cases, nasopharyngeal disease in 63%, cutaneous vasculitis in 45%, and vasculitis affecting the nervous system in 25%. Ocular disease occurs in up to 60% of patients with Wegener granulomatosis and includes scleritis with or without peripheral keratitis, orbital pseudotumor, and vasculitis-mediated retinal vascular or neuro-ophthalmic lesions. Serum antibodies that react with cytoplasmic components of neutrophils (ANCA) are present in the majority of patients. Approximately 80% of patients with Wegener granulomatosis are serum positive for C-ANCA. (See also BCSC Section 9, *Intraocular Inflammation and Uveitis*.)

Prior to the use of immunosuppressive drugs, Wegener granulomatosis was a uniformly fatal disease, with a mean untreated survival of 5 months. With corticosteroid treatment, the mean survival increased to 12.5 months; long-term survival was seen only in patients with limited disease. However, the use of cytotoxic drugs has dramatically improved the outcome for patients with Wegener granulomatosis.

Treatment generally consists of cyclophosphamide 1–2 mg/kg/day, and prednisone initially at 1 mg/kg/day, subsequently tapered to an every other day schedule and then discontinued. Cyclophosphamide is continued for 1 year after a complete remission has been achieved; the patient is then tapered off this drug. The best results with this treatment regimen have been reported by the National Institutes of Health, where 93% of patients successfully achieved a remission. Although some patients relapse when the cyclophosphamide is discontinued, a second remission can be achieved with reinduction therapy. Complications of this treatment include leukopenia, hemorrhagic cystitis, gonadal dysfunction, alopecia, and neoplasia.

Giant Cell (Temporal) Arteritis

Giant cell arteritis (GCA) has been described in all races, although whites are most often affected. It is a disease of the elderly, rarely occurring in patients under 50 years old. It is particularly common in northern climates such as Scandinavia, Great Britain, and the northern United States. Autopsy studies in Scandinavia have estimated the prevalence of GCA at 1.1% of the population.

The clinical features of giant cell arteritis include headache, polymyalgia rheumatica (PMR), jaw claudication, constitutional symptoms such as fever and malaise, and ophthalmic symptoms. The signs of GCA include tenderness over the temporal artery, a pulseless temporal artery, scalp tenderness, fever, and loss of vision. PMR is a symptom complex of proximal muscle pain and weakness that may occur by itself without overt GCA.

The laboratory test most commonly abnormal in GCA is the erythrocyte sedimentation rate (ESR), with more than 90% of patients showing an elevated ESR. A recent study suggested that a marked acute phase reactant response, defined by an elevated ESR and an elevated serum C-reactive protein, appears to have strong predictive value in identifying patients with GCA. Care must be taken in interpreting the ESR, as the method used must be known. For example, markedly elevated ESRs are obtained with the Westergren method. In patients with GCA tested by the Westergren method, the median ESR is 96 mm/hr, with a range of 50–132 mm/hr. Studies stating that the normal ESR in elderly patients can be as high as 40 mm/hr have used the Westergren method. The Wintrobe method uses a closed-end tube and produces lower ESR rates than the Westergren. The mean ESR in patients with GCA tested by the Wintrobe method is 51 mm/hr, with a range of 38–59 mm/hr.

The definitive test for the diagnosis of giant cell arteritis is the temporal artery biopsy. Approximately 18%–45% of patients with PMR have giant cell arteritis as defined by a temporal artery biopsy. The characteristic features in a temporal artery biopsy are occlusion of the vessel lumen with either thrombus or subintimal edema and cellular proliferation. There are fragmentations of the internal elastic lamina and a patchy degeneration of smooth muscle cells. Granulomatous inflammation of the vessel wall affects the media, adventitia, and subintima. The inflammatory material is composed of lymphocytes, plasma cells, histiocytes, epithelioid cells, and giant cells. Temporal artery biopsies can occasionally be negative on one side and positive on the other. Two studies have suggested that the prevalence of false-negative unilateral biopsies is in the 4%–5% range. These are due to the presence of skip areas in the temporal artery biopsy.

Giant cell arteritis is treated with systemic corticosteroids. Because untreated GCA has the potential to cause blindness, treatment should be initiated as soon as the diagnosis is suspected. The initial prednisone dosage is approximately 1 mg/kg/day (60–80 mg daily). Generally, the symptoms will respond promptly within several days. Alternate-day steroids are ineffective in the initial treatment of GCA.

Some studies have suggested that GCA is a self-limited disease that will run its course in 1–2 years. These studies recommend steroid therapy for 1–2 years. Treatment is generally instituted at the initial high dose and slowly tapered using the ESR and clinical symptoms to monitor disease. Occasionally, longer-lasting disease requiring longer-term treatment will be seen.

Ophthalmologic considerations The most frequent ocular manifestation of GCA is ischemic optic neuropathy. Other ocular manifestations include amaurosis fugax, ischemic retinopathy, occasionally diplopia and/or ophthalmoplegia due to ischemia to the extraocular muscles, the ocular ischemic syndrome, choroidal ischemia, and cortical blindness. (Ocular involvement by GCA is discussed in BCSC Section 5, *Neuro-Ophthalmology*.)

Takayasu Arteritis

Takayasu arteritis affects large arteries, particularly branches of the aorta. It occurs primarily in children and young women. The disease is rare in the Western world but common in the Far East, particularly Japan. Other names for Takayasu arteritis include *aortic arch arteritis, aortitis syndrome,* and *pulseless disease.*

The disease may involve the entire aorta or be localized to any segment of the aorta or its primary branches. The inflammatory process is characterized by a panarteritis with a granulomatous inflammation. The involved vessels may ultimately become narrowed or obliterated, resulting in ischemia to the supplied tissues. Areas of weakened vascular wall may develop dissections or aneurysms.

Systemic features such as fatigue, weight loss, or low-grade fever are common. Evidence of vascular insufficiency due to large-artery narrowing or reduction leads to the characteristic pulseless phase. The disease is most often diagnosed using arteriography. Treatment is generally with systemic corticosteroids, which may successfully suppress the disease. Cyclophosphamide or methotrexate are added in resistant cases. Surgical reconstruction of damaged vessels may be necessary.

Ophthalmologic considerations The most characteristic ocular findings are retinal arteriovenous anastomoses, best demonstrated by fluorescein angiography. Earlier, milder changes are small-vessel dilation and microaneurysm formation, while more severe ischemia may result in peripheral retinal nonperfusion, neovascularization, and vitreous hemorrhage.

Behçet Syndrome

Behçet syndrome was initially described as a triad of oral ulcers, genital ulcers, and uveitis with hypopyon. It is now recognized as a multisystem illness. The disease is most common in the Middle East and Far East, particularly Japan. Oral ulcers are the most common clinical feature, seen in 98%–99% of patients. Genital ulcers occur in 80%–87%; skin disease occurs in 69%–90% and includes erythema nodosum, superficial thrombophlebitis, and pyoderma. Some 44%–59% of patients have an asymmetric, nondeforming, large-joint polyarthritis that frequently is responsive to steroids.

Vascular disease, which occurs in 10%–35% of patients, can present as a migratory superficial thrombophlebitis, major vessel thrombosis, arterial aneurysms, or even peripheral gangrene. CNS disease, found in 10%–30% of patients, has been classically divided into three types: brain stem syndrome, meningoencephalitis, and confusional states. Most often patients present with combinations of the three. The major cause of mortality in Behçet syndrome is CNS involvement.

Treatment

The clinical impression of most authors is that corticosteroids can delay disease progression but do not alter the ultimate outcome. Since the early 1970s, immunosuppressive drugs have been used in the treatment of Behçet syndrome. *Chlorambucil* (0.1–0.2 mg/kg/day) has been the most frequently used drug. Other studies have used *cyclophosphamide* (1–2 mg/kg/day). In many cases, the use of such immunosuppressive drugs has arrested the disease process, and studies have suggested that a long-term remission can be induced with 1–2 years of treatment. The indications for the use of immunosuppressive drugs have been either ocular or neurologic Behçet syndrome. Cyclosporine has also been reported to be highly effective in the treatment of Behçet syndrome, but it has the side effect of nephrotoxicity.

Ophthalmologic Considerations

The most common ocular manifestations are iridocyclitis, with or without hypopyon, and retinal vasculitis. The natural history of retinal vasculitis in Behçet syndrome is poor. The majority of untreated patients will lose all or part of their vision within 5 years.

Medical Therapy for Rheumatic Disorders

Corticosteroids

The adrenal cortex synthesizes three types of corticosteroids: glucocorticoids, mineralocorticoids, and androgens. However, only the glucocorticoids have anti-inflammatory activity. Although the mechanism of the anti-inflammatory effect is complex, it appears to involve the inhibition of prostaglandin synthesis by preventing the release of the prostaglandin precursor, arachidonic acid, from membrane phospholipids.

In addition to their anti-inflammatory activity, glucocorticoids have a variety of other effects. Gluconeogenesis is promoted, with concomitant protein reduction and negative nitrogen balance. Fat oxidation, synthesis, storage, and mobilization are also affected. Glucocorticoids exert a broad range of effects on circulating leukocytes. They produce lymphocytopenia, which lasts for about 24 hours. Circulating neutrophils increase, because mature neutrophils are released from bone marrow and movement from blood to other tissues decreases. Other circulating leukocytes decrease after glucocorticoid administration. Associated mineralocorticoid activity increases sodium retention and potassium excretion.

The molecular structure of the steroid nucleus can be modified to dissociate glucocorticoid from mineralocorticoid activity. However, although synthetic glucocorticoids have been produced with variable levels of biological potency, the goal of dissociating beneficial anti-inflammatory effects from the harmful side effects of glucocorticoid activity has not been achieved. In some instances, undesirable metabolic effects can be reduced by administering the total 48-hour dose of corticosteroids during the early morning every other day. Alternate-day therapy is preferred for maintenance whenever feasible and is reported to be particularly effective in asthma, systemic lupus erythematosus, uveitis, and nephrotic syndrome. However, alternate-day therapy may not be adequate in severe conditions such as renal transplantation or certain hematologic and malignant disorders. Further, this regimen is not effective with steroids that have prolonged effects, such as those with substitution at the 16 position of the steroid nucleus (triamcinolone, paramethasone, betamethasone, and dexamethasone).

The ophthalmologist must be aware of both ocular and systemic toxicity in patients who are receiving systemic steroids. Ocular side effects of systemic steroids include development of posterior subcapsular cataracts, glaucoma, mydriasis, ptosis, papilledema associated with pseudotumor cerebri, reactivation or aggravation of ocular infection, and delay of wound healing. Systemic complications may include peptic ulceration, osteoporosis, compression fracture, negative nitrogen balance, aseptic necrosis of the femoral head, muscle and skin atrophy, hyperglycemia, hypertension, edema, weight gain, hyperosmolar nonketotic coma, hypokalemia, mental changes, pseudotumor cerebri, changes in body fat distribution seen in Cushing habitus, and growth retardation in children.

Another frequently overlooked complication of systemic steroid therapy is the effect of rapid withdrawal from the drugs. Several patterns of response to steroid withdrawal have been described. They include hypothalamic-pituitary-adrenal (HPA) axis suppression with or without symptoms, exacerbation of the disease being treated, and physical or psychological dependence with otherwise normal function. The rate of steroid withdrawal should be determined by the degree of HPA suppression (related to dose and duration of therapy) and the response of the underlying disease.

A variety of schedules have been suggested. Glucocorticoids given in large doses for 1–3 days probably suppress HPA function only temporarily, so they can be withdrawn suddenly or gradually over 1 week. After 1 or more months of treatment, a dosage-reduction protocol is usually followed. Otherwise, sudden withdrawal of steroid therapy may produce adrenal insufficiency, with the symptoms of fatigue, weakness, arthralgias, anorexia, nausea, orthostatic hypotension, fainting, dyspnea, and hypoglycemia. In severe cases, adrenal suppression may be fatal. After steroid therapy has been discontinued, it may take 1 year or more for adrenal function to return to normal; thus, supplementary steroids may be needed if the patient has a serious illness or undergoes a surgical procedure during this recovery period.

Some patients become psychologically dependent on glucocorticoids, particularly those who have been given repeated courses of therapy for recurring problems such as asthma or certain dermatological conditions. Since euphoria and rapid relief occur when glucocorticoid therapy is initiated, it may be difficult to convince the patient to accept repeated withdrawals of medication and the attendant discomforts.

Because of the likelihood of withdrawal symptoms, even physiologic doses of long-term steroids (20 mg of hydrocortisone or 5 mg of prednisone a day) should be gradually tapered off. Moreover, patients presently on long-term corticosteroid therapy or who have had significant corticosteroid therapy within the previous 9 months should wear an identification bracelet with information regarding the need for supplemental steroids during acute stress or illness and prior to any major surgical procedure.

Nonsteroidal Anti-Inflammatory Drugs

A wide variety of nonsteroidal anti-inflammatory agents have been developed in recent years to treat rheumatoid arthritis and other rheumatic diseases. The names of and starting dosages for some of these agents are listed in Table VIII-3. Aspirin and indomethacin are also included for comparison. All of these agents inhibit prostaglandin synthesis, although they may also have other actions that add to their therapeutic efficacy. These drugs are all analgesic, antipyretic, and anti-inflammatory. Their relative efficacy remains largely untested, and individual patients vary in their responsiveness to these drugs.

The exact role of nonsteroidal agents in treating ocular inflammation remains uncertain. Systemic *indomethacin*, for example, appears effective in treating scleritis. Many of the drugs have also been tried for postsurgical analgesia and as anti-inflammatory agents in patients with uveitis or cystoid macular edema. In general, these drugs are not as effective as corticosteroids. Several topical nonsteroidal anti-inflammatory agents have been approved for ocular use. *Flurbiprofen* (Ocufen) is used primarily to control intraoperative miosis during anterior segment surgery. *Diclofenac* (Voltaren) has been approved for the treatment of postoperative inflammation following cataract surgery. *Ketorolac tromethamine* (Acular) is approved for treating the symptoms of allergic conjunctivitis but has also been studied for the relief of pain following corneal injuries or erosions. Both ketorolac and diclofenac are used to relieve postoperative pain following excimer laser photorefractive keratectomy.

The most common side effects of oral nonsteroidal anti-inflammatory agents are gastrointestinal symptoms, including nausea, vomiting, diarrhea, anorexia, and abdominal pain. Gastrointestinal bleeding and ulceration may occur. *Misoprostol* (Cytotec), a synthetic prostaglandin E_1 analogue, is indicated for the prevention of NSAID-induced gastric ulcers in patients at high risk for this complication. It is contraindicated in pregnant women. Oral NSAID agents can interfere with platelet function and clotting. Some of these agents have also been reported to cause bone-marrow suppression, hepatic toxicity, depressed renal function, and CNS symptoms, including headache, dizziness, and confusion. Asthmatic attacks and other

TABLE VIII-3

NONSTEROIDAL ANTI-INFLAMMATORY DRUGS

DRUG	STARTING DOSE
Aspirin*	650 mg qid
Indomethacin (Indocin)	25 mg tid
Diclofenac (Voltaren)	50 mg bid
Etodolac (Lodine)	300 mg bid or tid
Ibuprofen (Motrin)*	400 mg qid
Ketoprofen (Orudis)*	75 mg tid
Nabumetone (Relafen)	1000 mg q day
Naproxen (Naprosyn)*	250 mg bid
Oxaprozin (Daypro)	1200 mg q day
Piroxicam (Feldene)	20 mg qid
Sulindac (Clinoril)	150 mg bid

* Available over the counter.

hypersensitivity reactions may occur in susceptible patients. Indomethacin has also been noted to cause corneal deposits and perhaps retinal toxicity, although this remains unproven. Ibuprofen has been reported to cause optic neuritis.

Hayreh SS, Podhajsky PA, Raman R, et al. Giant cell arteritis: validity and reliability of various diagnostic criteria. *Am J Ophthalmol.* 1997;123:285–296.

Manthorpe R, Asmussen K, Oxholm P. Primary Sjögren's syndrome: diagnostic criteria, clinical features, and disease activity. *J Rheumatol.* 1997;24(suppl50):8–11.

Schumacher HR, ed. *Primer on the Rheumatic Diseases.* 10th ed. Atlanta: Arthritis Foundation; 1993.

Vitali C, Bombadieri S, Moutsopoulos HM, et al. Preliminary criteria for the classification of Sjögren's syndrome. Results of a prospective concerted action supported by the European Community. *Arthritis Rheum.* 1993;36:340–347.

CHAPTER IX

Endocrine Disorders

Recent Developments

☐ Insulin-dependent diabetes mellitus is now considered to be an autoimmune disorder, with islet-cell and anti-insulin antibodies detectable in the serum of most patients.

☐ Metformin, a new oral agent for non–insulin-dependent diabetes mellitus, lowers blood glucose and improves insulin sensitivity. When used appropriately, it does not appear to cause hypoglycemia and has a low incidence of lactic acidosis.

☐ The TSH immunometric assay (TSH-IMA), or "sensitive TSH test," has simplified screening for hyperthyroidism.

Diabetes Mellitus

The definition and diagnosis of diabetes mellitus have undergone considerable change in recent years. The National Diabetes Data Group recommends that a diagnosis of diabetes in nonpregnant adults be made for those patients who fulfill one of the following three criteria:

☐ A random plasma glucose level of 200 mg/dL or greater, plus classic signs and symptoms of diabetes mellitus, including polydipsia, polyuria, polyphagia, and sudden or unexplained weight loss

☐ A fasting plasma glucose level of 140 mg/dL or greater on at least two occasions

☐ A fasting plasma glucose level of less than 140 mg/dL, plus sustained elevated plasma glucose levels during at least two oral glucose tolerance tests. The 2-hour plasma glucose level (and at least one other within 2 hours after the 75 g glucose dose) must be 200 mg/dL or greater.

In children, the diagnosis is made when polyuria, polydipsia, and glycosuria are present in conjunction with a random blood glucose value in excess of 200 mg/dL.

Classification

Diabetes is subdivided into three major groups: *insulin-dependent diabetes mellitus (IDDM), or type I; non–insulin-dependent diabetes mellitus (NIDDM), or type II;* and a third group associated with various other conditions and syndromes.

Insulin-dependent diabetes mellitus (IDDM)   Previously called *juvenile-onset diabetes,* this form of diabetes is now known to present at any age, although the peak onset is between 11 and 13 years of age. A second peak is noted at age 6–8 years. By the third decade of life, the incidence falls to a steady but substantial level, and it is unusual to see IDDM present past age 40. These patients demonstrate a lack of endogenous insulin production and are prone to ketoacidosis. Although the disorder is not inherited, genetic factors are important in the etiology of IDDM. These patients have an increased or decreased frequency of certain histocompatibility antigens (HLA) on chromosome 6. A child with an IDDM parent has only 2%–5% risk of developing this disease. If one child has IDDM, the average risk for another sibling is 5%–10%. This risk, however, is much greater if the second sibling is HLA-identical to the first, intermediate if HLA-haploidentical, and very low if HLA-nonidentical. The monozygotic twin of an IDDM patient has a 30%–50% risk of developing diabetes.

IDDM has been established as an autoimmune disorder in which there is immune-mediated destruction of the insulin-secreting beta cells in the islets of the pancreas. As many as 90% of patients with new-onset IDDM have demonstrable serum titers of islet-cell antibodies. Anti-insulin antibodies are also frequently present in the serum of these patients. In humans, islet-cell and anti-insulin antibodies can be detected years before clinical presentation of the disease. In addition to circulating antibodies, cell-mediated immune response may also be involved. Glutamate decarboxylase (GAD) has been identified as one of the cellular antigens. Alterations in T-lymphocyte subpopulations and increased K cells (killer lymphocytes) have been reported in IDDM. Both antibody-induced and cell-mediated immune phenomena, therefore, may be involved in the pathogenesis of IDDM.

In addition to strong genetic components, other factors may contribute to the etiology of IDDM. For example, certain viruses have been demonstrated to have an association with onset of this disease. These findings suggest that IDDM may be the result of numerous genetic and environmental factors, although the exact role each of these factors plays is not yet clear.

Non–insulin-dependent diabetes mellitus (NIDDM) Patients with NIDDM are not ketoacidosis prone, and only in rare cases do they require insulin. NIDDM patients are usually, but not always, older than age 40 at presentation. Obesity is a frequent finding and, in the United States, is seen in 80%–90% of patients with NIDDM. This form of diabetes tends to be dominantly inherited. Obesity by itself leads to insulin resistance and predisposes to or exacerbates the NIDDM state. In NIDDM patients, postbinding abnormalities are primarily responsible for the insulin resistance. When impaired insulin binding is present, it may be secondary to obesity or hyperinsulinemia; but, nevertheless, it may also contribute to impaired tissue insulin sensitivity. In a significant number of these patients, the elevated plasma glucose level can revert to normal with caloric restriction and weight loss.

In NIDDM, beta-cell function is impaired, but in response to fasting hyperglycemia, basal insulin secretion is normal or increased. Insulin resistance can lead to the development of a defect in insulin secretion, and, similarly, impaired beta-cell function can lead to a disturbance in insulin action. This explains why both impaired insulin secretion and insulin resistance are seen in patients with NIDDM once the disease is fully established.

Patients with NIDDM are usually treated with diet alone or with diet and oral agents. However, some patients may require treatment with insulin. The treatment regimen does not necessarily dictate the classification of diabetes.

Other types of diabetes The third subclass of diabetes mellitus—that associated with certain other conditions and syndromes—involves a relatively small number of patients but includes many different disease entities. Examples include pancreatic diseases, endocrinopathies, and certain drug-induced forms of diabetes mellitus.

Gestational diabetes mellitus (GDM) describes the condition of a small group of women who develop hyperglycemia while pregnant but have normal glucose tolerance at other times.

The use of the term *diabetes mellitus* has been discarded in all other conditions. Previously, patients with abnormalities of blood glucose levels (but without clinical diabetes) were penalized socioeconomically if classified as diabetic. These patients were often refused insurance or had their existing insurance premiums raised; they were frequently denied jobs or admission to the armed forces. Most of these individuals, however, did not develop clinical diabetes mellitus. Three of these additional categories are now labeled as follows:

☐ Impaired glucose tolerance (IGT)

☐ Previous abnormality of glucose tolerance (Prev AGT)

☐ Potential abnormality of glucose tolerance (Pot AGT)

IGT applies to a patient with a fasting plasma glucose level of less than 140 mg/dL, a 2-hour oral glucose tolerance test with a plasma glucose level between 140 and 200 mg/dL, and one intervening plasma glucose value of 200 mg/dL or greater. These patients were previously labeled as having chemical, latent, borderline, or subclinical diabetes. Few of these patients progress to IDDM, but development of atherosclerosis may be accelerated.

Prev AGT applies to patients who developed hyperglycemia during pregnancy or during the stress of infection, myocardial infarction, or surgery. Glucose intolerance may occur again later in life.

Patients in the category of Pot AGT include relatives of patients with diabetes and women who have given birth to babies weighing more than 4.5 kg.

Pathophysiology

In normal individuals, the mean fasting venous plasma glucose level measured by enzymatic methods (glucose oxidase or hexokinase) is 60–130 mg/dL. A level greater than 140 mg/dL is abnormal and consistent with the diagnosis of diabetes mellitus. Measurements of the level of arterial or capillary blood will give values approximately 20 mg/dL higher.

A number of homeostatic mechanisms act to maintain the plasma glucose level. The plasma glucose level is reduced by only one hormone, insulin. In contrast, there are six hormones that increase plasma glucose: somatotropin, adrenocorticotropin, cortisol, epinephrine, glucagon, and thyroxine. Each of these hormones combines with a specific receptor on the surfaces of responsive cells. The hormones are secreted as needed to maintain normal serum glucose levels. The interaction on the cellular surface initiates a chain of postreceptor enzymatic and biochemical events. In the fed state, anabolism is initiated by increased secretion of insulin and growth hormone. This leads to conversion of glucose to glycogen for storage in the liver and muscles, synthesis of protein from amino acids, and the combining of fatty acid and glucose in adipose tissue to form triglycerides.

In the fasting state, catabolism results from the increased secretion of contra-insulin hormones. In this set of interactions, glycogen is reduced to glucose in the liver and muscles; proteins are broken down into amino acids in muscles and other tissues and transported to the liver for conversion to glucose or ketoacids; and triglycerides are degraded into fatty acids and glycerol in adipose tissue for transport to the liver for conversion to ketoacids and glucose (or for transport to muscle for use as an energy source).

The normal lean adult secretes approximately 33 units of insulin per day. In the obese overfed adult, insulin secretion can increase almost fourfold to approximately 120 units per day. In this state, the plasma glucose may rise only slightly, but pancreatic beta-cell mass increases. When serum insulin levels are elevated, the number of insulin receptors on the surface of insulin-responsive cells actually decreases; and formerly insulin-sensitive tissues become resistant to the glucose-lowering effects of both endogenous and exogenous insulin, even in great amounts. This condition may progress to fasting hyperglycemia and NIDDM. Compared to people at ideal body weight, for those 20% above ideal body weight, the risk of hyperglycemia is 2 times as great; 40% above is 4 times as great; 60% above is 8 times as great; 80% above is 16 times as great; and 100% above is 32 times as great. Ninety percent of Americans who are at risk of developing fasting hyperglycemia can avoid it by maintaining ideal body weight or by losing excess weight.

Therapeutically induced weight loss can reverse the metabolic consequences of obesity. Insulin requirements are increased during the growth spurts of pregnancy and puberty and in the presence of excessive amounts of exogenously administered or endogenously produced anti-insulin hormones. Thus, hyperthyroidism, Cushing syndrome, acromegaly, pheochromocytoma, pregnancy, and puberty can all induce enough metabolic stress to precipitate fasting hyperglycemia.

Insulin production will fall if the pancreatic beta-cell mass is reduced below a critical level, as in IDDM. In such cases, sometimes less than 3 units per day will be produced. Fasting hyperglycemia and resultant persistent catabolism may lead to fatal diabetic ketoacidosis or hyperglycemic hyperosmotic coma if insulin therapy is not started. Cellular insulin receptors are increased in number, and tissues are sensitive to exogenous insulin.

Clinical Presentations

The classic findings of diabetes mellitus are polyuria, polydipsia, and polyphagia. When initially detected, however, most individuals, particularly those with NIDDM, are asymptomatic. Other important historical findings include complications of pregnancy or giving birth to large babies, reactive hypoglycemia, advanced vascular disease, impotence, leg cramps or pains, dry mouth, and burning feet.

Physical findings, particularly in NIDDM, may include obesity, hypertension, arteriopathy, neuropathy, genitourinary abnormalities (especially recurrent *Candida* infections or bacterial bladder or kidney infections), periodontal disease, foot abnormalities, skin abnormalities, and unusual susceptibility to infections.

Diagnosis

The recommendations of the National Diabetes Data Group for the diagnosis of diabetes mellitus are now widely accepted. Since the adoption of more uniform criteria, the diagnosis is more easily and reliably established than in the past. The diagnosis of diabetes mellitus is made when there are two fasting serum glucose levels over 140 mg/dL or when two postprandial readings exceed 200 mg/dL. When serum glucose levels exceed normal limits but have not reached 140 mg/dL in adults or 200 mg/dL in children, the oral glucose tolerance test may be useful in establishing the diagnosis.

To prepare the patient for the glucose tolerance test, any medications that could affect glucose metabolism should be withdrawn. The patient must not be in a state of metabolic stress, such as pregnancy, infection, or recent myocardial infarction. For 3 days prior to testing, at least 150 g of carbohydrates must be ingested daily. The National Diabetes Data Group suggests that fasting plasma glucose levels of less than 140 mg/dL plus sustained elevated plasma glucose levels during at least two oral glucose tolerance tests are diagnostic of diabetes mellitus. The 2-hour plasma glucose test and at least one other test within 2 hours after the 75 g glucose load must have values of 200 mg/dL or greater.

Therapy

When planning to initiate therapy, the physician must first determine whether the patient has IDDM or NIDDM. All hormones with an anti-insulin action should be eliminated, if possible.

Diet and exercise   If NIDDM is diagnosed, the next step is to reduce body weight to normal by a diet and exercise routine. Extensive counseling on weight reduction may be necessary.

Isotonic exercises requiring rhythmic and repetitive large-muscle activity over a continuous period of time increase endurance and fitness. These cardiovascular training programs must promote the use of oxygen (aerobic exercise). A good exercise program will assist with the weight-loss program and improve fitness as well. Before prescribing an exercise program for anyone over age 35, a determination must be made that the heart is normal and that there are no contraindications. Obviously, anyone who has been sedentary and out of condition should start slowly and work up to more demanding activities.

Insulin therapy   Approximately 1 million North Americans require insulin therapy. It is indicated in those diabetic patients who are at or below ideal body weight with sustained hyperglycemia, ketoacidosis, a hyperosmotic state, or pregnancy. The use of insulin in NIDDM actually decreases target-cell insulin receptors, increases food intake, and promotes weight gain. Therefore, patients who are above ideal body weight, who have not experienced ketoacidosis, and are not pregnant should not be treated with insulin initially.

The goal of insulin therapy is to maintain plasma glucose levels as close to the normal range (80–130 mg/dL fasting and 100–150 mg/dL postprandial) as possible without inducing significant hypoglycemia. Therapy should be instituted with a subcutaneously administered morning dose of intermediate-acting insulin. The magnitude of the excursion over a 24-hour period is then determined by frequent home blood glucose monitoring techniques or by frequent measurement during hospitalization. If fasting and other glucose levels return to normal on this regimen, it should be maintained with appropriate monitoring. However, if fasting glucose is high while other levels during the day are normal, the intermediate-acting insulin should be split into a morning dose (usually 50%–85%) and an evening dose (usually 15%–50%) 12 hours later. Some of the morning intermediate-acting insulin should be replaced by regular insulin if the plasma glucose peaks before lunch or in the early afternoon, with the other levels remaining normal. Table IX-1 shows the action and duration of various types of insulin.

TABLE IX-1

INSULINS BY RELATIVE ACTION CURVES

TYPE OF INSULIN	ONSET (HR)	PEAK (HR)	USUAL EFFECTIVE DURATION (HR)	USUAL MAXIMUM DURATION (HR)
Animal				
Insulin injection (regular)	0.5–2.0	3–4	4–6	6–8
Insulin suspension, isophane (NPH)	4–6	8–14	16–20	20–24
Insulin zinc suspension (lente)	4–6	8–14	16–20	20–24
Insulin zinc suspension, extended (ultralente)	8–14	Minimal	24–36	24–36
Human				
Insulin injection (regular)	0.5–1.0	2–3	3–6	4–6
Insulin suspension, isophane (NPH)	2–4	4–10	10–16	14–18
Insulin zinc suspension (lente)	3–4	4–12	12–18	16–20
Insulin zinc suspension, extended (ultralente)	6–10	?	18–20	20–30

The tight-control approach to normalization of blood sugar requires that insulin be administered to emulate both the basal and prandial components of normal beta-cell function. This is accomplished by using an intensive insulin strategy that incorporates multiple injections of short-, intermediate-, or long-acting insulin or, alternatively, continuous subcutaneous insulin infusions (CSII) by pump with insulin boluses at each meal. Tight control may be defined as maintenance of near euglycemia as often as possible without hypoglycemia.

Intensive therapy is very demanding, but it probably improves the patient's quality of life and allows for full development of the diabetic child whose parents are capable of accepting the responsibility. Other advantages of intensive insulin therapy include the reduction of macrosomia and fetal complications during pregnancy. Intensive insulin therapy will not reverse advanced complications. However, the Diabetes Control and Complications Trial (DCCT) found that intensive insulin therapy delayed the onset and the worsening of early retinopathy and decreased the progression to severe, visually threatening retinopathy.

Intensive insulin therapy also has certain disadvantages, including diabetic ketoacidosis, skin infection, hypoglycemia, weight gain, and an initial increase in diabetic retinopathy (which is a reversible phenomenon). In general, these complications occur more frequently with CSII than with multiple injections. Contraindications to intensive therapy include adrenal insufficiency, unawareness of hypoglycemia, psychiatric disturbances, autonomic dysfunction, hepatic and renal insufficiency, and adrenergic blockade.

Types of insulin. In the early years of insulin production, many extraneous pancreatic proteins and insulin precursors were present after extraction of insulin from animal pancreata. The proinsulin content of these preparations was about 3000 ppm. Today, several types of highly purified insulin preparations are available, all containing less than 10 ppm of proinsulin. These preparations may be derived from porcine, bovine, or semisynthetic or biosynthetic human sources. All mammalian insulin is structurally similar, containing 51 amino acids in two polypeptide chains: the A chain and the B chain. Most commercial insulins in the United States are human insulins.

Ingenious manufacturing methods now allow large amounts of insulin to be produced. A biosynthetic method developed by Eli Lilly and Company is a result of genetic engineering using recombinant DNA technology. Synthetic copies of a portion of the human insulin gene, encoding only the A or B chains, are inserted into an innocuous strain of *E coli.* Synthesized A and B peptides are extracted and then recombined, producing biosynthetic Humulin.

Highly purified monospecies pork insulin and human insulin are less antigenic than earlier forms of insulins and are thus beneficial to patients with local or systemic insulin allergy, with insulin resistance caused by insulin antibodies, and with lipoatrophy at injection sites. There is also evidence to support the use of purified insulin in pregnancy in order to reduce antibody formation and hence transplacental passage of anti-insulin antibodies to the fetus. The rationale, indications, and potential benefits of using human insulin are similar to those of using highly purified porcine insulin. For both forms of human insulin, the bioavailability, absorption, kinetics, metabolic clearance, plasma half-life, and hypoglycemic effects are virtually identical to those of highly purified pork insulin. At present, the cost of highly purified pork and human insulin is comparable. Analogues like Humalog regular insulin are now becoming available, which can be made to work with predesigned time courses of action.

Complications of insulin therapy. Hypoglycemia is the most significant complication of insulin therapy. Stimulation of adrenal medulla overactivity with hyperepinephrinemia may result in anxiety, palpitation, perspiration, pallor, tachycardia, hypertension, and dilated pupils. Neurologic dysfunction is manifested as headache, paresthesia, blurred vision, drowsiness, irritability, bizarre behavior, mental confusion, combativeness, and a variety of other symptoms. Short-term hypoglycemia can lead to accidental injury, criminal behavior, or death. Prolonged hypoglycemia can result in irreversible brain damage or death.

Hypoglycemia is usually caused by inadequate carbohydrate intake secondary to a missed or delayed meal, vigorous exercise, decreased hepatic gluconeogenesis, or an excessive dose of insulin. The condition needs to be promptly verified by testing for a venous plasma glucose level of lower than 50 mg/dL. If the patient is still able to swallow, candy, soft drinks, orange juice, food, or glucose are given. For those unable to swallow, 25 g of intravenous glucose or 1 mg of subcutaneous or intramuscular glucagon is administered. The patient needs to be observed until recovery is complete, and the plasma glucose test is repeated with additional food given.

The *Somogyi phenomenon* is the occurrence of posthypoglycemic rebound hyperglycemia. Somogyi (1959) postulated that stimulation of counterregulatory hormone secretion by hypoglycemia could lead to subsequent hyperglycemia. Critics have argued that hyperglycemia is merely the consequence of waning of insulin; however, it has been convincingly demonstrated that rebound hyperglycemia can occur in the absence of waning of insulin. The incidence of the Somogyi phenomenon is not known, but it is probably not frequent. Hypoglycemia as mild as 50–60 mg/dL of plasma glucose (which may be asymptomatic) can activate counterregulation. Current evidence indicates that catecholamines and growth hormone are the major factors involved.

Treatment of the Somogyi phenomenon requires elimination of the precipitating hypoglycemia by reducing insulin dosage or providing additional carbohydrates. Although the Somogyi phenomenon may occur at any time of day, when hypoglycemia occurs overnight it is often difficult to distinguish rebound hyperglycemia from the dawn phenomenon (see below). The treatment of these two conditions is quite different. Therefore, when there is doubt, it is expedient to check plasma glucose levels between 1:00 AM and 4:00 AM. A progressive increase in the plasma glucose with no values below 100 mg/dl suggests the dawn phenomenon or waning of insulin. On the other hand, a plasma glucose value below 80 mg/dL suggests the Somogyi phenomenon.

The *dawn phenomenon* is simply an exaggeration of a normal physiologic process, which can result in substantial hyperglycemia. It is characterized by early morning hyperglycemia not preceded by hypoglycemia or waning of insulin. The dawn phenomenon is thought to be caused by a surge of growth-hormone secretion shortly after the patient falls asleep, which leads to overproduction of glucose by the liver and diminished use of glucose by muscle tissue, without a compensatory increase in insulin secretion. Some patients with diabetes have excessive surges of growth-hormone secretion, producing severe morning hyperglycemia. This phenomenon can occur with equal frequency in IDDM and NIDDM, but its severity is variable, making it difficult to treat. Management consists of increasing a patient's before-supper intermediate-acting insulin or delaying the insulin administration to before bedtime. Thus, additional insulin is provided for the period in which growth hormone–induced insulin resistance occurs.

Allergies and local reactions to insulin. Lipoatrophy or lipohypertrophy may occur at sites of insulin injection. In the past, lipoatrophy (loss of fat) was due to lipolytic impurities in insulin preparations. This phenomenon is seen infrequently now with the use of purified human insulins. Lipohypertrophy consists of accumulation of fat at insulin injection sites. This condition can be eliminated by properly rotating injection sites so that no single site is injected more often than once a month.

True insulin allergy is caused by IgE antibodies and is characterized by a hard erythematous indurated area at the injection site, which is usually pruritic. It develops 1–4 weeks after initiation of insulin therapy and usually clears as therapy continues. Generalized anaphylaxis, hives, and angioedema may also develop and must be treated with desensitization techniques.

Immunologic insulin resistance may occur and is seen in patients who require more than 200 units of insulin per day for plasma glucose control. These patients also have an insulin-neutralizing antibody titer (IgG and IgA) greater than 30 units per liter of serum. Many cases of apparent insulin resistance are caused by downregulation of the number of receptors as a result of obesity. Congenital absence of these receptors and insulin receptor antibodies are rare causes of insulin resistance. In this situation, the use of highly purified pork or human insulin is indicated. The efficacy of human and pork insulins is equivalent. However, human insulin is less immunogenic than animal insulin when employed in cases of insulin resistance. Patients with insulin resistance requiring over 200 units per day have been successfully treated with U 500 regular insulin.

Oral agents The sulfonylureas (Table IX-2) have been widely used in the United States and Canada since 1967. Their major mechanism of action is stimulation of pancreatic insulin secretion, although some studies have suggested a peripheral augmentation of insulin action.

The major problem with sulfonylurea therapy is that approximately one third of patients who begin therapy will not become normoglycemic. Furthermore, over a 5-year period, 85% of those who initially responded to the drug will develop secondary failure to control blood sugar. Weight reduction is a far more effective method of normalizing blood sugar and is the method of choice. Further, the sulfonylureas are also contraindicated in diabetics who are pregnant or in those who have had ketoacidosis.

The most significant adverse effect of the sulfonylureas is hypoglycemia, which may be severe and prolonged. Extrapancreatic effects include blood dyscrasias, increased fibrinolytic activity, photosensitivity, corneal opacities, water retention, jaundice, liver enzyme inhibition, and increased stomach-acid secretion. Therapy also causes an altered EEG in epilepsy.

TABLE IX-2

CHARACTERISTICS OF SULFONYLUREA AGENTS

GENERIC NAME	BRAND NAME	DURATION OF ACTION (hr)	COMMENTS
Tolbutamide	Orinase	6–12	Metabolized by liver to an inactive product; given 2–3 times per day.
Chlorpropamide	Diabinese	60	Metabolized by liver (~70%) to less active metabolites and excreted intact (~30%) by kidneys; can potentiate ADH action; given once per day.
Acetohexamide	Dymelor	12–18	Metabolized by liver to active and inactive products; given 1–2 times per day.
Tolazamide	Tolinase	12–24	Metabolized by liver to both active and inactive products; given 1–2 times per day.
Glyburide	DiaBeta Micronase Glynase	12–24	Metabolized by liver to mostly inert products; given 1–2 times per day.
Glipizide	Glucotrol	12–24	Metabolized by liver to inert products; given 1–2 times per day.

Sulfonylureas compete for carrier-protein binding sites with many other drugs, including sulfonamides, salicylates, phenylbutazone, monoamine oxidase inhibitors, thiazides, and barbiturates. Because the pharmacological effect of these drugs may be increased when they are displaced from their albumin-combining sites, combination drug therapy may have unforeseen toxic consequences. It is also difficult to maintain stable anticoagulation therapy in a patient taking sulfonylureas, because these agents compete with anticoagulants for the same binding sites. In addition, the effects of alcohol are potentiated by sulfonylureas.

Two new second-generation sulfonylurea agents, *glipizide* (Glucotrol) and *glyburide* (DiaBeta, Micronase) have been approved by the Food and Drug Administration for the treatment of patients with NIDDM. These sulfonylureas differ from the first generation in structure and potency. On a weight-for-weight basis, glipizide and glyburide are approximately 50–100 times more potent than first-generation agents and are effective at nanomolar rather than micromolar blood levels. Although both glipizide and glyburide have very short half-lives (2–4 hours), blood levels and duration of action are dissociated so that these drugs generally need to be given only once daily. Glipizide and glyburide are certainly more potent than the first-generation sulfonylureas in facilitating insulin release. This enhanced beta-cytotrophic effect is not, however, associated with better control of hyperglycemia when either of these agents is compared to first-generation agents. Complications may be expected to occur less frequently with the second-generation agents because of their nonionic binding to albumin. Thus, patients may be less susceptible to drug interactions in that the second-generation sulfonylureas are not displaced by anionic drugs. The rates of primary and secondary failure with these new second-generation agents are virtually identical to those seen through the years with the first-generation drugs. If a patient has a primary or secondary failure of control with one sulfonylurea agent, a trial with another agent is indicated.

A major advance has recently become available for the treatment of NIDDM with the FDA's approval of *metformin* (Glucophage). This is a biguanide with a basic structure similar to phenformin, an oral antidiabetic agent taken off the market because of the risk of developing lactic acidosis. Metformin therapy improves insulin sensitivity, as shown by a reduction in fasting plasma glucose and insulin. The drug's glucose-lowering effect in NIDDM is attributed mainly to decreased hepatic glucose output and enhanced peripheral glucose uptake. Several other actions may contribute, such as increased intestinal use of glucose and decreased fatty acid oxidation.

Metformin can be used as either a first-line therapy or in combination with a sulfonylurea. When used appropriately, metformin appears to be a much safer agent, with an extremely low incidence of lactic acidosis. In addition, metformin apparently does not cause hypoglycemia. Labeling guidelines indicate that metformin should not be prescribed to patients with elevated serum creatinine.

Glucose Surveillance

Glycosylated hemoglobin   Diabetes mellitus is characterized by constant fluctuation of blood sugar. Thus, periodic blood sugar measurement is inadequate for assessing long-term metabolic control; it can indicate the blood sugar level only for the specific time at which the blood was drawn.

During the past two decades, the measurement of *glycosylated hemoglobin levels* has significantly improved long-term glucose-control surveillance. All serum- and membrane-bound proteins are exposed to glucose, and these proteins undergo a nonenzymatic postsynthetic modification that results in the attachment of glucose to the protein (glycosylation). Higher concentrations of glucose and longer periods of exposure result in a higher concentration of glycosylated proteins. The time period reflected by the glycosylated protein concentration depends upon the particular protein's turnover rate. Red blood cells and hemoglobin have a half-life of 60 days. Therefore, the glycosylated hemoglobin level reflects the mean blood glucose concentration over the preceding 2 months. Glycosylated hemoglobin has been called *fast hemoglobin* (HbA_1 or HbA_{1C}, depending upon the assay). Chromatographic methodology can separate the glycosylated fractions designated HbA_{1A}, HbA_{1B}, and HbA_{1C}, with the last being quantitatively the largest. Assays for glycosylated hemoglobin are expressed as a percentage of total hemoglobin.

The glycosylated hemoglobin assay is useful because it is relatively unaffected by transient fluctuations in serum blood glucose and does not require patient cooperation. The HbA_{1C} assay is used to monitor the degree of chronic glucose control in both IDDM and NIDDM patients. It is especially useful in uncooperative, unreliable patients. HbA_{1C} helps to differentiate transient glucose intolerance associated with stress from previously unrecognized diabetes and to clarify contradictory or confusing oral glucose tolerance tests.

Self–blood-glucose monitoring   Probably the most important advance in glycemic control is self–blood-glucose monitoring (SBGM). It potentially permits the patient to achieve blood sugars in the normal physiologic range, thus allowing more ambitious treatment strategies. Home use of blood-glucose analyzers facilitates the normalization or near-normalization of metabolic control in diabetic patients requiring insulin. The blood-glucose analyzers are small electronic devices that measure the glucose in the blood. The patient obtains a drop of capillary blood by a finger stick and places it on a glucose oxidase–impregnated paper strip and inserts the strip into the reflectance meter for the determination. Blood-glucose analyzers for home use are safe and reasonably accurate when used as directed.

SBGM is appropriate for any insulin-requiring diabetic who is well motivated and capable of adhering to a rigorous management program. It is also very helpful and is becoming the standard monitoring process for patients on oral agents who do not use insulin.

Acute Complications of Diabetes

The acute complications of diabetes are either *nonketotic hyperglycemic-hyperosmolar coma (NKHHC)* or *diabetic ketoacidosis (DKA)*. Either of these, if not recognized promptly and treated aggressively, can lead to death. Patients in severe ketoacidosis or in the nonketotic hyperosmolar state may have a marked increase in the serum osmolality, primarily because of hyperglycemia. In addition, an adult with DKA might have lost as much as 12 liters of water and up to 800 mEq of sodium and 80 mEq of potassium in the development of this imbalance. Patients typically present with a decreased pH, as manifested in a decreased CO_2 content.

In mild to moderate ketoacidosis, the imbalances may be corrected by administration of IV continuous insulin infusion, coupled with oral fluids containing potassium and sodium to replace water and electrolyte deficits. In anything but minimal ketoacidosis, an intravenous infusion of isotonic sodium chloride with potassium supplementation is begun and regular insulin administration is instituted. The subcutaneous route of insulin administration should be avoided initially in patients with marked dehydration, hypotension, or shock because of delayed absorption. Insulin treatment, beginning with an intravenous bolus of 5–10 units of regular insulin, followed by intravenous infusion of 1–10 units of regular insulin per hour, is recommended, depending on the response. Blood pressure, urine flow, serum glucose, potassium, and sodium must be monitored hourly. When plasma glucose reaches 300 mg/dL, 5% dextrose should be added to the intravenous infusion to prevent hypoglycemia.

Chronic Complications of Diabetes

The long-term complications of diabetes are usually secondary to vascular disease. Neuropathy, nephropathy, peripheral vascular disease, coronary atherosclerosis, secondary cerebral thrombosis, cardiac infarction, and retinopathy are all important causes of late morbidity.

Nephropathy Approximately 40% of patients who have had diabetes mellitus for 20 or more years will have nephropathy (demonstrated by a urinary protein level of more than 200 mg/day). Glomerular basement membrane thickening commonly occurs in diabetic patients, but changes in the mesangium are more predictive of the development of nephropathy. Currently, 25%–33% of all patients with end-stage renal disease are diabetics. Renal failure eventually occurs in approximately 50% of patients who develop diabetes before age 20 and in 6% of those with onset after age 40. Proteinuria is the most sensitive indicator of underlying renal disease. *Microalbuminuria,* defined as an abnormally elevated albumin excretion rate in the absence of clinical proteinuria, has been used as a sensitive predictor of incipient diabetic nephropathy. The clinical onset of asymptomatic proteinuria eventually evolves into the nephrotic syndrome characterized by massive edema, heavy proteinuria, and hypoalbuminemia. Almost invariably, nephropathy and retinopathy develop within a short time of each other. Hypertension, glycemic control, and, possibly, excess dietary protein intake determine the rate of function loss.

Typically, 20 years of clinically manifest diabetes pass before the patient develops end-stage renal disease. It is a common observation that, once begun, kidney failure proceeds in a predictable fashion, seemingly independent of the initiating disease process. However, recent studies suggest that tight-control insulin therapy and the use of angiotensin-converting enzyme inhibitors may reduce the level of proteinuria and slow the progression of renal failure. These drugs can be administered in conjunction with a diuretic or other antihypertensive drug. Additional evidence suggests that dietary protein restriction early in the course of renal insufficiency may possibly retard the progression of renal failure.

Neuropathy Diabetic neuropathy is a common problem. Electrophysiological diagnostic techniques indicate that 75%–80% of diabetic patients have neuropathological abnormalities at presentation. After 30 years of diabetes mellitus, 45%–50% of diabetic patients will have signs of neuropathy, and 15%–20% will have symptoms of distal symmetrical polyneuropathy. Changes in nerve metabolism and function are thought to be mediated through increased polyol-pathway activity; reduced cellular myoinositol concentrations, with alterations in Na^+, K^+-ATPase activities; reduced membrane fluidity; and reduced oxygen uptake. Schwann-cell synthesis of myelin is impaired, and axonal degeneration ensues. Thus, analogous to microvascular complications, the altered metabolic milieu leads to abnormal cell function. In addition, microangiopathy of the endoneural capillaries leads to vascular abnormalities and microinfarcts of the nerves, with multifocal fiber loss. Symptoms occur most commonly in the feet and lower legs. Foot pain, paresthesias, and loss of sensation occur frequently and are probably the result of both ischemic and metabolic abnormalities of nerves. Weakness may occur as part of mononeuritis or a mononeuritis multiplex and is usually associated with pain. There is no specific treatment for diabetic neuropathy. Aldose reductase inhibitors (not commercially available yet) may improve nerve conduction slightly but do not produce major clinical improvement. The pain often responds to amitriptyline or carbamazepine. Phenytoin and phenothiazines are ineffective and should not be used.

Cerebrovascular and peripheral vascular disease   Cerebral thrombosis is approximately twice as prevalent in the diabetic as in the nondiabetic population. Peripheral vascular disease is 40 times as prevalent in the diabetic population, and 25% of those with diabetic peripheral vascular disease have peripheral neuropathy. The tibial and peroneal vessels are more frequently involved in diabetics than in nondiabetics, and the macrovascular lesions are more diffuse and extensive. Intermittent claudication of the calf, thigh, or buttock is a common complaint. With more advanced disease, there may be pain at rest. Initial findings may include absent peripheral pulses. In more advanced states, findings include tight, shiny skin, hair loss, localized pallor or cyanosis, muscle atrophy, ulceration, gangrene, and diminished sensation. Delayed venous filling and delayed capillary flush may occur when the leg returns to a dependent position after several minutes of elevation.

Coronary artery disease   Coronary artery disease is the major cause of death in the United States. Diabetic patients are at higher risk; they are more likely to sustain a myocardial infarction and more likely to have complications. The Framingham Study showed that diabetic patients had a yearly risk of cardiovascular death 3.5 times that of nondiabetic persons. Hypertension adds significantly to the risk of cardiovascular disease for diabetics. It is widely accepted that diabetic infarcts are frequently painless. The mortality rate in diabetic patients with an anterior myocardial infarction is twice that of nondiabetics. It is generally agreed that coronary artery gross pathology is similar in diabetics and nondiabetics. It is essential to reduce all controllable risk factors. Metabolic management in the hospital must be directed toward avoiding both hypoglycemia and hyperglycemia. The physician may have to adjust myocardial infarction therapy because of coexisting diabetic complications.

Ophthalmologic Considerations

The most common *acute* ocular manifestation in diabetes is refractive change due to hyperglycemia. The most important *chronic* features of diabetes include retinopathy and accelerated cataract formation. Additional problems, such as cranial mononeuropathies and an increased incidence of other retinal vaso-occlusive phenomena, are seen with chronic diabetes. Chronic and acute vaso-occlusive disease can lead to rubeosis and glaucoma. Diabetic retinopathy and associated conditions are discussed at length in BCSC Section 12, *Retina and Vitreous.*

Aiello LA. *Evaluation and Treatment of Diabetic Retinopathy* (Continuing Ophthalmic Video Education videotape). San Francisco: American Academy of Ophthalmology; 1990.

Diabetes 2000 Program. *Progression of Retinopathy* (clinical handout card). San Francisco: American Academy of Ophthalmology; 1993.

Surgical Considerations in Diabetes

The stress of surgery exacerbates the metabolic abnormalities of diabetes mellitus; meticulous attention to plasma glucose control is necessary. The goals of treatment are to prevent hypoglycemia and ketoacidosis by keeping the plasma glucose levels between 150 and 250 mg/dL and to maintain fluid and electrolyte balance. The key to achieving these goals is frequent assessment of plasma glucose and plasma electrolytes. Additional regular insulin is given if plasma glucose exceeds 300 mg/dL, and the rate of glucose infusion is increased if the plasma glucose is less than 150 mg/dL. The choice of therapy is guided by the patient's usual treatment and the extent of surgery. All regimens require frequent plasma glucose measurement and appropriate modification of therapy. Rapid bedside methods of blood glucose determination facilitate management. Sliding-scale methods of insulin administration based on urine tests should be abandoned.

Patients treated with diet may not require specific therapy, but small doses of regular insulin should be given if the blood sugar exceeds 300 mg/dL. If temporary insulin therapy is needed, human insulin should be used to minimize the future risk of insulin allergy or resistance.

In patients treated with sulfonylureas, the drug should be omitted on the day of surgery. For minor operations, insulin is required only if the plasma glucose exceeds 300 mg/dL. For major operations, 15–20 units of isophane insulin suspension (NPH insulin) should be given on the morning of surgery and 5% dextrose infused at approximately 75–125 ml/hr. Additional regular insulin should be given as necessary.

In *insulin-treated patients* undergoing minor procedures, the morning insulin dose may be delayed until the procedure is completed and the patient is fed; this delayed dose should be reduced by about one third. For major surgery, a 5% dextrose infusion should be instituted prior to surgery, and one half the usual daily insulin dosage should be given subcutaneously as isophane insulin suspension. Additional regular insulin is given as indicated by frequent plasma glucose measurements, and dextrose should be administered intravenously. As long as the patient is unable to eat, isophane insulin suspension may be given daily in the preceding dosage and supplemented with regular insulin if the plasma glucose exceeds 300 mg/dL.

Bailey CJ, Turner RC. Metformin [review article]. *N Engl J Med.* 1996;334:574–579.

DeFronzo RA, Goodman AM. Efficacy of metformin in patients with non–insulin-dependent diabetic mellitus. The Multicenter Metformin Study Group. *N Engl J Med.* 1995;333:541–549.

Diabetes in America. 2nd ed. National Diabetes Data Group. Bethesda, MD: National Institutes of Health; 1995. NIH Publication No. 95-1468.

The effect of intensive treatment of diabetes on the development and progression of long-term complications in insulin-dependent diabetes mellitus. The Diabetes Control and Complications Trial (DCCT) Research Group. *N Engl J Med.* 1993;329: 977–986.

Keller RJ, Eisenbarth GS, Jackson RA. Insulin prophylaxis in individuals at high risk of type I diabetes. *Lancet.* 1993;341:927–928.

National Diabetes Data Group. Report of the Expert Committee on Glycosylated Hemoglobin. *Diabetes Care.* 1984;7:602–606.

Olefsky JM. Diabetes mellitus. In: Wyngaarden JB, Smith LH Jr, Bennett JC, eds. *Cecil Textbook of Medicine.* 19th ed. Philadelphia: Saunders; 1992:1291–1310.

Physician's Guide to Insulin Dependent (Type I) Diabetes. Alexandria, VA: American Diabetes Association; 1988.

Physician's Guide to Non–Insulin Dependent (Type II) Diabetes. 2nd ed. Alexandria, VA: American Diabetes Association; 1989.

Skyler JS. Human insulin of recombinant DNA origin. Clinical potential. *Diabetes Care.* 1982;5(suppl2):181–186.

Somogyi M. Exacerbations of diabetes by excess insulin action. *Am J Med.* 1959;26: 169–191.

Thyroid Disease

Physiology

Functionally, the thyroid gland can be thought of as having two parts. The *parafollicular* (or C) cells secrete calcitonin and do not play a role in thyroid physiology. Thyroid *follicles* are made up of a single layer of epithelial cells surrounding colloid, which consists mostly of thyroglobulin, the storage form of the thyroid hormones T_4 and T_3.

T_4 (thyroxine), the main secretory product of the thyroid gland, contains four iodine atoms; deiodination of T_4, which occurs mainly in the liver and kidney, gives rise to T_3, the metabolically active form of thyroid hormone. Eighty percent of serum T_3 is derived through deiodination; the remainder is secreted by the thyroid. Only a small fraction of the hormones circulate free in the plasma (0.02% of total T_4 and 0.3% of total T_3); the remainder is bound to the proteins thyroxine-binding globulin (TBG), transthyretin, and albumin.

Thyroid function is regulated by the interrelationships of hypothalamic, pituitary, and thyroid activity. Thyrotropin-releasing hormone (TRH) is secreted by the hypothalamus, causing the synthesis and release of thyrotropin (or thyroid-stimulating hormone, TSH). TSH, in turn, stimulates the thyroid, leading to release of T_4 and T_3. T_4 and T_3 inhibit the release of TSH and the TSH response to TRH at the level of the pituitary.

The main role of the thyroid hormones is the regulation of tissue metabolism through effects on protein synthesis. Normal development of the central nervous system requires adequate amounts of thyroid hormone during the first 2 years of life. Hypothyroidism results in irreversible mental retardation (cretinism). Normal growth and bone maturation are also dependent on sufficient hormone levels.

Testing for Thyroid Disease

Detection of thyroid disease and evaluation of the efficacy of therapy require the use of various combinations of laboratory tests (see Table IX-3). Recent advances—specifically, greater availability of direct measurement of free T_4 and the "sensitive" TSH test—have greatly simplified the testing process.

Measurement of serum T_4 Total serum T_4 is composed of two parts: protein-bound and free hormone. Total T_4 levels can be affected by changes in serum thyroxine-binding protein (TBG) levels while maintaining euthyroidism and normal free T_4 levels. TBG and total T_4 are elevated in pregnancy and with use of oral contraceptives, while free T_4 levels remain normal. Low TBG and total T_4 levels are associated with chronic illness, protein malnutrition, hepatic failure, and use of glucocorticoids.

For many years, laboratory determination of *total T_4* by radioimmunoassay was the most commonly used direct measurement of thyroid function. *Free T_4* was then calculated indirectly by multiplying total T_4 by the T_3 resin uptake (itself an indirect determination of the fraction of unbound thyroid hormone in the serum). Recently, however, direct determination of free T_4 has become widely available, improving the accuracy of thyroid function testing.

Measurement of serum T_3 Serum T_3 levels may not accurately reflect thyroid gland function for two reasons: first, because T_3 is not the major secretory product of the thyroid; and second, because many factors influence T_3 levels, including nutrition, medications, and mechanisms regulating the enzymes which convert T_4 to T_3. Determination of T_3 levels is indicated in patients who may have *T_3 thyrotoxicosis*. This is an uncommon condition in which clinically hyperthyroid patients have normal T_4 and free T_4 but elevated T_3 levels.

Measurement of serum TSH TSH secretion by the pituitary is tightly controlled by negative feedback mechanisms regulated by serum T4 and T3 levels. TSH levels begin to rise early in the course of hypothyroidism and fall early in hyperthyroidism, even before free T4 levels are outside the normal range. Therefore, the serum TSH level is a very sensitive indicator of thyroid dysfunction.

Until recently, available tests were not sufficiently sensitive to differentiate between normal and reduced TSH levels, requiring the use of the thyroid-releasing hormone (TRH) test to make the distinction. In recent years immunometric assays of TSH levels (TSH-IMA, "sensitive" TSH test), which can detect TSH levels down to 0.01 µ/ml, have made possible differentiation of hyperthyroid from euthyroid patients. TSH levels will be essentially undetectable in hyperthyroid patients when measured by the sensitive assays.

The sensitive TSH test is useful for (1) screening for thyroid disease; (2) monitoring replacement therapy in hypothyroid patients (TSH levels respond 6–8 weeks after changes in hormone replacement dosage); and (3) monitoring suppressive therapy for thyroid nodules or cancer.

In screening for thyroid disease, the combination of free T_4 and sensitive TSH assays has a sensitivity of 99.5% and a specificity of 98%.

Serum thyroid hormone-binding protein tests TBG concentrations can be measured directly by immunoassay. However, it is rarely necessary to determine the levels of circulating TBG and transthyretin in the clinical setting. Estimates of thyroid hormone binding can be obtained by employing the T_3 resin uptake test.

TABLE IX-3

LABORATORY EVALUATION OF THYROID DISEASE

DIAGNOSIS	TSH	TOTAL T$_4$	FREE T$_4$	T$_3$	RAIU	COMMENTS
Euthyroid	Normal	↓, normal, ↑	Normal	–	Normal	Total T$_4$ may be ↑ or ↓ due to alterations in TBG levels
Graves disease	Undetectable	↑	↑	↑	↑	
Subacute thyroiditis	Low or undetectable	Usually ↑	↑	↑	↓	RAIU very low
Toxic nodular goiter	Low	↑	↑	↑	Normal, ↑	
T$_3$ thyrotoxicosis	Low	Normal	Normal	↑	↑	
Secondary hyperthyroidism	High	↑	↑	–	–	Elevated TSH and free T$_4$, caused by TSH-secreting pituitary tumor (rare)
Primary hypothyroidism	High	↓	↓	↓	Usually low	
Secondary hypothyroidism	Low	↓	↓	↓	Usually low	Decreased TSH and free T$_4$, caused by hypothalamic or pituitary disease

↑ = elevated; ↓ = reduced

Radioactive iodine uptake (RAIU)   A 24-hour test of the thyroid's ability to concentrate a dose of radioactive iodine, RAIU is not always accurate enough to assess thyroid metabolic status. Its main use is in determining whether a patient's hyperthyroidism is due to Graves disease (elevated RAIU, >30%–40%), toxic nodular goiter (normal to elevated), and subacute thyroiditis (low to undetectable, <2%–4%).

Testing for antithyroid antibodies   Several antibodies related to thyroid disease can be detected in the blood. The most common is *thyroid microsomal antibody (TMAb),* found in approximately 95% of patients with Hashimoto thyroiditis, 55% of those with Graves disease, and only 10% of adults with no apparent thyroid disease. Antibodies to thyroglobulin are also found in thyroid disease of varied causation, including Hashimoto thyroiditis, Graves disease, and thyroid carcinoma. Graves patients may have antibodies against thyroid TSH receptors, which results in stimulation of those receptors and, thus, hyperthyroidism. Assays are being developed to detect antibodies against antigens present on extraocular muscles in Graves ophthalmopathy.

Thyroid scanning   This technique allows imaging of the thyroid's ability to trap radioactive iodine, usually ^{123}I. It is useful in distinguishing functioning (hot) from nonfunctioning (cold) thyroid nodules and in evaluating chest and neck masses for the presence of metastatic thyroid cancer.

Thyroid ultrasound   Ultrasonography is used to establish the presence of thyroid nodules in suspicious cases that cannot be determined by palpation; nodules as small as 1 mm can be detected, though nodules this size are not of clinical significance. It is also useful in assessing the response of thyroid nodule size to suppressive therapy.

Biopsy or fine-needle aspiration biopsy   These techniques are used to obtain tissue samples for the evaluation of thyroid nodules. Fine-needle aspiration specimens require interpretation by an experienced cytopathologist. Needle aspiration is also used to drain fluid from cystic thyroid nodules.

Hyperthyroidism

Hypermetabolism caused by excessive quantities of circulating thyroid hormones results in the clinical syndrome of hyperthyroidism. The syndrome has many etiologies. Graves disease accounts for about 85% of cases of thyrotoxicosis. Toxic nodular goiter and thyroiditis account for most of the remaining cases.

Graves disease   Patients with Graves disease exhibit various combinations of hypermetabolism, diffuse enlargement of the thyroid gland, ophthalmopathy, and pretibial myxedema. Although the exact cause is not known, it is believed to be an autoimmune disorder: 85%–90% of patients have circulating TSH receptor antibodies (TRAb). Patients with ophthalmopathy usually have high titers of TRAb; antibodies to soluble human eye muscle antigens have also been found in these patients but not in Graves patients without eye involvement.

Graves disease is common, with a 10:1 female preponderance. Peak incidence is in the third and fourth decades of life, and there is a strong familial component. The clinical syndrome is well known, consisting of nervousness, tremor, weight loss, palpitations, heat intolerance, emotional lability, muscle weakness, and gastrointestinal hypermotility. Clinical signs include tachycardia or atrial fibrillation, increased systolic and decreased diastolic blood pressure (widened pulse pressure), and thyroid enlargement. Pretibial myxedema—brawny, nonpitting swelling of the pretibial area, ankles, or feet—is present.

One notable situation for the ophthalmologist is *euthyroid* Graves disease. These patients present with ophthalmopathy but without coexisting hyperthyroidism. This clinical picture may appear in thyroid gland destruction by Hashimoto thyroiditis or in delayed-onset hyperthyroidism, in which other systemic manifestations appear months to years later. In some cases, however, patients have ophthalmic manifestations without ever demonstrating thyroid abnormalities.

Thyroid storm, a potentially fatal complication seen in some patients with hyperthyroidism, is a medical emergency. It presents with fever, abdominal pain, change in mental status, and tachycardia or other arrhythmias. Often brought on by superimposed stress or infection, thyroid storm formerly had a mortality of 20%–40%; with current treatment, mortality is much lower. Treatment includes IV fluids, body cooling, antithyroid drugs (propylthiouracil, methimazole), sodium iodide (to inhibit release of preformed thyroid hormone), steroids, beta blockers, and treatment directed at any underlying precipitating factors.

Treatment of Graves disease is aimed at returning thyroid function to normal. A significant proportion of patients (30%–50%) will experience remission in association with drug treatment directed at the thyroid. Both relapse and/or hypothyroidism may occur later in the course of the disease in these patients.

The first step in treatment is to suppress thyroid secretion with the use of the thiourea derivatives *propylthiouracil (PTU)* or *methimazole (Tapazole).* The drugs work by inhibiting the organification of iodine by the gland. Treatment is continued until improvement in clinical and laboratory indices is apparent. Side effects include rash (common), liver damage, vasculitis (both rare), and agranulocytosis (0.02%–0.05% of patients).

Long-term therapy of Graves disease involves several options. The aforementioned antithyroid drugs can be continued for 12–24 months in hopes of a remission. Partial surgical removal of the gland is frequently successful, although about half of such patients will eventually become hypothyroid. The third and most commonly employed choice is the use of radioactive iodine. [131]I is highly effective, resulting in hypothyroidism in 80% of patients within 6–12 months; some of the remainder will require a second treatment. Side effects are minimal, with no increased risk of thyroid carcinoma or leukemia.

Toxic nodular goiter   In this condition, thyroid hormone–producing adenomas (either single or multiple) make sufficient quantities of hormone to cause hyperthyroidism. Hot nodules (those shown to be functioning on thyroid scan) are almost never carcinomatous and often result in hyperthyroidism. Toxic nodules may be treated with radioactive iodine or surgery.

Hypothyroidism

Hypothyroidism is a clinical syndrome resulting from a deficiency of thyroid hormone. *Myxedema* is the nonpitting edema caused by subcutaneous accumulation of mucopolysaccharides in severe cases of hypothyroidism; the term is sometimes used to describe the entire syndrome of severe hypothyroidism.

Primary hypothyroidism accounts for more than 95% of cases and may be acquired or congenital. Most primary cases are due to Hashimoto thyroiditis (discussed below, under Thyroiditis), "idiopathic" myxedema (felt by many to be end-stage Hashimoto thyroiditis as well), and iatrogenic causes (after ^{131}I or surgical treatment of hyperthyroidism). *Secondary hypothyroidism,* caused by hypothalamic or pituitary dysfunction (usually after pituitary surgery), is much less common. As in hyperthyroidism, there is a significant female preponderance among adults with hypothyroidism.

Clinically, the patient with hypothyroidism presents with signs and symptoms of hypometabolism and accumulation of mucopolysaccharide in the tissues of the body. Many of the symptoms are nonspecific, and their relationship to thyroid dysfunction may not be recognized for quite some time: weakness, fatigue, lethargy, decreased memory, dry skin, deepening of the voice, weight gain (despite loss of appetite), cold intolerance, arthralgias, constipation, and muscle cramps.

Clinical signs include bradycardia, reduced pulse pressure, myxedema, loss of body and scalp hair, and menstrual disorders. In severe cases, personality changes ("myxedema madness") and death (following "myxedema coma") may occur.

Treatment of hypothyroidism is straightforward, requiring the normalization of circulating hormone levels with oral thyroid replacement medication. Levothyroxine is the most commonly used preparation. Serum T_4 and TSH levels are monitored at regular intervals to ensure euthyroidism is maintained.

Thyroiditis

Thyroiditis may be classified as acute, subacute, or chronic. *Acute thyroiditis,* caused by bacterial infection, is extremely rare. *Subacute thyroiditis* occurs in two forms: granulomatous and lymphocytic. There are also two types of *chronic thyroiditis*: Hashimoto and Riedel.

Subacute granulomatous thyroiditis presents with a painful, enlarged gland associated with fever, chills, and malaise. The patient may be hyperthyroid due to release of hormone from areas of thyroid destruction; pathologic examination reveals granulomatous inflammation. The disease is self-limited and treatment is symptomatic, with either analgesics or, in severe cases, oral corticosteroids. Following resolution, transient hypothyroidism, which becomes permanent in 5%–10% of patients, may occur. *Subacute lymphocytic thyroiditis* ("painless" thyroiditis), which commonly occurs 2–4 months postpartum, presents with symptoms of hyperthyroidism and a normal or slightly enlarged but nontender gland. Pathology shows lymphocytic infiltration resembling Hashimoto thyroiditis, suggesting an autoimmune cause. This disease is also self-limited, generally lasting less than 3 months, and subsequent hypothyroidism may occur. Treatment is symptomatic.

Hashimoto thyroiditis is an autoimmune disease that appears to be closely related to Graves disease. It has been found to be associated with specific HLA antigens (B46, DR3, DR4, DR5, DR9, and DRw53). Patients have antibodies to one or more thyroid antigens and an increased incidence of other autoimmune diseases such as Sjögren syndrome, systemic lupus erythematosus, idiopathic thrombocytopenic purpura, and pernicious anemia. Rarely, other endocrine organs—the adrenals, parathyoids, pancreatic islet cells, pituitary, and gonads—may be involved as well.

Patients with Hashimoto thyroiditis may present with hypothyroidism, an enlarged thyroid, or both. Pathologic examination reveals lymphocytic infiltration. Treatment is aimed at normalizing hormone levels with thyroid replacement therapy. Patients with enlarged glands and airway obstruction that do not respond to TSH suppression may require surgery. There is a small increased risk of primary thyroid lymphoma in patients with Hashimoto thyroiditis.

Riedel thyroiditis is a very rare disease consisting of a sclerosing fibrous infiltration of the thyroid gland associated with hypothyroidism, tracheal obstruction, retroperitoneal fibrosis, and sclerosing cholangitis. Surgery is required to relieve airway obstruction.

Thyroid Tumors

Virtually all tumors of the thyroid gland arise from glandular cells and are, therefore, adenomas or carcinomas. Functioning adenomas have been discussed previously (see *Toxic nodular goiter,* under Hyperthyroidism).

On thyroid scan, 90%–95% of thyroid adenomas are nonfunctioning ("cold" nodules) and come to attention only if large enough to be physically apparent. Diagnostic testing involves a combination of approaches including ultrasonography (cysts are benign and simply aspirated), fine-needle aspiration, and surgery, depending on the clinical situation. Treatment options for benign cold nodules are suppressive therapy, in which thyroid hormone replacement is used to suppress TSH secretion and its stimulatory effect on functioning nodules, and surgery.

Carcinomas of the thyroid are of four types: papillary, follicular, medullary, and anaplastic (undifferentiated). Non-Hodgkin's lymphoma accounts for about 5% of thyroid malignancies. Treatment involves surgical excision or ^{131}I ablation.

Papillary carcinoma is the most common form of thyroid tumor. It is 2–3 times more common in women than men. Tumors removed prior to extension outside the capsule of the gland appear to have no adverse effect on survival; extrathyroidal papillary carcinomas have a 20-year survival rate of about 40%.

Follicular carcinoma is also more common in women than in men. When noninvasive, such tumors are compatible with a normal life span. They tend to spread via blood vessel invasion; metastases may appear years after apparent complete excision. The 10-year survival in patients with vascular invasion at the time of surgery is 30%.

Medullary carcinoma arises from the C cells and produces calcitonin. It can occur as a solitary malignancy or as part of the multiple endocrine neoplasia syndrome, type 2B (MEN 2B), in which it is associated with enlarged corneal nerves.

Anaplastic carcinoma, though fortunately rare, is the most malignant tumor of the thyroid gland and is found mainly in patients over the age of 60. The giant-cell form has a survival time of less than 6 months from time of diagnosis; the small-cell form has a 5-year survival of 20%–25%.

Behnia M, Gharib H. Primary care diagnosis of thyroid disease. *Hosp Pract.* 1996;31: 121–134.

Kennedy JW, Caro JF. Managing hyperthyroidism in the older patient. *Geriatrics.* 1996; 51:22–32.

Larsen PR. The Thyroid. In: Wyngaarden JB, Smith LH, Bennett JC, eds. *Cecil Textbook of Medicine.* 19th ed. Philadelphia: Saunders; 1992:1248–1271.

Socolow EL, Fleischer N. Thyroid disease and the heart. In: Hurst JW, ed. *Current Therapy in Cardiovascular Disease.* 4th ed. St Louis: Mosby; 1994.

CHAPTER X

Osteoporosis

Recent Developments

☐ Dual-photon x-ray absorptiometry (DXA) has become the technique of choice for evaluation of bone density, shortening examination time and improving accuracy compared to older techniques.

☐ Bisphosphonates have become an important part of therapeutic regimens.

☐ A slow-release form of sodium fluoride, which stimulates bone formation, will soon be available in the U.S.

Introduction

Osteoporosis is a condition of varied etiology in which there is a decrease in the mass of bone per unit volume (reduced bone density), leading to increased bone fragility and risk of fracture. It is the most common bone disorder confronting the clinician.

Osteoporosis is a significant, worldwide public health problem whose prevalence seems to be increasing. The disease is rare among black women and females of southern European ancestry. About 25% of white women over 60 years of age have documented spinal compression fractures in association with osteoporosis. As many as 50% of women will develop vertebral fractures by age 75. After age 45, the incidence of distal forearm fractures increases markedly. By age 60, there are ten times as many forearm fractures in women as in men of comparable age. The risk of hip fractures increases with age and, among women, reaches 20% by age 90; 80% of hip fractures are associated with preexisting osteoporosis. Approximately 17% of women with hip fractures die within 3 months of the fracture. In the United States, it is estimated that osteoporosis causes 1.5 million fractures each year at a cost of $10 billion.

Bone Physiology

Bone is a two-component system, with an organic and an inorganic phase. The organic phase (osteoid) is a matrix of collagen, glycoproteins and phosphoproteins, mucopolysaccharides, and lipids. The inorganic phase (hydroxyapatite) is an insoluble calcium-phosphate mineral. There are three types of bone cells: *osteoclasts,* which resorb bone; *osteoblasts,* which form bone; and *osteocytes,* which maintain bone structure and function. The outer portion of bone (*cortical bone*) composes 80% of total bone volume and consists of less than 5% soft tissue, while the inner portion of bone (*trabecular bone*) is more porous and includes 75% soft tissue.

Bone is metabolically active and continually remodels throughout life along lines of mechanical stress. During late adolescence, bone mineral content increases rapidly. Bone mass peaks in the third decade. With age, the balance between bone resorption and bone formation is altered, and bone mass decreases. By age 60, skeletal mass may be as little as 50% of that at age 30.

Risk Factors

Many risk factors are associated with osteoporosis. Peak bone mass (the maximum bone density reached by an individual, normally in young adulthood) appears to be the strongest correlate to lifetime fracture risk. Racial and sexual differences in peak bone mass at skeletal maturity may explain the high relative risk in white women, compared with black women and white men (intermediate peak density and risk) and black men (highest peak bone density and lowest risk).

Sex hormones play a significant role: high rates of osteoporosis are seen in women after menopause or oophorectomy, in girls with gonadal dysgenesis, and in female long-distance runners with functional hypogonadism. Age-related factors include decreased formation of new bone, impaired calcium absorption (with secondary hyperparathyroidism and increased bone loss), and nutritional vitamin D deficiency. Other associated factors include insufficient dietary calcium intake, sedentary lifestyle, nulliparity, alcohol abuse, and cigarette smoking.

In addition, glucocorticoid excess, thyrotoxicosis of Graves disease, acromegaly, diabetes mellitus, and a variety of other systemic diseases and drugs are all associated with bone loss.

Clinical Features

The typical clinical picture in osteoporosis includes back pain, spinal deformity, loss of height, and fractures of the vertebrae, hips, and less commonly, other bones. Multiple vertebral fractures over a period of years can lead to severe kyphosis, with a loss of height of 4–8 inches, and cervical lordosis ("dowager's hump.")

Diagnostic Evaluation

Radiographic Evaluation

Patients at risk with a history of back pain are evaluated for radiographic evidence of vertebral fracture. At least 30% of bone mass must be lost before radiographic changes can be seen. The changes may be subtle, since osteoporosis represents a generalized reduction in bone mass. The amount of loss necessary for detection by conventional x-ray depends upon the bone involved. The spinal column exhibits the most characteristic radiographic features of osteoporosis, with accentuation of the vertebral end plates, anterior wedging in the thoracic spinal column, biconcave compression ("ballooning," or "codfish vertebrae") in the lumbar region, and disc herniation into the vertebral body. The long bones exhibit cortical thinning with irregularity of endosteal surfaces. Osteoporosis caused by glucocorticoid excess presents a somewhat different picture, with radiographic changes in the skull, ribs, and pelvic rami.

Several other techniques allow more accurate measurement of bone density than can be obtained through conventional x-rays. All of these methods measure the degree of attenuation of a beam of photons from an x-ray tube by targeted bones and surrounding soft tissues. Measurements of the spine are used to predict vertebral fractures, of the femoral neck for hip fractures, and of the wrist or heel for peripheral fractures. Results are compared to mean values in young adults, the normal for women being within one standard deviation (SD) of this reference mean (the T score). The risk of fractures increases with age and with each SD below the mean; below 2 SD, the risk rises exponentially. *Osteoporosis* is defined as values more than 2.5 SD below the mean, *osteopenia* as a value 2.0 SD below the mean.

Dual-photon x-ray absorptiometry (DXA) is presently the technique of choice, as it allows for shorter examination time (a few minutes with current machines), greater accuracy, improved resolution, and longer source life. The radiation dose of this test is less than 5 millirem.

Dual-energy quantitative computed tomography (QCT) scans the lower thoracic and upper lumbar vertebral bodies in cross section at numerous levels, and the CT values obtained are compared with standards for soft tissue, fat, and mineral. QCT is very accurate but is more expensive than DXA and may be less reproducible. The x-ray dose is less than 3 millirem.

Clinical Evaluation

If densitometric studies confirm the diagnosis of osteoporosis, a medical evaluation should be undertaken to rule out secondary causes (Table X-1). Serum calcium and phosphorus levels are usually normal, although slight hyperphosphatemia may be present in postmenopausal women. Alkaline phosphatase is usually normal but may be slightly elevated following a fracture. Sustained elevation of alkaline phosphatase in the absence of liver disease suggests osteomalacia or skeletal metastasis.

Treatment

General Considerations

All patients with osteoporosis should have a diet that supplies adequate amounts of calcium, protein, and vitamins. Weight-bearing exercise such as walking, jogging, and weight lifting is important in the maintenance of bone mass. Limitation of alcohol intake and cessation of smoking are also beneficial. Back pain is treated with analgesics and physical therapy.

Drug Therapy

Calcium and vitamin D   Ingestion of elemental calcium is important for the maintenance of bone mass. The incidence of hip fractures appears to be significantly less in female populations where dietary calcium intake is high. The recommended daily intake is 1000 mg/day for premenopausal women and 1500 mg/day for postmenopausal women (roughly the equivalent of four 8-ounce glasses of milk), but the average intake in women is only about 375 mg/day. During pregnancy and lactation, much more calcium may be needed. This calcium may be obtained from dietary as well as pharmacological sources. Patients who receive long-term steroids to treat an underlying disease should have calcium and vitamin D supplementation. Vitamin D replacement in vitamin-deficient older patients reverses secondary hyperparathyroidism, but its value in patients without documented vitamin deficiency is unclear.

Calcium is available in a variety of preparations, including calcium carbonate, citrate, gluconate, lactate, and phosphate. Calcium carbonate and phosphate have

TABLE X-1

CAUSES OF SECONDARY OSTEOPOROSIS

Primary osteoporosis	Bone-marrow disorders
Juvenile	Multiple myeloma
Idiopathic (young adults)	Systemic mastocytosis
Involutional	Disseminated carcinoma
Endocrine	**Connective tissue diseases**
Hypogonadism	Osteogenesis imperfecta
Ovarian agenesis	Homocystinuria
Glucocorticoid excess	Ehlers-Danlos syndrome
Hyperthyroidism	Marfan syndrome
Hyperparathyroidism	**Miscellaneous**
Diabetes mellitus (?)	Immobilization
Gastrointestinal	Chronic obstructive pulmonary disease
Subtotal gastrectomy	Chronic alcoholism
Malabsorption syndromes	Rheumatoid arthritis (?)
Chronic obstructive jaundice	Chronic heparin administration
Primary biliary cirrhosis	Chronic use of anticonvulsant drugs
Severe malnutrition	

the highest concentration of elemental calcium, about 40%; calcium citrate has 21%, lactate 13%, and gluconate 9%. Calcium therapy may cause constipation, nausea, flatulence, bloating, hypercalcuria, and renal stones. Hypercalcemia does not occur in patients with normal renal function. However, massive doses of vitamin D can lead to dangerous hypercalcemia.

Hormone therapy   Numerous clinical studies have established that estrogens are useful in the prevention of osteoporosis. Estrogens produce significant calcium retention, decrease the imbalance between bone formation and resorption, and tend to decrease the progression of osteoporosis by slowing bone turnover. A recent study showed an increase in bone mineral density in women taking estrogen or combination estrogen-progestin treatment (see below) compared to those taking placebo.

Estrogen therapy may preserve height, reduce the rate of vertebral and hip fracture (by 70% and 50%, respectively in some studies), prevent vertebral deformity, and stabilize bone loss in postmenopausal women, amenorrheic premenopausal women, and post-oophorectomy patients. Their effectiveness may be enhanced when combined with calcium supplementation. Maximum benefit from estrogen treatment appears to be achieved by starting therapy at the onset of menopause and continuing for at least 7–10 years, although it has also been shown to have some benefit in older women with established osteoporosis.

Unopposed estrogen treatment increases the risk of endometrial carcinoma, but concurrent progestin therapy reduces this risk to that of the general population. Whether hormone therapy increases the risk of breast carcinoma remains controversial, but its use is contraindicated in patients with proven breast cancer or a positive family history. Estrogen therapy may cause nausea, weight gain, glucose intolerance, and breast tenderness. It also increases the risk of hypertension and cholelithiasis.

Other drugs *Calcitonin* interferes with osteoclast function and inhibits bone resorption. Derived from salmon, it has been used in the treatment of osteoporosis for many years but could only be given by subcutaneous or intramuscular injection. Recently, however, calcitonin nasal spray (*Miacalcin*) has become available. It is well tolerated and has shown some effectiveness in increasing bone density and reducing fractures. Adequate concomitant intake of calcium and vitamin D is necessary.

Bisphosphonates are a class of drugs that bind strongly to hydroxyapatite crystals, are adsorbed onto new bone matrix, and prevent bone resorption by inhibiting osteoclast activity. Bisphosphonates shift the balance between bone formation and resorption toward formation. High doses, however, interfere with the process of bone mineralization.

Alendronate (Fosamax), a bisphosphonate recently approved by the FDA, has a much more favorable ratio between suppression of resorption and inhibition of mineralization than previously available drugs in this class. Its main side effects are gastrointestinal. As with other treatments for osteoporosis, calcium and vitamin D intake must be adequate.

Sodium fluoride, unlike other available treatments, stimulates osteoblast proliferation and increases bone formation. In fact, when fluoride is used the demand for calcium created by the osteoblastic response is so great that bone can be resorbed if calcium intake is insufficient, leading to increased bone fragility and increased incidence of fractures. Plain sodium fluoride can have significant gastrointestinal side effects; a slow-release preparation is available and will soon be marketed in the United States.

Thiazide diuretics reduce the excretion of urinary calcium and may enhance positive calcium balance.

Osteoporosis in Men

Osteoporosis is perceived primarily as a disease of postmenopausal females. It should be noted, however, that women have only twice the incidence of hip fracture as men. Cigarette smoking, alcohol consumption, steroid therapy, and hypogonadism are associated with an increased incidence of osteoporosis in men, who also seem to benefit from the above-cited protective measures (with the exception of estrogen therapy).

Bellantoni MF. Osteoporosis prevention and treatment. *Am Fam Physician.* 1996;54: 986–992.

Bone densitometry. In: Abramowicz M, ed. *The Medical Letter.* 1996;38:103–104.

Calcium supplements. In: Abramowicz M, ed. *The Medical Letter.* 1996;38:108–109.

Cauley JA, Lucas FL, Kuller LH, et al. Bone mineral density and risk of breast cancer in older women. Study of Osteoporotic Fractures Research Group. *JAMA.* 1996;276: 1404–1408.

Effects of hormone therapy on bone mineral density: results from the postmenopausal estrogen/progestin intervention (PEPI) trial. The Writing Group for the PEPI Trial. *JAMA.* 1996;276:1389–1396.

New drugs for osteoporosis. In: Abramowicz M, ed. *The Medical Letter.* 1996;38:1–3.

Riggs BL. Osteoporosis. In: Wyngaarden JB, Smith LH, Bennett JC, eds. *Cecil Textbook of Medicine*. 19th ed. Philadelphia: Saunders; 1992:1426–1431.

Sturtridge W, Lentle B, Hanley D. Prevention and management of osteoporosis: consensus statement from the Scientific Advisory Board of the Osteoporosis Society of Canada. 2. The use of bone density measurement in the diagnosis and management of osteoporosis. *CMAJ*. 1996;155:924–929.

CHAPTER XI

Cancer

Recent Developments

☐ Genetic profiling of tumors may contribute significantly to their potential treatment.

☐ Antiangiogenesis may prove to be a significant form of cancer therapy in humans.

Incidence

Cancer is the second leading cause of death in the United States. About 1,170,000 new cases are diagnosed, and some 550,000 deaths occur annually. More than 3 million Americans have survived cancer, and in more than 2 million of these the diagnosis was established longer than 5 years ago. About 23% of all deaths in the United States are due to cancer.

Cancer is actually many different diseases; questions of etiology, cancer prevention, and cancer cure must address the specific types of tumors. Nonmelanotic skin cancers are the most common tumors, but these cancers rarely produce major clinical problems. After these types, the most common forms of cancer in adult Americans (in decreasing order of incidence) are lung, breast, prostate, and colorectal. About 80% of adult cancers arise from the epithelial tissues; leukemias and sarcomas are relatively rare.

The incidence of cancer in children has increased some 20% over the last two decades and accounts for 10% of deaths from ages 1 to 14. In that age group, cancer is second to accidents as a leading cause of death. Leukemias, CNS tumors, and soft tissue tumors account for the majority of cancers in this age group.

Etiology

Cancer is a genetic disease. It is caused by multiple mutations in genes that control cell division. Some of these genes, called *oncogenes,* stimulate cell division while others, called *tumor-suppressor genes,* slow this process. In the normal state, both types of genes work together, enabling the body to replace dead cells and repair damaged ones. Mutations in these genes cause the cell to proliferate out of control. Such mutations can be inherited or acquired through environmental insults. (Cancer causes, therefore, are explained on the basis of chemical, viral, or radiation-related etiologies that occur in a complex milieu, including host genetic composition and immunobiological status). Between 60% and 90% of cases are understood on the basis of environmental origin. Several examples of this are cigarette smoking (lung cancer), asbestos (lung cancer and mesothelioma), vinyl chloride (hepatic angiosarcoma), benzidine (leukemia), dietary nitrates (gastrointestinal carcinoma), and lye injury (esophageal carcinoma).

Carcinogenic Factors

Chemical Over the past 40 years, definite changes have occurred in the cancer mortality rates in the United States. For example, lung cancer death rates have increased markedly in both men and women. This increase parallels the rise in cigarette smoking, but the higher death rate lags about 20 years behind the increase in smoking. The increased incidence of and mortality from lung cancer are particularly striking in women, in whom mortality is increasing at the rate of about 6% per year. Even though breast cancer remains more prevalent, lung cancer kills more women than does breast cancer. Most cases of lung cancer can be attributed to cigarette smoking.

The mortality rates from breast, colon, and rectal cancer have remained essentially unchanged over the past 40 years. Stomach cancer has become fairly rare in the United States, presumably because of a decrease in human exposure to exogenous agents such as dietary nitrites and an increase in dietary vitamins.

In the United States and Western Europe, there is a high mortality rate from lung, colon, and breast cancer and a low mortality rate from stomach cancer. In Japan, stomach cancer predominates and colon and breast cancer are relatively rare. Descendants of Japanese individuals who migrated to the United States will, after several generations, show a decreased incidence of stomach cancer and acquire the high incidence of colon cancer characteristic of the United States. Similarly, Japanese in Japan who adopt a Western diet and lifestyle have an increased rate of colon cancer and a decreased rate of stomach cancer, while people of Japanese ancestry in the United States who marry Japanese spouses and do not adopt a Western diet continue to show high stomach cancer and low colon cancer rates. These examples support the argument for the predominant role of environmental factors as opposed to genetic or inborn factors in the etiology of most human cancers.

The incidence of specific cancers in different subsets of the American population shows considerable variation. For example, the black population has a higher incidence of cancer of the prostate, uterine cervix, lung, esophagus, and oropharynx than does the white population; however, the black population also has a lower incidence of cancer of the breast and corpus uteri than does the white population.

Epidemiologic data suggest that up to 80% of human cancers may be due to exogenous chemical exposure. If they could be properly identified, a major proportion of human cancers could be prevented by reducing host exposure or by protecting the host. A number of industrial processes or occupational exposures and numerous chemicals or groups of chemicals have been implicated in various forms of human cancer. Specific causes of major cancers such as large bowel and breast cancer have not been identified with certainty. Important questions needing resolution are

□ The extent to which cancers are caused by naturally occurring substances versus manmade chemicals

□ The role of chemical versus viral agents

□ The role of general nutritional factors

□ The role of multifactor interactions

Radiation The carcinogenic effects of ionizing radiation were discovered at the turn of the century when radiation caused an epidermoid carcinoma on the hand of a radiologist. The general population is exposed to both naturally occurring ionizing radiation and manmade ionizing radiation.

Levels and doses of radiation are measured in various units. Units expressing absorbed doses are the *rad* and the *gray (Gy)*, an SI unit equal to 100 rad. The *rem* and *sievert (Sv)* are units that measure biological effect. One rem is that dose of any radiation that produces a biological effect equivalent to 1 rad of x-rays or gamma rays. Similarly, the sievert (an SI unit) is that dose of any radiation that produces the biological effect equivalent to 1 gray of x-rays. (Thus, 1 Sv equals 100 rem.)

Natural radiation comes from cosmic rays; thorium, radium, and other radionuclides in the earth's crust; and potassium 40, carbon 14, and other naturally occurring radioactive elements in the body. The average dose for a person living at sea level is 0.8 mSv (80 mrem) per year. The average dose may be double for persons living at higher elevations (e.g., Denver) because of more intense cosmic rays. It may also be larger where the content of radioactive material in the soil and subterranean rock is greater.

Manmade sources deliver an average of 106 mrem per year to each person. These sources include medical diagnostic equipment, technologically altered natural sources (such as phosphate fertilizers and building materials containing small amounts of radioactivity), global fallout from atmospheric testing of atomic weapons, nuclear power, high-altitude jet flight, occupational exposure, and consumer products such as color television sets, smoke detectors, and luminescent clocks and instrument dials.

Radiation exposure has been associated with cancer of almost every organ, system, and tissue in human and animal models. The carcinogenic effects result from molecular lesions caused by random interactions of radiation with atoms and molecules. Most molecular lesions induced in this way are of little consequence to the affected cell. However, DNA is not repaired with 100% efficiency, and mutations and chromosomal aberrations accrue with increasing radiation dose. Although these changes in genes and chromosomes have been postulated to account for the carcinogenic effect of radiation, the precise molecular mechanisms are unknown. Parameters that influence response of the target tissue include the total radiation dose, the dose rate, the quality of the radiation source, the characteristics of certain internal emitters (such as radioiodine), and individual host factors such as age at the time of radiation exposure and sex.

Viral   The role of viruses in the etiology of cancer has been studied extensively, but evidence is still too weak to permit the unequivocal conclusion that viruses cause tumors in humans. The inoculation of animals with specific viruses may produce tumors, and certain naturally occurring tumors in animals may be transmitted horizontally from animal to animal by viruses (for example, Lucké renal adenocarcinoma in the leopard frog, Marek lymphomatous disease in chickens, leukemia in cats and cattle). In humans, some papillomavirus infections produce warts that can become cancerous, and particles resembling viruses associated with the transmission of leukemia in animals have been found in human cancer patients. In addition, several human cancers show a definite correlation with viral infection and the presence and retention of specific virus nucleic acid sequences and virus proteins in the tumor cells (Burkitt lymphoma, nasopharyngeal carcinoma, carcinoma of the cervix, and hepatocellular carcinoma).

All of the DNA virus groups except the parvovirus family have been associated with cancer. This is notable because all the DNA viruses associated with cancer contain double-stranded DNA, whereas the parvoviruses contain only single-stranded

DNA. The DNA tumor-causing viruses are of varying shapes, sizes, and molecular weights. All are icosahedral; some are enveloped and some are not.

There are nine RNA virus groups, but only one is associated with oncogenicity: the retrovirus group. The retroviruses differ from all other RNA viruses in that they require a DNA intermediate to replicate. Retroviruses contain and specify an enzyme called *reverse transcriptase*. In the presence of the four nucleoside triphosphates, reverse transcriptase can synthesize DNA complementary to the single-stranded RNA contained in the virion, producing an RNA-DNA hybrid. The RNA in this RNA-DNA hybrid is then degraded, and a double-stranded linear DNA molecule forms. This double-stranded DNA molecule moves into the cell nucleus and is integrated into the cellular DNA as a provirus. Retrovirus virions are 70–100 nm in diameter, spherical, and enveloped. They are icosahedral with a single-stranded genome.

The papillomavirus of the papovavirus group has been associated with squamous cell carcinoma and laryngeal papilloma in humans. The hepatitis B virus has been associated with primary hepatocellular carcinoma in humans.

The human herpesviruses associated with disease include Epstein-Barr virus (EBV), herpes simplex virus type 1 (HSV-1), herpes simplex virus type 2 (HSV-2), cytomegalovirus (CMV), and varicella-zoster virus (VZV). The EBV that causes infectious mononucleosis has been associated with Burkitt lymphoma and nasopharyngeal carcinoma. The HSV-1 that causes gingivostomatitis, encephalitis, keratoconjunctivitis, neuralgia, and labialis has been associated with carcinoma of the lip and oropharynx. The HSV-2 that causes genital herpes, disseminated neonatal herpes, encephalitis, and neuralgia has been associated with cancer of the uterine cervix, vulva, kidney, and nasopharynx. The CMV that causes CMV disease, transfusion mononucleosis, interstitial pneumonia, and congenital defects has been associated with prostate cancer, Kaposi sarcoma, and carcinoma of the bladder and uterine cervix. The VZV that causes chickenpox, shingles, and varicella pneumonia has not yet been associated with specific human cancers.

Genetic and familial factors   Host susceptibility is an established but poorly defined concept in understanding human carcinogenesis. A heritable component may be more important in some forms of cancer (colon cancer) and less important in others (esophageal cancer). Certain cancers show an ethnic predilection.

Cancers may aggregate in a nonrandom manner in certain families. These cancers may be of the same type or dissimilar. Such cancer-cluster families may have several children with soft-tissue sarcoma and relatives with a variety of cancers, especially of the breast in young women. Multiple endocrine neoplasia (MEN-I and -II) is yet another example of familial cancer. The recognition of family cancer syndromes permits early detection that may be lifesaving.

Genetic abnormalities are a feature of many cancers. These may be single-gene disorders or inborn chromosomal abnormalities. Heritable retinoblastoma is due in part to a 13q14 deletion. Other forms of cancer may be caused by mutation of multiple alleles, some of which are pleiotropic (e.g., they may induce more than one form of cancer). An example is osteosarcoma occurring in the lower femurs of children with bilateral retinoblastoma. Such persons may also be unusually susceptible to the carcinogenic effect of radiotherapy for the eye tumor and develop a second primary tumor after an indefinite latency.

Therapy

Radiation

Ionizing radiation interacts with host tissues and malignant tumors by an energy transfer and a chemical reaction, with the release of free radicals and the decomposition of water into hydrogen, hydroxyl, and perhydroxyl ionic forms. These ionic forms probably react with DNA and RNA in vital enzymes, producing biological injury. The injuries noted to date include mitotic-linked death and chromosomal aberrations such as breakage, sticking, and cross-bridging. Consequent cell death occurs in both normal tissue and malignant lesions. In radiotherapy, biochemical recovery and biological repair occur in the normal host, maintaining the integrity of vital systems.

The poorly differentiated lymphoid cells, intestinal epithelium, and reproductive cells are more readily damaged and recover more quickly than do the highly differentiated normal cells. Lymphocytes are therefore damaged by 100 rads and CNS tissue by 5000 rads. Surface irradiation of approximately 1000 rads produces skin erythema. The most serious damage is the late development of postradiation malignant changes in as many as 21% of patients, manifesting as squamous cell carcinoma and basal cell carcinoma. Bone absorption can produce osteogenic sarcomas and fibrosarcomas.

Radiation teratology is an area of ongoing interest. The most radiosensitive stage occurs during the period of organogenesis, 6–12 weeks following conception. The most common site of radiation damage is the CNS, producing microcephaly and mental retardation. Ocular manifestations of fetal irradiation in the first trimester include microphthalmos, congenital cataracts, and retinal dysplasia. Congenital anomalies may occur in an irradiated fetus at a 5 rad dose. Fetal exposure to approximately 30–80 rads doubles the incidence of congenital defects; while 500 rads, or the LD 50 for humans, will generally induce an abortion.

Effects of radiation on tumors (Table XI-1) In general, more anaplastic carcinomas are more radioresponsive. However, some tumors that are relatively radiosensitive may not be radiocurable because of their diffuse state, e.g., lymphosarcoma. Alternatively, radioresistant tumors are not necessarily radioincurable if they are sufficiently localized, e.g., renal cell carcinoma or melanoma. The radiocurability of malignant tumors depends upon

- The state of the host's defenses and immunologic factors
- The anatomic extent of the tumor, and
- The therapeutic ratio

This last term, *therapeutic ratio,* refers to the relationship between the normal tissue tolerance dose (measured in rads) and the tumor LD measured in rads. If the dose of radiation necessary to eradicate the tumor is substantially greater than the 5000 rads normally tolerated by the surrounding tissues, radiocurability becomes unlikely. The exact tissue diagnosis is therefore critical if radiation therapy is being considered.

Effects of radiation on the eye and adnexa The ocular effects of radiation depend not only upon total dose, fractionation, and treatment portal size but also upon associated systemic diseases such as diabetes and hypertension. Concomitant chemotherapy has an additive effect.

TABLE XI-1

TUMORS IN DECREASING ORDER OF RELATIVE RADIOSENSITIVITY

TUMORS	RELATIVE RADIOSENSITIVITY	TISSUES
Lymphoma, leukemia, seminoma dysgerminoma, granulosa cell carcinoma, retinoblastoma	High	Lymphoid, hematopoietic (marrow), spermatogenic epithelium, ovarian follicular epithelium, intestinal epithelium
Squamous cell cancer of the oropharyngeal epithelium, esophageal epithelium, bladder epithelium, skin epithelium, cervical epithelium	Fairly high	Oropharyngeal stratified epithelium, epidermal epithelium, hair follicle epithelium, sebaceous gland epithelium, bladder epithelium, esophageal epithelium, optic lens epithelium, gastric gland epithelium, ureteral epithelium
Vascular and connective tissue elements of all tumors, secondary neovascularization, astrocytomas	Medium	Ordinary interstitial connective tissue, neuroglial tissue (connective tissue of the nervous system), fine vasculature, growing cartilage, bone tissue
Adenocarcinoma of breast epithelium, serous gland epithelium, salivary gland epithelium, hepatic epithelium, renal epithelium, pancreatic epithelium, thyroid epithelium, colon epithelium; liposarcoma; chondrosarcoma; osteogenic sarcoma	Fairly low	Mature cartilage of bone tissue, mucous or serous gland epithelium, salivary gand epithelium, sweat gland epithelium, nasopharyngeal simple epithelium, pulmonary epithelium, renal epithelium, hepatic epithelium, thyroid epithelium, adrenal epithelium
Rhabdomyosarcoma, leiomyosarcoma, ganglioneurofibrosarcoma, melanoma	Low	Muscle tissue, neuronal tissue

The lens is the most radiosensitive structure in the eye, followed by the cornea, the retina, and the optic nerve. The orbit is completely included in the treatment portal in diseases such as large retinoblastomas and melanomas or partially included in diseases such as small melanomas and retinoblastomas and tumors of adjacent structures, such as the maxillary antrum, nasopharynx, ethmoid sinus, and nasal cavity. Usual doses range from 2000 to 10,000 rads. The total dose is usually fractionated during the treatment.

Doses to the lens as low as 200 rads in one fraction may cause a cataract. However, cataracts caused by low doses may not be symptomatic and may not progress. Cataracts caused by higher doses (700–800 rads) may continue to progress, causing considerable visual loss. The average latent period for the development of radiation-induced cataracts is 2–3 years.

The clinical picture of radiation retinopathy resembles diabetic retinopathy, and it is very rare below the fractionated dose of 5000 rads over 5–6 weeks. At higher fractionated doses (7000–8000 rads), the majority of patients develop radiation retinopathy. The usual interval between radiation and the development of radiation-induced retinopathy is 2–3 years. Patients who are diabetic or on chemotherapy may develop radiation retinopathy earlier. The earliest clinical manifestation of radiation retinopathy is usually cotton-wool spots. After several months they fade away, leaving large areas of capillary nonperfusion. Telangiectatic vessels grow in the retina into the areas of capillary nonperfusion. Microaneurysms may also develop. These ischemic changes may cause rubeosis iridis, which in turn may lead to rubeotic glaucoma.

Histologically, the capillary endothelial cell is the first type of cell to be damaged, followed closely by the pericytes and then the endothelial cells of the larger vessels. The new intraretinal telangiectatic vessels have thick collagenous walls. There may be spotty occlusion of the choriocapillaris.

Doses to the optic nerve in the range of 6000–7000 rads can cause some injury in a small number of patients. Damage to the distal end of the optic nerve is called *radiation optic neuropathy*. Clinically, these patients have disc pallor with splinter hemorrhages. If the injury occurs to the more proximal part of the optic nerve, it resembles a retrobulbar optic neuropathy. Such patients may complain of unilateral headaches and ocular pain; the disc may not reveal edema or hemorrhage.

The effect of radiation on lacrimal tissue depends upon the total dose. Permanent damage is not common below 5000 rads. With doses of 6000–7000 rads, some patients may develop a dry eye syndrome. This syndrome usually develops within a year and may occasionally progress to corneal ulceration and severe pain.

Chemotherapy

The goal of cancer chemotherapy is to destroy cancer cells by taking advantage of their increased metabolic activity compared to normal cells. Effective drugs should have minimal long-term impact on normal cells, especially those with a rapid rate of turnover such as bone marrow and mucous membrane. A model treatment plan should allow normal cells to regrow more rapidly than tumor cells, to permit re-treatment at appropriate intervals. Cancer inhibition takes place at several levels: (1) macromolecular synthesis, (2) cytoplasmic organization, and (3) cell membrane synthesis. Most drugs destroy cells by first-order kinetics; that is, they kill a constant percent (or log) of cells with each treatment.

It has been estimated that approximately 10^9, or 1 g, of tumor cells are required to be detected. A lethal number of cells is 10^{12}, or 1 kg. If a drug can kill 2–3 log, three to five treatments would still be required after all clinical disease has disappeared to achieve a cure. This is the basis for continuing treatment after an apparent complete remission. Chemotherapy may fail in some instances because tumor populations are not homogeneous; some cells are less sensitive to drugs, and therefore the log or percent kill is lower.

The sensitivity of a tumor population is largely dependent on the growth characteristics of the tumor cells. Some of the factors involved are cell cycle time, growth fraction (the percent of cells undergoing division), number of tumor cells present, and tumor cell natural death rate.

Chemotherapeutic agents can be divided into the following basic groups: alkylating agents, antimetabolites, hormones, and natural products (Table XI-2).

Alkylating agents Alkylating agents form covalent bonds within the nuclei, which cause cross-linking and abnormal base-pairing, producing lethal errors in dividing cells. Examples are *mechlorethamine* (nitrogen mustard), *cyclophosphamide* (Cytoxan), *chlorambucil* (Leukeran), *melphalan* (Alkeran), and *busulfan* (Myleran). Toxicity causes cytopenia, nausea, alopecia, hemorrhage, and pulmonary fibrosis. Cyclophosphamide is a precursor to its active metabolites, phosphoamide mustard and acrolein. It is well absorbed orally (90% bioavailability). Its active products are

TABLE XI-2

ANTINEOPLASTIC DRUGS

DRUGS BY CLASS	MECHANISM OF ACTION	TUMORS COMMONLY RESPONSIVE	TOXICITY AND REMARKS
Alkylating agents Mechlorethamine (nitrogen mustard) Chlorambucil (Leukeran) Cyclophosphamide (Cytoxan) Melphalan (Alkeran) Ifosfamide (Ifex)	Alkylation of DNA with restriction of strands' uncoiling and replication	Hodgkin's, malignant lymphoma, small cell lung Ca, Ca of breast and testis, CLL	Alopecia with high IV dosage; nausea and vomiting; myelosuppression; hemorrhagic cystitis (especially with ifosfamide), which can be ameliorated with Mesna; muto- and leukemogenic; aspermia; permanent sterility possible
Antimetabolites Folate antagonist (Amethopterin) Methotrexate (MTX)	Folate antagonist with binding to dehydrofolate reductase and interference with (pyrimidine) thymidylate synthesis	Choriocarcinoma (female), Ca of head and neck, ALL, Ca of ovary, malignant lymphoma, osteogenic sarcoma	Mucosal ulceration; bone marrow suppression; toxicity increased with renal function impairment or ascitic fluid (with pooling of drug). Leucovorin rescue can reverse toxicity at 24 h (10–20 mg q 6 h × 10 doses).
Purine antagonist 6-Mercaptopurine (6-MP)	Blocks de novo purine synthesis	Acute leukemia	Myelosuppression, alopecia
Pyrimidine antagonist 5-Fluorouracil (5-FU)	Interferes with thymidylate synthase to reduce thymidine production	GI neoplasms, Ca of breast	Mucositis, alopecia, myelosuppression, diarrhea and vomiting, hyperpigmentation. When given after MTX, synergistic effect is significant.
Cytarabine (Ara-C)	DNA polymerase inhibition	Acute leukemia (especially nonlymphocytic), malignant lymphoma	Myelosuppression, nausea and vomiting, cerebellar and conjunctival toxicities at high dosage, skin rash

ALL = acute lymphocytic leukemia; Ca = cancer; CLL = chronic lymphocytic leukemia; CML = chronic myeloid leukemia; IFN = interferon; SIADH = syndrome of inappropriate antidiuretic hormone secretion.

TABLE XI-2

ANTINEOPLASTIC DRUGS (Continued)

DRUGS BY CLASS	MECHANISM OF ACTION	TUMORS COMMONLY RESPONSIVE	TOXICITY AND REMARKS
Plant Alkaloids			
Vincas			
Vinblastine (Velban)	Mitotic arrest by alteration of microtubular proteins	Lymphomas, leukemias, Ca of breast, Ewing's sarcoma, Ca of testis	Alopecia, myelosuppression, peripheral neuropathy, ileus
Vincristine (Oncovin)	As above		Peripheral neuropathy, SIADH. Dose commonly "capped" at total of 2 mg in adults.
Podophyllotoxins			
Etoposide (VP-16)	Inhibition of mitosis by unknown mechanisms	Lymphoma, Hodgkin's, Ca of testis, Ca of lung (especially small cell), acute leukemia	Nausea, vomiting, myelosuppression, peripheral neuropathy. Etoposide cleared by liver (teniposide by kidney); increased toxicity in renal failure.
Antibiotics			
Doxorubicin (Adriamycin)	Intercalation between DNA strands inhibits uncoiling of DNA	Acute leukemia, Hodgkin's, other lymphomas, Ca of breast, Ca of lung	Nausea and vomiting, myelosuppression, alopecia. Cardiac toxicity at cumulative dosage >500 mg/m^2. Higher dosage tolerated when given by continuous IV.
Bleomycin	Incision of DNA strands	Squamous cell Ca, lymphoma, Ca of testis, Ca of lung	Anaphylaxis, chills and fever, skin rash; pulmonary fibrosis at dosage >200 mg/m^2; requires renal excretion
Mitomycin	Inhibits DNA synthesis by acting as a bifunctional alkylator	Gastric adenocarcinoma; colon, breast, and lung Ca; transitional cell Ca of the bladder	Local extravasation causes tissue necrosis; myelosuppression, with leukopenia and thrombocytopenia 4–6 wk after treatment; alopecia; lethargy; fever; hemolytic-uremic syndrome
Nitrosureas			
Carmustine (BiCNU)	Alkylation of DNA with restriction of strands' uncoiling and replication	Brain tumors, lymphoma	Myelosuppression, pulmonary toxicity (fibrosis), renal toxicity
Lomustine (CeeNU)	Carbamoylation of amino acids in proteins	As above	As above

Table XI-2

Antineoplastic Drugs (Continued)

DRUGS BY CLASS	MECHANISM OF ACTION	TUMORS COMMONLY RESPONSIVE	TOXICITY AND REMARKS
Inorganic ions			
Cisplatin (Platinol)	Intercalation and intracalation between DNA strands inhibits uncoiling of DNA	Ca of lung (especially small cell), testis, breast, and stomach; lymphoma	Anemia, ototoxicity, peripheral neuropathy, myelosuppression
Biologic response modification			
IFN (Intron-A, Roferon-A)	Antiproliferative effect	Hairy-cell leukemia, CML, lymphomas, Kaposi sarcoma (AIDS), renal cell Ca, melanoma	Fatigue, fever, myalgias, arthralgias, myelosuppression, nephrotic syndrome (rarely)
Enzymes			
Asparaginase (Elspar)	Depletion of asparagine, on which leukemic cells depend	ALL	Acute anaphylaxis, hyperthermia, pancreatitis, hyperglycemia, hypofibrinogenemia
Hormones			
Tamoxifen (Nolvadex)	Places cells at rest: binding of estrogen receptor	Ca of breast	Hot flushes, hypercalcemia, deep vein thrombosis
Flutamide (Eulexin)	Binding of androgen receptor	Ca of prostate	Decreased libido, hot flushes, gynecomastia

ALL = acute lymphocytic leukemia; Ca = cancer; CLL = chronic lymphocytic leukemia; CML = chronic myeloid leukemia; IFN = interferon; SIADH = syndrome of inappropriate antidiuretic hormone secretion.

(Adapted from *The Merck Manual of Diagnosis and Therapy.* 16th ed. Rahway, NJ: Merck Research Laboratories; 1992:1278–1280.)

excreted in the urine and cause two unusual adverse effects, hemorrhagic cystitis and inappropriate retention of water. Nitrosoureas are a form of alkylating agent that is lipid soluble and crosses the blood-brain barrier; therefore, drugs of this type have some effect on CNS tumors. Cisplatin also binds and cross-links (interfering with DNA synthesis) and acts like an alkylating agent. Its unique toxicity is renal failure, which can be reduced with hydration.

Antimetabolites   *Antimetabolites* interfere with metabolic pathways of dividing cells, especially with DNA synthesis. They are commonly structural analogues or precursor molecules of cofactors and, therefore, interfere with biosynthetic enzymes or become incorporated into abnormal or nonfunctional products lethal to the cells.

Antimetabolites include three basic groups. The *antifolates* (methotrexate) interfere with dihydrofolate reductase, an enzyme important in the reduction of folate and dihydrofolate to tetrahydrofolate and in the one-carbon metabolism of adenine, guanine, and thymidine. Antifolates are not metabolized in the body but are excreted into the urine and are therefore not useful in patients with renal impairment.

A second group of antimetabolites, *antipurines,* includes *6-mercaptopurine* (6-MP) and its imidazole derivative, *azathioprine* (Imuran). These drugs interfere with multiple sites of purine biosynthesis (adenine and guanine) and the interconversion of purines. 6-mercaptopurine analogue (a hypoxanthine) is given orally and is generally effective in acute leukemias. The circulating leukocyte reduced by chemotherapeutic agents is not specific. Cyclophosphamide primarily reduces recirculating small lymphocytes; 6-MP reduces polymorphonuclear leukocytes and large mononuclear cells.

A third group of antimetabolites, the *antipyrimidines,* interferes with biosynthesis of uridine or thymidine, and includes *6-azauridine, cytarabine,* and *5-fluorouracil* (5-FU). Cytarabine may compete with deoxycytidine for one or more enzymes and thereby inhibit DNA synthesis. It is currently used against acute leukemia. 5-FU is an inhibitor of thymidylate synthase and, consequently, DNA production. It is a widely used drug, effective against colon and breast carcinoma, and significantly palliative in gastrointestinal malignancies. 5-FU is converted to two cytotoxic metabolites: fluorouridine triphosphate (FUTP) and 5-fluorodeoxyuridine monophosphate (5-FDUMP). The former is incorporated into RNA and inhibits RNA processing and function, and the latter binds tightly to thymidylate synthase and inhibits the eventual formation of the DNA precursor deoxythymidine triphosphate (dTTP). 5-FU is usually administered intravenously; plasma levels vary considerably after oral administration. The primary toxicities of 5-FU are bone-marrow suppression, stomatitis, and diarrhea. It can cause acute and chronic conjunctivitis, as well as punctal and canalicular stenosis.

Hormones   The hormone class of chemotherapeutic agents is used in pharmacological doses of 10–100 times the normal physiological replacement dose to inhibit growth of tumor cells. These compounds include the *nonsteroidal antiestrogen, tamoxifen,* used in progressive prostate carcinoma and breast cancer. The *androgens,* including *testosterone propionate* and *fluoxymesterone* (Halotestin), are useful in metastatic breast cancer and some renal cell carcinomas. The *progesterones,* including *hydroxyprogesterone* and *medroxyprogesterone acetate* (Provera), are useful in adenocarcinoma of the endometrium and occasionally in patients with renal cell or prostate carcinoma. The *corticoids,* such as *prednisone,* are useful in higher doses in acute lymphocytic leukemias, lymphoma, and hypercalcemia of malignancy.

Natural products The natural products include a wide variety of agents. The most common are vinca alkaloids, podophyllin derivatives, and antitumor antibodies.

Vinca alkaloids are derived from the periwinkle plant and include *vincristine* (Oncovin), *vinblastine* (Velban), and several investigational agents. These agents block incorporation of orotic acid and thymidine into DNA and cause arrest and inhibition of mitosis.

Podophyllin derivatives and semisynthetic plant derivatives arrest cells in the G_2 phase. VP-16 *(etoposide)* and VM-26 *(teniposide)* are gaining new acceptance in many treatment protocols.

Antitumor antibiotics are compounds produced by species of *Streptomyces* in culture. These agents interfere with the synthesis of nucleic acid. A partial list includes:

- *Anthracyclines* (Adriamycin and derivatives), which interfere with template function of DNA (a unique side effect is cardiac muscle degeneration leading to cardiomyopathy)

- *Bleomycin,* which causes DNA-strand scission

- *Dactinomycin* (actinomycin-D), which inhibits DNA-directed RNA synthesis

- *Mitomycin,* which impairs replication by alkylating and cross-linking DNA strands

The major dose-limiting toxicity of mitomycin is myelosuppression, and it has also been implicated as a cause of the hemolytic-uremic syndrome (HUS).

Several drugs have been used, all with limited effectiveness, for the treatment of systemic involvement of malignant melanoma of the choroid. The highest response rates are with the nitrosoureas and dacarbazine (DTIC). *Dacarbazine* is thought to act like an alkylating agent. Although objective responses of 12%–26% have been reported, the responses are of short duration with little, if any, survival benefit. Regressions of metastatic ocular melanoma have also been seen with biological response modifiers (immune therapy), an area which warrants further investigation.

Other Approaches

The treatment of cancer in general is evolving at a very rapid rate. In some instances the treatment approaches are entirely new, while in others, previously known therapies are used, either individually or in combination to be more specific and effective. An example of the latter approach is the combination of chemotherapy and bone marrow transplantation. Patients receive either their own marrow (previously withdrawn) or marrow from a suitable donor, after large doses of chemotherapy destroy malignant cells to the point of marrow suppression. This approach has been successful against a significant number of tumors such as breast and medulloblastoma that failed to respond to all other conventional treatments. Combining chemotherapy and radiation may significantly improve the survival of patients with advanced cancer of the nose and throat. Further, the combined use of immune-system stimulants such as interferons and interleukins appears to increase their potency.

A totally new approach to cancer therapy may lie in the use of *antiangiogenic factors,* which prevent tumors from developing the blood vessels necessary for their growth and survival. When angiogenesis is inhibited, tumors remain in check and, in some instances, disappear.

In the future, rather than classifying tumors based on their organ of origin, we may group them together based on their genetic profiles. An example of this is differentiation between those tumors with a normal or an abnormal tumor-suppressor gene p53. Tumor cells with normal p53 genes are far more sensitive to chemotherapy than those with mutant p53.

Ophthalmologic Considerations

The eye and its adnexa are frequently involved in systemic malignancies, as well as in extraocular malignancies that extend into ocular structures (including local malignancies of skin, bone, and sinuses). Breast and lung cancers frequently metastasize to the eye and represent the second most common intraocular tumors in adults. Acute myelogenous and lymphocytic leukemias frequently have uveal and posterior choroidal infiltrates as part of their generalized disease. In children, these manifestations are often signs of CNS involvement and suggest a poor prognosis. Although malignant lymphomas do not usually involve the uveal tract, histiocytic lymphoma is one type that often involves the vitreous and presents as uveitis. The retina and choroid may also be involved. Tumors of the eye and adnexa are discussed in several other BCSC books, including Section 4, *Ocular Pathology and Intraocular Tumors;* Section 6, *Pediatric Ophthalmology and Strabismus;* Section 7, *Orbit, Eyelids, and Lacrimal System;* and Section 8, *External Disease and Cornea.*

DeVita VT Jr, Hellman S, Rosenberg SA, eds. *Cancer. Principles and Practice of Oncology.* 5th ed. New York: Lippincott-Raven; 1997.

Holland JF, Frei E, Bast RC, et al, eds. *Cancer Medicine.* 5th ed. Baltimore: Williams & Wilkins; 1997.

CHAPTER XII

Behavioral Disorders

Recent Developments

☐ The latest edition of the *Diagnostic and Statistical Manual of Mental Disorders (DSM-IV)*, published in 1994, has changed the designation of *organic mental syndromes* to *mental disorders due to a general medical condition.*

Introduction

The field of psychiatry deals with a wide variety of conditions that have in common the disordered functioning of personality. These disturbances range from mild reactions to the events or circumstances of an individual's life to debilitating, life-threatening illnesses. Although the practicing ophthalmologist will not be called on to treat mental illness, it may have profound effects on the diagnosis and treatment of ocular diseases. In addition, some of the medications used to treat psychiatric disorders have significant ophthalmic side effects. The illnesses and medications discussed below are those most likely to affect the practice of ophthalmology.

Mental Disorders Due to a General Medical Condition

Formerly called *organic mental syndromes,* this category has been renamed in the *Diagnostic and Statistical Manual of Mental Disorders* (DSM-IV). The essential feature of *mental disorders due to a general medical condition* is a psychological or behavioral abnormality associated with transient or permanent dysfunction of the brain. Causes include any disease, drug, or trauma that directly affects the CNS and systemic illnesses that indirectly interfere with brain function; Alzheimer disease is included in this category. Patients have impairment of orientation, memory, and other intellectual functions. Psychiatric symptoms may occur, including hallucinations, delusions, depression, obsessions, and personality changes.

Patients with mental disorder due to a general medical condition with or without cognitive impairment are often unable to remember instructions and therefore unable to comply with treatment regimens. Depression, which frequently accompanies the syndrome, can complicate the situation. Medications with CNS side effects, such as beta blockers and carbonic anhydrase inhibitors, must be used with care, as these patients are frequently sensitive to these agents.

Schizophrenia

The term *schizophrenia* actually encompasses a group of disorders with similar features. These are some of the most devastating mental illnesses in terms of personal and societal cost. Usually beginning at a young age and continuing to a greater or lesser extent throughout their lives, schizophrenics invariably display thought disturbances, bizarre behavior, and deterioration in their general level of function. Incidence is estimated at 0.5%–1.0% of the population.

The classic manifestations are delusions and hallucinations in a clear sensorium. *Delusions* are disturbances in thought: firmly held beliefs that are untrue. Other thought abnormalities include loosening of associations and tangential thinking. *Hallucinations* are abnormal perceptions, experienced without any actual external stimulus. The affect is often flattened or inappropriate.

Motor disturbances range from uncontrolled, aimless activity to catatonic stupor, in which the patient may be immobile, mute, and unresponsive yet fully conscious. Repetitive, purposeless mannerisms and inability to complete goal-directed tasks are also common.

Treatment involves the use of antipsychotic medications (discussed later in this chapter), psychosocial support, and hospitalization for acute exacerbations.

Mood Disorders

Also known as *affective disorders,* this group ranges from appropriate reactions to negative life experiences to severe, recurrent, debilitating illnesses. Common to all of these disorders is either depressed mood or elevated mood (mania) or alternations of the two. The classic term *manic depression* has been replaced by *bipolar disorder,* now used to describe any illness in which mania is present, whether or not depression occurs. Milder symptoms resulting from stressful life experiences are called *adjustment disorders* and are discussed separately.

Mania is a period of abnormally and persistently elevated or irritable mood sufficiently severe to cause impairment in social or occupational functioning. It is slightly more common in females and is estimated to affect 0.6%–0.9% of the population. Typical symptoms include euphoria or irritability, grandiosity, decreased need for sleep, increased talkativeness, flight of ideas, and increased goal-directed activity. *Lithium* is the cornerstone of pharmacological treatment of bipolar illness and may be used alone or in combination with antipsychotic drugs. Psychotherapy is used as an adjunct.

Major depression is far more common than mania (estimates range from 5%–9% for women, 2%–4% for men) and therefore has a greater impact on all aspects of society. It may occur at any age but is most common in the middle-aged and the elderly. Affective changes include a feeling of sadness, emptiness, and nervousness. Thought processes are typically slowed and reflect low self-esteem, pessimism, and feelings of guilt. Social withdrawal and psychomotor retardation are seen, although agitation also occurs. Basic physical functions are impaired, as manifested by sleep disturbances, changes in appetite with associated weight loss or gain, diminished libido, and an inability to experience pleasure (anhedonia). Somatic complaints are common, such as fatigue, headache, and other nonspecific symptoms. Up to 15% of seriously depressed individuals may commit suicide.

For the nonpsychiatric clinician, depression creates a number of problems. There may be no apparent mood change, the illness being manifested in somatic complaints leading to time-consuming, expensive workups. Conversely, patients known to be depressed may have organic disease overlooked as psychosomatic. Appropriate recommendations for psychotherapeutic intervention may be met with resistance, anger, or denial, disrupting the patient-physician relationship. Compliance with diagnostic and treatment regimens for medical and surgical disorders can be problematic. Drugs with CNS side effects may exacerbate depressive symptoms. Treatment consists of psychotherapy and antidepressant medications. Electroconvulsive therapy is effective in selected cases.

Adjustment Disorders

Adjustment disorder is defined as a psychological reaction to a known psychosocial stress, resulting in suffering or dysfunction out of proportion to the degree of stress; the diagnosis implies the absence of other mental disorders. The causative stress may be single or multiple, recurrent or continuous. Clinical features may occur singly or in combination; are less severe than in major mood disorders; and include depression, anxiety, behavioral misconduct, withdrawal, somatic complaints, and inability to perform job-related or academic tasks. Psychotherapy is the mainstay of treatment, although occasionally short-term adjunctive drug therapy can be helpful. Prognosis is variable, ranging from complete remission to prolonged illness; if prolonged, the diagnosis of another mental illness may be applied.

Somatoform Disorders

The essential feature of these disorders is the presence of symptoms that suggest physical disease in the absence of physical findings or a known physiological mechanism to account for the symptoms. The symptoms in somatoform disorders are considered not to be under the patient's voluntary control. The practicing physician should be aware of these syndromes, as encounters with these patients are common.

Several somatoform disorders are recognized. *Conversion disorders* are characterized by temporary and involuntary loss or alteration of physical functioning due to psychosocial stress. Symptoms are typically neurologic in nature and include functional visual loss ("hysterical blindness"). In *somatoform pain disorder,* prolonged, severe pain is the only symptom. Psychotherapy is the primary therapeutic modality.

Somatization disorder is usually seen in women and consists of multiple somatic complaints. Patients are often histrionic in their description of their symptoms and may have had multiple hospitalizations and surgery. The incidence of associated psychiatric illness is high. Treatment is aimed at providing psychological support and minimizing the expenditure of medical resources. Psychotherapy is typically met with resistance and is therefore unsuccessful. Psychopharmacological treatment of underlying psychiatric disorders may be of benefit.

Hypochondriasis is a preoccupation with the fear of having or developing a serious disease. Physical examination fails to support the patient's belief, and reassurance by the examining physician fails to allay the fear. Treatment principles are the same as for somatization disorder. In *body dysmorphic disorder* the patient believes that his or her body is deformed in the absence of a physical defect or has an exaggerated concern about a mild physical anomaly. This illness is rare, and treatment regimens are not well defined.

Two other disorders that are not part of the somatoform disorders bear mentioning here. *Factitious disorders* are characterized by willful production of physical or psychological signs or symptoms in the absence of external incentives. It is believed that these patients feign illness solely because of a psychological need to assume the sick role. Treatment requires discovery of the true nature of the physical illness, a carefully planned confrontation, and psychotherapy. Prognosis for recovery is guarded. *Malingering* is the intentional production of physical or psychological symptoms for the purpose of identifiable secondary gain. It is not considered a primary psychiatric illness.

Ophthalmologists should be familiar with techniques for detecting malingerers who feign loss of vision, as they are not uncommonly encountered in practice. (See BCSC Section 5, *Neuro-Ophthalmology,* for some of these techniques.)

Substance Abuse Disorders

Substance abuse is one of the major public health problems in the United States. Alcohol-related deaths rank third in frequency behind heart disease and cancer. The cost of illness, death, and crime related to alcohol and drug abuse in the United States has been estimated in the tens of billions of dollars.

Drug dependence is the abuse of a drug causing a threat to physical health, psychological functioning, or the ability to exist within the demands of society. Common to all types of drug dependence is *psychic dependence,* that is, a psychic drive or a feeling of satisfaction requiring periodic or continuous drug administration in order to avoid discomfort, produce pleasure, relieve boredom, or facilitate social interaction. *Physical dependence* occurs when repeated administration of a drug causes an altered physiological state in the CNS so that sudden cessation of the drug causes an *abstinence syndrome* (a physical illness whose symptoms are determined by the specific drug). *Tolerance* occurs when increasing amounts of a drug are necessary to achieve the same desired effect. The drugs causing dependence fall into several groups, as listed in Table XII-1.

Opiates

Heroin is the opiate most commonly abused in the United States. Diagnosis of heroin use is made by history, and findings may include puncture sites on the skin and miotic pupils. Symptoms of abstinence include restlessness, yawning, rhinorrhea, pupillary mydriasis, hyperthermia (38°–40°C), vomiting, and diarrhea. Withdrawal, although not fatal to people with no other serious illness, can be dangerous in ill or elderly people. A total plan of withdrawal as well as support (economic, social, and psychiatric) must be employed to prevent the patient from returning to drug dependence. Because many former heroin abusers are unable to remain drug-free, methadone maintenance is sometimes used.

Methadone maintenance is the most common form of treatment in the United States for heroin dependence. Methadone is absorbed orally, prevents drug craving and abstinence symptoms for 24–36 hours, and causes tolerance (blockage of other opiates). Administered by the government, methadone allows patients to function better in society by freeing them from the need to secure heroin, the mind-altering euphoria of heroin, and IV drug administration. Vocational, educational, and psychiatric rehabilitation services are also available through methadone maintenance programs. Unfortunately, drug-free status is difficult to maintain for long periods of time; 90% of patients who leave methadone treatment programs will be incarcerated, deeply involved in drugs, readmitted to the program, or dead within 1 year.

Hypnotic Drugs

Hypnotic drugs may be used for nonmedical purposes by teenagers and adults. These drugs elevate the threshold of excitation of neurons, thereby resulting in

TABLE XII-1

CLASSIFICATION OF DEPENDENCE- PRODUCING DRUGS

Class I—Drugs producing both psychic and physical dependence

    A. Opiate type

        1. Morphine group: opium, morphine, diacetylmorphine (heroin), hydromorphone (Dilaudid), codeine, dihydrohydroxycodeinone
        2. Morphinans: oxycodone (Percodan)
        3. Benzomorphans: phenazocine (Prinadol)
        4. Meperidine group: meperidine (Demerol)
        5. Methadone group: methadone, propoxyphene (Darvon)

    B. Alcohol-barbiturate type

        1. Ethyl alcohol
        2. Barbiturates
        3. Paraldehyde
        4. Chloral hydrate
        5. Meprobamate (Miltown, Equanil)
        6. Piperidinediones: glutethimide, methyprylon (Noludar)
        7. Benzodiazepines: chlordiazepoxide (Librium), diazepam (Valium)
        8. Tertiary carbinols: methylpentynol (Dormison), ethchlorvynol (Placidyl)

    C. Opiate agonist-antagonist type

        1. Nalorphine
        2. Levallorphan
        3. Cyclazocine
        4. Pentazocine (Talwin)

    D. Amphetamine type

        1. dl-amphetamine (Benzedrine), dextroamphetamine (Dexedrine)
        2. Phenmetrazine (Preludin)
        3. Methylphenidate (Ritalin)
        4. Diethylpropion (Tenuate)
        5. Pipradrol (Meratran)

    E. Cocaine type: coca leaf, cocaine

Class II—Drugs producing psychic dependence but not physical dependence

    A. Hallucinogens

        1. Lysergic acid diethylamide (LSD)
        2. Mescaline
        3. Tryptamines: psilocybin, dimethyltryptamine, diethyltryptamine
        4. Hallucinogenic amphetamines

    B. Cannabis type: cannabis leaf (marijuana), hashish

    C. Bromides

lethargy, ataxia, nystagmus, impaired judgment, and emotional lability. Cessation of the drug causes anxiety, restlessness, convulsions, delusions, and hyperthermia; it may even be fatal. Diagnosis of drug abuse is made from history and confirmed by a blood or urine level of the drugs. Hypnotic drug abuse should be suspected in anyone appearing drunk without evidence of alcohol ingestion. Treatment consists of a monitored hospital withdrawal with posthospital support.

Alcohol

Alcohol is by far the most commonly abused drug, owing to its social acceptance and widespread availability. It is estimated that 7% of adults in the U.S. are alcoholics. Although multiple factors contribute to an individual's alcoholism, twin and adoption studies have shown a genetic influence. According to several studies, approximately 25% of fathers and brothers of alcoholics are themselves alcoholics.

Like hypnotic drugs, alcohol depresses the CNS and gives similar clinical findings; blood levels of ethyl alcohol should be obtained in suspicious cases. An alcoholic patient may experience restlessness, hallucinations, and even seizures 72–96 hours after admission to the hospital (or withdrawal) in the alcohol abstinence syndrome. Treatment consists of a supported, controlled withdrawal using a sedative-hypnotic drug. In addition, the patient needs long-term support such as Alcoholics Anonymous.

Alcohol crosses the placental barrier, and children born to alcoholic mothers may be affected by the fetal alcohol syndrome. Some of the ocular manifestations of this syndrome are blepharophimosis, telecanthus, ptosis, optic nerve hypoplasia or atrophy, and tortuosity of the retinal arteries and veins. (See also BCSC Section 6, *Pediatric Ophthalmology and Strabismus.*)

Amphetamines

Amphetamine-type drugs are sympathomimetic amines that are widely abused. Diagnosis of drug abuse should be suspected in a person who shows paranoid behavior that clears in a few days. Acute use produces euphoria, a heightened sense of effectiveness, tachycardia, and paranoia. Treatment consists of hospital observation until the abstinence syndrome, especially depression, passes.

Cocaine

Cocaine has become an increasingly abused drug in the United States since the mid-1970s. At one time believed not to be addictive, cocaine is now known to cause both psychological and physical dependence.

Cocaine hydrochloride is a white crystal powder derived from coca leaves, which can be taken intranasally or intravenously. Intranasal cocaine has a half-life of less than 90 minutes, its euphoric effects lasting 15–30 minutes. Removal of the hydrochloride salt produces freebase cocaine, an 80% pure alkaloid form of cocaine. "Crack," or "rock," cocaine is a freebase derivative that is smoked, producing intense euphoria within seconds. The widespread availability of inexpensive crack has dramatically increased the scope of the cocaine abuse problem.

The symptoms of cocaine abstinence are not as stereotypical as those of opiate withdrawal. In general, there is a dysphoric state consisting of depression, anhedonia, insomnia, and anxiety lasting about 3 days. As these symptoms wane, cocaine craving persists, often leading to binge cycles at 3–10 day intervals. If the cycle of abuse can be broken, craving tends to wane over a 3-week period. Symptoms of major depression are common during this period but eventually clear.

Cocaine addiction among pregnant women is a growing problem. Premature labor, abruptio placentae, and fetal asphyxia may occur. "Crack babies" may show intrauterine growth retardation, microcephaly, seizures, sudden infant death syndrome (SIDS), rigidity, developmental delay, and learning disabilities.

The Psychology of Aging

The psychology of aging is influenced by a wide range of factors including physical changes, adaptive mechanisms, and psychopathology. Each elderly patient has a unique psychological profile resulting from his or her own psychological and social life history. Deleterious changes are not universal; in fact, in the absence of disease, growth of character and the ability to learn continue throughout life.

As we age, the issue of loss becomes more prevalent. Losses—of status, physical abilities, loved ones, and income—become more frequent. A fear of loss of social and individual power, and with it an attendant loss of independence, is common. In addition, the reality of death has increasing influence on an individual's psychological status.

Normal Aging Changes

Age-related changes in sensation and perception can have great influence, isolating an individual from the surrounding environment and requiring complex psychological reactions. There may be diminution of hearing and vision (see Ophthalmologic Considerations, below), slowing of intellectual and physical response time, and increasing difficulty with memory.

Many physical and intellectual abilities, however, are retained throughout life, and their loss should not be assumed to be part of the normal aging process. These include the senses of taste and smell, intelligence, the ability to learn, and sexuality. Any change in physical, intellectual, or emotional capabilities may reflect underlying organic or psychological disease.

Psychopathology

Functional disorders *Depression* is common in the elderly; very often a clear precipitant (e.g., physical ailments, bereavement) can be identified. Suicide rates in older men are very high; for reasons that are unclear, older women commit suicide much less commonly. The signs and symptoms of depression are similar to those seen in younger age groups, although there may be a greater emphasis on physical complaints. *Paranoia* is usually the result of social isolation or reduced cognitive and sensory capabilities rather than the severe personality disorganization seen in younger patients. For example, a hearing-impaired individual may have difficulty understanding what is being said and may imagine hostile motivations on the part of others. Although it may begin in adolescence, *hypochondriasis* more often begins in middle-to-late adulthood and is seen relatively frequently in the older population.

Organic disorders The clinical symptoms of organic brain disorders (now also called *mental disorders due to a general medical condition*) relate to deficits in intellectual and cognitive performance. Disorientation, memory loss, and inability to assimilate new information are typical. It is important to recognize that these disorders may be acute—related to metabolic disorders, drug effects, or treatable systemic disease—and thus, treatment of the underlying cause may completely or partially resolve the mental symptoms. Chronic cognitive impairment may be associated with alcoholism, Alzheimer disease, cerebrovascular disease, hypothyroidism, and Parkinson disease.

Some elderly, depressed patients may have "pseudodementia." These patients manifest prominent symptoms resembling dementia, with several important differences. Impairment of memory and orientation in pseudodementia has a sudden onset and rapid progression. There is often a prior history of depression, and depressive symptoms are present. Most important, the intellectual deficits are relieved by successful treatment of the depression.

Treatment

Functional disorders in the elderly are as amenable to treatment as in younger patients. Psychotherapy and pharmacologic therapy are quite effective and should be offered to all individuals. Acute mental disorders due to a general medical condition (organic brain syndromes) may also be treatable and thus should be thoroughly worked up.

Ophthalmologic Considerations

Diminishing visual capabilities of any cause can contribute to behavioral disorders in the elderly. Depression, paranoia, and organic brain syndromes may be exacerbated. Optimizing visual function through optical correction, medical therapy of vision-impairing disorders, surgical correction of cataract, and low-vision aids can reduce symptoms of behavioral disorders and greatly improve the quality of life in many individuals.

Compliance

The term *compliance* refers to a person's behavior as it relates to medical or health advice. Compliance with therapy means a positive behavior, in which the patient is motivated to adhere to a prescribed treatment (medication, diet, exercise, lifestyle changes) because of a perceived self-benefit.

Noncompliance is a major problem for both patients and health care professionals. Studies have shown that compliance rates are fairly constant, at about 50%, across all demographic categories (age, gender, socioeconomic class, level of education) and that physicians are unable to acccurately estimate patient compliance. In chronic disease states, compliance with treatment regimens also averages about 50%, regardless of the illness or setting. Noncompliance has been linked to an increased number of clinic visits, hospital admissions, emergency room visits, and nursing home admissions. An estimated 125,000 deaths and several hundred thousand hospitalizations are caused annually by noncompliance problems among patients with cardiovascular disease.

Factors Associated With Noncompliance

Surprisingly, most studies show little correlation between disease characteristics and compliance rates. Contrary to what would be expected, compliance tends to decrease as disease symptoms increase. Psychiatric patients tend to comply poorly, as do patients with depression or dementia.

Duration of therapy can influence compliance. Short-term treatments tend to be better followed than long-term regimens, but rapid declines in compliance occur even during the first 10 days of short-term therapy. Increased complexity of treatment regimens (more frequent dosing, more medications), adverse medication reactions, and increasing cost of medications are all associated with decreased compliance.

Factors That Tend to Improve Compliance

Many strategies have been shown to improve compliance rates. In general, none of these works well in isolation; rather, a multifactorial approach is necessary to increase the chances of success. The strategies fall into two categories: compliance aids and health-professional intervention. *Compliance aids* include simplification of treatment regimens (combination drugs, long-acting drugs), proper labeling, medication calendars and drug reminder charts, special medication containers and caps, and compliance packaging. *Health-professional intervention* consists of patient education, patient involvement in health care decisions, psychological support, and medication refill reminder cards.

Pharmacological Treatment of Psychiatric Disorders

Antipsychotic Drugs (Major Tranquilizers)

Antipsychotic drugs, or major tranquilizers, are also called *neuroleptics* because of their potential to induce neurologic side effects. The classes of drugs having antipsychotic activity include the phenothiazines, thioxanthenes, butyrophenones, dihydroindolones, dibenzoxazepines, and dibenzodiazepines (Table XII-2).

The *major tranquilizers* effectively reduce many of the symptoms of acute and chronic psychoses. Their value has been established in reducing fear, panic, hostility, and destructive, antisocial, or withdrawn behavior occurring in patients with schizophrenia, manic reactions, and involutional, senile, organic, and toxic psychoses. Their use has allowed many more patients to function outside the walls of psychiatric institutions.

Antipsychotic medications are indicated for the signs and symptoms of major emotional disturbances with loss of reality testing and for the signs of thought disorders. Such signs and symptoms include profound sleep disturbance, racing thoughts, inability to concentrate, thought blocking, ideas of reference, delusions, and hallucinations. The major tranquilizers are *not* antianxiety agents and are not used to treat neurotic or existential anxieties. In the management of organic and toxic psychoses, these drugs should be used in small doses and only as an adjunct to treatment of the underlying disorder. These drugs have also found wide use as preoperative and postoperative medications because of their antiemetic effects and potentiation of hypnotics and anesthetic agents.

Although their mechanism of action has not been demonstrated clearly, antipsychotic drugs block the uptake of dopamine by the postsynaptic membranes in

TABLE XII-2

ANTIPSYCHOTIC DRUGS

CHEMICAL CLASSIFICATION	DRUGS
Phenothiazine	
Aliphatic compound	Triflupromazine (Vesprin)
	Chlorpromazine (Thorazine)
Piperidine compound	Mesoridazine (Serentil)
	Thioridazine (Mellaril)
Piperazine compound	Fluphenazine (Permitil, Prolixin)
	Trifluoperazine (Stelazine)
	Perphenazine (Trilafon)
	Prochlorperazine (Compazine)
	Acetophenazine (Tindal)
Thioxanthene	Thiothixene (Navane)
	Chlorprothixene (Taractan)
Butyrophenone	Haloperidol (Haldol)
Dihydroindolone	Molindone (Moban)
Dibenzoxazepine	Loxapine (Loxitane)
Dibenzodiazepine	Clozapine (Clozaril)

the CNS. A wide range of side effects is associated with these agents, including extrapyramidal reactions, drowsiness, orthostatic hypotension, and anticholinergic effects. Less commonly, cholestatic jaundice, blood dyscrasia, photosensitive dermatoses, and sudden death may occur. In addition, ocular side effects include anticholinergic problems, keratopathy, lens pigmentation, and retinal pigmentary degeneration.

Each of the phenothiazines varies from its congeners in the incidence of the different side effects. A particular agent may be selected because of a high or low incidence of a specific side effect. Withdrawal symptoms may occur but usually involve only mild gastrointestinal disturbances. Tardive dyskinesias are seen at a rate of 2%–4% per year over the first 7 years of exposure and can worsen on withdrawal after long-term therapy; elderly women are the highest risk group.

Antianxiety and Hypnotic Drugs

Benzodiazepines The benzodiazepines are usually the drugs of choice when an antianxiety, sedative, or hypnotic action is needed. Other indications for selected benzodiazepines include preanesthetic medication, alcohol withdrawal, seizure disorders, spasticity, localized skeletal muscle spasm, and nocturnal myoclonus. The benzodiazepines have distinct advantages over other agents with respect to adverse reactions, abuse or dependence liability, drug interactions, and lethality. The pharmacokinetics of these medications greatly affect their efficacy and adverse reactions and thus influence drug selection (Table XII-3).

TABLE XII-3

ANTIANXIETY AND HYPNOTIC DRUGS

Benzodiazepines

Compounds with active metabolites

Chlordiazepoxide (Librium)
Clorazepate (Tranxene)
Diazepam (Valium, Valrelease)
Flurazepam (Dalmane)
Halazepam (Paxipam)
Prazepam (Centrax)

Compounds with weakly active, short-lived, or inactive metabolites

Alprazolam (Xanax)
Clonazepam (Klonopin)
Lorazepam (Ativan)
Midazolam (Versed)
Oxazepam (Serax)
Quazepam (Doral)
Temazepam (Restoril)
Triazolam (Halcion)

Barbiturates

Phenobarbital
Mephobarbital (Mebaral)
Amobarbital (Amytal)
Pentobarbital (Nembutal)
Secobarbital (Seconal)

Nonbenzodiazepine-nonbarbiturates

Antianxiety agents

Buspirone (BuSpar)
Hydroxyzine (Atarax, Vistaril)
Meprobamate (Equanil, Miltown)

Hypnotic agents

Chloral hydrate
Ethchlorvynol (Placidyl)
Ethinamate (Valmid)
Glutethimide (Doriden)
Methyprylon (Noludar)
Paraldehyde

All benzodiazepines alleviate the uncomplicated anxiety of generalized anxiety disorder and improve situational anxiety. Some patients with chronic anxiety benefit from long-term administration of these drugs. Such patients must be monitored carefully, however, to assure the need for continuing medication as well as the continuing efficacy and safety of the drug. Flurazepam, triazolam, and temazepam are used most commonly to treat insomnia, although diazepam, oxazepam, and lorazepam are also effective hypnotic agents.

Daytime or residual sedation (hangover) is the most common initial untoward effect of the benzodiazepines, but it appears to occur less frequently than with the barbiturates. Common dose-related side effects with oral use are dizziness and ataxia; respiratory depression, apnea, and cardiac arrest have occurred, usually following intravenous administration. Products available in parenteral form, such as diazepam and midazolam, must be administered with careful monitoring and only by personnel trained and equipped to handle cardiorespiratory emergencies.

The abuse potential of benzodiazepines is mild compared to drugs such as pentobarbital, hydromorphone, and cocaine. Nevertheless, long-term administration of these agents can cause physical dependence. Once physical dependence is established, withdrawal reactions may occur if the drugs are discontinued abruptly. Psychological dependence is more common than physical dependence and can occur with any dose. This type of drug reliance is difficult to distinguish from a recurrence of the original anxiety disorder. Consequently, good medical practice demands that these agents be prescribed initially only when a disorder known to respond to such therapy can be diagnosed with reasonable assurance, and their use should be continued only for the shortest time required.

Barbiturates   Derivatives of barbituric acid possess sedative, hypnotic, and anticonvulsant activity. Of the longer-acting barbiturates, phenobarbital and mephobarbital are administered principally for seizure disorders; phenobarbital and butabarbital are also labeled for use as sedatives. The use of barbiturates and these latter compounds as antianxiety agents and sedative-hypnotics has been largely superseded by the benzodiazepines. The benzodiazepines have lower potential for abuse and dependence and a greater therapeutic index.

Side effects with the barbiturate sedative-hypnotics are common and include drowsiness and lethargy, particularly in the elderly or in patients taking large doses; residual sedation is common after hypnotic doses. For these reasons, ambulatory patients should be specifically warned to avoid or be cautious of activities that require mental alertness, judgment, and physical coordination. Allergic reactions, Stevens-Johnson syndrome, and gastrointestinal symptoms are also seen. Paradoxic effects such as restlessness and excitement may be seen in some patients, particularly in the elderly and those patients with mental disorder due to a general medical condition. Because barbiturates may aggravate acute intermittent porphyria by inducing the enzymes responsible for porphyrin synthesis, their use is contraindicated in patients with this disease.

Chronic intoxication occurs most commonly with use of the short-acting barbiturates; symptoms are similar to those of alcohol intoxication. Prolonged, uninterrupted use of escalating doses of barbiturates, particularly the short-acting drugs, may result in physical and psychological dependence. Barbiturates also remain one of the leading causes of fatal drug poisoning.

The barbiturates frequently interact with other agents. Their dosage must be reduced when they are given with other CNS depressants, such as alcohol, other hypnotic and antianxiety agents, opiate analgesics, antipsychotics, and antihistamines. Barbiturates must be used with caution in patients receiving monoamine oxidase inhibitors, since these drugs may potentiate the depressant effects of the barbiturates.

Antidepressants

In patients with major depression, antidepressants usually improve symptoms, increase the chances and rate of recovery, reduce the likelihood of suicide, and help social and occupational rehabilitation. Psychotherapy is the first line of intervention in patients whose depression is based on external or environmental situations such as the loss of a job or family problems.

In general, antidepressants take 3–6 weeks to show significant effect. Most studies find that these drugs can result in mood elevation, improved appetite, better sleep, and increased mental and physical activity. Treatment is usually necessary for 3–6 months after recovery is apparent.

There are two groups of antidepressants: the *heterocyclic antidepressants* and the *monoamine oxidase (MAO) inhibitors* (Table XII-4). In addition to their utility in treating acute depressive episodes, the heterocyclic antidepressants are effective as maintenance therapy in preventing relapses and recurrences of major depressive episodes. Moreover, some heterocyclic compounds are effective in the treatment of panic or phobic disorders.

All heterocyclic compounds are well absorbed orally, extensively metabolized, and slowly eliminated. Because half-lives are prolonged in patients over age 55 years, the initial dose for older patients may require modification. The initial treatment period is considered to be the 4–8 weeks needed for the patient to become nearly symptom-free. Outpatient treatment is usually instituted at the lower dose range and increased gradually if required. An excessive initial dosage regimen can cause a combination of oversedation, orthostatic hypotension, and anticholinergic effects during the first few days; such unpleasant effects can lead to patient noncompliance and, thus, inadequate treatment. Following initial therapy, the treatment is continued approximately 6 months.

TABLE XII-4

ANTIDEPRESSANT DRUGS

Heterocyclic antidepressants
    Amitriptyline (Elavil)
    Amoxapine (Asendin)
    Bupropion (Wellbutrin)
    Desipramine (Norpramin)
    Doxepin (Adapin, Sinequan)
    Fluoxetine (Prozac)
    Imipramine (Tofranil)
    Maprotiline (Ludiomil)
    Mirtazapine (Remeron)
    Nefazodone (Serzone)
    Nortriptyline (Aventyl, Pamelor)
    Paroxetine (Paxil)
    Protriptyline (Vivactil)
    Sertraline (Zoloft)
    Trazodone (Desyrel)
    Trimipramine (Surmontil)
    Venlafaxine (Effexor)

Monoamine oxidase (MAO) inhibitors
    Isocarboxazid (Marplan)
    Pargyline (Eutonyl)
    Phenelzine (Nardil)
    Tranylcypromine (Parnate)

A subclass of the heterocyclic antidepressants is the *selective serotonin reuptake inhibitors,* including fluoxetine (Prozac), sertraline (Zoloft), and paroxetine (Paxil). These drugs, which affect levels of serotonin, have fewer side effects than the tricyclic compounds and are therefore better tolerated.

The MAO inhibitors have long been considered second-line drugs in the treatment of mood disorders; however, recognition of their usefulness has increased with refinement of the classification of these disorders and with greater understanding of the need to titrate doses carefully. Nevertheless, the significant risk of hypertensive crisis caused by interactions between MAO inhibitors and various foods and drugs must be taken into account when they are prescribed.

A common side effect of both groups of drugs is a general anticholinergic action. Cholestatic jaundice, hepatitis, agranulocytosis, and cardiac arrhythmias are uncommon side effects. The MAO inhibitors, when combined with food and beverages of high tyramine content, may produce severe hypertension that can lead to subarachnoid or cerebral hemorrhage. Foods to be avoided include cheese, herring, chicken liver, yeast, and yogurt. Red wine and beer also have high tyramine content.

Because MAO inhibitors prevent catabolism of catecholamines, patients taking these substances have exaggerated responses to drugs containing vasopressors, such as cold remedies, nasal decongestants, and even topical or retrobulbar epinephrine. These drugs may produce seizures, particularly in patients prone to such disorders, including those with a history of severe alcoholism. The MAO inhibitors prolong and intensify the actions of CNS depressants, narcotics, and anticholinergics. Tricyclic antidepressants may also potentiate narcotics.

Lithium Carbonate

Lithium carbonate is effective in the treatment of bipolar disorder and in some patients with recurrent unipolar depression. It has a very narrow therapeutic ratio, making close monitoring of plasma levels mandatory. Side effects include renal, thyroid, parathyroid, cardiac, and neurologic toxicity. Weight gain and gastrointestinal upset are common. Toxic plasma levels due to renal dysfunction, concurrent use of diuretics, or overdose can lead to persistent nausea and vomiting, coma, circulatory failure, and death.

Ophthalmologic Considerations

Although behavioral disorders do not directly affect the eye, a number of related issues are of importance to the ophthalmologist. Noncompliance is a common problem among patients with psychiatric illness, dementia, and depression. Malingering and functional visual loss require a high index of suspicion and special diagnostic skills on the part of the clinician. A number of medications used to treat eye disease, including beta blockers, carbonic anhydrase inhibitors, and oral corticosteroids, may induce or exacerbate depression.

Antipsychotic drugs have several ocular side effects. Corneal and lenticular pigmentations, although not visually significant, are common. Pigmentary retinopathy, which can lead to irreversible blindness, has been reported with prolonged use of several different neuroleptics but is most closely associated with thioridazine (Mellaril). The anticholinergic effects of these drugs can produce pupillary dilation and angle-closure glaucoma in susceptible individuals. Blepharospasm can occur as an extrapyramidal side effect associated with phenothiazine use.

Substance abuse is associated with an increased incidence of ocular trauma. Toxic optic neuropathy is seen in alcoholics, either as a direct effect or related to accompanying malnutrition. Corneal epithelial defects and infectious keratitis have been reported with increasing frequency in otherwise healthy cocaine and crack abusers.

American Psychiatric Association. *Diagnostic and Statistical Manual of Mental Disorders.* 4th ed. Washington, DC: American Psychiatric Association; 1994.

Bond WS, Hussar DA. Detection methods and strategies for improving medication compliance. *Am J Hosp Pharm.* 1991;48:1978–1988.

Brocklehurst JC, Tallis RC, Fillit HM, eds. *Textbook of Geriatric Medicine and Gerontology.* Edinburgh: Churchill Livingstone; 1992.

Goodwin DW, Guze SB. *Psychiatric Diagnosis.* 4th ed. New York: Oxford University Press; 1989.

Morris LS, Schulz RM. Patient compliance—an overview. *J Clin Pharm Ther.* 1992; 17:283–295.

Sclar DA. Improving medication compliance: a review of selected issues. *Clin Ther.* 1991;13:436–440.

Talbott JA, Hales RE, Yudofsky SC, eds. *Textbook of Psychiatry.* Washington, DC: American Psychiatric Press; 1988.

PART 2

GENERAL MEDICAL CONSIDERATIONS

CHAPTER XIII

Preventive Medicine

Screening Procedures

The goal of preventive medicine is not only the reduction of premature morbidity and mortality but also the preservation of function and quality of life.

Screening techniques can be used both for research and for practical disease prevention or treatment. Screening for nonresearch purposes is useful if the disease in question is

☐ Detectable with some measurable degree of reliability

☐ Treatable or preventable

☐ Significant because of its impact (frequency or severity)

☐ Generally asymptomatic (or has symptoms a patient might deny or might not recognize)

The decision to apply screening techniques to a certain population should take into consideration sensitivity and specificity of the test, ease of administration, cost of finding a problem, and cost of not finding a problem. Cost can and should be measured in both economic and human terms, including the cost of suffering, losing function, or dying.

The term *sensitivity* describes how often a test is positive among persons with a target disease. *Specificity* measures the test's ability to exclude true negatives. *Relative risk* is the probability of a disease based on a specific finding divided by the probability of that disease in the absence of that specific finding.

Screening can be done as a one-time venture or by the sequential application of screening tests. Initially, a more *sensitive* test is administered; when appropriate, it is followed by a more *specific* test (which is often more costly or difficult to use). In judging the predictive value of the screens for an individual patient, the physician should take into account the patient's clinical history and current medications.

Cardiovascular Diseases

Hypertension   The consequences of uncontrolled hypertension include significantly increased risk of strokes, congestive heart failure, and renal failure. More than 50 million Americans are hypertensive, about half diagnosed and one third on some form of therapy. Hypertension meets all four of the criteria mentioned above for screening: it is detectable, treatable, and highly prevalent; and it is characteristically asymptomatic until late in its course.

Control of hypertension has been demonstrated to decrease the risk of stroke, congestive heart failure, and renal failure. There is some debate whether reducing blood pressure reduces the risk of myocardial infarction.

The Framingham Study and other older insurance industry literature tell us that elevated blood pressure *is* predictive of long-term cardiovascular risk. Morbidity and mortality are proportional to the systolic and diastolic pressures. Arbitrary cutoff points for the upper limits of "normal" are generally the levels associated with 50% or more increase in mortality compared with the lowest levels. In individuals younger than 45 years of age, the target level is 130/90; in those older than 45, the target level is 140/95. For older patients, 160/90 is an appropriate cutoff, given the risk of orthostatic hypotension.

The primary screening method is blood pressure measurement. Abnormal measurements, unless urgently high, should be confirmed on two more occasions. Once hypertension is detected, the etiology should be sought in order to determine possible treatment.

Elevations in either systolic and diastolic readings are associated with cardiovascular risk; elevated systolic pressure is perhaps the greatest cardiovascular risk factor in older adults.

Atherosclerotic cardiovascular disease   Atherosclerosis is involved in about half of all deaths in the United States and one third of deaths between ages 35 and 65. Three fourths of deaths related to atherosclerosis are from coronary artery disease. Atherosclerosis is the leading cause of permanent disability and accounts for more hospital days than any other illness.

The rationale for early screening emerged with the demonstration that reducing risk factors does reduce the incidence of coronary disease events. The Coronary Primary Prevention Trial of the Lipid Research Clinics Program showed that each 1% of reduction in total cholesterol produced a 2% reduction in the risk of coronary disease events including, but not limited to, fatal and nonfatal myocardial infarctions. Several recent studies reveal reduced cardiovascular morbidity and mortality and total mortality in patients with previous coronary heart disease.

Established risk factors include family history of early-onset coronary disease, increasing age, male sex, elevated plasma cholesterol (and elevated LDL cholesterol and low HDL cholesterol levels), hypertension, smoking, physical inactivity, and stress. Patients in the top 20th percentile for risk factors had about 50% of fatal and nonfatal atherosclerotic events. Determining whether the patient is a smoker and providing simple advice about cessation should be an important element of all visits.

Hypertriglyceridemia alone, without elevated cholesterol level, is not associated with a significant incidence of coronary disease; but, together, cholesterol and triglyceride elevations carry a greater risk of coronary disease than cholesterol elevation alone.

Dyslipoproteinemia has become an important concept. We now recognize that excesses or deficiencies of specific lipoproteins and apolipoproteins are more significantly correlated with atherosclerosis than the more general category of lipids. Indeed, screening for cholesterol and triglycerides alone will miss 50% of cases of hyperlipoproteinemia. Therefore, it is valid and important to measure the HDL cholesterol every 5 years.

The presence of xanthelasma and corneal arcus, especially in young patients, increases the odds of concomitant dyslipoproteinemia. While these signs are low in specificity, they are easily detected during a routine eye examination, and the patient should be advised to have a more specific lipid-lipoprotein screening.

Screening for significant coronary artery atherosclerosis as such is more expensive and time-consuming than screening for associated reversible risk factors. In general, it is reasonable to screen for a history of cardiovascular symptoms and events (chest pain, dyspnea, syncope, arrhythmias, claudication, stroke) and reserve more specific testing (e.g., exercise testing in one of its various forms) for people who are in increased risk categories.

Lipid Research Clinics Program. The Lipid Research Clinics Coronary Primary Prevention Trial results. I. Reduction in incidence of coronary heart disease. *JAMA*. 1984; 251:351.

Lipid Research Clinics Program. The Lipid Research Clinics Coronary Primary Prevention Trial results. II. The relationship of reduction in incidence of coronary heart disease to cholesterol lowering. *JAMA*. 1984;251:365.

Scandinavian Simvastatin Survival Study Group. Randomized trial of cholesterol lowering in 4444 patients with coronary heart disease. *Lancet*. 1994;344:1383–1389.

The Lipid Research Clinics Program Prevalence Study. *Circulation*. 1986;73:Monograph 118.

Cancer

In women, the most common cancers are breast, lung, and colorectal. In men, they are lung, prostate, and colorectal. The types of cancer most amenable to screening are (in order) cervical cancer, breast cancer, urologic cancer, lung cancer, and gastrointestinal and colorectal cancer. Table XIII-1 shows a set of recommendations for early cancer detection.

Cervical cancer   Cervical cancer is the most common gynecological cancer in patients between the ages of 15 and 34. Overall, about 15,000 cases of invasive cancer of the cervix and 45,000 cases of carcinoma-in-situ occur each year in the United States. Early detection and appropriate treatment markedly reduce the morbidity and mortality from invasive cancer of the cervix. Cervical cancer is asymptomatic when it occurs in situ, and the most effective screening technique remains the Papanicolaou smear (Pap test).

Breast cancer   Breast cancer is the most common malignancy in women and the most common cause of death in women over 40. The overall incidence of breast cancer in the United States is 10%–12%; 50% of these patients are curable.

The importance of specific screening is increased by the presence of known risk factors, all of which are identifiable by history: (1) first-degree relative with breast cancer, (2) prior breast cancer, (3) nulliparity, (4) first pregnancy after age 30, and (5) early menarche or late menopause. Fibrocystic disease is not a risk factor unless there is demonstrated hyperplasia or atypia on biopsy. Oral contraceptives and postmenopausal estrogens have not been demonstrated to be independent risk factors.

About 42% of breast cancers detectable by mammography are not detectable by physical exam alone, and one third of those found by mammographic screening are noninvasive or less than 1 cm in size if invasive. Since false-negative mammograms do occur, the best detection strategy involves a physical exam plus mammography, with biopsy if either reveals an abnormality. Mammograms have been shown to be safe as well as effective, with current low-dose radiation not inducing added cancer risk. Mammographic screening should be performed yearly in women beyond age 50. Between the ages of 40 and 50, mammography should be a patient-physician decision. A woman should have mammographic screening until at least age 70.

TABLE XIII-1

AMERICAN CANCER SOCIETY RECOMMENDATIONS FOR EARLY CANCER DETECTION
IN ASYMPTOMATIC PATIENTS

| TEST OR PROCEDURE | POPULATION | | FREQUENCY |
	SEX	AGE (YEARS)	
Sigmoidoscopy	M, F	> 50	After two negative exams 1 year apart, perform every 3–5 years
Stool guaiac slide test	M, F	> 50	Annual
Digital rectal exam	M, F	> 40	Annual
Papanicolaou test	F	20–65; < 20, if sexually active	After two negative exams 1 year apart, perform at least every 3 years
Pelvic examination	F	20–40 > 40	Every 3 years Annual
Endometrial tissue sample	F	Women at high risk* and at menopause	At menopause
Breast self-examination	F	> 20	Monthly
Breast physical examination	F	20–40 > 40	Every 3 years Annual
Mammography	F	35–40 40–49 > 50	Baseline Every 1–2 years Annual
Chest x-ray			Not recommended
Sputum cytology			Not recommended
Health counseling and cancer checkup**	M, F M, F	> 20 > 40	Every 3 years Annual

* History of infertility, obesity, failure to ovulate, abnormal uterine bleeding, or estrogen therapy.

** To include examination for cancers of the thyroid, testis, prostate, ovary, lymph nodes, oral region, and skin.

Urologic cancer   The prostate, bladder, kidney, and testes yield about 16% of new cancer cases per year, with most of the common malignancies in middle-aged and older men. Screening remains controversial. Early detection can be accomplished by digital examination of the prostate, serum prostate-specific antigen (PSA) measurements, and physical examination of the testes. It is now generally accepted that a PSA should be performed yearly on men over 50 years of age.

Lung cancer   Lung cancer is the leading form of cancer in adults. Among male patients with lung cancer, 93% are smokers. The number of cases and percentage of incidence in women have risen with the increased incidence of smoking in women. In one study of patients with lung cancer, 40% were detected by a change on chest x-ray and 60% were detected by symptoms. The usefulness of radiographic and sputum cytology screening is generally considered to be low.

Gastrointestinal cancer (See below for colorectal carcinoma.) Risk factors for esophageal cancer are excessive alcohol and cigarette use, accounting for perhaps 80%–90% of esophageal cancers. Treatment has poor results; thus, prevention or elimination of the risk factors is worthwhile.

Gastric cancer appears to be associated with certain geographic areas, high ingestion of nitrates, loss of gastric acidity, and blood type A. Pancreatic cancer is two to three times more common in heavy smokers, and hepatocellular cancer is more common in people with preexisting liver disease, especially cirrhosis.

Colorectal cancer Colorectal cancer is a major killer in Western society, second only to lung cancer in incidence and mortality. The cumulative lifetime probability of developing colon cancer is roughly 6%, with a 3% probability of dying from it. The chance for survival 5 years after diagnosis remains only 40%, despite the optimistic theory that early detection would lead to curative surgery. Potentially modifiable risk factors such as fiber and fat intake are important in primary prevention.

Most authorities accept the theory that colorectal cancer develops from an initially benign polyp in a mitotic process that occurs over 5–10 years. Supportive evidence shows that many operative specimens containing colon cancer have at least one adenoma and that invasive cancer frequently occurs in close proximity to adenomatous tissue. Histologic studies have shown that growth of adenomas is associated with increasing cellular atypia. Additional supportive observations for this theory have been the malignant potential of adenomas in familial polyposis; further, patients who refuse removal of polyps frequently develop cancer at the same site and at other sites in their colon.

Studies to date lack the necessary longevity to prove definitively that polyp removal prevents development of carcinoma. Yet colonoscopic removal or ablation of all polyps has become the standard of care where facilities and trained personnel are available.

A national polyp study is under way to define the biology of these tumors, to identify factors that seem to promote invasive carcinoma, and to clarify whether early removal prevents development of invasive cancer. A recent study reported characteristics associated with high-grade dysplasia in colorectal adenomas; the major independent risk factors were adenoma size and extent of the villous component in the adenoma. Increasing age was associated with increased risk for high-grade dysplasia. Gender was not an independent factor.

Detection must be improved with more widespread use of screening studies such as Hemoccult slides, flexible sigmoidoscopy, and barium enema, with aggressive follow-up of positive cases.

Periodic sigmoidoscopy (every 3 years) and annual digital rectal examination with fecal occult blood testing have been recommended in asymptomatic adults older than 50. Recommendations remain controversial because of a lack of randomized trials. Sigmoidoscopy offers good specificity but misses proximal cancers. Nevertheless, several case-control studies have demonstrated a 50%–70% reduction in risk of colorectal cancer in patients screened with sigmoidoscopy. Similarly, fecal occult blood testing every two years has been shown to decrease mortality by 40%.

The overall sensitivity of the barium enema is the main disadvantage; historically, it has been ineffective in examination of the rectum. Double-contrast or air-contrast barium enema is still not the standard examination in many radiology offices.

Use of complete colonoscopy as a screening test for asymptomatic patients has been suggested. However, this has not been practical because of the expense of the procedure, the number of trained personnel required, and the risk of colonic perforation (approximately 0.2%).

Allison JE, Feldman R, Tekawa IS. Hemoccult screening in detecting colorectal neoplasm: sensitivity, specificity, and predictive value. *Ann Intern Med.* 1990;112:328–333.

de Roos A, Hermans J, Shaw PC, et al. Colon polyps and carcinomas: prospective comparison of the single- and double-contrast examination in the same patients. *Radiology.* 1985;154:11–13.

Mandel JS, Bond JH, Church TR, et al. Reducing mortality from colorectal cancer by screening for fecal occult blood. *N Engl J Med.* 1993;328:1365–1371.

Neugut AI, Forde KA. Screening colonoscopy: has the time come? *Am J Gastroenterol.* 1988;83:295–297.

O'Brien MJ, Winawer SJ, Zauber AG, et al. The National Polyp Study: Patient and polyp characteristics associated with high-grade dysplasia in colorectal adenomas. *Gastroenterology.* 1990;98:371–379.

Selby JV, Friedman DG, Quesenberry CP, et al. A case-control study of screening sigmoidoscopy and mortality from colorectal cancer. *N Engl J Med.* 1992;326:653–657.

Stryker SJ, Wolff BG, Culp CE, et al. Natural history of untreated colonic polyps. *Gastroenterology.* 1987;93:1009–1013.

Metabolic Diseases

Diabetes   The prevalence of diabetes mellitus is difficult to determine accurately because of problems of diagnosis. Rates differ according to race, age, and sex. Prevalence in the United States is thought to be about 1%; one fourth of the total cases are insulin-dependent disease, while three fourths of patients have other forms, mainly primary non–insulin-dependent diabetes. Specific screening has greater importance in the presence of risk factors such as family history, obesity, and pregnancy, and in blacks and Native Americans.

The time at which blood samples are obtained complicates the logistics of mass screening. The diagnosis of diabetes or the gradations of milder glucose intolerance can be made with a fasting blood sugar test and, ideally, a 2-hour postprandial blood sugar test. If only one blood specimen can be obtained, drawing the sample 2 hours after a large breakfast may allow the most useful screening. A fasting blood sugar of 140 mg/dL on two separate occasions or a glucose tolerance test of 200 mg/dL is diagnostic of diabetes. There is no evidence that early treatment of asymptomatic hyperglycemia is beneficial in non–insulin-dependent individuals.

Thyroid diseases   There is a high prevalence of abnormal thyroid test results, particularly in older individuals. Up to 15% of women over 60 have asymptomatic elevated TSH levels or low T_4 levels. A low percentage of such persons progress to clinical hypothyroidism. While no clinical trials justify widespread screening, it would be reasonable to test older women. As discussed in chapter IX, the availability of the new TSH-IMA test has simplified screening for thyroid disease.

Infectious Diseases

The major public health screening efforts in the United States have been for tuberculosis and sexually transmitted diseases. Hepatitis screening is used primarily for blood donation rather than for general population screening.

Tuberculosis   The prevalence of tuberculosis has recently increased in the United States, reversing decades of steady decline. High-incidence clustering is seen in certain subgroups: HIV-infected patients; inner city, economically disadvantaged males; nursing-home residents (3.5% incidence of skin test conversion to positive); health care workers, including physicians; people over age 50; recent immigrant groups; drug- and alcohol-dependent groups; and patients with gastrectomies and debilitating diseases. Tuberculosis skin testing should be performed in these high-risk groups. Such testing is sensitive, although interpretation of results may be complicated by coinfection with HIV. Positive skin tests should lead to a chest x-ray and consideration of chemoprophylaxis. Some experts advocate routine skin testing of all people below age 35 at the time of routine health exams, for detection as well as for baseline data. OSHA requires annual tuberculosis skin testing of all health care workers.

Syphilis   Syphilis is almost always transmitted sexually; congenital disease transmitted in utero is now rare. In fact, the incidence of congenital syphilis has dropped 90% since the 1940s as the result of required premarital screening and pregnancy screening.

Latent, untreated cases of syphilis in which the primary or secondary mucocutaneous lesion is no longer present can be detected only by screening. It is important to detect early latent disease, because about 25% of cases experience spontaneous reemergence of infectious mucocutaneous lesions in the first 2 years. Late latent disease should be detected and treated because of the long-term destructive effects on the CNS, the aorta, and the skeletal system.

Screening is generally performed with the more sensitive, but less specific, nontreponemal antigen tests (VDRL, RPR) to rule out false positives that can occur with treponemal antigen tests (FTA-ABS, MHA-TP, HATTS), which are also generally more expensive.

Immunization

The development of immunization as a means of preventing the spread of infectious disease began in 1796, when Edward Jenner injected cowpox virus, which causes a mild disease, into a child to prevent smallpox, a severe, potentially fatal illness. Immunization today still relies on Jenner's inoculation methods in protecting against the development of disease. There are two types: active and passive.

In *active immunization,* the recipient develops an acquired immune response to inactivated or killed viruses, viral subfractions, bacterial toxoids or antigens, or synthetic vaccines. Once the immune response has developed to a particular pathogen, it will protect the host against infection. The persistence of acquired immunity depends upon the perpetuation of cell strains responsive to the target antigenic stimulus, and booster inoculations may be required for certain immunogens.

In general, live inactivated vaccines produce longer-lasting immunity; however, they are contraindicated in immunocompromised individuals or pregnant women because the pathogen can potentially replicate in the host. Ideally, active immunization should be completed before exposure; however, life-saving postexposure immunity can be developed through combining active and passive immunization.

Passive immunization depends upon the transfer of immunoglobulin in serum from a host with active immunity to a susceptible host. Passive immunity does not result in active immunity and may even block the development of active immunity in some circumstances. Passive immunity is short-lived and without immune memory; however, it confers immediate protection on the recipient who has been exposed to the pathogen. Pooled human globulin, antitoxins, or human globulin with high antibody titers for specific diseases are the usual products available for passive immunization.

Immunization should be avoided in individuals who have allergic reactions to the vaccine or its components. Idiopathic autoantibody or cross-reacting antibody development may occur after vaccination, resulting in systemic disease such as Guillain-Barré syndrome, a rare but devastating complication of vaccination. Immunization should be avoided during a febrile illness. Multidose immunization schedules that are interrupted can be resumed; however, doses given outside the schedule should not be counted toward completion of the vaccination sequence.

Hepatitis B

Approximately 100,000 symptomatic cases of hepatitis B occur annually in the United States. Between 6% and 10% of adult hepatitis B patients become carriers. Chronic active hepatitis occurs in 25% of carriers. Of those patients with chronic active disease, 20% will die of cirrhosis, and 5% will die of hepatocellular carcinoma. Two forms of a hepatitis B vaccine are available: a plasma-derived form and the presently preferred vaccine—a recombinant yeast–derived vaccine. The plasma vaccine is formulated from pooled human plasma, which undergoes three inactivation steps, each of which will independently completely inactivate the human immunodeficiency virus (HIV-1). No nucleic acids related to HIV-1 can be detected in the vaccine, and recipients do not develop antibodies to HIV-1. Clinical, laboratory, and epidemiologic data have not demonstrated any significant risk associated with the plasma-derived vaccine. A new yeast-derived vaccine (Engerix-B), produced by cells that carry the surface antigen (HBsAg), is considered the hepatitis vaccine of choice. It is the only recombinant vaccine with a recommended standard dose of 20 μg that results in high antibody levels most closely approximating those seen with the plasma-derived vaccine. The new vaccine is the only recombinant approved for hemodialysis patients, and it can be administered in an accelerated dosing schedule when rapid protection is desired.

With either vaccine, antigen is usually administered in three sessions, with the second and third occurring 1 and 6 months after the initial injection. On this regimen, 90% of recipients develop protective antibody levels for at least 3 years. The recombinant vaccine can also be given on an accelerated dosing schedule. This schedule requires vaccination at 0, 1, and 2 months followed by a booster dose at 12 months. Development of adequate antibody levels occurs in more than 90% of recipients after the third injection at 3 months, versus 6 months with the usual schedule. Hemodialysis patients should receive 40 μg doses of the recombinant vaccine at 0, 1, 2, and 6 months to achieve adequate antibody response. Antibody levels greater than 10 mIU/ml are considered to be adequate protection. The need for booster injections for individuals whose antibody levels are lower is controversial. Approximately 3%–4% of healthy individuals lack the immune response gene needed to produce antibodies after receiving the vaccine. Repeat vaccination results in the development of protective antibodies in only 50% of the nonresponders.

Vaccination before exposure is indicated in certain high-risk groups: health care workers, hemodialysis patients, residents and staff of institutions for the retarded, household and sexual contacts of chronic carriers of hepatitis B, hemophiliacs, users of illicit injectable drugs, prison inmates, and sexually active homosexual men. Vaccination can be combined with passive immunization for postexposure prophylaxis without affecting the development of active immunity.

Postexposure prophylaxis with hepatitis B immune globulin should be considered when there is perinatal exposure of an infant born to a carrier, accidental percutaneous or permucosal exposure to blood positive for hepatitis B surface antigen, or sexual exposure (within 14 days) to a carrier of hepatitis B. Hepatitis B immune globulin should be given as soon as possible after exposure in a single intramuscular dose of 0.06 ml/kg body weight; the recombinant hepatitis B vaccine should be concurrently administered in an accelerated dosing schedule as previously described. If hepatitis B immune globulin is unavailable or the hepatitis B status of the blood is unknown, then the recipient can be given immune globulin and accelerated recombinant hepatitis B vaccination. The previous recommendations for postexposure prophylaxis should then be followed if the test for hepatitis B in the blood is positive or within 24 hours, once the hepatitis B immune globulin becomes available.

Influenza

Although influenza is usually a self-limited disease with rare sequelae, it can be associated with severe morbidity and mortality in elderly individuals or individuals with chronic diseases. Influenza vaccines produce long-lasting immunity; however, antigenic shifts, primarily in type A rather than type B influenza virus, necessitate yearly reformulation of the vaccine to contain the antigens of strains considered most likely to cause disease. Protection is correlated with the development of antihemagglutinin and antineuraminidase antibodies, which when present decrease both the patient's susceptibility and the severity of the disease. Annual vaccination is recommended for adults and children with chronic diseases requiring medical care, nursing-home residents, children who require long-term aspirin therapy (in whom influenza could lead to the development of Reye syndrome), individuals over 65, and medical personnel with extensive contact with high-risk patients. Influenza vaccine should not be administered to persons with anaphylactic hypersensitivity to eggs or to pregnant women in their first trimester.

Varicella Zoster

It is generally recommended that health care workers who have not been exposed to chickenpox be vaccinated with Varivax.

Measles

Vaccination has dramatically reduced the incidence of measles, along with its associated encephalitis, mental retardation, and mortality. The initial vaccine introduced in 1963 was an inactivated virus that did not provide a long duration of protection; therefore, many young adults are at risk of contracting measles, which is more severe as an adult disease. Vaccination before 1 year of age with any form of vaccine is ineffective, as maternal antibodies block the development of immunity. In 1967, a live attenuated vaccine was introduced that causes long-lasting immunity. Vaccination with the attenuated strain should be routine not only at 15 months of age but also for individuals born between 1957 and 1967 who were neither vaccinated nor infected and for individuals who received the inactivated viral vaccine. Individuals born before 1957 are considered immune by virtue of natural infection. Post-exposure prophylaxis with immune globulin should be considered within 6 days for individuals who cannot have the vaccine, which should be given within 72 hours of exposure. The vaccine is contraindicated for individuals with hypersensitivity to eggs.

Mumps

The occurrence of reported cases of mumps in the United States has decreased steadily since the introduction of live mumps vaccine in 1967. Although mumps is generally self-limited, meningeal signs may appear in up to 15% of cases and orchitis in up to 20% of clinical cases in postpubertal males. Mumps vaccination is indicated in all children and all susceptible adults, particularly postpubertal males.

Rubella

Rubella immunization is intended to prevent fetal infection and consequent congenital rubella syndrome, which can occur in up to 80% of fetuses of mothers infected during the first trimester of pregnancy. The number of reported cases of rubella in the United States has decreased steadily from more than 56,000 in 1969, the year rubella vaccine was licensed, to 954 cases in 1983. A single subcutaneously administered dose of live, attenuated rubella vaccine provides long-term (probably lifetime) immunity in approximately 95% of persons vaccinated.

Rubella vaccine is recommended for adults, particularly women, unless proof of immunity is available (documented rubella vaccination on or after the first birthday or a positive serologic test), or if the vaccine is specifically contraindicated. Rubella vaccine should be given at least 14 days before administration of immune globulin or deferred for 3 months after administration. Because of the theoretical risk to the fetus, women of childbearing age should receive the vaccine only if they are not pregnant.

Polio

Before the introduction of the first polio vaccine in 1955, polio caused thousands of cases of paralysis. Despite widespread immunization with oral vaccine in 1962, there has been a steady decline in polio immunization and a growing number of susceptible individuals. Although the incidence of polio is low, the possibility for large-scale outbreaks increases as the number of susceptible individuals increases. There are two forms of the vaccine: an oral form that is a live attenuated virus (Sabin vaccine) and a subcutaneous injectable form of killed virus (Salk vaccine). Vaccination with the oral form is indicated for all children; however, it is contraindicated in pregnant women, who should receive the killed virus vaccine.

Tetanus and Diphtheria

The combined tetanus and diphtheria toxoid (Td) vaccine is highly effective. It is used for both the primary and booster immunization of adults. The pediatric vaccine, diphtheria-pertussis-tetanus (DPT), should not be given to adults, because there is a significant incidence of adverse neurologic reactions among adults to the pertussis component. All young adults should have completed a primary series of tetanus and diphtheria toxoids. Persons who have completed a primary series of tetanus and diphtheria immunization should receive a booster dose every 10 years. If serious doubt exists about the completion of a primary series of immunization, two doses of 0.5 ml of the combined toxoids should be given intramuscularly at monthly intervals, followed by a third dose 6–10 months later. Thereafter, a booster dose of 0.5 ml should be given at 10-year intervals.

In wound management for tetanus, previously immunized persons with severe wounds should receive a booster if more than 5 years have elapsed since the last injection. The management of previously unimmunized patients with severe wounds should include tetanus immune globulin as well as Td. Though uncommon, more than 60% of tetanus cases occur in persons older than 60. Older adults should be given a single booster at age 65.

Pneumococcal Pneumonia

Pneumococcal pneumonia is the most serious and prevalent of the community-acquired respiratory infections. Although pneumococcal disease affects children and adults, the incidence of pneumococcal pneumonia increases over the age of 40. Pneumococci that are resistant to penicillin have emerged since 1974. The mortality rate from bacteremic pneumococcal infection exceeds 25%, despite treatment with antibiotics.

The current pneumococcal vaccine contains polysaccharide antigens from 23 of the types of pneumococci most commonly found in bacteremic pneumococcal disease. The 23-valent vaccine has been designed to induce a protective level of serum antibodies in immunocompetent adults. The vaccine is highly effective in healthy young adults, but its effectiveness in the elderly and the infirm has not been precisely determined. However, the vaccine is well tolerated, and it is recommended for the elderly, for patients who have cardiac or respiratory disease, and for other patients who are at high risk for pneumococcal infection, including those with sickle cell disease, splenic dysfunction, renal and hepatic disease, or immunodeficiency. The pneumococcal vaccine is given subcutaneously or intramuscularly as a 0.5 ml dose. In most circumstances, persons who have previously received the 14-valent vaccine should not be revaccinated with the 23-valent vaccine because it may be associated with increased local and systemic reactions. The duration of protection afforded by primary vaccination with pneumococcal vaccine seems to be 9 years or more. Persons who received pneumococcal vaccine before age 65 should be reimmunized at 65 if more than 6 years have passed since the initial vaccination.

Haemophilus Influenzae

A vaccine against *Haemophilus influenzae* type B has been endorsed by the Committee on Infectious Diseases of the American Academy of Pediatrics and the Immunization Practices Advisory Committee. They have recommended that the vaccine be given to all children at 24 months of age. The current vaccine is not expected to have any impact on infections caused by nontypable *H influenzae,* such as 20% of the cases of acute otitis media in children. The vaccine is purported to prevent infections caused by encapsulated *H influenzae* type B strain, which affects 1 in every 200 children in the United States during the first 5 years of life. Approximately 60% of these infections are meningitis, amounting to about 10,000 cases each year. The type B capsule, often referred to as PRP (polyribosylribitol), enhances the *H influenzae* invasive potential. These encapsulated strains may result in life-threatening bacteremic infections. A critical test factor that determines an individual's susceptibility to systemic *H influenzae* type B infection is the presence or absence of serum antibodies to PRP. Thus, the induction of serum antibodies by immunization with PRP is a reasonable strategy.

It is hoped that the vaccine will reduce the overall risk of a child's contracting systemic *H influenzae* type B infection by about one quarter to one third. The vaccine should be protective in preventing epiglottitis and orbital cellulitis, because the great majority of children who contract these *H influenzae* type B infections are over 2 years of age. The vaccine is estimated to be 90% effective when given at 24 months of age. Compared to other routine immunizations, PRP is expensive; however, it is important to note that PRP appears to be one of the safest vaccine products approved for use in children.

Centers for Disease Control. General recommendations on immunization. *Ann Intern Med.* 1989;111:133–142.

Guide for Adult Immunization. 2nd ed. Philadelphia: American College of Physicians; 1990.

Moxon ER. *Haemophilus influenzae* vaccine. *Pediatrics.* 1986;77:258–260.

CHAPTER XIV

Medical Emergencies

Although only occasionally called upon to manage a patient in acute distress, the ophthalmologist must be aware of the diagnostic and therapeutic steps necessary for proper care of these emergencies. Infrequent use of these techniques makes periodic review of life-support techniques particularly important. The American Red Cross and the American Heart Association both offer courses in, and periodic review of, basic life support (BLS) and advanced cardiac life support (ACLS).

Cardiopulmonary Arrest

Cardiopulmonary resuscitation (CPR) is intended to rescue patients with acute circulatory or respiratory failure or both. The most important determinant of short- and long-term neurologically intact survival is the interval from the onset of the arrest to the restoration of effective spontaneous circulatory and respiratory function. Numerous studies have demonstrated that early defibrillation is the most important factor influencing survival and the minimization of sequelae. The following sequences have been developed to optimize treatment and are useful guidelines for the majority of patients. They do not, however, preclude other measures that may be indicated for individual patients. The most crucial aspects of treatment are **A**irway maintenance, **B**reathing, and **C**irculation (ABC).

When one encounters an unconscious patient, the following steps should be performed:

1. Determine unresponsiveness: Attempt to arouse the patient by shaking the shoulders and saying, "Are you OK?" Do not shake the head or neck unless trauma to this area has been ruled out.

2. Activate the EMS system if there is no response (911 where available). Be prepared to give the location and nature of the emergency and condition of the victim(s).

3. Position the victim supine on a firm, flat surface.

4. Open the airway. The head-tilt, chin-lift maneuver is preferred, since it is most likely to provide a good airway opening; the jaw thrust and the neck lift are alternative maneuvers (Fig XIV-1). The chin lift is used to tilt the head backward by applying firm pressure to the forehead while the fingers of the other hand are placed under the chin, supporting the mandible. The modified jaw thrust should be used if a neck injury is suspected.

5. Determine breathlessness: If spontaneous respiration is not present, gently pinch the nose closed with the index finger and thumb of the hand that is on the forehead (Fig XIV-2). Make a tight seal over the patient's mouth and ventilate twice with slow, full breaths (1.5–2.0 seconds each). A 2-second pause should be observed between breaths. Slow breaths will result in less gastric distension.

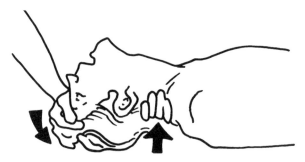

FIG XIV-1—Head-tilt method of opening airway.

Health care professionals should be proficient in the use of barrier devices for basic life support. A face shield can help prevent transmission of most infections and exposure to the human immunodeficiency virus (HIV) in saliva. (One such device is the Microshield, from Medical Devices International.) The mouth-to-nose technique is recommended when it is impossible to ventilate through the victim's mouth. Masks are more effective than face shields in delivering adequate ventilation. Features can include a non-rebreathing (one-way) valve, an extension tube to eliminate close proximity, low resistance, a bacterial filter, transparency, and ease in maintaining a seal over the mouth (for example, the Seal-Easy Mask, from Respironics Inc).

6. Determine presence or absence of pulse: Palpate the carotid pulse for at least 5 seconds to assure that a pulse is not missed due to bradycardia.

7. Call for help again. If a carotid pulse is present, rescue breathing should be continued at a rate of 10–12 ventilations per minute. If there is no pulse, begin chest compressions.

8. To assure good hand placement necessary to perform chest compressions, the heel of one hand should be placed at the midsternal region with the bottom of the hand 1–2 fingerbreadths above the xiphoid process.

9. Recommended cardiac compression rates of between 80 and 100 per minute maximize cardiac output. Cardiac output varies, but on average, 30% of normal cardiac output can be expected with CPR. The depth of chest compression is critical; compressions of 1.0–1.5 inches for children and 1.5–2.0 inches for adults are optimal. Duration of chest compression should be at least 50% of the total duration of the cycle.

10. For one-rescuer CPR (Fig XIV-3), 15 compressions should be performed before ventilating twice. About 3–5 seconds should be taken for 2 ventilations, and there should be a pause between ventilations.

11. For two-rescuer CPR (Fig XIV-4), the compression-ventilation ratio is 5:1, with a 1.5–2.0 second pause for ventilation after every 5 cardiac compressions. The rescuer responsible for airway management should assess the adequacy of compressions by periodically palpating for the carotid pulse. Once the patient is intubated, ventilations are continued at a rate of 12–15 per minute, without

FIG XIV-2—Mouth-to-mouth resuscitation.

pausing for compressions. The rescuer should stop and check for return of pulse and spontaneous breathing every few minutes.

12. Cardiopulmonary resuscitation is most effective when started immediately after cardiac arrest. If cardiac arrest has persisted for more than 10 minutes, CPR is unlikely to restore the victim to the prearrest CNS status. If there is any question about the exact duration of cardiac arrest, the victim should be given the benefit of the doubt and resuscitation started.

The following adjuncts are helpful in CPR and are suggested components for a medical emergency tray, crash cart, or tackle box:

☐ Oxygen, to enhance tissue oxygenation and to prevent or ameliorate a hypoxic state.

☐ Airways, adult and child, oral and nasal, to be used on unconscious or sedated patients.

☐ A barrier device such as a face shield or mask-to-mouth unit to prevent disease transmission. Both can be used with supplemental oxygen and are especially useful if the rescuer is unfamiliar in the use of a standard bag-valve device (i.e., AMBU BAG), which should also be included as standard equipment to help secure the airway.

☐ Intravenous drugs (Table XIV-1).

☐ Intravenous solutions: 5% dextrose and water (D5W), D5 lactated Ringer's (LR), normal saline.

☐ Syringes (1, 5, and 10 cc), hypodermic needles (20, 22, and 25 gauge), and venous catheters.

☐ A suction apparatus, tourniquet, taped tongue blade, and tape.

☐ Laryngoscope and endotracheal tubes (adult and child).

In the absence of a 911 community emergency phone system, it is essential to have the phone number of the local paramedic emergency squad posted near all office telephones.

TABLE XIV-1

MEDICATIONS USED IN ACUTE MEDICAL EMERGENCIES

DRUGS	INDICATIONS	ADULT DOSE (IV)	ADVERSE EFFECTS
Epinephrine (1:1000)	Anaphylaxis	0.3–0.5 mg subcutaneously every 5 minutes	Tachycardia, hypertension
Epinephrine (1:10,000)	Asystole, ventricular fibrillation, EMD	Bolus 0.5–1.0 mg every 5 minutes	Hypertension in excess doses
Lidocaine	PVCs, ventricular tachycardia, ventricular fibrillation	Bolus 1.0 mg/kg with subsequent doses of 0.5 mg/kg to a maximum total dose of 3.0 mg/kg	Focal and grand mal seizures in excess doses
Atropine	Bradycardia, EMD, asystole	Bolus 0.5–1.0 mg every 5 minutes	Induced ventricular fibrillation, ventricular tachycardia, or supraventricular tachycardia
Diphenhydramine HCl (Benadryl)	Anaphylaxis and anaphylactoid reactions	10–20 mg	Drowsiness
Diazepam (Valium)	Seizures	5–10 mg	Sedation
Hydrocortisone sodium succinate (Solu-Cortef)	Anaphylaxis and anaphylactoid reactions	500 mg every 6 hours	Adrenal-pituitary axis suppression
Sodium bicarbonate	Severe metabolic acidosis	Bolus 1 mEq/kg	Hypernatremia, hypocalcemia, and metabolic alkalosis
Calcium chloride (ampule of 10% solution)	Acute hyperkalemia and hypocalcemia, calcium-channel blocker toxicity	2–4 mg/kg	Bradycardia
Aminophylline	Bronchospasm	6 mg/kg (loading dose)	Tachycardia
Glucose (D 50)	Profound hypoglycemia	Bolus 10 ml	Hyperglycemia

Basic life support also outlines methods for aiding choking victims, including the Heimlich maneuver and appropriate manual techniques for removing foreign bodies from the oral pharynx. Epigastric thrusts should be attempted; up to 10–12 thrusts may be necessary. Thereafter, ventilation should be attempted. If these efforts are unsuccessful, the mouth should be cleared with a finger sweep and ventilation attempted again. Transtracheal ventilation by means of cricothyrotomy may be necessary.

In addition to basic CPR, the American Heart Association has established guidelines and procedures for advanced cardiac life support (ACLS). ACLS includes intubation, defibrillation, cardioversion, pacemaker placement, administration of drugs and fluids, and communication with ambulance and hospital systems. Protocols and

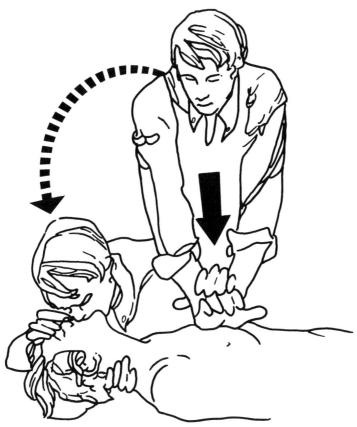

FIG XIV-3—One-rescuer CPR.

algorithms have been established in critical cardiac care for ventricular fibrillation, ventricular tachycardia, asystole, electrical-mechanical dissociation (EMD), premature ventricular contractions (PVCs), atrial tachycardia, and bradycardia. The provider of ACLS must have a precise understanding of the actions, indications, doses, and adverse effects of the cardiac drugs used in the specific protocols. Except in dire emergencies, these drugs should be administered to treat cardiac arrhythmias *only* by physicians who use them on a routine basis.

Because of the comprehensive and changing nature of the ACLS algorithms, it is beyond the scope of this chapter to describe ACLS procedures.

Shock

Shock is a state of generalized inadequacy of tissue perfusion that leads to impaired cellular metabolism and progresses, if uncorrected, to multiple organ failure. The clinical syndrome is usually characterized by an altered sensorium, relative hypotension, tachycardia, tachypnea, oliguria, metabolic acidosis, weak or absent pulse, pallor, diaphoresis, and cool skin (however, warm skin may be present in septic shock).

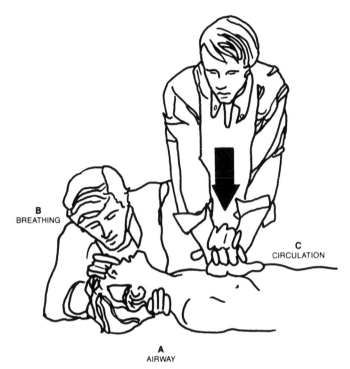

B
BREATHING

C
CIRCULATION

A
AIRWAY

FIG XIV-4—Two-rescuer CPR.

Classification

Shock is classified according to the four primary pathophysiological mechanisms involved:

- Oligemic or hypovolemic (e.g., hemorrhage, diabetic ketoacidosis, burns, or sequestration)
- Cardiogenic (e.g., myocardial infarction or arrhythmia)
- Obstructive (e.g., pericardial tamponade, pulmonary embolus, or tension pneumothorax)
- Distributive, characterized by maldistribution of the vascular volume secondary to altered vasomotor tone (e.g., sepsis, anaphylaxis, spinal cord insult, beriberi, or an arteriovenous fistula)

The type of shock present can often be determined by history, physical examination, and appropriate diagnostic tests. Regardless of the event that precipitated the state of shock, microcirculatory failure is the common factor that eventually leads to death in advanced shock. Ventilatory failure appears to be the most significant factor in the morbidity and mortality of shock, with subsequent hypoxemia and metabolic acidosis leading to many complications.

If one rules out vasovagal syncope (by virtue of its short duration and the situations that produce such an occurrence), the basic life-support measures for the initial emergency care of the unconscious patient are very similar. The most important aspects of treatment are **A**irway maintenance, **B**reathing, and **C**irculation (ABC): the same principles as in CPR.

Failure of respiratory gas exchange is the most frequent single cause of death in patients with shock. One must first rule out respiratory obstruction. Oxygen is then given by mask, and if respiratory movements are shallow, mechanical ventilation will be necessary. If laryngeal edema is present, as with anaphylaxis, then endotracheal intubation (if possible), tracheotomy, or cricothyrotomy is indicated. Respiratory obstruction can be assumed if there is stridor with respiratory movements or if cyanosis persists even when adequate ventilatory techniques have been applied. A conscious patient in distress who cannot speak but is developing cyanosis may be choking on food or a foreign body; the Heimlich maneuver has been shown to be an effective means of treatment for the "cafe coronary."

Assessment

The vital signs must be monitored. Tachycardia, tachypnea, arrhythmia, hypothermia, and hypotension are the hallmarks of shock. Decreased pulse pressure is often an early sign of shock, and systolic pressures of less than 90 mm Hg are often associated with vital organ hypoperfusion. Blood pressure, however, is not always a reliable indicator of tissue perfusion. The following tests and procedures are useful:

☐ Arterial blood gases (ABG).

☐ Electrocardiogram (ECG).

☐ Pulmonary artery (Swan-Ganz) catheter monitoring.

☐ Complete blood count (CBC). A low hematocrit may indicate blood loss; a high hematocrit may indicate intravascular volume depletion.

☐ Serum electrolytes and creatinine.

☐ Renal function: Oliguria, increased urinary osmolarity, and urinary sodium less than 20 mEq/liter are signs of tissue hypoperfusion.

Treatment

Treatment of shock is indicated for a patient with a systolic blood pressure less than 90 mm Hg, urinary output less than 0.5 ml/kg/hour, or metabolic acidosis. Following are general guidelines for the treatment of shock.

1. The patient should lie in Trendelenburg's position or with the legs elevated.

2. Supplemental oxygen should be administered to all patients in shock to enhance tissue oxygenation. Mechanical ventilation should be used as needed to maintain the pO_2 at more than 60 mm Hg and to prevent respiratory acidosis.

3. Volume expansion with an IV infusion is of primary importance in maintaining circulation. Initially, a crystalloid solution (i.e., normal saline or Ringer's lactate) should be administered rapidly. In shock secondary to acute blood loss, hypotension that persists after infusion of 2 liters of crystalloid solution may respond to whole blood or packed red cells. An IV infusion line also provides an immediate route for administering drugs used to treat other specific causes of shock.

4. Sodium bicarbonate, given IV over 5–10 minutes, is indicated for correction of severe metabolic acidosis. The dosage should be titrated according to ABG results to achieve and maintain an arterial blood pH of greater than 7.2.

5. Vasopressor drugs (norepinephrine bitartrate [Levophed] or dopamine) may be needed for augmentation of cardiac output and perfusion of vital organs, but generally these drugs are to be used only after an adequate circulating volume is established. Drugs to treat cardiac arrhythmias should not be administered (except in dire emergencies) by individuals who do not use them on a routine basis.

6. Antibiotic therapy should be initiated promptly if sepsis is suspected.

Anaphylaxis

One specific cause of shock that requires immediate and specific therapy is anaphylaxis. *Anaphylaxis* is an acute allergic reaction following antigen exposure in a previously sensitized person. It is usually mediated by immunoglobulin E (IgE) antibodies and involves release of chemical mediators from mast cells and basophils. *Anaphylactoid reactions,* which are more common yet less severe, are the result of direct release of these chemical mediators triggered by nonantigenic agents. Anaphylaxis or anaphylactoid reactions may occur after exposure to pollen, drugs, foreign serum, insect stings, diagnostic agents such as iodinated contrast materials or fluorescein, vaccines, local anesthetics, and food products. The most important parameter for prediction of such an attack is a history of a previous allergic reaction to any other drug or possible antigen. Unfortunately, a history of known sensitivity may not always be elicited.

Anaphylaxis is particularly important to the ophthalmologist, in view of the increasing number of surgical procedures and fluorescein angiograms being performed in the office setting. It is estimated that allergic reactions to fluorescein (including urticaria) occur in up to 1% of all angiograms. In a recent survey, the overall risk of a severe reaction was 1 in 1900 patients, including a risk of respiratory compromise in 1 in 3800 subjects. Reactions can occur with doses as small as 5 ml of 25% oral fluorescein sodium (1.23 g) in 100 ml of orange juice. Any patient developing diaphoresis, apprehension, pallor, and/or a rapid and weak pulse after administration of a drug should be considered to have an allergic reaction until proven otherwise. The diagnosis is certain if there is associated generalized itching, urticaria, angioedema of the skin, dyspnea, wheezing, or arrhythmia. This process may lead rapidly to loss of consciousness, shock, cardiac arrest, coma, or death. Once an acute allergic reaction is suspected, prompt treatment is indicated.

1. A vasopressor is indicated to manage hypotension unresponsive to volume expansion. Epinephrine (0.3–0.5 ml of 1:1000 injected subcutaneously or IM in a limb opposite to the antigenic agent injection site or, with a tourniquet applied, proximal to the antigen injection site) is usually quite effective.

2. Volume expansion, with either 5% dextrose in normal saline or Ringer's lactate solution, may be needed to restore and maintain tissue perfusion.

3. Oxygen should be administered to all patients in respiratory distress.

4. Aminophylline, 6 mg/kg as a loading dose, may be infused IV over 20–30 minutes to treat bronchospasm.

5. Tracheostomy or cricothyrotomy is indicated for laryngeal edema unresponsive to the above methods or when oral intubation cannot be performed.

6. Hydrocortisone sodium succinate (Solu-Cortef), 500 mg IV every 6 hours (or its equivalent), should be administered for serious or prolonged reactions. Corticosteroids are not first-line drugs; however, when given early, they help in controlling possible long-term sequelae. Antihistamines are also helpful in slowing or halting the ongoing allergic response but are of limited value in treating acute anaphylaxis.

7. All patients with anaphylaxis or anaphylactoid reactions should be observed for at least 6 hours.

In cases of mild allergic reactions, the physician can give 10–50 mg of diphenhydramine (Benadryl) orally or intramuscularly and observe the patient closely to determine if further treatment is necessary. Pretreating high-risk patients with an antihistamine and/or corticosteroids prior to a fluorescein angiogram may reduce the risk of an allergic reaction. In all cases of anaphylaxis, supportive treatment should be maintained until the emergency medical team arrives.

Personal emergency kits containing epinephrine are available for patients with a known history of anaphylaxis to use while awaiting medical help. The kits are designed to allow self-treatment by the patient or administration by a family member or an informed bystander. The Ana-Kit contains a syringe and needle preloaded with 0.6 ml of 1:1000 epinephrine. The physician who prescribes this kit must give detailed instructions concerning the use of the device. The EpiPen or EpiPen Jr contains a spring-loaded automatic injector, which does not permit graduated doses to be given but automatically injects 0.3 mg of epinephrine (0.15 mg in the junior version) when the device is triggered by pressure on the thigh. The epinephrine ampules contained in these self-treatment kits have a limited shelf life. They should be replaced prior to the expiration date, or if the solution becomes discolored.

Eisenberg MS, Copass MK. *Emergency Medical Therapy.* 3rd ed. Philadelphia: Saunders; 1988

Guidelines for cardiopulmonary resuscitation and emergency cardiac care. Emergency Cardiac Care Committee and Subcommittees, American Heart Association. *JAMA.* 1992;268:2171–2392.

Kinsella FP, Mooney DJ. Anaphylaxis following oral fluorescein angiography. *Am J Ophthalmol.* 1988;106:745–746.

Lipson BK, Yannuzzi LA. Complications of intravenous fluorescein injections. *Int Ophthalmol Clin.* 1989;29:200.

Roth CS, Weaver DT, eds. *Pocket Manual of Emergency Medical Therapy.* 4th ed. Toronto: Decker; 1987

Seizures and Status Epilepticus

A *seizure* is a paroxysmal episode of abnormal electrical activity in the brain resulting in involuntary transient neurologic, motor activity, behavioral, or autonomic dysfunction. Seizures can present with many different clinical manifestations, but most fit into the categories of simple-partial, complex-partial, or generalized tonic-clonic.

As in the treatment of all medical emergencies, the first consideration is airway maintenance. This becomes particularly important if the seizure progresses to status epilepticus. *Status epilepticus* is defined as a prolonged seizure or multiple seizures without intervening periods of normal consciousness. Status epilepticus, like seizures, may have a local onset with secondary generalization or be generalized from onset. A seizure is considered status epilepticus when it lasts for 30 minutes or longer. Status epilepticus is often found concomitantly with hyperthermia, acidosis, hypoxia, tachycardia, hypercapnia, and mydriasis and, if persistent, may be associated with irreversible brain injury. Status epilepticus that is completely stopped within 2 hours usually has relatively minor morbidity compared to episodes lasting longer than 2 hours.

Major causes of seizures and status epilepticus include:

- Drug withdrawal, such as from anticonvulsants, benzodiazepines, barbiturates, or alcohol
- Metabolic abnormalities, such as hypoglycemia, hyponatremia, hypocalcemia, or hypomagnesemia
- Conditions that affect the CNS, such as infection, trauma, stroke, hypoxia, ischemia, or sleep deprivation
- Toxic levels of various drugs

In management, it is important not only to stop the seizure activity but also to identify and treat the underlying cause. A general treatment protocol is outlined below.

1. Note time. Monitor airways, vital signs, and electrocardiograph.

2. Establish IV line. Position patient on his or her side to allow gravity drainage of saliva. Insert oral airway if possible. Some experts advocate using a washcloth or taped tongue blade as a bite block.

3. Draw blood immediately and check glucose, electrolytes, calcium, magnesium, sodium, and toxicology screen. Also check drug levels if patient is known to be taking medicines associated with seizures (e.g., anticonvulsants, theophylline, lithium, etc). CBC, ABG, and urinalysis are also potentially helpful tests. Additional tests that may be warranted following control of seizures include liver and renal function tests, CT or MRI scan, and lumbar puncture.

4. Give 50 ml of 50% dextrose IV push (or 1 ml/kg).

5. Administer a benzodiazepine such as diazepam (Valium) or lorazepam (Ativan) slowly by IV, titrated to an effective dose, usually 5.0 mg/min up to 20–30 mg in adults to a total dose of 0.5 mg/kg.

6. Proceed immediately to administer phenytoin at an IV rate of 50 mg/min to a loading dose of 15–18 mg/kg. Monitor pulse, blood pressure, and ECG. Watch especially for hypotension. Fosphenytoin (Cerebyx) has recently become available; it can be administered more rapidly (150 mg/min) and is stable in dextrose-containing IV solutions (phenytoin should not be given with dextrose solutions).

7. If seizures continue for 20 minutes, administer a loading dose of phenobarbital (10–15 mg/kg) at 50 mg/min intravenously.

8. If seizures persist, consider transferring the patient to ICU for general anesthesia/paralysis with EEG monitoring.

TABLE XIV-2

MAXIMUM RECOMMENDED LOCAL ANESTHETIC DOSES

AGENT	COMMERCIALLY AVAILABLE CONCENTRATIONS (%) 1% = 10 mg/cc	PLAIN SOLUTIONS (mg)	EPINEPHRINE-CONTAINING SOLUTIONS (mg)
Chloroprocaine	1.0, 2.0, 3.0	800	1000
Lidocaine	0.5, 1.0, 1.5, 2.0, 4.0, 5.0	300	500
Mepivacaine (Carbocaine)	1.0, 1.5, 2.0	300	225
Bupivacaine	0.25, 0.5, 0.75	175	225
Tetracaine	1.0	100	100

Toxic Reactions to Local Anesthetics and Other Agents

Toxic overdose is an additional cause of unconsciousness or of acute distress in a conscious patient, and it must be considered whenever the patient is having a procedure performed that requires local anesthesia. Table XIV-2 lists commonly used local anesthetics with their maximum safe dose.

Reactions following the administration of local anesthetics are almost always toxic and only rarely allergic. A high blood level of local anesthetic can be produced by the following: too large a dose, unusually rapid absorption (including inadvertent IV administration), and/or unusually slow detoxification or elimination (especially in liver disease). Hypersensitivity (i.e., decreased patient tolerance) and idiosyncratic reactions are rare, but they may occur with local anesthetic agents, as with any drug. Although true allergic or anaphylactic reactions are also rare, they may occur, particularly with agents belonging to the aminoester class.

Toxic reactions cause overstimulation of the CNS, which may lead to excitement, restlessness, apprehension, disorientation, tremors, and convulsions (cerebral cortex effects), as well as nausea and vomiting (medulla effects). Cardiac effects initially include tachycardia and hypertension. Ultimately, however, depression of the CNS and cardiovascular systems occurs, which may result in sleepiness and coma (cerebral cortex effects) as well as in nausea, vomiting, irregular respirations, sighing, dyspnea, and respiratory arrest (medulla effects). Cardiac effects of CNS depression are bradycardia and hypotension.

When signs of cortical stimulation occur, treatment must be started immediately, before progressive changes to cortical and medullary function and cardiac depression occur. Increased metabolic activity of the CNS and poor ventilatory exchange lead to cerebral hypoxia. Treatment consists of oxygenation, supportive airway care, and titrated IV administration of midazolam, which is used to suppress cortical stimulation. Respiratory stimulants are to be avoided, as the medullary respiratory center has already been stimulated by the local anesthetic, and these drugs lead to eventual respiratory depression.

In cases of toxic overdose, other emergency procedures include suctioning if vomiting occurs and use of taped tongue blade if convulsions develop. If shock develops, the appropriate drugs can be administered by IV infusion.

The addition of *epinephrine* to the local anesthetic can also cause adverse reactions. Epinephrine can produce symptoms similar to early CNS stimulation by local anesthetic, such as anxiety, restlessness, tremor, hypertension, and tachycardia. Unlike local anesthetics, however, epinephrine does not produce convulsions or bradycardia as the toxic reaction proceeds. Oxygen is useful in the treatment of epinephrine overdoses.

A recent study looked at the effect of intraocular epinephrine irrigation at a concentration that maintained pupillary dilation during routine extracapsular cataract surgery. The study found that no additional risk of significant interval changes in either arterial blood pressure or heart rate was incurred by patients with or without hypertension.

The administration of retrobulbar *bupivacaine* has been associated with respiratory arrest. This reaction may be caused by intra-arterial injection of the local anesthetic, with retrograde flow to the cerebral circulation. It could also result from puncture of the dural sheath of the optic nerve during retrobulbar block, with diffusion of the local anesthetic along the subdural space in the midbrain. A large prospective study comparing retrobulbar injection of 0.75% bupivacaine plus 2.0% lidocaine to 0.75% bupivacaine plus 4.0% lidocaine found that those patients receiving 4.0% lidocaine mixed with bupivacaine had an almost 9 times greater risk of respiratory arrest than the patients receiving 2.0% lidocaine mixed with bupivacaine. (See also chapter XV, Perioperative Management of the Ocular Surgery Patient, for further discussion of reactions to local anesthetics.)

The use of *edrophonium chloride* (Tensilon) in the diagnosis of myasthenia gravis can have toxic side effects. The signs and symptoms are the result of cholinergic stimulation and may include nausea, vomiting, diarrhea, sweating, increased bronchial and salivary secretions, muscle fasciculations and weakness, and bradycardia. Some of these signs may be transient and self-limited because of the very short half-life of IV Tensilon. Whenever a Tensilon test is to be performed, a syringe containing 0.5 mg of atropine sulfate must be immediately available. (Some physicians routinely pretreat all patients undergoing Tensilon testing with atropine.)

If signs of excess cholinergic stimulation occur, 0.4–0.5 mg of atropine sulfate should be administered intravenously. This dosage may be repeated every 3–10 minutes if necessary. The total dose of atropine necessary to counteract the toxic effects is seldom more than 2 mg. If toxic signs progress, the treatment described above for toxic overdose may be necessary.

Firestone LL, Lebowitz PW, Cooke CE, eds. *Clinical Anesthesia Procedures of the Massachusetts General Hospital.* 3rd ed. Boston: Little, Brown; 1988.

Wittpenn JR, Rapoza P, Sternberg P, et al. Respiratory arrest following retrobulbar anesthesia. *Ophthalmology.* 1986;93:867–870.

Yamaguchi H, Matsumoto Y. Stability of blood pressure and heart rate during intraocular epinephrine irrigation. *Ann Ophthalmol.* 1988;20:58–60.

Drug Interactions

Because of the development of compartmentalized medical specialties and the proliferation of specific therapeutic agents, patients frequently have multiple simultaneous drug regimens. Often, no single physician (among the several to whom a patient may relate) is aware of all of the drugs the patient is taking. In the last decade, the problem of drug interactions has been recognized as becoming increasingly serious.

The clinical problem is compounded by several factors. For example, the physician is often not aware of what other drugs the patient uses or might not be familiar with agents used outside of his or her own specialty. In addition, the interaction may affect a bodily system not usually monitored by a given specialist. Moreover, many of the myriad interactions reported in the literature may be seen infrequently or are more theoretical than real. Finally, the patient might not associate a symptom with a particular drug if that symptom is not related to the system for which the drug was given. For example, the association between ophthalmic epinephrine therapy and cardiac arrhythmia might not be readily apparent to the patient.

Mechanisms for drug interaction, where known, vary greatly. Some of these mechanisms and some clinically significant examples of each mechanism are given in Table XIV-3. The examples are those of greatest significance to the ophthalmologist, since they involve drugs that the ophthalmologist uses or that are commonly used by ophthalmic patients.

Obviously, it is impossible to commit to memory all possible drug interactions. The ophthalmologist can minimize adverse effects from multiple drug therapy by:

☐ Maintaining a high level of suspicion for drug interactions

☐ Questioning the patient closely about other drug therapy and general symptomatology

☐ Encouraging all patients to carry a card listing the drugs they use

☐ Keeping in close communication with the patient's primary physician

☐ Consulting with a clinical pharmacologist or internist whenever a question of drug interaction arises

Hansten PD, Horn JR. *Drug Interactions and Updates* (loose-leaf binder format). Philadelphia: Lea & Febiger; 1993.

Mehta M. *PDR Guide to Drug Interactions, Side Effects, Indications.* Montvale, NJ: Medical Economics; 1993.

TABLE XIV-3

EXAMPLES OF DRUG INTERACTION

MECHANISM OF INTERACTION	IF TAKING DRUG #1	AND ADDING DRUG #2	EFFECT WILL BE
1. Physiochemical reaction	Ascorbic acid	Penicillin	Precipitate in IV solution
2. Alteration of gastro-intestinal absorption	Antacids or food	Tetracycline	Reduced serum tetracycline due to decreased absorption
	Belladonna-like drugs	Many drugs	Reduced absorption
3. Alteration of protein binding	Sulfonylureas, diphenylhydantoin	Coumarin anticoagulants	Release of coumarin from protein-binding sites, causing increased anticoagulation
	Aspirin	Tolbutamide	Release of tolbutamide from protein-binding sites, causing increased hypoglycemia
	Acetazolamide	Salicylates	Increased plasma un-ionized salicylate, with increased brain levels and increased CNS toxicity
4. Interactions at receptor sites	MAO inhibitors	Epinephrine, phenylephrine, apraclonidine	Excessive pressor effects due to lack of detoxifying enzyme
	Belladonna alkaloids or phenothiazines	Pilocarpine	Reduced effect on intraocular pressure due to competition at receptor sites
	Halothane	Phenylephrine, epinephrine, apraclonidine	Arrhythmias due to increased myocardial irritability

TABLE XIV-3

EXAMPLES OF DRUG INTERACTION (Continued)

MECHANISM OF INTERACTION	IF TAKING DRUG #1	AND ADDING DRUG #2	EFFECT WILL BE
5. Alterations of drug metabolism	Barbiturates	Coumarin, diphenylhydantoin, digitoxin	Reduced effect of drug #2 due to increased metabolism by induction hepatic enzymes
	Coumarin anticoagulants	Diphenylhydantoin, tolbutamide, chlorpropamide	Enhanced effect of drug #2 due to reduction in metabolic detoxification rate
6. Alteration of drug excretion	Anticoagulants, sulfonamides, phenylbutazone	Hypoglycemic agents	Enhanced hypoglycemic effect due to reduced excretion of drug #2
	Propranolol	Lidocaine	Increased lidocaine effect
	Methotrexate	Salicylates	Increased methotrexate effect
7. Alteration of blood pH or electrolytes	Acetazolamide	Diuretics, corticosteroids	Enhanced potassium excretion and digitalis effect
8. Antimicrobial synergy and antagonism	Penicillin	Streptomycin	Synergism for *Streptococcus viridans*
	Erythromycin	Chloramphenicol	Antagonism for gram-positive organisms
9. Additive side effects	Acetazolamide	Echothiophate	Increased gastrointestinal disturbance
	Corticosteroids	Aspirin	Increased irritation of gastric mucosa and increased likelihood of gastric bleeding
	Psychotropic drugs	Alcohol, hypnotics, narcotics	Increased CNS depression

CHAPTER XV

Perioperative Management of the Ocular Surgery Patient

Preoperative Evaluation

Adult Patients

Current recommendations for laboratory screening for all adult patients before "major" surgery include hemoglobin determination and an ECG if the patient is older than 40 years of age. In addition, patients taking diuretics or digoxin should have their serum potassium levels determined. Any patient with cardiac or pulmonary disease or a history of recent upper respiratory infection or anyone with a history of smoking who is over the age of 50 should have a chest x-ray if general anesthesia is anticipated. Fasting blood glucose level should be checked in any diabetic patient or any patient over 50 years of age (Table XV-1). These recommendations apply to all ophthalmic patients, even those having "just a cataract." Although the need to convert to general anesthesia is quite rare, it significantly increases morbidity in the ophthalmic population.

In the past, potassium abnormalities were a source of concern in patients taking diuretics or digoxin. However, current evidence suggests that asymptomatic patients (no congestive heart failure, no ischemic cardiac symptoms) can undergo elective surgery if their potassium level is between 2.8 and 5.9 mEq/L.

Marked elevations of fasting blood glucose (greater than 300 mg/dL) or the discovery of new onset of diabetes at the time of glucose screening should delay elective eye surgery. The sequela of an unexpected neurologic event occurring during the perioperative period is worse in patients with hyperglycemia.

Even the most stable patient can become hypertensive, hypotensive, tachycardic, or bradycardic in response to potentially disturbing stimuli such as injection of local anesthetic or placement of drapes that may cause claustrophobia. Common abnormalities of the ECG that pose problems are apparently "new" onset of atrial fibrillation, "new" ST-T segment depression that suggests new ischemia, or "new" myocardial infarction, premature ventricular contractions, or severe bradycardia or heart block.

When ST-T segment changes are found on the preoperative ECG, it is important to compare it with an old ECG if possible. Changes in an asymptomatic patient are less ominous than changes in a patient with chest pain. The exact date that a previous myocardial infarction occurred is medically important in that the incidence of reinfarction decreases to 5% in 6 months after the original cardiac infarct. New onset atrial fibrillation can be benign or be a sign of significant systemic disease such as pulmonary emboli, myocardial ischemia, or incipient congestive heart failure. Although more than five premature ventricular contractions per minute are associated with increased perioperative morbidity, premature ventricular contractions

TABLE XV-1

MINIMAL PREOPERATIVE TEST REQUIREMENTS AT THE MAYO CLINIC

AGE (YR)	TESTS REQUIRED*
<40	None
40–59	Electrocardiography, measurement of creatinine and glucose
≥60	Complete blood cell count, electrocardiography, chest roentgenography, measurement of creatinine and glucose

*In addition, the following guidelines apply:

A complete blood cell is indicated in all patients who undergo blood typing and who are screened or crossmatched.

Measurement of potassium is indicated in patients taking diuretics or undergoing bowel preparation.

Chest roentgenography is indicated in patients with a history of cardiac or pulmonary disease or with recent respiratory symptoms.

A history of cigarette smoking in patients older than 40 years of age who are scheduled for an upper abdominal or thoracic surgical procedure is an indication for spirometry (forced vital capacity).

(Reproduced from Narr BJ, Hansen TR, Warner MA. Preoperative laboratory screening in healthy Mayo patients: cost-effective elimination of tests and unchanged outcomes. *Mayo Clin Proc.* 1991;66:155.)

should be considered in the context of the patient's history. If electrolyte levels are normal, the ECG is stable, and there are no symptoms of ischemia, the judgment may be to proceed with surgery. Premature ventricular contractions also occur in the setting of alcohol, caffeine, or cocaine use.

Pediatric Patients

Different considerations apply to pediatric eye patients. There is no evidence that abnormalities appearing on a CBC really affect the choice of anesthetic management for asymptomatic children. In general, if the child is healthy and does not take chronically prescribed medications, no laboratory tests are necessary even for general anesthesia. However, a family history of sickle trait or sickle disease *is* significant because some aspects of anesthetic management will change in these patients. Bleeding time or routine urinalysis is unnecessary in the healthy child and only serves to traumatize the patient.

The issue of performing elective eye surgery on a child with an upper respiratory infection is controversial. A child who is already ill will feel even worse after surgery, and the significance of a postoperative fever may be difficult to interpret. Further, contaminated nasal discharge could possibly enter the ocular area. If a child has a fever above 101° F, has purulent nasal discharge, or appears systemically ill, the likelihood of a bacterial lower respiratory infection should be considered. This would argue for a delay to avoid increased risk of laryngospasm and bronchospasm with general anesthesia. However, in the absence of such findings—e.g., a child who appears well except for a runny nose—many anesthesiologists will elect to proceed.

Specific Preoperative Concerns

Obstructive pulmonary disease   Chronic obstructive pulmonary disease can pose a distinct problem in ophthalmic surgery. Cessation of smoking is extremely helpful in reducing intra- and postoperative coughing. Preoperative bronchopulmonary care with chest physiotherapy can decrease the susceptibility to infection and improve air exchange. General anesthesia may be preferred to local anesthesia since the anesthesiologist may have better control over tracheal bronchial secretions and the cough reflex. (See also chapter VI, Pulmonary Diseases.)

Malignant hyperthermia   Malignant hyperthermia (MH), which will be discussed at greater length on pages 248–249, is a serious intraoperative complication triggered by certain anesthetic agents. MH can be fatal if diagnosis and treatment are delayed. It can occur as an isolated case or as a dominantly inherited disorder with incomplete penetrance. Physical disorders associated with MH include strabismus, muscular dystrophy, or congenital ptosis. The incidence is reported variously as between 1:6000 and 1:30,000 and is generally thought to be higher in children. It can occur in all age groups, however.

The preoperative personal and family history is helpful in determining if the patient is at risk for malignant hyperthermia. Patients with a history of masseter muscle rigidity after the administration of succinylcholine during anesthesia induction may be at risk for malignant hyperthermia. If the patient or other family members have a history of sudden onset of tachycardia, breathing problems, or high fever during anesthesia or a history of ventricular arrhythmias or cardiac failure during anesthesia, the diagnosis of malignant hyperthermia should be considered.

Muscle biopsy with in-vitro halothane and caffeine contraction testing is the most specific test to confirm the clinical diagnosis. Patients who have an unconfirmed but suspicious history for MH or a relative with MH should undergo testing to see if they are susceptible. The measurement of creatine kinase should not be relied upon. Although levels are elevated in up to two thirds of MH patients, normal results have no predictive value.

Malignant hyperthermia occurs most commonly with the use of succinylcholine, often in combination with the administration of an inhalation anesthetic such as halothane. Safer agents include nitrous oxide, barbiturates, narcoleptics, antipyretics, nondepolarizing muscle relaxants, propofol, and droperidol. However, even the stress of having surgery itself can trigger malignant hyperthermia. See pages 248–249 for further information and a treatment protocol.

Latex allergy   Latex allergy is a condition that has caused growing concern in the last few years. The overall prevalence of latex allergy has not been determined, but certain populations appear to be at particular risk for reactions. Health care workers and hospital employees can experience progressive sensitization to latex because of repeated occupational exposure. This sensitivity is accentuated if the health care worker has a history of atopy. Certain medical populations also have significant risks for latex allergy and anaphylaxis, including patients with myelodysplasia or spina bifida and those who have undergone repeated urinary catheterization or frequent surgical procedures. A cross-reactivity with bananas, avocados, mangoes, and chestnuts has been demonstrated, and allergies to these foods have also been associated with latex allergy. Other implicated foods include apricots, celery, figs, grapes, papayas, passion fruit, peaches, and pineapples. A history of reactivity to balloons is also suggestive of a latex allergy.

Any patient suspected of having latex allergy should be referred to an allergist, and the surgery should be delayed until this concern can be evaluated. The entire operating-room environment must be changed to care for the latex-allergic patient. Further, the allergic patient should be the first case of the day in that particular operating room.

Local anesthetic allergies   A patient reporting an allergy to all the "-caines" might actually have experienced an intravascular injection of epinephrine, a vasovagal attack, or even a panic attack rather than a true allergic reaction. True allergic reactions occur but account for less than 1% of all local anesthetic reactions. A true allergic reaction to a -caine medication includes wheezing, urticaria, and respiratory distress. A history of sweating, tachycardia, headache, or hypertension suggests intravascular injection of epinephrine. However, an overdose of local anesthetic produces tinnitus, a bad taste in the mouth, or central nervous system changes such as confusion, slurred speech, or respiratory arrest. An overdose is unlikely in ophthalmic anesthesia given the relatively small volumes used.

A true allergy to local anesthetics is more likely with the *ester derivatives* such as procaine, tetracaine, chloroprocaine, and benzocaine. An allergy can even occur to the preservative Paraben, which is widely used in multidose vials of local anesthetics, as well as in other medicines, cosmetics, and foods.

If a patient is suspected of having a true allergy to local anesthetics, preoperative skin testing by appropriate personnel with adequate monitoring and resuscitation equipment nearby is recommended. If the patient proves to have true ester allergy, *amides* (lidocaine, bupivacaine, or mepivacaine) can be used as an alternative. Conversely, if the patient has a true allergy to amides, then an ester-type of anesthetic can be used such as chloroprocaine or tetracaine. Preservative-free agents are also available. (Allergic or toxic reactions to local anesthetics are discussed more fully on pages 235–236 in chapter XIV, Medical Emergencies; and on pages 247–248 of this chapter.)

Preoperative Fasting

Questions often arise as to how long the patient must be kept on NPO status before surgery. A pediatric patient who is kept on NPO status for 10–12 hours preoperatively may become hypotensive as a result of dehydration. It has been shown that use of clear liquids orally up to 2 hours prior to surgery does not lead to any higher incidence of aspiration or other gastrointestinal complications of general anesthesia or local anesthesia.

The purpose of preoperative fasting is to reduce the particulate matter in the stomach and to lower the gastric fluid volume and acidity in case aspiration of stomach contents occurs. Diabetics, particularly those with autonomic neuropathy, are at risk for gastroparesis. Pregnant patients have a higher-than-normal risk of aspiration. Additionally, patients with known gastroesophageal reflux and those with peptic ulcer disease may also have some increased risk of aspiration.

Oral administration of an H_2 blocker such as *ranitidine* or *famotidine* 2–4 hours prior to surgery reduces the percentage of patients with low gastric pH or high gastric volume. *Metoclopramide* or *cisapride* also promotes intestinal motility and decreases reflux; these drugs are especially useful in a nonfasting patient who requires urgent surgery. Cisapride may be more beneficial in that it is devoid of antidopaminergic effects and has a lower incidence of side effects than metoclopramide. (See Table XV-2 for selected perioperative medications.)

TABLE XV-2

SELECTED PERIOPERATIVE MEDICATIONS

NAME (GENERIC AND BRAND)	USES
Metoclopramide (Reglan)	Relief of gastric paresis, reduction of gastro-esophageal reflux, perioperative antiemetic
Cisapride (Propulsid)	Reduction of gastroesophageal reflux
Midazolam (Versed)	Preoperative sedation
Propofol (Diprivan)	Preoperative sedation/general anesthesia
Diazepam (Valium)	Preoperative sedation
Alfentanil (Alfenta)	Analgesic/anesthetic
Fentanyl citrate (Sublimaze)	Analgesic/anesthetic
Methohexital (Brevital Sodium)	Analgesic/anesthetic
Sufentanil (Sufenta)	Analgesic/anesthetic
Ondansetron (Zofran)	Postoperative antiemetic
Ketorolac (Toradol)	Postoperative analgesic

Management of Concurrent Medications

It is important to know which chronically administered medications should be taken, and which should be withheld, on the day of surgery. The following are general guidelines, although individual practice can vary from locality to locality.

Antihypertensive medications should be continued until the time of surgery to avoid rebound hypertensive crises and the risk of end-organ damage associated with uncontrolled hypertension (specifically myocardial ischemic diseases). Such medications include clonidine (both dermal patch and orally administered), beta blockers, and angiotensin-converting-enzyme inhibitors. Oral antihypertensive medications can be taken with a sip of water the day of surgery whether or not the patient is on NPO status.

Digoxin can be withheld the day of surgery for many patients, given its long half-life. However, if a patient is receiving digoxin to control the ventricular response to atrial fibrillation, it is important to be sure that the resting heart rate is appropriate on the morning of surgery; digoxin should be given if the resting heart rate is more than 90 beats per minute.

Anticonvulsant medications should be administered (with sips of water) on the patient's usual schedule, since stress and particularly general anesthesia can lower the seizure threshold.

The patient who has taken *systemic corticosteroids* for more than 1 month within the previous 6 months before surgery is customarily "covered" with the equivalent of 300 mg per day of hydrocortisone perioperatively. At the start of the procedure, 100 mg is given intravenously, an additional 100 mg is given at the end of the procedure, and the last 100 mg is administered 6 hours after the end of surgery.

Lower doses can be administered for procedures associated with minimal physiologic stress, in the range of 25–30 mg of hydrocortisone intravenously in the first 24 hours after surgery.

In general, *antimicrobial prophylaxis* of bacterial endocarditis in patients with cardiac valvular disease is not necessary for ocular surgery. An exception to this guideline is when there is a chance of exposure to pathogens in the upper respiratory system such as during dacryocystorhinostomy, orbital surgery, or an incision and drainage of infected tissue. Prophylaxis is not recommended for elective oral endotracheal intubation. Mitral valve prolapse, without valvular regurgitation, is not an indication for prophylaxis (see Tables I-1 through I-4, pp 10–13).

If a patient does require prophylactic antibiotic treatment for prevention of endocarditis, either the intravenous or oral route can be used, depending on the individual situation. IV *ampicillin* or oral *amoxicillin* can be used. In case of penicillin allergy or intolerance, *clindamycin* can be substituted. For children, consultation with the patient's pediatrician or anesthesiologist should be considered. Recommendations for prophylactic drugs and dosages are listed in Tables I-3 and I-4, pp 12–13.

As previously mentioned, *management of blood glucose* is important to avoid CNS dysfunction. Whenever possible, insulin-dependent patients should have surgery early in the day to allow for postoperative insulin management. For patients who are on insulin and undergoing procedures shorter than 2 hours, the "no insulin, no glucose" regimen works well preoperatively on the morning of surgery. Perioperative monitoring of blood glucose before, during, and after surgery is important. The availability of one-touch monitoring makes such measurements very easy, even in the operating room. During the procedure, intravenous solutions without dextrose (lactated Ringer's or saline) are given. After the surgical procedure, the patient should receive a portion (usually one half or one third) of the usual insulin dose, once oral intake is established.

If a procedure lasts more than 2 hours, insulin will have to be given as an infusion of at least 4 units per hour, with monitoring of the blood glucose level every 30–60 minutes. Alternatively, one fourth to one half of the patient's usual long-acting daily insulin can be administered at the beginning of the procedure, with frequent monitoring of the glucose level thereafter. The anesthesiologist and primary care physician should be involved in managing the blood glucose level in such patients.

Oral hypoglycemic medications are usually withheld the day of surgery. These medications have a relatively long duration of action, which could lead to hypoglycemia late in the day if the patient's oral caloric intake is inadequate. Surgical considerations for diabetic patients are also discussed in chapter IX, Endocrine Disorders.

Thyroid medications can be held the day of surgery given their long half-life.

Certain medications should be *omitted* the day of surgery. These include *diuretics*. A patient having a procedure performed under local anesthesia may become uncomfortable from a full bladder caused by a preoperative dose of diuretic. A patient undergoing general anesthesia who continues diuretic use on the morning of surgery may become hypotensive because of the intravascular volume depletion that occurred prior to surgery.

Drugs that interfere with platelet function, such as *aspirin* or the *nonsteroidal anti-inflammatory agents*, should, if at all possible, be discontinued for the duration of one platelet lifespan, at least 7 days.

Warfarin can be discontinued until the prothrombin time has returned to normal, or the INR to 1.5, unless the patient has an artificial heart valve or unstable atrial fibrillation. In the case of an artificial heart valve, especially a mitral valve, warfarin is discontinued until the prothrombin time is around 15 seconds or the INR drops to 1.5. *Heparin* can be restarted 12–14 hours after the procedure. There is recent evidence that postoperative heparin administration increases morbidity from bleeding in surgical procedures. It is important that an internist, cardiologist, or primary care provider continue to be involved in the management of patients with such complex problems.

Nicotinic acid should be discontinued before general anesthesia because it can cause an exaggerated hypotensive response from vasodilation. It is generally taught that *MAO inhibitors* should be discontinued 2–3 weeks before elective surgery, because these medications are associated with an exaggerated hypertensive response to systemically released vasopressors during general anesthesia. In addition, the ephedrine or dopamine that are sometimes needed to increase blood pressure intraoperatively can cause marked elevation in blood pressure in patients who are on MAO inhibitors. The administration of meperidine to patients who are taking MAO inhibitors can result in hyperpyrexia, muscle rigidity, seizures, coma, hypotension, and respiratory depression, probably in response to an increase in cerebral serotonin occurring secondary to MAO inhibition. Nevertheless, there is some debate as to whether MAO inhibitors need to be discontinued, in that anesthetic techniques with vasoactive medications other than ephedrine and dopamine can be used to avoid the chance of hypertension or sympathetic stimulation. This is an issue best discussed with the anesthesiologist.

Though rarely used today, the administration of *echothiophate iodide* eyedrops will affect the choice of muscle relaxant prior to endotracheal intubation. Ideally, the drops should be stopped 3 weeks before the elective surgery to allow recovery of the cholinesterase enzyme system. However, if echothiophate iodide must be continued, succinylcholine *cannot* be used during intubation. Fortunately, alternative medications are available for use in such cases.

Preoperative Sedation

Preoperative sedation is an important part of comfortable regional or general anesthesia in a patient undergoing elective surgery. Anxiolytics such as *midazolam* can be given intramuscularly (2–4 mg) 30–60 minutes before the procedure or intravenously (0.5–1.0 mg) 2–3 minutes before the stimulus of the anesthetic block. Midazolam is a more appropriate sedative than *diazepam* for outpatient surgery, because its elimination half-life is 2–4 hours, while diazepam's is 20–40 hours. Midazolam can also be reversed with *flumazenil*. Careful IV titration of sedatives and narcotics is very important in the elderly to avoid oversedation or respiratory depression.

Alfentanil can be given intravenously in titrated doses of 100–500 mg with appropriate anesthesia monitoring. Its peak effect occurs in 1–2 minutes and lasts 10–20 minutes. *Fentanyl citrate,* which has a peak effect in 3–5 minutes and lasts about 30 minutes, is given in titrated doses of 25–50 mg for ophthalmic monitored anesthesia. The effects of narcotics can be reversed with the antagonist *naloxone,* intravenously. The duration of naloxone reversal is 1 hour or less.

Thiopental sodium in 10–25 mg increments every 30 seconds can be used to ensure amnesia and hypnosis for regional anesthesia or local infiltration of anesthetic agents. It should be remembered that too rapid or too large a dose can depress hemodynamics and respiration. *Methohexital* can be similarly used in increments of 10 mg titrated intravenously every 20–30 seconds.

Propofol is a drug with unique properties of rapid hypnosis and a tendency to produce bradycardia, but it has rapid clearance with very little hangover. It must be given through a large-bore vein or administered after a lidocaine flush of the IV line to avoid significant burning on administration.

Preoperative sedation for children can include midazolam in a dose of .05 mg/kg given in 5–10 cc of the child's favorite clear liquid or oral acetaminophen. Methohexital (20–25 mg/kg) can be administered rectally through a french catheter for preoperative sedation.

Intraoperative Complications

Adverse Reactions to Local Anesthesia

Screening for possible allergies to local anesthetic agents has already been discussed as part of the preoperative evaluation of the patient. Other types of adverse reactions are discussed below.

Local anesthetic injection into the retrobulbar space can lead to apnea, respiratory arrest, and cranial nerve palsies on the side being injected or even on the opposite side. Anatomic studies of the position of the retrobulbar needle in relation to the optic nerve when the adducted or supraducted position of the eye is used during injection show that it is possible to inject anesthetic into the subdural space with a standard Atkinson-type needle. Cases of cranial nerve palsies in association with respiratory difficulties represent actual brain stem anesthesia from injection of the anesthetic agent into the subdural space, with subsequent diffusion into the circulating cerebrospinal fluid.

Several suggestions have been made to avoid such complications, including changing the traditional positioning of the eye during the retrobulbar anesthetic injection so that the nerve is rotated away from the track of the needle, for example, by having the patient look straight ahead. Using less-sharp, nondisposable retrobulbar needles less than 1¼ inch long also reduces the chance of perforating the optic nerve sheath. Although the concentration of the anesthetic has been implicated as the cause of respiratory arrest in one series, it is more likely that a larger volume and, therefore, a larger total dose of anesthetic was delivered to the brain stem through an inadvertent subdural injection. The peribulbar technique was devised, in part, to avoid such complications. If apnea, respiratory arrest, or cranial neuropathies occur after a retrobulbar injection, the patient's airway must be supported with mask ventilation. Intubation and mechanical ventilation may be necessary. Apnea seldom lasts more than 30–50 minutes, but it is important that the patient be stabilized during this time by experienced medical personnel.

Respiratory distress and dysphagia can occur from the Nadbath block, an injection into the stylomastoid foramen that is used to provide facial akinesia. These complications occur when the anesthetic agent is injected deeply into the area of the facial nerve as it exits the stylomastoid foramen, and the anesthetic bathes cranial nerves IX, X, and XI as they exit the jugular foramen. This leads to paralysis of these nerves, and the patient becomes dysphagic, begins to cough or has a hoarse voice, and may develop stridor or severe respiratory insufficiency. These complications tend to occur in thin individuals in whom it is easier to bury the needle deeply.

Management of the respiratory distress requires suctioning the pharynx, positioning the patient on his or her side, and supplementing the patient's inspired gases with oxygen or even intubation. Recommendations for avoiding this complication are using a short hypodermic needle, advancing it only partway into the area to be injected, and injecting a small volume (less than 3 cc).

Anesthetic toxicity can occur when high concentrations of anesthetic agent per cc are given. For example, if 4% lidocaine is used for a peribulbar injection, the total volume that can be safely given to a 70 kg patient is limited to 8 cc. A smaller individual would be able to tolerate no more than 5 cc of 4% lidocaine without risking complications of systemic toxicity, including confusion, cardiac arrhythmias, and respiratory depression.

Seizures have occurred from the intra-arterial injection of local anesthetic agent into the ophthalmic artery. Such seizures are instantaneous with injection; supportive measures should include airway maintenance and blood pressure support. These seizures of are short duration.

Malignant Hyperthermia

As discussed earlier in this chapter, preoperative evaluation can help to identify some patients who are at risk for MH. Nevertheless, such preoperative screening is not infallible, and the surgeon should be prepared to respond to this complication.

Malignant hyperthermia is a disorder of calcium binding by the sarcoplasmic reticulum of skeletal muscles. In the presence of an anesthetic triggering agent, there is an increase in unbound intracellular calcium, which stimulates muscle contracture. This increased metabolism outstrips oxygen delivery, and anaerobic metabolism develops with the production of lactate and subsequent massive acidosis. Hyperthermia thus occurs as a result of the hypermetabolic state.

The earliest signs of MH include tachycardia that is greater than expected for the patient's anesthetic and surgical status and elevated end-tidal carbon dioxide level when the patient is monitored by capnography. Labile blood pressure, tachypnea, sweating, muscle rigidity, blotchy discoloration of skin, cyanosis, and dark urine all signal progression of the disorder. Temperature elevation, which can reach extremely high levels, is a relatively late sign. Ultimately, respiratory and metabolic acidosis, hyperkalemia, hypercalcemia, myoglobinuria, and renal failure can occur as well as disseminated intravascular coagulation and death.

Although volatile anesthetics such as halothane, enflurane, isoflurane, and intravenous succinylcholine are all known to trigger malignant hyperthermia, haloperidol, trimeprazine, and promethazine also can cause malignant hyperthermia.

If a surgeon wishes to avoid the use of succinylcholine, a laryngeal mask airway can be considered for strabismus surgery in adults if muscle relaxation is not otherwise required. The use of the laryngeal mask airway reduces the soreness and irritation of the throat that occurs after oral endotracheal intubation.

Treatment   Malignant hyperthermia is treated as a medical emergency (see Table XV-3 for the treatment protocol). The Malignant Hyperthermia Association of the United States staffs a 24-hour hotline to advise medical personnel on the diagnosis and treatment of malignant hyperthermia at (800) 644-9737.

TABLE XV-3

1. Stop the triggering agents immediately, and conclude surgery as soon as possible.

2. Hyperventilate with 100% oxygen at high flow rates.

3. Administer:
   a. Dantrolene: 2–3 mg/kg initial bolus with increments up to 10 mg/kg total. Continue to administer dantrolene until symptoms are controlled. Occasionally, a dose greater than 10 mg/kg may be needed.
   b. Sodium bicarbonate: 1–2 mEq/kg increments guided by arterial pH and pCO_2. Bicarbonate will combat hyperkalemia by driving potassium into cells.

4. Actively cool patient:
   a. If needed, IV iced saline (not Ringer's lactate) 15 ml/kg q 10 minutes × 3. Monitor closely.
   b. Lavage stomach, bladder, rectum, and peritoneal and thoracic cavities with iced saline.
   c. Surface cool with ice and hypothermia blanket.

5. Maintain urine output. If needed, administer mannitol 0.25 gm/kg IV, furosemide 1 mg/kg IV (up to 4 doses each). Urine output greater than 2 ml/kg/hr may help prevent subsequent renal failure.

6. Calcium channel blockers *should not* be given when dantrolene is administered, as hyperkalemia and myocardial depression may occur.

7. Insulin for hyperkalemia: Add 10 units of regular insulin to 50 ml of 50% glucose and titrate to control hyperkalemia. Monitor blood glucose and potassium levels.

8. Postoperatively: Continue dantrolene 1 mg/kg IV q 6 hours × 72 hours to prevent recurrence. Lethal recurrences of MH may occur. Observe in an intensive care unit.

9. For expert medical advice and further medical evaluation, call the MHaus MH hotline consultant at (800) 644-9737. For nonemergency professional or patient information, call (800) 986-4287.

Postoperative Care of the Ophthalmic Surgery Patient

The use of balanced general anesthesia—in which small amounts of several different types of medications are titrated to avoid the side effects of large dose of any one type—has been effective in reducing prolonged anesthesia and prolonged recovery time. Neuromuscular blocking agents of short duration (12 minutes for mivacurium and 30 minutes for atracurium and vecuronium) administered with an infusion pump allow the anesthesiologist to fine-tune the degree of neuromuscular blockade during balanced anesthesia.

The shorter-acting narcotics such as sufentanil have potencies up to 1000 times that of morphine. These agents help provide short-term stability of hemodynamics during intense stimulation without the cost of prolonged excessive sedation postoperatively. Their use immediately before intubation as part of an anesthetic induction has become nearly universal.

Management of postoperative nausea and vomiting after general anesthesia has become easier with more powerful antinausea medications such as ondansetron and metoclopramide. Ondansetron and metoclopramide do not cause sedation as droperidol does, thus speeding recovery of the patient in same-day surgery settings.

Postoperative pain can be prophylactically treated during the procedure with IV ketorolac in a 30–60 mg dose or with small titrated doses of IV fentanyl in the range of 25–50 mg. Because of the reported gastrointestinal complications of higher doses of ketorolac, patients over the age of 60 should receive no more than 30 mg of IV ketorolac, total. Longer-acting narcotics such as morphine or meperidine can delay the patient's discharge because of excessive sedation. Also, there is evidence that IV ketorolac, because of its pain-reducing qualities, can reduce the amount of postoperative nausea and vomiting in strabismus and other general anesthetic patients. There is no evidence that the use of this particular nonsteroidal anti-inflammatory increases postoperative bleeding in ophthalmic surgery patients.

Everett LL, Kallar SK. Current status of treatment to prevent aspiration in outpatients. *Anesthesiol Clin North Am.* 1996;14:679–693.

Haberkern CM, Lecky JH. Preoperative assessment and the anesthesia clinic. *Anesthesiol Clin North Am.* 1996;14:609–630.

Kay MC, Kay J. Complications of anesthesia for ocular surgery. In: *Ophthalmic Surgery Complications: Prevention and Management.* Philadelphia: Lippincott; 1995.

Van Norman G. Preoperative management of common minor medical issues in the outpatient setting. *Anesthesiol Clin North Am.* 1996;14:655–677.

ACKNOWLEDGMENT

We would like to acknowledge Jonathan Kay, MD, for his contributions to this chapter.

CHAPTER XVI

Epidemiology and Statistics

Introduction

The role of clinical research is vital in establishing a standard of care for patients. Such research is best performed using an interdisciplinary approach that combines the efforts of the clinician, statistician, and epidemiologist from the conception of the study through data analyses and interpretation. The choice of study design depends upon the research questions to be answered, the population available, the resources and effort to be expended. If the findings of a study reveal a statistical association, the validity of this association may be accepted after carefully ruling out alternate explanations such as chance, bias, and confounding. Further, the association may be more credible if it is a consistent finding in other studies, as well.

The goal of this chapter is to provide a general overview of the different types of epidemiological studies and the more common statistical tests and terms used in clinical research. We hope this discussion will serve as a stimulus for interested investigators to further explore the field of epidemiologic research. More important, it is intended to encourage the clinician to critically review the results of clinical research found in the medical literature.

Epidemiology: Definition and Design Strategies

Epidemiology is defined as the study of the occurrence of disease in human populations. Epidemiologic methodology, a powerful tool for clinical research, can be broadly categorized into either descriptive or analytic components. *Descriptive epidemiology,* employed by practitioners for centuries, is the practice of describing the symptoms and quantifying the occurrence of disease. Information is gathered on the distribution of a disease with respect to what part of the population gets the disease and when and where the disease occurs. With this knowledge, hypotheses concerning the etiology and treatment of the disease can then be developed. Such hypotheses can be analytically tested using appropriate epidemiologic study designs. Thus, *analytic epidemiology* evaluates factors that may cause or prevent disease by testing the hypotheses generated from descriptive studies.

The analysis of the data collected systematically in epidemiologic studies includes the determination of whether a statistical association exists between the presence or absence of a factor and the disease (*observational studies*) or whether a difference exists between "treated" and "control" groups (*experimental studies*). If a statistical association is observed, it is important to rule out alternate explanations such as the luck of the draw (*chance*), systematic errors in collecting or interpreting the data (*bias*), or the effects of other associated variables (*confounding*).

A number of types of epidemiologic studies are used in clinical research (Table XVI-1). The choice of which to use depends on the question to be answered, the population available, and the resources and effort to be expended. The various epi-

TABLE XVI-1

CLINICAL RESEARCH DESIGNS: TYPES OF STUDIES

	OBSERVATIONAL				EXPERIMENTAL
	CASE REPORTS/SERIES, NATURAL HISTORY	SURVEYS (POPULATION BASED)	COHORT STUDIES	STUDIES OF CASES AND CONTROLS	CLINICAL TRIALS
Object*	Diagnostic characteristics, complications, limited natural history, etiology	Prevalence, association between disease and factor (etiology)	Incidence, association between disease and factor (etiology)	Association between disease and factor (etiology)	Evaluation of therapy, diagnostic procedures, preventive measures
Information sought for study analysis*	Variable	Previous and present risk factors, disease status at the time of the survey	Follow-up for development of disease	Disease status, previous and present risk factors	Occurrence for the defined outcome following randomized treatment, complications of therapy
Use of old records*	Possible	Possible	Possible	Possible	No
Dependent on patient's memory*	Possible	For historical questions	Not usually	Usually	No
Study groups	Persons with disease	Total population	Persons with and without factor	Diseased (cases) and not diseased (controls)	Treated and controls
Sample size (depends on likelihood of disease outcome)*	Variable	Large	Large	Small	Variable (depending on treatment efficacy and likelihood of "events" in the controls)
Risk estimate	Absolute and relative risk of developing complications	Absolute and relative risk of having disease	Absolute and relative risk of developing disease	Relative risk of developing disease	Risks and benefits of therapy

*This is usual; variations are possible.

demiologic approaches to clinical research, their strengths and weaknesses, and the appropriate situation in which to use each are summarized in Table XVI-2.

MacMahon B, Pugh TF. *Epidemiology: Principles and Methods.* Boston: Little, Brown & Co; 1970.

Epidemiologic research design strategies can be categorized as descriptive or analytic. *Descriptive studies* are concerned with the distribution of the disease in relation to person, time, and place. Such descriptive data provide valuable information to health care providers and administrators for developing effective prevention and education programs as well as for allocating appropriate resources. Furthermore, they are useful in the formulation of hypotheses that may be tested in analytic studies. In *analytic studies* a direct comparison is designed by the investigator to determine whether or not the risk of disease is different for individuals exposed or not exposed to a factor of interest. The appropriate use of a comparison group allows for testing of epidemiologic hypotheses. Depending on the role of the investigator, analytic studies are further divided into *observational* (the investigator observes the outcome in subjects with self-selected factors) and *experimental,* or *interventional,* studies (the investigator purposely manipulates factors that might influence the outcome).

TABLE XVI-2

STRENGTHS AND WEAKNESSES OF CLINICAL RESEARCH DESIGNS

DESIGN	STRENGTHS	WEAKNESSES
Case report or series	Description of a new aspect of an old disease, or description of clinical characteristics of a new disease	Cannot assess the effects of treatment or risk factor without a concurrent control group
Cohort studies	Useful for common diseases, especially with respect to outcomes; internal comparison group present	Generally requires large sample size and lengthy follow-up; costly in terms of time and money
Case-control studies	Suitable for rare diseases and for studying a variety of risk factors; efficient in use of time and money	Subject to bias (selection bias of cases and controls and information bias)
Clinical trial	Randomization of subjects to treatment provides concurrent controls who are comparable to the treated group in every aspect except for treatment. This comparison group is essential in the assessment of therapeutic effects.	Costly in terms of money and time; potential for loss to follow-up

Descriptive Studies

Case reports and case series   A *case report* is the simplest type of descriptive study. A *case series* is a systematic grouping of case reports. These descriptive studies organize information concerning a new disease or raise suspicion about the possible influence of a particular factor or treatment on the disease. Further formulation of hypotheses may then lead to the design of analytic studies to test these hypotheses.

An example of a case report is the initial description of acute uveitis with retinal periarteritis and detachment. Subsequent case series of such patients have established the defined syndrome of acute retinal necrosis (ARN). From this knowledge, an etiologic factor such as herpes zoster has been implicated.

Case series of untreated patients with available follow-up data have also been used to define the natural history of a disease. This process, however, has its limitations, since many published case series do not have clearly defined eligibility and exclusion criteria, and follow-up is often incomplete in a sizable proportion of the patients. An example of a successful case series that illustrates the natural history of a disease is the natural history portion of the Diabetic Retinopathy Vitrectomy Study. This study was designed to assess the risk of visual loss in persons with a specified level of severe diabetic retinopathy. It was considered necessary to ascertain the natural history prior to considering a clinical trial of vitrectomy with retinopathy this severe. Patients with the defined degree of severe diabetic retinopathy were entered into the study and examined at regular visits. This study demonstrated that eyes with specific characteristics of severe diabetic retinopathy are at high risk of developing severe visual loss. These characteristics, found in a descriptive study, were then used to develop major eligibility criteria for entry into a randomized clinical trial (analytic design strategy) to evaluate the beneficial effects of vitrectomy in such eyes.

> Culbertson WW, Blumenkranz MS, Haines H, et al. The acute retinal necrosis syndrome. Part 2: Histopathology and etiology. *Ophthalmology.* 1982;89:1317–1325.
>
> Diabetic Retinopathy Vitrectomy Study Research Group. Two-year course of visual acuity in severe proliferative diabetic retinopathy with conventional management. *Ophthalmology.* 1985;92:492–502.
>
> Diabetic Retinopathy Vitrectomy Study Research Group. *DRVS Manual of Operations.* (Available from DRVS Coordinating Center, 2829 University Ave SE, Minneapolis, MN 55414.)

Surveys   Surveys measure the *prevalence* of a disease, that is, the number of cases of a disease present in a defined population at a specified time. In addition, information on the characteristics of the disease as well as on characteristics of the population may be used to study possible associations between the disease and various risk factors. However, this type of study can only demonstrate associations and not impute cause and effect, because the risk factor found may be the cause of the disease or the result of the disease, or it may simply coexist with the disease. Associations observed may be used to formulate hypotheses to be tested by analytic studies.

Since surveys are population based, they require either the examination of each person in the population or everyone in a specifically defined subgroup. To the extent that some persons may not be available for examination, the accuracy of the prevalence estimate is diminished. Other factors limiting the success of a survey are the techniques used to identify the population to be studied and the methods used to motivate those selected to participate in the examination process and/or interview.

An example of a successful cross-sectional survey is the Wisconsin Epidemiologic Study of Diabetic Retinopathy. Attempts were made to identify all known diabetic individuals in several counties in southern Wisconsin. A random sample of this group was then selected, and efforts were made to examine each of these identified persons. The main goal of this study was to determine the prevalence of various types of retinopathy in this population of diabetic persons and to identify risk factors, such as the degree of hyperglycemia or hypertension, that might be associated with more severe retinopathy.

If the goal of a survey is to determine disease prevalence for a general population rather than for a segment of the population such as diabetics, the sample to be examined must be drawn from the overall population. The Health and Nutrition Examination Survey and the Visual Acuity Impairment Study, both performed in cooperation with the United States Bureau of the Census, are examples of population-based studies. As noted above, the success of a survey depends upon appropriately identifying a representative sampling of the population to be studied and motivating the selected individuals to participate in the study.

Another population-based study is the Baltimore Eye Survey. In this study, the prevalence of primary open-angle glaucoma was compared between black residents and white residents of east Baltimore. Previous clinical studies had supported a growing acceptance that blacks were at a higher risk of glaucoma than whites, and this clinical impression was confirmed by the Baltimore Eye Survey. Using comprehensive examination techniques in population-based samples of blacks and whites, researchers found the rate of primary open-angle glaucoma in black Americans to be four to five times higher than in whites. The comprehensive examination techniques maximized the sensitivity and specificity of the diagnosis of primary open-angle glaucoma.

Ganley J, Roberts J. Eye conditions and related need for medical care among persons 1–74 years of age. *United States: Vital and Health Statistics,* Series 11, No 2287. Washington, DC: Department of Health and Human Services Pub No 83-1678.

Klein R, Klein BEK, Moss SE, et al. The Wisconsin epidemiologic study of diabetic retinopathy. II. Prevalence and risk of diabetic retinopathy when age at diagnosis is less than 30 years. *Arch Ophthalmol.* 1984;102:520–526.

Klein R, Klein BEK, Moss SE, et al. The Wisconsin epidemiologic study of diabetic retinopathy. III. Prevalence and risk of diabetic retinopathy when age at diagnosis is 30 or more years. *Arch Ophthalmol.* 1984;102:527–532.

Tielsch JM, Sommer A, Katz J, et al. Racial variations in the prevalence of primary open-angle glaucoma. The Baltimore Eye Survey. *JAMA.* 1991;266:369–374.

Visual Acuity Impairment Survey Pilot Study. *Biometry & Epidemiology.* National Eye Institute/National Institutes of Health, Department of Health and Human Services. Washington, DC: US Government Printing Office; 1984.

Analytic Design

Observational   Analytic studies can be experimental or observational. There are two basic types of observational analytic studies: cohort and case-control.

Cohort studies. In cohort, or follow-up, studies, persons who are initially free of the disease under study are followed over a period of time, during which some subjects develop the disease. Groups are defined at study entry on the basis of the presence or absence of exposure to possible risk factors. Examples could be those who are hypertensive versus those who are not or those with elevated hemoglobin A_1C versus those with less elevated hemoglobin A_1C.

The analysis of data from cohort studies results in a calculation of the incidence of the disease in the cohort. The number of new cases observed during the specified period of follow-up is divided by the number of individuals at risk of developing the disease. The incidence in the group with a positive exposure or with a specific risk factor divided by the incidence in the group without the risk factor is called the *relative risk,* which is a primary statistic used to assess whether the risk factor is associated with the disease. When the relative risk is significantly greater than 1.0, the factor is thought to be associated with the development of the disease; when it is significantly less than 1.0, the factor is associated with not developing the disease.

Since all individuals in a cohort study are disease free at the outset of the study, the researcher can document that exposure to a risk factor predated development of the disease. However, cohort studies require following large numbers of individuals over long periods of time to observe an adequate number of cases developing the disease. The cost in terms of money and time is a major drawback of the cohort study. In addition, because individuals must be followed for long periods of time, even as long as decades, there is a great potential for introducing bias as a result of losses in follow-up. This study design is best suited for a relatively common disease that can be expected to develop in a large proportion of the study group during the follow-up period.

An early and important example of a cohort study is the Framingham Heart Study. In it, 5209 residents of Framingham, Massachusetts, between the ages of 30 and 62 at the start of the study were followed every 2 years to assess a wide variety of possible cardiovascular risk factors such as hypertension, cigarette smoking, and blood cholesterol levels. The subjects were all initially free of cardiovascular disease. Over the next 35 years, all cardiovascular events were ascertained, and incidence rates and relative risks were calculated. For example, the incidence rate of myocardial infarction, adjusted for age and sex, among persons with diastolic blood pressure (at first examination) ≥ 90 mm Hg was several times the rate among persons with diastolic blood pressure < 90 mm Hg. This was one of the earliest studies to demonstrate the association between the development of cardiovascular disease and hypertension.

An example of a cohort study concerning eye diseases is the Wisconsin Epidemiologic Study of Diabetic Retinopathy already mentioned. Persons who were diagnosed with diabetes mellitus and examined in the original survey were reexamined 4 years later. The objectives of this cohort study were to examine the incidence and progression of diabetic retinopathy and to determine the relationships between incidence and progression of diabetic retinopathy and risk factors. In patients diagnosed with diabetes mellitus at age of 30 years or more who were free of retinopathy at the baseline examination, 47% of insulin users and 34% of nonusers had developed retinopathy by the 4-year visit. Other studies have shown that the most potent risk variable for prevalence and incidence of diabetic retinopathy is the duration of diabetes. In the Wisconsin cohort study, this characteristic was found to be an important predictor during the 4 years of observation, but it did not have a consistent linear effect on the rate of development or on the rate of progression. A likely explanation could be the increasing rates of mortality in the older patients. This cohort study was composed of subjects whose diagnosis of diabetes mellitus was made at 30 years or more of age. Because 25% had died during the 4-year interval, only 72% of this group of patients participated in the follow-up visit. In the studies of patients with onset of diabetes at a younger age, 82% participated in the follow-up examination. Death accounted for the majority of the nonparticipation rate in this cohort study. Nevertheless, the incidence and progression rates for diabetic retinopathy provided important information for future studies, i.e., clinical trials, and for planners of health care.

The Framingham Study. An Epidemiological Investigation of Cardiovascular Disease. Department of Health, Education & Welfare (National Institutes of Health). Washington, DC: US Government Printing Office; 1975. Pub No 74-478.

Klein R, Klein BEK, Moss SE, et al. The Wisconsin Epidemiologic Study of Diabetic Retinopathy. IX. Four-year incidence and progression of diabetic retinopathy when age at diagnosis is less than 30 years. *Arch Ophthalmol.* 1989;107:237–243.

Klein R, Klein BEK, Moss SE, et al. The Wisconsin Epidemiologic Study of Diabetic Retinopathy. X. Four-year incidence and progression of diabetic retinopathy when age at diagnosis is 30 years or more. *Arch Ophthalmol.* 1989;107:244–249.

Studies of cases and controls. In a *case-control study,* sometimes referred to as a *retrospective study,* subjects are selected on the basis of the presence (case) or absence (control) of disease. The two groups are then compared with respect to the proportion having a particular characteristic or exposure factor. A statistic called the *odds ratio* is calculated from the data, based on the presence or absence of the exposure factor among the cases and the controls. The odds ratio is similar to the relative risk calculated in a cohort study. If statistically it is significantly greater or less than 1.0, the factor is said to be either positively or negatively associated with the disease. If the odds ratio is not significantly different from 1.0, there is no evidence from this study that the factor and the disease are associated.

A type of case-control study that determines the presence or absence of a risk factor at the time of the examination is called a *cross-sectional study.* Both case-control and cross-sectional studies use cases and controls. They differ in that within the case-control study format an effort is made to ascertain that the exposure to the suspected risk factor (e.g., history of cigarette smoking) predated the onset of the disease, while in the cross-sectional format the factor and the disease coexist (e.g., current cigarette smoking regardless of past history, or the measurement of current blood pressure or serum cholesterol). Often, retrospective and cross-sectional elements are combined in a single study of cases and controls.

A study of age-related macular degeneration by Hyman et al (1983) is one example of a study of cases and controls. Patients with age-related macular degeneration were identified at 34 ophthalmologists' offices. An equal number of age- and sex-matched controls were also selected from the same ophthalmologists' offices. Presence or absence of age-related macular degeneration was documented by retinal photographs. Historical information such as family history of age-related macular degeneration, history of various medical problems, and exposure to a number of environmental risk factors was ascertained. In addition, present conditions such as refractive errors, current blood pressure, hand grip strength, and iris color were collected in the cross-sectional aspect. A positive association was found between several of the factors studied and the presence of age-related macular degeneration.

Hyman L, Lilienfield AM, Ferris FL 3rd, et al. Senile macular degeneration: a case-control study. *Am J Epidemiol.* 1983;118:213–227.

A disadvantage of the case-control study is the difficulty of establishing the temporal relationship between an exposure factor and a disease, despite efforts to ascertain risk factors that might have predated the disease. Iris color, for example, is a risk factor that can be assessed after disease diagnosis but that almost certainly predated the development of the disease. In contrast, intraocular pressure could well be modified by the presence of a disease and cannot be assumed to have been the same prior to the development of the disease. An effective method used to minimize such problems is the selection of cases prospectively as they occur *(incident cases)*. An example of such a technique is seen in a case-control study of the relative risk of ulcerative keratitis among users of soft contact lenses. Cases were defined to be soft contact lens users with newly diagnosed ulcerative keratitis who were evaluated at six university ophthalmologic centers during the months between November 1986 and November 1987. The use of these incident cases provided advantages in that the risk factors examined in the study were more likely to be related to the development of the disease and not to the duration of the disease once it had developed (i.e., prognosis). In addition, the use of incident cases minimized the time between the development of the condition and the interview, which provided more accurate reporting of the information on prior exposures.

> Schein OD, Glynn RJ, Poggio EC, et al. The relative risk of ulcerative keratitis among users of daily-wear and extended-wear soft contact lenses. a case-control study. Microbial Keratitis Study Group. *N Engl J Med.* 1989;321:773–778.

Of all the analytic studies, the case-control study has the greatest potential for bias, especially in the selection of cases and controls. It is important to consider possible sources of bias prior to starting a case-control study. In the study of risk factors for cataract (The Lens Opacities Case-Control Study), cases were not selected from patients undergoing cataract surgery because the reasons that lead to patient selection and referral for surgery may cause biases that are difficult to assess. In addition, the selection of controls for such cases may be difficult. The cases and controls for the cataract study were selected from the same general eye services of outpatient clinics in order to increase comparability on socioeconomic, demographic, health utilization, and other factors. Misclassification of these cases and controls was minimized by using a system of lens classification based on clinical examination and centralized grading of lens photographs. Among the factors found to be associated with less extensive lens opacities were use of multivitamins and dietary intake of antioxidant vitamins. This association was further tested and confirmed by adjusting for age, sex, race, and education. This finding demonstrates an association of vitamin use and lens opacities; but because of possible biases or confounding, it does not necessarily imply that decreased intake of antioxidant vitamins potentially causes cataracts, nor does it follow that the disease process will be prevented or retarded by the use of such vitamins. A randomized clinical trial must be designed to address such questions.

> Leske MC, Chylack LT Jr, Wu SY, et al. The Lens Opacities Case-Control Study. Risk factors for cataract. *Arch Ophthalmol.* 1991;109:244–251.

In the Eye Disease Case-Control Study, patients with high serum levels of carotenoids had a reduced rate of neovascular age-related macular degeneration compared to patients with low serum levels of carotenoids. This association was statistically significant at the level of $P<0.0001$. However, this association does not imply a causal relationship of carotenoids to age-related macular degeneration.

Again, the only way to prove that antioxidants may play an etiological role in age-related macular degeneration is by assessing them in a randomized, controlled clinical trial. The Age-Related Eye Disease Study is such a study designed to evaluate the role of antioxidants and minerals in the treatment of both age-related macular degeneration and cataract. Until this study and similar clinical trials have concluded, the above observational data cannot be used to recommend taking antioxidants and minerals for the prevention and treatment of cataracts or age-related macular degeneration.

> Eye Disease Case-Control Study Group. Antioxidant status and neovascular age-related macular degeneration. *Arch Ophthalmol.* 1993;111:104–109.

> Sperduto RD, Ferris FL 3rd, Kurinij N. Do we have a nutritional treatment for age-related macular degeneration? *Arch Ophthalmol.* 1990;108:1403–1405.

When potential sources of bias in selection of cases and controls and in the ascertainment of historical information are recognized and minimized in both the design and the analysis of the study, case-control studies are a very valuable tool in clinical research. Unlike cohort studies, they are efficient in time and expense. This design is suitable for studying rare diseases. It is also useful in testing a variety of exposure factors among the diseased and controls, making it particularly suitable for early investigations of the risk factors of a disease.

Experimental, or interventional, study (clinical trial)   The experimental, or interventional, study is a prospective study in which the investigator assigns the exposure factor or the treatment. This type of study is also known as a *clinical trial.* It is defined as a prospective study comparing the effect and value of intervention(s) against a control in human subjects. Rarely does the introduction of a new therapy or procedure produce such unequivocal results as that of penicillin in the treatment of pneumococcal pneumonia. More often, the effects of therapy are much smaller but still clinically important and significant. Observational studies may fail to demonstrate such a beneficial effect, whereas randomized clinical trials will reveal the strongest epidemiological evidence of the beneficial effect.

> Friedman LM, Furberg CD, DeMets DL. *Fundamentals of Clinical Trials.* 3rd ed. St Louis: Mosby; 1996.

> Meinert CL, Tonascia S. *Clinical Trials. Design, Conduct, and Analysis.* New York: Oxford University Press; 1986.

Generally, in a clinical trial the researcher selects a study population that has a high risk of developing the outcome or response variable. Eligibility criteria for inclusion in the study must be clearly defined at the beginning of the study. Treatment, which should be administered in a standard fashion, is ideally allocated by randomization, helping to ensure that the treatment group(s) are similar to the control group in all respects except for treatment. Data from baseline and subsequent visits must be collected in a systematic fashion, preferably by trained personnel. The response or outcome variable that is to be measured must also be clearly defined. To prevent bias, the outcome variable should be objectively assessed by someone who is unaware of the treatment assignment.

Sample size calculations must be performed in the initial development phase of all analytic studies, but they are particularly important in a clinical trial. A trial must have a sufficiently large sample size to have adequate statistical power to detect differences between groups considered to be of clinical interest. These calculations are an essential part of planning a clinical trial. (Sample size calculations and power are explained later in this chapter.)

During follow-up, the proportion of individuals in each study group(s) that develop the predetermined outcome is calculated, and the effects of the intervention are compared. Monitoring of noncompliance and adverse side effects is an important aspect of the study. The problem of loss to follow-up must be addressed when the selection of the study population and the nature of the intervention are being considered, because a high follow-up rate is essential to the success of the study.

The analysis of clinical trials is similar to that of cohort studies, where the comparison is between the rates of the outcome of interest in the treated (exposed) group(s) and the corresponding rates in the control (unexposed) group. As a result of randomization, the comparison groups are likely to be quite similar in all aspects other than the treatment. A crucial initial step in analysis involves comparing the groups to ensure that important baseline characteristics are indeed balanced. Once subjects are randomized to a particular group, they will remain in that group for analysis, regardless of whether they drop out or become noncompliant ("once randomized, always analyzed"). It is important to minimize noncompliance and dropout rates and to attempt to ascertain complete information.

The disadvantage of interventional studies is the enormous cost in expense and time. However, carefully designed clinical trials, involving adequate numbers of randomized subjects, provide the most powerful epidemiologic evidence of the effects of an intervention.

One example of an interventional study in ophthalmology is the Diabetic Retinopathy Study (DRS), a randomized, controlled clinical trial to evaluate photocoagulation treatment for proliferative diabetic retinopathy. (This study is also discussed in BCSC Section 12, *Retina and Vitreous*.) Between 1972 and 1975, 1758 patients were enrolled and follow-up was continued until 1979. Eligible patients had proliferative diabetic retinopathy in at least one eye or severe nonproliferative retinopathy in both eyes and visual acuity of 20/100 or better in each eye. One eye was randomized to immediate photocoagulation with either xenon arc or argon laser photocoagulation, while the fellow untreated eye acted as the control. At 4-month intervals, an examiner who was not aware of the treatment status of the eyes obtained best-corrected visual acuity. The primary outcome variable measured was "severe visual loss," defined as visual acuity <5/200 at two or more consecutively completed follow-up visits.

In 1976 a change of protocol was implemented because the incidence of severe visual loss in the treated eyes was reduced by 50% or more in comparison to the control eyes. At this change of protocol, eyes with certain characteristics were observed to be at a particularly high risk of severe visual loss. The data and safety monitoring committee recommended that treatment no longer be withheld from eyes with high-risk characteristics that had initially been randomized to no treatment. Thus, the DRS, a randomized, controlled clinical trial, successfully demonstrated the efficacy of photocoagulation in the treatment of proliferative diabetic retinopathy and identified a high-risk group of persons with diabetes for whom photocoagulation was indicated.

Adverse side effects, such as visual field loss and persistent decrease of visual acuity associated with argon and xenon photocoagulation, were also carefully documented in the DRS. The rates of adverse side effects for these two different types of treatments were also compared; the xenon group was found to have higher rates of harmful effects.

The subsequent clinical trial of treatment of diabetic retinopathy, the Early Treatment Diabetic Retinopathy Study (ETDRS), evaluated the timing of photocoagulation during the course of diabetic retinopathy, the efficacy of photocoagulation for diabetic macular edema, and the role of aspirin in altering the course of diabetic retinopathy. (This study is discussed in BCSC Section 12, *Retina and Vitreous*.)

The aspirin portion of the ETDRS consisted of randomly assigning each patient to 650 mg of aspirin or placebo. Compliance with study medication was assessed with laboratory studies such as serum thromboxane B_2 and urine salicylate levels at annual visits and with counts of pills and patient interviews at each clinic visit. The results of these tests showed that 80% of the patients were taking prescribed study medications, a compliance level similar to that reported for other trials of aspirin. The primary end point for assessing the effect of aspirin on the course of diabetic retinopathy was the development of high-risk proliferative retinopathy. The relative risk of developing high-risk proliferative retinopathy for patients assigned to aspirin compared with patients assigned to placebo is 0.97 with a 99% confidence interval of 0.85–1.11. Thus, there was no difference between the treated and untreated group, as the confidence interval included 1.0.

The power of this study to detect a 25% treatment effect as estimated during the design phase of the study was 99%, given the sample size and projected event rates of 40%. After adjusting for noncompliance with study medications and the actual outcome rates, the study had power to detect a 25% treatment effect. When negative results of a clinical trial are presented, it is important to report the study's power to detect the proposed clinical difference. (For an explanation of *confidence interval* and *power*, see pp 269 and 272–273.)

The Diabetes Control and Complications Trial (DCCT) was another important clinical trial of diabetic retinopathy, which evaluated the role of intensive management and control of hyperglycemia in preventing the development or progression of diabetic retinopathy. Previous observational studies in humans and animal studies of experimental models of diabetes suggested that intensive treatment of hyperglycemia was important in preventing the progression of diabetic retinopathy. Only through this randomized, controlled clinical trial were the beneficial effects of intensive treatment of hyperglycemia proven. The incidence of development and progression of diabetic retinopathy, loss of vision, and the need for photocoagulation were reduced with intensive treatment. Other secondary end points including diabetic nephropathy, neuropathy, and macrovascular diseases were also significantly reduced by intensive management of hyperglycemia. This clinical trial provided important guidelines for the treatment of complications for persons with type I diabetes mellitus. (Again, this trial is also discussed in BCSC Section 12, *Retina and Vitreous*.)

Another clinical trial in ophthalmology evaluated the common use of corticosteroids to treat optic neuritis. (This trial is discussed in BCSC Section 5, *Neuro-Ophthalmology*.) The following research questions were posed by the investigators:

□ Does treatment with either oral prednisone or intravenous methylprednisolone improve visual outcome in acute optic neuritis?

□ Does either treatment speed the recovery of vision?

□ What are the complications of treatment in relation to its efficacy?

Visual field, the primary measure of outcome, was graded in a masked fashion by a central reading center. Best-corrected visual acuity was obtained by technicians who were unaware of the treatment assignment. Results of this clinical trial showed that intravenous methylprednisolone followed by oral prednisone accelerated the recovery of visual loss from optic neuritis and resulted in slightly better vision at 6 months. However, oral prednisone alone actually increased the risk of new episodes of optic neuritis. These findings were somewhat surprising, since a mail survey performed in 1986 of ophthalmologists and neurologists in Michigan and Florida indicated that 65% of the ophthalmologists and 90% of the neurologists prescribed corticosteroids for optic neuritis.

As mentioned, the case-control study can provide valuable information about the possible association of certain risk factors with the disease being studied, but such observational studies cannot provide conclusive data as to the causal role of the risk factor. An example of this is seen in the Alpha-Tocopherol, Beta Carotene Cancer Prevention Study performed in Finland. Rates of lung cancer were higher in patients with lower serum levels of both vitamin E and beta carotene at baseline (a nested case-control evaluation). However, when these patients were randomly assigned these two antioxidants and followed for 5–8 years, no beneficial effect in reducing the rates of lung cancer was found in the treated group. In fact, the patients receiving beta carotene had increased rates of lung cancer and mortality. These results emphasize the need for randomized, controlled clinical trials to evaluate the validity of associations seen in observational studies such as the case-control studies.

The Alpha-Tocopherol, Beta Carotene Cancer Prevention Study Group. The effect of vitamin E and beta carotene on the incidence of lung cancer and other cancers in male smokers. N Engl J Med. 1994;330:1029–1235.

Beck RW, Cleary PA, Anderson MM, et al. A randomized, controlled trial of corticosteroids in the treatment of acute optic neuritis. N Engl J Med. 1992;326:581–588.

The Diabetes Control and Complications Trial Research Group. The effect of intensive treatment of diabetes on the development and progression of long-term complications in insulin-dependent diabetes mellitus. N Engl J Med. 1993;329:977–986.

The Early Treatment Diabetic Retinopathy Study Research Group. Effects of aspirin treatment on diabetic retinopathy. ETDRS Report Number 8. Ophthalmology. 1991;98: 757–765.

Sommer A. Epidemiology and Statistics for the Ophthalmologist. New York: Oxford University Press; 1980.

Statistical Terminology

In order to critically review the medical literature, the reader should have an understanding of the more commonly used statistical terms and methodology.

Mean   The mean (arithmetic mean) is one of the most widely used and understood ways of describing the *average,* or central, tendency of a set of data. The sum of values of a set of individual observations is divided by the number of values. For example, the mean age for cataract extraction is 65.7 years.

Median   The median has the connotation of the "middlemost" or "most central" value of a set of numbers; it is the value that divides the set so that one half is smaller and one half is larger. With an odd number of observations, the median is directly ascertainable. With an even number of items, there are two central values; by convention, the arithmetic mean of these two central values is designated the median.

Mode   The mode is a conceptually useful term, but often it is not calculated explicitly. The mode is the observation that occurs with the greatest frequency. The mode of a frequency distribution has the connotation of a "typical" or representative value, a location in the distribution at which there is maximal clustering. In this application, if a frequency distribution is symmetrical (a bell curve), then the mode, the median, and the mean coincide. However, in a skewed distribution, the mean is pulled away from the mode toward the extreme values. If more than one mode appears, the frequency distribution is described as *multimodal.* If there are two modes, the frequency distribution is called *bimodal.* Bimodal distributions would result, for example, by merging the weight data for men and women. Often, the observation of a bimodal distribution suggests that two different "causes" are present and that two distinct distributions should be recognized.

Distribution   A *normal curve, normal distribution,* or *gaussian distribution* describes a symmetric distribution (e.g., mean, median, and mode are the same) of great utility in statistics. The graph of the normal distribution forms a bell-shaped curve, symmetrical around an ordinate erected at the mean (which, of course, lies at the center of the distribution). If the total area under the graph of a normal curve is equal to 1.0, then one half of the area (representing probability) lies to the left or right of the mean, and the probability is 0.5 that a value will fall below or above the mean (μ).

Variance and standard deviation   Although the central tendency, as measured by the various averages already discussed, is an important descriptive characteristic of statistical data, it is not the only measure required to completely specify the distribution of observations. The most common probability distribution encountered in medical literature is the normal distribution. Although the specification of the normal distribution's average or mean is important, some measure of the spread of the observations must also be given. The most commonly used measures of an average dispersion from some measure of central tendency are the variance and the standard deviation:

$$\sigma = \left[\frac{\Sigma\,(x - \mu)^2}{(N-1)} \right]^{1/2}$$

The *standard deviation* (σ) of a normal distribution may be used with the mean to indicate the percentage of items that fall within specified ranges. The following relationships apply for a population of observations that form a normal distribution:

μ (mean) + σ includes 68.3% of all items
μ (mean) + 2σ includes 95.5% of all items
μ (mean) + 3σ includes 99.7% of all items

For populations with normal distribution, 5% of values lie at least 1.96 standard deviations (σ) away from the mean. This concept is important, because it is the basis for many statistical tests. Since the curve is symmetric, 2.5% of the population are at this distance either above or below the mean. The variance of a distribution is the square of its standard deviation, σ^2.

The *variance* (σ^2) of observations in a population is the arithmetic mean of the squared deviations of each observation (x) from the population mean (μ). However, the observer rarely knows the true population mean. More likely, the observer has some estimate of this quantity, the sample mean (x). Thus, just as the population mean is estimated by the sample mean, so the population variance is estimated by the sample variance (σ^2). Although the sample variance measures the extent of variation in values of a set of observations, it is described in units of squared deviation or squares of the original numbers.

In order to obtain a measure of dispersion in terms of the units of the original data, the positive square root of the variance is taken. The resultant measure is known as the standard deviation. Numerically, the *standard error* of the mean of a sample is calculated as the estimated standard deviation divided by the square root of the number of observations:

$$\text{Standard error} = \frac{\text{Standard deviation}}{\sqrt{n}}$$

Statistical Analyses

Chi-Square Tests

Chi-square (χ^2) tests provide a basis for judging whether more than two sampled population proportions can be considered equal. The mathematical derivations behind chi-square tests are beyond the scope of this text. However, two fundamental generalities are at its heart: tests of goodness of fit and tests of independence. Tests of *goodness of fit* provide the method for deciding whether a particular theoretical probability distribution (such as a normal curve) is a close enough approximation to a sample frequency distribution for that theoretical distribution to describe the population from which the sample was drawn. Tests of *independence* help the statistician to decide whether a hypothesis of independence between different variables is tenable. The entire chi-square sequence tests the equality of more than two population proportions. Thus, chi-square tests may reveal that a set of observed frequencies differs so greatly from a set of theoretical frequencies that the hypothesis under which the theoretical frequencies were derived should be rejected.

The chi-square test is a useful, simple test, but it has limited power. For example, following cataract extraction, the expected incidence of cystoid macular edema (CME) is 15%. In a series of 100 patients pretreated with aspirin, CME occurred in 10 patients. Does that observation indicate a statistically significant benefit for treatment? (Chi-square = 0.25, $P<0.70$.) This result means that 7 out of 10 times this result would be caused by chance alone, with no real benefit from the aspirin pretreatment. If only 5 patients developed CME ($\chi^2= 1.1$, $P<0.30$), the same results would occur less than 30% of the time just from chance. In contrast, if only one patient developed CME ($\chi^2= 13.32$, $P<0.001$), it could mean that if the experiment were repeated 1000 times, this result would occur less than once by chance alone.

In general, statistical significance is considered reasonable by chi-square testing at the $P<0.05$ level or less. Since the sampling distribution of the chi-square statistic is only an approximation to a theoretical random distribution, the sample size usually must be large enough for a good approximation to be obtained. Therefore, in the case of contingency tables, samples with expected frequencies of less than 5 in any cell should be measured with a more exact test.

t-Tests

The Student's *t*- and paired *t*-tests are more powerful tests of statistical significance. They attempt to answer the question of whether the *means* of two normally distributed populations are far enough apart to conclude that the distributions are different. From the *t*-statistic, a *P* value is generated. If the *P* value is sufficiently small, the observer concludes that there is sufficient evidence to reject the hypothesis and that there is no difference in the means. What makes this *t*-test useful is the underlying assumption that populations treated differently will tend to have different means and that populations treated in an identical manner (i.e., a treatment had no effect) will have the same means. The *t*-test examines the difference between the means obtained from samples from two normal populations. Note that this difference is weighed only in a statistical fashion. Statistical significance does not imply clinical importance, which must be scrutinized by the clinical investigator.

Researchers must know something about the variability of a normal population in order to completely specify it, so the *t*-test has different forms depending on the assumption made about the variances of the two groups. The two groups themselves may differ in character. For example, two data samples may consist of pairs of observations made on the same individual. Under these circumstances, the values of observations in one sample may not be independent of values in the other. The researcher may take advantage of this interdependence in the construction of the statistical test, thereby serving to increase the power of the test. In the paired *t*-test, increased power is a result of the incorporation of the correlation between the two samples into the statistical test.

For example, consider a researcher who measures the intraocular pressure of 10 patients before and after each patient is given a mydriatic eyedrop in the hope of determining if, on the average, the mydriatic changes the IOP. That researcher can analyze the data by computing the average IOP before instillation of the mydriatic and again after instillation and then comparing these two means by using a Student's *t*-test. However, in doing so, the researcher assumes that the two samples are independent (i.e., knowledge of a patient's IOP prior to mydriatic instillation does not help predict the postinstillation result). Since this assumption is false, any statistical test based on it can be misleading.

The appropriate procedure in this example would be to compute the difference between the premydriatic and postmydriatic IOP of each patient. The analysis is still based on the mean difference between the pressures before and after instillation, but by computing the variance of the mean difference from the difference obtained from each patient, the researcher will reduce the variance of the estimate considerably, depending on the correlation between premydriatic and postmydriatic IOP. By decreasing the variance of the estimate, the researcher has increased the likelihood of detecting a mydriatic effect and has thus enhanced the power of the test.

Analysis of variance   A powerful generalization of the *t*-test, analysis of variance simultaneously examines samples from several normal distributions by asking if the means of these normal distributions are identical. A researcher starting with samples from each of *k* populations could address this question by doing *t*-tests on all of the possible sample pairings from the k distributions. However, this process would result in k(k − 1) *t*-tests, each of which would require interpretation, a tedious task that often results in misleading conclusions. The analysis of variance test leads to just one *P* value, examining whether the means of the *k* normal distributions are identical. Thus, despite its name, the analysis of variance test is really a test of means. Many different types of analysis of variance tests can be used (e.g., Latin squares, repeated measures), but they all address essentially the same question: are the means of the groups under observation different?

Correlation Coefficient

The fundamental objective of *correlation analysis* is to obtain a measure of the degree of association between two variables; that is, to find out how well the variables are correlated to each other. *Regression analysis*, by contrast, provides the basis for predicting values of a variable from values of one or more other variables. In general, for many medical and biological systems, a simple two-variable correlation model is assumed. One objective of regression analysis is to provide estimates of values of the dependent variable from values of the independent variable. Most commonly, this estimation is accomplished by a *regression line*, a line "best fitted" to the scattered entries of data. This regression line displays mean values of Y for given values of X. Since the line has a simple equation of the form $Y = mX + b$, the equation will provide estimates of the dependent variable when values of X are inserted.

Correlation analysis attempts to measure the degree of association or correlation between two variables. The coefficient of correlation measures, in part, the strength of the linear relationship between two variables: a coefficient of 1.0 would indicate a perfect correlation, whereas a coefficient of 0 would indicate no correlation. The slope of the "best-fitted" straight line is the correlation coefficient multiplied by the ratio of the standard deviation of the dependent variable to the standard deviation of the independent variable. It is important to note the difference between correlation and causation. Variables may be uncorrelated but strongly related.

Multivariable Analysis

Many researchers have come to realize that relationships between variables can be complicated. For example, the likelihood of a patient suffering from a myocardial infarction depends not only on that patient's age but also on gender, smoking habits, glucose metabolism, cholesterol and triglyceride levels, blood pressure, and family history of vascular disease and diabetes, among other factors. All of these factors must be examined simultaneously to fully appreciate their total impact on the outcome event. To this end, a number of multivariable procedures have been developed. *Multiple regression analysis, logistic regression,* and *Cox hazard functions* represent a subset of a class of powerful statistical procedures. Their definitions and applications are beyond the scope of this summary. However, when combined with the computing capability of the mini- or microcomputer, these procedures provide a readily available set of tools with which the clinical investigator can further elucidate the complicated interdependencies of many pertinent risk factors on the outcome of the variable of interest.

Data From Follow-up Studies

Survival, or Life-Table, Analysis

In describing the results from long-term follow-up studies, more complex statistical methods besides simple frequency distributions and estimates of the mean may be necessary. Patients are enrolled at various points in time and observed for months or years for the occurrence of the outcome measurement, e.g., vision loss. Unfortunately, investigators often summarize the results of such a study with a statement like this: "125 patients with retinal disease were observed from 6 months to 7 years (mean follow-up, 26.5 months). 25 of the 125 patients (20%) experienced severe visual loss during the follow-up period." Such statements are not informative and may be misleading.

Survival, or life-table, analyses are more appropriate, as they have the advantage of using the full information on patients followed for varying lengths of time. In these analyses all patients are followed until the *event,* or outcome measurement of interest, occurs or until the date of the analysis. The length of follow-up is then computed for each patient from enrollment to the event or date of analysis. Life tables are usually presented in graph form displaying either the cumulative proportion with an event or the proportion surviving without an event. Figure XVI-1 is an example of such a life-table analysis of patients with the resolution of vitreous hemorrhage in the Early Treatment Diabetic Retinopathy Study.

Chew EY, Klein ML, Murphy RP, et al. Effects of aspirin on vitreous/preretinal hemorrhage in patients with diabetes mellitus. Early Treatment Diabetic Retinopathy Study Research Group. *Arch Ophthalmol.* 1995;113:52–55.

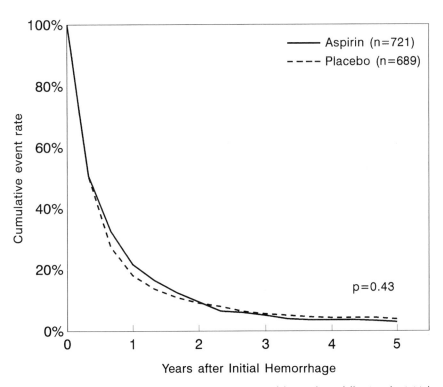

FIG XVI-1—Life-table rates of persistent vitreous/preretinal hemorrhage following the initial clinically observed hemorrhage in 1410 eyes assigned to deferral of photocoagulation at each study visit.

The Use of One or Two Eyes in Data Analyses

A common statistical problem encountered by the clinical researcher in the field of ophthalmology is the issue of using one eye versus two eyes in the same individual. Because eyes are highly correlated in the same individual, each eye is not counted twice in the sample size calculation because they are not independent entities. How does the researcher deal with such data? The following options are available:

□ Use right eye

□ Use left eye

□ Select one eye randomly

□ Use the mean of two eyes

□ Use both eyes, accounting for correlation between the eyes

The final option has the advantage of accommodating all the available data. Methodology such as *generalizing estimating equations (GEE)* is beginning to be used in the ophthalmic literature. The explanation of the theories behind the use of such methodology is beyond the scope of this chapter. The interested reader is referred below to other literature available. The use of GEE is also helpful in situations in which the data collected are not "independent" but are correlated, such as longitudinal studies in which a patient is examined at several time points, familial studies, and multiple measurements at a single time. A study of familial aggregation of lens opacities in the Framingham Eye Study used such methodology to show the strong associations between siblings for nuclear and posterior subcapsular opacities.

Finally, if one eye is randomly assigned to receive the treatment while the fellow eye is designated to be the control eye, the sample size may be reduced because the basic systemic parameters are identical in the same individual. Such paired analyses may be very useful in studies in which the treatment is local and does not have a cross-over or systemic effect.

The Framingham Offspring Eye Study Group. Familial aggregation of lens opacities: the Framingham Eye Study and the Framingham Offspring Eye Study. *Am J Epidemiol.* 1994;140:550–564.

Glynn RJ, Rosner B. Accounting for the correlation between fellow eyes in regression analysis. *Arch Ophthalmol.* 1992;110:381–387.

Statistical Association

Using descriptive studies, researchers can generate hypotheses based on data that demonstrate significant etiologic or therapeutic factors. Such hypotheses can be tested by an analytic study, which ultimately leads to the determination of the presence or absence of a *statistical association*. This association may be correct, but alternate explanations such as chance, bias, and confounding must be ruled out.

Chance

In epidemiologic studies it is not feasible to study every member of the population of interest. Instead, a subgroup of the entire population is studied. Inferences about the characteristics of the population are made based on information collected on the subgroup. Such inferences may not be correct because of random sampling variability or chance (the luck of the draw). The deviation of the sample values from the true population values will decrease as the sample size and the representativeness of the subgroup increases.

Tests of statistical significance and quantification of the sampling variability are involved in evaluating the role of chance. Hypothesis testing begins with the *null hypothesis,* which states that there is no association between the factor and the disease. The *alternative hypothesis* states that there is indeed a relationship between the factor and the disease. For example, the investigators in the Diabetic Retinopathy Study hoped to be able to demonstrate the efficacy of treatment and thus reject the null hypothesis that there is no difference between the rates of severe visual loss in the treated and untreated groups.

Tests of significance generally lead to a probability statement, or *P* value. This *P* value is the probability of obtaining by chance alone a result at least as extreme as that observed. A *P* value of 0.05 means that there is a 5% probability of mistakenly rejecting the null hypothesis. That is, in "truth" there is no association between the disease and the risk factor studied, but a difference as large as that found in the study could be found by chance alone, 1 time out of 20. Chance can never be completely excluded as an explanation for a study's findings, and thus the null hypothesis can never be unequivocally rejected. However, as the *P* values become smaller, such as 0.01 or 0.001, it becomes less likely that the difference found in the experiment is a result of chance. The smaller the *P* value, the less likely the null hypothesis is true and the less likely random chance is the explanation for the findings.

The calculated *P* value is related to the size of the difference found in the study and the standard error of that difference. Small *P* values are the result of large study differences, small standard errors, or both. The *standard error* is related both to the variability of observation and the total number of individuals in the study (the study *sample size*). In general, a study involving a small number of individuals can reach a *P* value small enough to reject the null hypothesis only if a large study difference (difference between the study groups) is present. However, a small study difference may result in a statistically significant *P* value in a study with a large sample size, because the standard error decreases with increasing sample size. Thus, a study could attain statistical significance, and the null hypothesis rejected, but the difference between the groups could be so small as to be essentially meaningless clinically. For example, a researcher might undertake a large study to evaluate the side effects of intracapsular versus extracapsular cataract surgery. The study might show that 94% of one group compared to 93% of the other group had good visual acuity outcomes. If the sample size was large enough, this difference would be statistically significant, but such a difference is unlikely to be clinically meaningful.

Another way of evaluating a statistical association is through the use of the *confidence interval.* The study difference is bracketed by a range of values known as the confidence interval. A 95% confidence interval indicates that if the experiment were repeated 20 times, 19 out of the 20 tries would result in a value within this interval. If the null value (no difference) is included in the confidence interval, it is inappropriate to reject the null hypothesis at the $P \leq 0.05$ level. The confidence interval will decrease with a larger sample size, which leads to less variability and more precision. Both the *P* value and its close relative, the confidence interval, provide an estimate of the role of chance in the results of a study.

Bias

Bias is any systematic error in a study that results in an incorrect measurement of the association between the disease and the risk factor. Bias may be introduced by the investigator or by participants in the study. Generally, it can be divided into selection or information bias.

Selection bias   Selection bias occurs when the individuals enrolled in the study are not representative of the proposed study population. Measurements made on this study group will not be representative of treatment effects or associations that would be true for the targeted study population. Some study designs are more likely to suffer from selection bias than others. In a cohort study, the population of individuals free of the disease under study is defined at the outset. They are followed over a period of time for the development of this disease, and the prevalence of various risk factors in those who develop the disease is then compared with the prevalence in those who did not develop the disease. These associations are not affected by selection bias since the population was selected prior to the development of disease.

Studies of cases and controls, in contrast, are particularly vulnerable to selection bias. Generally, all available cases are selected, most of them having been referred because of the presence of the disease. Matching these referred cases with individuals who are comparable is a difficult task. Ideally, the control should be randomly drawn from the same population that the cases came from, but this is generally not possible. When evaluating the associations found in case-control studies, the researcher must always keep in mind that the association may be a result of the fact that a variable is a risk factor for the disease or that the control group was selected from a special subgroup of the population. Consider a case-control study of open-angle glaucoma in which the controls were selected from a retina clinic. The finding of an increased prevalence of myopia in the control group compared to the cases with glaucoma could indicate that hyperopia is associated with the development of glaucoma or could indicate that myopia is especially prevalent among patients with retinal disease. In this example, the increased prevalence of myopia in the control group is probably a result of the special subgroup that served as the source of controls.

Information bias   Information bias is introduced into a study when completeness or comparability is lacking in the manner the data are collected in each of the study groups. Both the subjects and the examiners are potential sources of this bias. One type of subject bias is called *recall bias,* typically a problem in studies of cases and controls when historical information is being collected. Individuals who have a disease are often more likely to remember possible factors associated with the development of the disease than are individuals in the control group. For example, a subject with an ocular malignancy may tend to report completely or even overestimate exposure to x-rays as compared with an individual who does not have a malignancy. Similarly, a subject with age-related macular degeneration may be more likely to be aware of a family member with the disease than would the normal control. The affected subject is more likely to have asked family members about signs and symptoms of the disease, and they are more likely to have discussed this disease with their eye doctors, than are family members of individuals without age-related macular degeneration.

Exposure identification is often determined through an interview. If the interviewer knows the identity of the cases and controls, his or her prejudices concerning potential risk factors and aggressiveness in ascertaining the histories in the cases and controls may distort the collection of data.

As information bias can also occur in clinical trials, *masking* is an important aspect of the randomized clinical trial. Sometimes it is possible to maintain the *double-blind,* or *double-masked,* situation. In surgical trials, patients undergoing surgical treatment know that they are in the treated group. Having undergone surgery, they may be particularly likely to try harder during testing and to minimize losses on historical data collection. Individuals collecting data in a trial can also be affected by the knowledge of whether an ocular or a systemic treatment has been given. They may urge the treated patients to try harder in the measurement of the outcome variable in an attempt to find beneficial results of treatment. This effort may be on a subconscious level with no intent to purposely distort the data, but their honest desire to find a successful treatment prejudices their attempts to collect the data. If the double blind is not possible, attempts should be made to assure that the person assessing the outcome variable is masked as to the treatment status.

Sommer A. *Epidemiology and Statistics for the Ophthalmologist.* New York: Oxford University Press; 1980.

Confounding

Confounding can occur when multiple factors are associated with the development of the disease or the outcome under study. To affect the study results, the confounder must be associated with both the exposure under study and the disease. In a case-control study of smoking and age-related macular degeneration (AMD), age may be a confounding factor. The researcher might find a definite association between smoking and AMD. However, a strong relationship between age and AMD may also be found. If age and smoking were related (e.g., if older patients were more likely to smoke than young patients), then the association of smoking and AMD could be the result of the confounding factor age rather than a direct relationship between smoking itself and macular degeneration. That is, smoking itself has an *apparent* association to AMD but actually has nothing to do with the development of AMD; rather, both smoking and AMD are more common in older people than in younger people. This confounding effect can be tested by stratifying the study group by age and looking in groups matched for age for an increased prevalence of smoking in the cases compared to the controls. If confounding had been responsible for the original association, no new association within age strata would then be observed.

Confounding has also been termed the *mixing of effects.* The mixing of factors both positively and negatively associated with the disease can mask true associations. Thus, confounders can be responsible for positive or negative associations and can be responsible for apparent lack of association.

In the design of studies, confounding is controlled by three methods: randomization, restriction, and matching. *Randomization* in a clinical trial of sufficient sample size makes it likely that all potential confounding factors, both recognized and unrecognized, are equally distributed in the study groups. When the confounding factors are balanced, differences between the groups cannot be related to the confounding factor. *Restriction* is a term that describes the enforcement of strict eligibility criteria in the creation of homogenous study groups. The price paid for restriction is the reduction of eligible subjects, making recruitment difficult. Also, when the study group is restricted, e.g., to a group of a specific age, then age cannot be evaluated as a potential factor. Generalizability of study results may also be limited in the restricted study. *Matching,* the pairing of an affected case to one or more controls, is a technique used frequently in case-control studies and occasionally in clinical trials. With this technique, individuals (either cases and controls in a case-control study or treated and untreated patients in a clinical trial), are paired on the basis of their similarity with respect to specific selective variables such as age, sex, race, etc. This is a laborious, expensive technique to control for confounding, and it can also seriously limit recruitment. Furthermore, in a case-control study, matching prevents the researcher from evaluating the effect of a factor that has been matched on.

Confounding may be controlled retrospectively in the analysis phase of the study by *stratification,* the evaluation of the association within groups or within the strata of the confounding variable. Age-, sex-, and race-adjusted strata-specific estimates would be calculated. The disadvantage with this method is that only a small number of potential known confounders can be controlled simultaneously. Multivariable analysis, however, allows for the determination of association while controlling for a larger number of known factors simultaneously.

Validity, Generalizability, Consistency

In order to assess the validity of the study, these factors of chance, bias, and confounding must be evaluated as possible alternative explanations for the results of the study. Once validity is established, the results are then considered for their generalizability to populations other than the targeted study population. For example, the Framingham Heart Study involved a mostly white population. Generalizability of the Framingham results to the black population would be a matter of speculation. The consistency of associations between risk factors and a particular disease from one study to another provides further evidence that a relationship is true and not a chance association. For example, the association of hyperopia to age-related macular degeneration found in the case-control study of Hyman et al was also found in two other case-control studies. This consistent finding supports the credibility of a probably true association between hyperopia and AMD.

> Delaney WV Jr, Oates RP. Senile macular degeneration: a preliminary study. *Ann Ophthalmol.* 1981;14:21–24.

> Hennekens CH, Buring JE, Mayrent SL. *Epidemiology in Medicine.* Boston: Little, Brown & Co; 1987.

> Maltzman BA, Mulvihill MN, Greenbaum A. Senile macular degeneration and risk factors: a case-control study. *Ann Ophthalmol.* 1979;11:1197–1201.

Sample Size and Power

As previously mentioned, the sample size of a study greatly influences the magnitude of the study's *P* value. An important initial aspect of a study design includes the sample size and power calculations to determine the number of individuals required to detect a statistically significant effect of a given magnitude. The *Type I error,* or α *error,* is associated with the null hypothesis. The probability of making a Type I error is equal to the *P* value. For example, at the 5% level, there is a 5% risk (or 1 in 20) of erroneously rejecting the null hypothesis when the null hypothesis is indeed true. The *Type II error,* or *β error,* is the chance of erroneously failing to reject the null hypothesis when it is false. In other words, it is the chance of failing to show a difference that in fact exists.

The *power* of a study is the probability of rejecting the null hypothesis when indeed there is a difference of specified size between the study groups. The power is the complement of the β error or:

$1 - β$ = power of the study

If $β = 0.20$, then the power of the study is $1.00 - 0.20 = 0.80$, indicating an 80% chance of detecting a difference if the "true" difference between groups is equal to or greater than the magnitude of the difference specified during the study design phase.

The *sample size calculation* begins with the alternate hypothesis, that is, the expected magnitude of the effect of the treatment or of the association with the risk factor being studied. These values are often estimated from previously published reports or, if such reports are unavailable, the investigators may choose a minimum effect that might be considered clinically meaningful. This is an important step, requiring the clinician's careful judgment. The total sample size is related to the significance level, or $α$; the power $(1 - β)$; and the magnitude of the effect. The necessary sample size increases if the power of the study increases or the significance level $α$ decreases.

The medical literature, including ophthalmic literature, unfortunately has a sizable number of studies with negative results, frequently the consequence of inadequate sample size. Studies that fail to find a clinical and statistical difference should include the intended sample size and power calculation. Numerous formulas are found in statistical textbooks and computer programs that can generate sample size calculations. It is beyond the scope of this section to provide such material. More important, it must be stressed that clinical research is a collaborative effort among clinicians, statisticians, and epidemiologists. Expertise from each of these disciplines should be used in the development phase of any study.

Colton T. *Statistics in Medicine.* Boston: Little, Brown & Co; 1974.

Snedecor GW, Cochran WG. *Statistical Methods.* 6th ed. Ames: Iowa State University Press; 1968.

BASIC TEXTS

General Medicine

Adams RD, Victor M, Ropper AH, eds. *Principles of Neurology.* 6th ed. New York: McGraw-Hill, 1997.

Bennett JC, Plum F, eds. *Cecil Textbook of Medicine.* 20th ed. Philadelphia: Saunders; 1996.

Berkow R, Fletcher AJ, eds. *The Merck Manual of Diagnosis and Therapy.* 16th ed. Rahway, NJ: Merck Research Laboratories; 1992.

Braunwald E, ed. *Heart Disease: A Textbook of Cardiovascular Medicine.* 5th ed. Philadelphia: Saunders; 1997.

Cancer: Rates and Risks. 4th ed. Bethesda, MD: National Institutes of Health; 1996.

Diabetes in America. 2nd ed. Bethesda, MD: National Institutes of Health; 1995.

DeVita VT Jr, Hellman S, Rosenberg SA, eds. *Cancer: Principles and Practice of Oncology.* 5th ed. Philadelphia: Lippincott-Raven; 1997.

Fauci AS, Braunwald E, Isselbacher KJ, et al, eds. *Harrison's Principles of Internal Medicine.* 14th ed. New York: McGraw-Hill; 1998.

Kelley WN, Harris ED Jr, Ruddy S, et al, eds. *Textbook of Rheumatology.* 5th ed. Philadelphia: Saunders; 1997.

Mandell GL, Bennett JE, Dolin R, eds. *Mandell, Douglas and Bennett's Principles and Practice of Infectious Diseases.* 4th ed. New York: Churchill Livingstone; 1995.

Wilson J, Foster DW, Kronenberg H, et al, eds. *Williams Textbook of Endocrinology.* 9th ed. Philadelphia: Saunders; 1998.

CREDIT REPORTING FORM

BASIC AND CLINICAL SCIENCE COURSE
Section 1

1998–1999

CME Accreditation

The American Academy of Ophthalmology is accredited by the Accreditation Council for Continuing Medical Education to sponsor continuing medical education for physicians.

The American Academy of Ophthalmology designates this educational activity for a maximum of 30 hours in category 1 credit toward the AMA Physician's Recognition Award. Each physician should claim only those hours of credit that he/she has actually spent in the educational activity.

If you wish to claim continuing medical education credit for your study of this section, you must complete and return the study question answer sheet on the back of this page, along with the following signed statement, to the Academy office. This form must be received within 3 years of the date of purchase.

I hereby certify that I have spent _____ (up to 30) hours of study on the curriculum of this section, and that I have completed the study questions. (The Academy, *upon request,* will send you a transcript of the credits listed on this form.)

☐ *Please send credit verification now.*

Signature _____

                                                                  Date

Name:_____

Address: _____

City and State:_____ Zip: _____

Telephone: (_____) _____ *Academy Member ID# _____
            area code

* *Your ID number is located following your name on any Academy mailing label, in your Membership Directory, and on your Monthly Statement of Account.*

Section Evaluation

Please indicate your response to the statements listed below by placing the appropriate number to the left of each statement.

1 = agree strongly
2 = agree
3 = no opinion
4 = disagree
5 = disagree
   strongly

_____ This section covers topics in enough depth and detail.

_____ This section's illustrations are of sufficient number and quality.

_____ The references included in the text provide an appropriate amount of additional reading.

_____ The study questions at the end of the book are useful.

In addition, please attach a separate sheet of paper to this form if you wish to elaborate on any of the statements above or to comment on other aspects of this book.

Please return completed form to: **American Academy of Ophthalmology**
P.O. Box 7424
San Francisco, CA 94120-7424
ATTN: Clinical Education Division

SECTION COMPLETION FORM

BASIC AND CLINICAL SCIENCE COURSE

ANSWER SHEET FOR SECTION 1

Question	Answer	Question	Answer	Question	Answer
1	a b c d	18	a b c d e	35	a b c d e
2	a b c d	19	a b c d e	36	a b c d e
3	a b c d e	20	a b c d e	37	a b c d
4	a b c d	21	a b c d e	38	a b c d
5	a b c d	22	a b c d	39	a b c d e
6	a b c d	23	a b c d	40	a b c d
7	a b c d e	24	a b c d	41	a b c d e
8	a b c d	25	a b c d	42	a b c d e
9	a b c d e	26	a b c d e	43	a b c d e
10	a b c d e	27	a b c d e	44	a b c d
11	a b c d e	28	a b c d e	45	a b c d e
12	a b c d e	29	a b c d e	46	a b c d e
13	a b c d e	30	a b c d e	47	a b c d
14	a b c d e	31	a b c d	48	a b c d
15	a b c d e	32	a b c d	49	a b c d e
16	a b c d e	33	a b c d	50	a b c d e
17	a b c d e	34	a b c d		

STUDY QUESTIONS

STUDY QUESTIONS

1. Antiphospholipid antibodies

    a. Are found in the majority of patients with systemic lupus.
    b. Have been associated with vascular diseases of the eye.
    c. May cause serious systemic bleeding episodes.
    d. Are associated with positive tuberculin skin testing.

2. The International Normalized Ratio (INR)

    a. Modifies standard partial thromboplastin time (PTT) reporting.
    b. Should be higher when treating deep venous thrombosis than when using anticoagulants for patients with prosthetic cardiac valves.
    c. Should be 1.5–2.5 in patients with mechanical replacement valves.
    d. Was developed to standardize both intra- and interlaboratory measurement of the effect of anticoagulation therapy.

3. Which of the following statements regarding patient compliance is true?

    a. Approximately 75% of patients with chronic illnesses can be expected to comply with treatment recommendations.
    b. Compliance aids such as proper labeling, reminder charts, and special medication containers do not help improve compliance.
    c. Long-term therapy is more likely to be followed than short-term therapy.
    d. Strategies employing multiple compliance aids are no better at improving compliance rates than those using only a single aid.
    e. As disease symptoms increase, compliance tends to decrease.

4. Which of the following statements regarding the elderly population is true?

    a. Deleterious psychological changes are universal.
    b. The suicide rate is much higher among women than men.
    c. Treatment of depression may reverse symptoms of dementia.
    d. Psychotherapy is usually ineffective.

5. Which of the following statements about the development of osteoporosis is true?

    a. Systemic diseases do not influence the rate of bone loss.
    b. Racial and sexual differences affect the relative risk of developing the disease.
    c. Sedentary lifestyle, nulliparity, and cigarette smoking all reduce the incidence.
    d. Lifetime fracture risk is independent of peak bone mass.

6. Which of the following statements regarding the diagnostic evaluation of osteoporosis is true?

   a. Medical evaluation is not usually necessary.
   b. Radiographic changes can be detected when approximately 10% of bone mass has been lost.
   c. Exposure to radiation limits the usefulness of x-ray absorptiometry.
   d. The diagnosis of osteoporosis is made when bone density measurements fall more than 2.5 SD below the mean normal value established for young adults.

7. Laboratory evaluation of thyroid function has been greatly improved in recent years by

   a. Wide availability of direct determination of free T_4.
   b. Development of immunometric assays of TSH levels (TSH-IMA).
   c. Improved testing of serum T_3 levels.
   d. a and b.
   e. b and c.

8. Hashimoto thyroiditis

   a. Is associated with specific HLA antigens.
   b. Is unrelated to other autoimmune diseases.
   c. Presents with symptoms of hyperthyroidism.
   d. Causes eosinophilic infiltration of the thyroid gland.

9. Clinical manifestations of cerebral ischemia include:

   a. Paresis
   b. Amaurosis fugax
   c. Diplopia
   d. All of the above
   e. a and b only

10. The most sensitive diagnostic modality for determining the presence of intracranial hemorrhage is

    a. Magnetic resonance imaging (MRI)
    b. Magnetic resonance cerebral angiography (MRA)
    c. Computed tomography (CT)
    d. Duplex ultrasonography
    e. Diffusion-weighted echo-planar MR imaging

11. Elevated plasma homocysteine levels have been linked to

    a. Extracranial carotid stenosis
    b. Increased risk of stroke
    c. Increased risk of occlusive vascular disease
    d. Folate deficiency
    e. All of the above

12. All of the following are examples of recent emergence of bacterial resistance to antibiotics except:

    a. Vancomycin-resistant enterococci
    b. Penicillin-resistant pneumococci
    c. Penicillin-resistant gonococci
    d. Penicillin-resistant beta-hemolytic streptococci
    e. Cephalosporin-resistant *Haemophilus influenzae*

13. Each of the following drugs has been used for the treatment of CMV retinitis except:

    a. Cidofovir
    b. Famciclovir
    c. Foscarnet
    d. Ganciclovir
    e. Fomivirsen

14. Which of the following is not a useful biochemical marker for the detection of myocardial infarction?

    a. Troponin T
    b. Aldose reductase
    c. Troponin I
    d. Creatinine kinase MB isoenzyme
    e. Myoglobin

15. A 52-year-old man is experiencing shortness of breath, palpitations, and light-headedness as a result of paroxysmal atrial tachycardia. Which of the following is the best agent for immediate treatment?

    a. Propranolol
    b. Procainamide
    c. Adenosine
    d. Sotalol
    e. Amiodarone

16. What is the recommended initial therapy for a 33-year-old man with no other cardiac risk factors who has an LDL-cholesterol level of 200 mg/dL?

    a. Nicotinic acid
    b. Step-one diet
    c. Gemfibrozil
    d. Lovastatin
    e. Colestipol

17. Which of the following statements is false?

    a. Moderate alcohol consumption has been shown to increase HDL-cholesterol levels.
    b. Alpha-adrenergic blockers may reduce cholesterol levels.
    c. Beta-adrenergic blockers may reduce cholesterol levels.
    d. Simvastatin is one of the HMG-CoA reductase inhibitors.
    e. Cholestyramine is a bile acid sequestrant.

18. Which of the following is not a risk factor for hypertension?

    a. Sodium intake
    b. Alcohol consumption
    c. Sedentary lifestyle
    d. Obesity
    e. Smoking

19. All of the following drugs may be used in the treatment of asthma except:

    a. Albuterol
    b. Propranolol
    c. Cromolyn
    d. Beclomethasone
    e. Salmeterol

20. The most effective nonsteroidal anti-inflammatory drug is

    a. Indomethacin
    b. Aspirin
    c. Naproxen
    d. Sulindac
    e. Cannot answer the question with the information given

21. Reiter syndrome develops in a genetically susceptible host following an infection by any of the following bacteria except:

    a. *Chlamydia trachomatis*
    b. *Salmonella*
    c. *Yersinia*
    d. *Campylobacter*
    e. *Staphylococcus aureus*

22. The following study design is well suited for evaluating rare diseases efficiently:

    a. Cohort study
    b. Survey
    c. Case-control study
    d. Case series

23. The study that provides the strongest epidemiological evidence of the beneficial effect of a new treatment is

    a. Case report
    b. Randomized, controlled clinical trial
    c. Case-control study
    d. Cohort study

24. The number of cases of a disease present in a defined population at a specified time is the

    a. Incidence
    b. Relative risk
    c. Prevalence
    d. Null hypothesis

25. The potential for bias in epidemiologic studies is the greatest in the following study design:

    a. Case-control
    b. Case series
    c. Cohort
    d. Survey

26. Data from both eyes of the same individual patient may be used in the analyses if

    a. One eye is randomly selected for analyses.
    b. Separate analyses are done for the right eye or the left eye.
    c. The mean of the two eyes is assessed.
    d. Correlation between both eyes is accounted for.
    e. All of the above.

27. Following retrobulbar anesthesia using 5 cc of 2% lidocaine with 1:1000 epinephrine, a 68-year-old male experienced disorientation, nausea, vomiting, convulsions, hypotension, and respiratory arrest. Possible etiologies include all of the following except:

    a. Optic nerve sheath penetration with injection of local anesthesia
    b. Intravascular injection of local anesthesia
    c. Toxic overdose of epinephrine
    d. Hypersensitivity to lidocaine
    e. Idiosyncratic reaction to lidocaine

28. Initial treatment of the patient in the question above should be:

    a. 1:1000 epinephrine, subcutaneously or IM
    b. Oxygenation, supportive airway care, and titrated midazolam
    c. Sodium bicarbonate 50 mEq IV
    d. Demerol 50 mg IV
    e. Potassium chloride 20 mEq IV

29. A healthy 50-year-old man becomes diaphoretic and pale and collapses during a fluorescein angiogram. When called to his aid, you note a rapid, weak pulse and generalized urticaria. All of the following are appropriate therapeutic steps except:

    a.   Epinephrine (1:1000) 0.3 ml subcutaneously
    b.   Oxygen by face mask
    c.   Aminophylline 6 mg/kg IV
    d.   Hydrocortisone 500 mg IV
    e.   Diphenhydramine 50 mg IM or IV

30. A healthy 36-year-old woman is scheduled to undergo a Tensilon test (edrophonium chloride) to rule out myasthenia gravis. In discussing the possible side effects of edrophonium, you mention all of the following except:

    a.   Dry mouth
    b.   Nausea
    c.   Diaphoresis
    d.   Bradycardia
    e.   Muscle fasciculations

31. Which malignancy is responsible for producing the most cancer deaths in women in the US?

    a.   Breast
    b.   Colorectal
    c.   Lung
    d.   Ovarian

32. Which statement concerning cancer therapy is false?

    a.   Tumor cells with normal p53 genes are far more sensitive to chemotherapy than those with mutant p53 genes.
    b.   Bleomycin causes DNA-strand scission.
    c.   Antiangiogenic factors are promising new agents in the treatment of solid tumors.
    d.   New hormone chemotherapeutic agents (e.g., tamoxifen) are used in physiologic doses to inhibit growth of tumor cells.

33. Which of the following statements is true?

    a.   Hypertriglyceridemia alone, without elevated cholesterol levels, is not associated with significant incidence of coronary disease.
    b.   The presence of xanthelasma and corneal arcus in young patients is not associated with dyslipoproteinemia.
    c.   Lung cancer is the most common malignancy in women.
    d.   The prevalence of tuberculosis has remained unchanged in the United States in the last 10 years.

34. Which of the following statements about insulin-dependent diabetes mellitus (IDDM) is false?

   a. IDDM is a disorder in which there is immune-mediated destruction of the insulin-secreting beta cells of the pancreas.
   b. Anti-insulin antibodies are frequently found in the serum of these patients.
   c. Certain viruses have been demonstrated to have an association with onset of this disease.
   d. Fewer than 50% of patients with new onset IDDM have demonstrable serum titers of islet-cell antibodies.

35. In patients with AIDS, treatment of *Pneumocystis carinii* pneumonia with sulfamethoxazole-trimethoprim is frequently associated with all of the following except:

   a. Drug fever
   b. Rash
   c. Bronchospasm
   d. Thrombocytopenia
   e. Abnormal hepatic function

36. Which of the following is the *least* important as a factor influencing systolic function of the left ventricle?

   a. Aortic pressure
   b. Preload
   c. Contractility
   d. Pericardial disease
   e. Afterload

37. Which of the following ocular structures is the most radiosensitive?

   a. Retina
   b. Cornea
   c. Optic nerve
   d. Lens

38. All of the following statements about anemia of chronic disorders are true except:

   a. It results from decreased RBC survival, impaired iron metabolism, and inadequate bone marrow response.
   b. It presents as a normocytic or microcytic anemia.
   c. Hemoglobin levels are usually less than 9 g/dL in anemia of chronic disorders.
   d. It is seen in the clinical setting of chronic infections and chronic inflammatory diseases.

39. Functional visual loss is a manifestation of:

    a. A somatoform disorder
    b. An adjustment disorder
    c. Major depression
    d. Schizophrenia
    e. Malingering

40. Lyme disease histopathology is characterized by

    a. Necrotic perivascular granulomas.
    b. Sarcoid-type tissue lesions.
    c. Subdermal fat necrosis with acute and chronic inflammatory cells.
    d. Lymphocytic perivascular infiltration.

41. Which of the following antibiotics achieves an extremely high serum concentration when given orally (75% of what would be seen with intravenous administration)?

    a. Tetracycline
    b. Ampicillin
    c. Penicillin V
    d. Ciprofloxacin
    e. Sulfamethoxazole-trimethoprim

42. In treating diabetic patients with hypertension, which one of the following types of antihypertensive agents may also have a special protective effect on the kidneys?

    a. Beta blockers
    b. Direct-acting vasodilators
    c. Calcium channel blockers
    d. Diuretics
    e. ACE inhibitors

43. Which of the following groups of antihypertensive agents should be avoided in insulin-dependent diabetes mellitus patients?

    a. Diuretics
    b. Calcium channel blockers
    c. Direct-acting vasodilators
    d. Beta blockers
    e. ACE inhibitors

44. A diabetic patient taking tolbutamide is given a systematic sulfonamide for treatment of inclusion conjunctivitis. The physician should watch for:

    a. Inadequate sulfa levels, because tolbutamide interferes with sulfa absorption
    b. Hypokalemia, because sulfa potentiates excretion of potassium
    c. Hypoglycemia, because sulfa interferes with tolbutamide excretion and thus potentiates the hypoglycemic action
    d. Respiratory depression

45. Which of the following forms of therapy is considered appropriate for the patient with chronic obstructive pulmonary disease (COPD) following cataract surgery?

   a. Nasal oxygen, 10 L/minute
   b. Morphine
   c. Vigorous chest physical therapy
   d. Codeine
   e. None of the above

46. All of the following disorders are pathogenetically linked except:

   a. Rheumatoid arthritis
   b. Ankylosing spondylitis
   c. Reiter syndrome
   d. Recurrent acute iridocyclitis
   e. Psoriatic spondylitis

47. A nonimmunized individual splashed in the eye with blood that is positive for hepatitis B should

   a. Receive hepatitis B immune globulin, followed in 6 months by a full hepatitis B vaccination schedule.
   b. Receive immune globulin, followed by hepatitis B immune globulin in 1 week.
   c. Concurrently receive hepatitis B immune globulin and begin accelerated hepatitis B vaccination schedule.
   d. Concurrently receive hepatitis B vaccination and immune globulin.

48. Which statement is true regarding the pretreatment of high-risk patients prior to a fluorescein angiogram?

   a. Pretreatment has no effect on the number of repeat allergic reactions.
   b. H1 antihistamines (e.g., diphenhydramine), corticosteroids, or a combination of both greatly reduce the number of repeat allergic reactions.
   c. Vasopressors (dopamine and epinephrine) virtually eliminate repeat allergic reactions.
   d. Pretreatment is indicated only if the physician's office is not equipped with an advanced cardiac life support crash cart.

49. Regular insulin may be used in the treatment of malignant hyperthermia to:

   a. Lower body temperature
   b. Prevent myoglobin casts in the kidney
   c. Prevent the release of calcium from the sarcoplasmic reticulum
   d. Lower potassium levels
   e. Prevent metabolic alkalosis

50. Early signs of malignant hyperthermia include all of the following except:

   a. Tachycardia
   b. Skeletal muscle swelling
   c. Muscle rigidity
   d. Rapid increase in temperature
   e. Cyanosis

ANSWERS

1. Answer—b. Retinal vein and artery occlusions, retinal vasculitis, choroidal infarction, and arteritic anterior ischemic optic neuropathy have all been attributed to antiphospholipid antibodies. About 10% of lupus patients test positive for the antibodies. Clinical bleeding is rare, and the antibodies may be responsible for false-positive VDRL testing.

2. Answer—d. The INR modifies the standard prothrombin time (PT) ratio to reflect the particular thromboplastin reagent used by each laboratory, allowing standardization of therapeutic dosages. It should be lower in patients with deep venous thrombosis or tissue valves (2.0–3.0) than in those with mechanical valves (2.5–3.5).

3. Answer—e. Studies have shown that, contrary to what would be expected, patients are less likely to continue treatment as their symptoms worsen. Compliance rates in chronic illness average 50%. Compliance aids do improve compliance, more so in combination than singly.

4. Answer—c. In some elderly patients, depression may cause pseudodementia, in which symptoms of dementia are prominent. Treatment of the underlying depression can reverse these intellectual deficits. Deleterious psychological changes are not universal in the elderly, and psychotherapy and pharmacologic treatment can be highly successful. For unknown reasons, elderly men commit suicide much more commonly than elderly women.

5. Answer—b. The relative risk of developing osteoporosis is highest in white women. The risk is lower in black women and white men and lowest in black men. These differences may be explained by differences in peak bone mass, the strongest correlate of lifetime fracture risk. A variety of systemic illnesses increase the rate of bone loss, as do sedentary lifestyle, nulliparity, cigarette smoking, alcohol abuse, and insufficient dietary calcium intake.

6. Answer—d. Medical evaluation for secondary causes of osteoporosis should be pursued when the diagnosis is newly established. At least 30% of bone mass must be lost before radiographic evidence can be seen. The radiation dose of dual-photon x-ray absorptiometry is small—less than 5 millirem.

7. Answer—d. Direct measurement of free T_4 levels has greatly improved the accuracy of thyroid function testing. The TSH-IMA ("sensitive" TSH test) can differentiate between normal and reduced TSH levels. Serum T_3 levels may not accurately reflect thyroid gland function.

8. Answer—a. Hashimoto thyroiditis has been associated with specific HLA antigens (B46, DR3, DR4, DR5, and DRw53) and an increased incidence of numerous other autoimmune diseases. Patients usually present with hypothyroidism, an enlarged gland, or both. Pathologic examination shows lymphocytic infiltration.

9. Answer—e. Diplopia is a manifestation of vertebrobasilar, not cerebral, ischemia.

10. Answer—c. Of the other modalities, MRI and diffusion-weighted echo-planar MRI are best in early cerebral ischemia. MRA is best for defining structural vascular lesions (e.g., aneurysms), while duplex ultrasonography is used to determine stenotic carotid disease.

11. Answer—e. Dietary folic acid reduces plasma homocysteine levels.

12. Answer—d. Beta-hemolytic streptococci remain highly sensitive to penicillin. All of the other answers represent cases of bacterial resistance to antibiotics that have been reported in recent years.

13. Answer—b. Famciclovir is used for the treatment of herpes zoster and herpes simplex infections. All of the other drugs have been found to be useful in the treatment of CMV retinitis.

14. Answer—b. Aldose reductase is an enzyme important in the pathogenesis of diabetic microangiopathic complications. All of the others are useful biochemical markers in detecting myocardial infarction or injury.

15. Answer—c. Adenosine is currently the drug of choice for symptomatic paroxysmal atrial tachycardia.

16. Answer—b. Dietary restriction of cholesterol and saturated-fat intake is the recommended therapy for this level of hypercholesterolemia in a patient of this age with no other risk factors.

17. Answer—c. Beta blockers often cause elevation of cholesterol levels. The other statements are true.

18. Answer—e. Although smoking is a strong risk factor in the development of atherosclerotic disease and coronary heart disease, it is not a risk factor for hypertension itself.

19. Answer—b. As a beta-adrenergic blocker, propranolol is associated with bronchospasm.

20. Answer—e. Individual patients vary considerably in their responsiveness both to specific NSAIDs and dosages.

21. Answer—e. *S aureus* has not been implicated in Reiter syndrome. Fragments of *Chlamydia, Salmonella,* and *Yersinia* have been identified in the synovial tissue of patients with Reiter syndrome, but intact organisms have not been cultured.

22. Answer—c. Case-control study. It would be both difficult and inefficient to gather sufficient cases of rare diseases in other types of studies, such as surveys, to do statistical analyses.

23. Answer—b. Randomized, controlled clinical trials can balance both the known and unknown confounding factors in both the control and treated groups to provide valid conclusions regarding the efficacy of a new treatment. The other studies, observational in nature, may rarely provide answers to evaluate a new treatment.

24. Answer—c. *Prevalence* is the number of affected cases in the population at any point in time. *Incidence* is the development of disease over a defined period of time.

25. Answer—a. Case-control studies are the most prone to bias because they are usually retrospective, which often can lead to recall bias. Selection of controls may also be subject to bias.

26. Answer—e. All the methods listed in the responses deal appropriately with data from both eyes of the same individual. The researcher cannot simply pool the data from both eyes and double the sample size because of the high correlation between eyes.

27. Answer—c. Epinephrine does not produce convulsions. Although rare, hypersensitivity and idiosyncratic reactions to local anesthesia do occur. Bupivacaine and higher concentrations of lidocaine are more commonly responsible for respiratory arrest, but lower concentrations of local anesthesia may produce midbrain anesthesia.

28. Answer—b. Oxygen and supportive airway care are given to avoid cerebral hypoxia. Midazolam is now the drug of choice to suppress cortical stimulation because it has a much shorter half life than diazepam.

29. Answer—e. Antihistamines are of limited value in the treatment of acute anaphylaxis.

30. Answer—a. All of the other items are signs of cholinergic stimulation. However, administration of atropine—either as prophylaxis against, or antidote to, the cholinergic effects of edrophonium—can cause dry mouth and tachycardia.

31. Answer—c. Lung cancer causes the most cancer deaths among both men and women, even though breast cancer is the most common malignancy in women.

32. Answer—d. The hormone class of chemotherapeutic agents is used in dosages 10–100 times the normal physiologic replacement dose to inhibit growth of tumor cells.

33. Answer—a. Hypertriglyceridemia alone is not associated with a significant incidence of coronary disease. However, when hypertriglyceridemia is coupled with an elevated cholesterol level, the risk of coronary disease increases significantly.

34. Answer—d. As many as 90% of patients with new-onset IDDM have demonstrable serum titers of islet-cell antibodies.

35. Answer—c. Bronchospasm. Treatment of *Pneumocystis carinii* pneumonia in patients with AIDS is characterized by an unusually high incidence of side effects associated with sulfamethoxazole-trimethoprim therapy.

36. Answer—d. The three factors that determine ventricular systolic function are preload, afterload, and intrinsic ventricular contractility. Aortic blood pressure determines afterload and, therefore, is also a determining factor. Pericardial disease and infiltrative diseases have a greater influence on the relaxation, or diastolic, function of the ventricle.

37. Answer—d.

38. Answer—c. Anemia of chronic disorders is typically mild. A hemoglobin level of less than 9 g/dL or a hematocrit of less than 27% requires an investigation into other causes of anemia.

39. Answer—a. Functional visual loss is an example of a conversion disorder, a type of somatoform disorder. The symptoms are not under the patient's control. It is not a component of the adjustment disorders, major depression, or schizophrenia. Malingering is the intentional production of symptoms for a secondary gain.

40. Answer—d. Histopathologically, Lyme disease resembles syphilis.

41. Answer—e. After a single oral dose of sulfamethoxazole-trimethoprim, serum levels are about 75% of the concentration that would be achieved if the antibiotics were given intravenously. Sulfamethoxazole-trimethoprim is an extremely broad-spectrum antibiotic, having activity against Enterobacteriaceae usually comparable to that of a third-generation cephalosporin or even an aminoglycoside.

42. Answer—e. Studies of diabetic nephropathy suggest that ACE inhibitors may possess specific advantages in decreasing proteinuria and slowing progression of renal failure.

43. Answer—d. Beta blockers interfere with the catecholamine-induced counter-regulatory response to insulin-induced hypoglycemia. Symptoms of hypoglycemia, such as palpitation, tremor, and feelings of anxiety, may be blunted and hypoglycemia prolonged.

44. Answer—c. The mechanism of drug interaction is alteration of drug excretion. Notifying the patient's family physician or internist regarding the ocular treatment may help alleviate this problem.

45. Answer—e. High-flow nasal oxygen, morphine, vigorous chest physical therapy, and codeine are all hazardous to a patient with COPD following cataract surgery. High-flow nasal oxygen would depress the brain respiratory centers; morphine and codeine similarly suppress breathing. Vigorous chest physical therapy would be contraindicated in a recent postoperative cataract patient.

46. Answer—a. Ankylosing spondylitis, Reiter syndrome, recurrent acute iridocyclitis, and psoriatic spondylitis are all associated with HLA-B27. Ankylosing spondylitis has the strongest association, with 90% of patients being HLA-B27 positive; Reiter syndrome has a two-thirds association; and in recurrent acute iridocyclitis and psoriatic spondylitis, half of patients are HLA-B27 positive. Furthermore, the characteristic ocular lesion in ankylosing spondylitis, Reiter syndrome, and psoriatic spondylitis is recurrent acute iridocyclitis. Rheumatoid arthritis is not an HLA-B27–associated disease and has no association with iridocyclitis.

47. Answer—c. Individuals previously immunized with hepatitis B vaccine should have their protective antibody levels checked and, if they are not sufficiently elevated, should follow the recommended postexposure prophylaxis protocol.

48. Answer—b. Pretreatment with H1 antihistamines, such as diphenhydramine, and/or corticosteroids, has been shown to greatly reduce the number of repeat allergic reactions. Vasopressors such as dopamine or epinephrine may be used to support blood pressure once anaphylaxis has begun; however, they have no role in pretreatment.

49. Answer—d. Ten units of regular insulin may be added to 10 ml of 50% dextrose in water and given as an IV bolus if hyperkalemia occurs.

50. Answer—b. Skeletal muscle swelling, left heart failure, and disseminated intravascular coagulopathy are late clinical signs of malignant hyperthermia.

INDEX

Amantadine, 60t
Amaurosis fugax, in carotid stenosis, 80–81
Amethopterin, 189t
Amikacin, 57t
Amiloride, 73t
Aminocyclitols. *See* Aminoglycosides
Aminoglycosides, 42, 57t. *See also specific agent*
Aminopenicillins, 40
Aminophylline, for medical emergencies, 228t
Amiodarone, for arrhythmias, 110t
Amlodipine
  adverse effects of, 74t
  for angina, 93
Amoxicillin, 40, 50t
  with clavulanic acid, 42, 51t
  for endocarditis prophylaxis, 12–13t
    guidelines for use on day of surgery and, 245
Amphetamines, abuse of, 199t, 200
Amphotericin B, 59t
Ampicillin, 40, 50t
  for endocarditis prophylaxis, 12–13t
    guidelines for use on day of surgery and, 245
  with sulbactam, 42, 50t
Amrinone, for heart failure, 101
Amyloidosis, 132
Ana-Kit, 233
Analysis of variance, 265
Analytic studies, 251, 253, 255–262
Anaphylactoid reactions, 232
Anaphylaxis, 232–233
  local anesthetics causing, 235
Anaplastic carcinoma, of thyroid gland, 175
Androgens, in cancer chemotherapy, 192
Anemia, 128–130
  of chronic disorders, 129
  in elderly patients, 129
  ophthalmologic considerations and, 129–130
  physiologic, 129
  sickle cell, 129
Anesthetics, local, adverse reactions to, 235–236, 243, 247–248
  allergic, 235, 243
  toxic, 235–236, 248

Aneurysms
  berry, 79
  ruptured, intracranial hemorrhage caused by, 78, 80
Angiitis, Churg-Strauss (allergic granulomatosis), 147–148
Angina pectoris, 85. *See also* Ischemic heart disease
  functional classification of, 85, 86t
  medical management of, 92–93
  stable, 86
  surgical management of, 93–94
  unstable, 86
  variant (Prinzmetal), 87
    positive ergonovine response in, 90
Angiography
  cerebral
    magnetic resonance, in cerebrovascular ischemia/infarction, 77
    in subarachnoid hemorrhage, 80
  coronary, 90–91
Angioid streaks, in pseudoxanthoma elasticum, 132
Angioplasty, percutaneous transluminal coronary
  for acute myocardial infarction, 95
  for ischemic heart disease, 93
Angiotensin-converting enzyme inhibitors
  adverse effects of, 74t
  guidelines for use on day of surgery and, 244
  for heart failure, 100–101
  for hypertension, 65, 66t, 70t, 74t
  interactions of, 67–68t
  renal failure in diabetes prevented by, 166
Angiotensin II receptor antagonists, for hypertension, 70t
Anisoylated plasminogen streptokinase activator complex (APSAC), for acute myocardial infarction, 94–95
Ankylosing spondylitis, 140–141
Antacids, drug interactions and, 238t
Anterior uveitis, in seronegative spondyloarthropathies, 39
Anthracyclines, in cancer chemotherapy, 193
Antiangiogenic factors, in cancer treatment, 193

Antianxiety drugs, 204–206, 205*t*
Antiarrhythmic drugs, 108, 110*t*
Antibacterial agents, 37–45, 49–58*t. See also specific agent*
Antibiotic-associated diarrhea, 12
Antibiotics, 37–48, 49–60*t. See also specific agent*
  beta-lactam, 38–42
  in cancer chemotherapy, 190*t,* 193
  resistance to, 39
  update on, 37–45
Anticardiolipin antibodies, 136
Anticholinergics, for pulmonary diseases, 124, 124*t*
Anticoagulants
  circulating
    hemostatic abnormalities and, 135–136
    lupus, 136
  therapeutic, 136. *See also specific agent*
    drug interactions and, 238*t,* 239*t*
    for threatened stroke, 77–78
Anticonvulsant drugs, guidelines for use on day of surgery and, 244
Antidepressants, 206–208, 207*t*
  heterocyclic, 207–208, 207*t*
Antifolates, in cancer chemotherapy, 189*t,* 192
Antifungal agents, 47, 59*t*
Antigenic surface variation, as microbial virulence factor, 8
Antihypertensive drugs, 65–69, 70–71*t. See also specific agent*
  adverse effects of, 73–75*t*
  brand names of, 72*t*
  combination, 70–71*t*
  guidelines for initial therapy with, 66*t*
  guidelines for use on day of surgery and, 244
  interactions of, 67–68*t*
Anti-inflammatory drugs, for pulmonary diseases, 125
Anti-insulin antibodies, in diabetes mellitus, 156
Antimetabolites, in cancer chemotherapy, 189*t,* 192
Antimicrobial prophylaxis for endocarditis, 10–13*t*
  guidelines for use on day of surgery and, 245

Antimicrobial susceptibility testing, 39
Antineutrophil cytoplasmic antibodies, in Wegener granulomatosis, 148
Antinuclear antibodies
  in juvenile rheumatoid arthritis, 142
  in systemic lupus erythematosus, 142
Antiphospholipid antibodies, 136
Antiplatelet therapy. See also *Aspirin*
  for threatened stroke, 78
Antipsychotic drugs, 203–204, 204*t*
  ocular side effects of, 208
Antipurines, in cancer chemotherapy, 189*t,* 192
Antipyrimidines, in cancer chemotherapy, 189*t,* 192
Antithyroid antibodies, testing for, 172
Antitrypsin deficiency, alpha-1, in emphysema, 121
Antitumor antibiotics, 190*t,* 193
Antiviral agents, 45–47, 60*t*
Anxiety, drugs for management of, 204–206, 205*t*
Aortic arch arteritis (Takayasu arteritis), 147*t,* 150
Aortic coarctation, hypertension in, 63
Aortic valve stenosis, percutaneous balloon valvuloplasty for, 102
Aortitis syndrome (Takayasu arteritis), 147*t,* 150
Aplastic anemia, chloramphenicol causing, 43–44
Apraclonidine, drug interactions and, 238*t*
Aprindine, for arrhythmias, 110*t*
APSAC. *See* Anisoylated plasminogen streptokinase activator complex
Aqueous penicillin, 49*t*
ARC. *See* AIDS-related complex
Argon laser, for atheromatous lesion removal, 93
Arithmetic mean, 262
  standard deviation used with, 263
Arrhythmias, 103–109, 110*t. See also specific type*
  after myocardial infarction, 95
Arteriography. *See* Angiography
Arteriovenous anastomoses, retinal, in Takayasu arteritis, 150
Arteriovenous malformation, subarachnoid hemorrhage caused by, 79–80

Carotid bruits, 80–82. *See also* Carotid
    artery disease
Carotid endarterectomy, for carotid
    stenosis, 80–82
Carotid stenosis, 80–82. *See also* Carotid
    artery disease
Case-control studies, 252*t*, 257–259
    strengths and weaknesses of, 253*t*
Case reports/series, 252*t*, 254
    strengths and weaknesses of, 253*t*
Cataract
    in diabetes, 167
    radiation causing, 187
CAV. *See* Cytomegalovirus
CD4+ T cells, in HIV infection/AIDS, 27
Cefaclor, 53*t*
Cefadroxil, 52*t*
    for endocarditis prophylaxis, 12*t*
Cefamandole, 52*t*
Cefazolin, 52*t*
    for endocarditis prophylaxis, 12*t*
Cefepime, 54*t*
Cefixime, 54*t*
Cefmetazole, 54*t*
Cefonicid, 52*t*
Cefoperazone, 53*t*
Cefotaxime, 53*t*
Cefotetan, 53*t*
Cefoxitin, 52*t*
Cefpodoxime, 54*t*
Cefprozil, 54*t*
Ceftazidime, 53*t*
Ceftibuten, 54*t*
Ceftizoxime, 54*t*
Ceftriaxone, 53*t*
Cefuroxime, 53*t*
    axetil, 53*t*
Cellular immunity, 8
    deficient, in HIV infection/AIDS, 27
Cephalexin, 52*t*
    for endocarditis prophylaxis, 12*t*
Cephalosporins, 40–41, 52–54*t*. *See also*
    specific agent
Cephamycins, 54*t*
Cerebral angiography
    magnetic resonance, in cerebrovascular
        ischemia/infarction, 77
    in subarachnoid hemorrhage, 80

Cerebral ischemia/infarction, 76–78. *See
    also* Stroke
    in diabetes, 167
Cerebrovascular disorders, 76–83. *See also
    specific type*
    in diabetes, 167
    hypertension and, 61*t*
Cervical cancer, screening for, 215
CFU-C. *See* Colony-forming unit-culture
CFU-E. *See* Colony-forming unit-erythroid
CFU-L. *See* Lymphoid stem cell
CFU-S. *See* Colony-forming unit-spleen
Chance (statistical), 251, 268–269
Chancre, syphilitic, 16
Chemical carcinogenesis, 183
Chemotherapy (cancer), 188–193,
        189–191*t*. *See also specific agent*
Chest compressions, in CPR, 226
Chest physiotherapy, postoperative, 123
Chest x-ray, in pulmonary diseases, 122
CHF. *See* Congestive heart failure
Chi-square tests, 264
Chickenpox (varicella), 24
Children
    preoperative evaluation in, 241
    preoperative sedation for, 247
Chlamydia trachomatis, 21
Chlorambucil, 188, 189*t*
    for Behçet syndrome, 151
Chloramphenicol, 43–44, 58*t*
    drug interactions and, 239*t*
Chloroprocaine, maximum safe dose
        of, 235*t*
Chlorpropamide, 163*t*
    drug interactions and, 239*t*
Cholesterol, serum levels of
    elevated. *See also* Hypercholesterolemia
        classification of, 112, 113*t*
    testing, 112–114, 113*t*, 214
Cholestyramine, for hypercholesterolemia,
        116, 117*t*
Chondritis, auricular or nasal, in relapsing
        polychondritis, 146–147
Chronic disorders, anemia of, 129
Chronic obstructive pulmonary disease,
        121–122
    in ocular surgery candidate, 242
Churg-Strauss angiitis (allergic
        granulomatosis), 147–148

Cidofovir, 46, 60*t*
  for cytomegalovirus retinitis in HIV
      infection/AIDS, 35, 46
  for herpes simplex infection, 24, 46
Cigarette smoking
  hypertension and, 64
  in pulmonary diseases, 121
    cessation and, 123
Cilastin, imipenem with, 41
Ciprofloxacin, 45, 57*t*
Cisapride, preoperative administration of,
    243, 244*t*
Cisplatin, 191*t*, 192
CK. *See* Creatinine kinase
CK-MB isoenzyme, in myocardial
    infarction, 88
CKR-5, defective genes for, HIV immunity
    and, 32
Clarithromycin, 44, 56*t*
  for endocarditis prophylaxis, 12*t*
Clavulanic acid, antibiotics combined
    with, 42. *See also specific type*
Clindamycin, 44, 56*t*
  for endocarditis prophylaxis, 12*t*
    guidelines for use on day of surgery
        and, 245
Clinical trials, 251–253, 252*t*, 259–262
  strengths and weaknesses of designs
      for, 253*t*
Clofibrate, for hypercholesterolemia,
    116, 117*t*
Clonidine
  adverse effects of, 74*t*
  guidelines for use on day of surgery
      and, 244
  for heart failure, 101
Clostridium difficile, 12
Clotrimazole, 59*t*
Cloxacillin, 40, 50*t*
Coagulation
  disorders of
    acquired, 134–136
    hereditary, 134
  intravascular, and fibrinolysis
      (disseminated intravascular
      coagulation), 135
  laboratory evaluation of, 130–132
  pathways for, 130, 131*i*
Coagulation factors, 130
  abnormalities/deficiencies of, 134

Cocaine abuse, 199*t*, 200–201
Cogan syndrome, 148
Cohort studies (follow-up studies), 252*t*,
    255–257
  analysis of data from, 266–268, 267*i*
    one vs. two eyes used in, 268
  strengths and weaknesses of, 253*t*
Colestipol, for hypercholesterolemia,
    116, 117*t*
Colitic (enteropathic) arthritis, 141
Colitis
  antibiotic-associated, 12
  granulomatous (Crohn disease), 141
  ulcerative, 141
Colonoscopy, in cancer screening, 218
Colony-forming unit-culture (CFU-C), 127
Colony-forming unit-erythroid
    (CFU-E), 127
Colony-forming unit-spleen (CFU-S), 127
Color flow Doppler echocardiography, in
    myocardial infarction, 89
Colorectal cancer, screening for, 217–218
Coma
  myxedema, 174
  nonketotic hyperglycemic-
      hyperosmolar, 165
Commissurotomy, mitral, surgical, 102
Complete (third-degree) atrioventricular
    block, 104
Completed stroke, 76
Compliance with therapy, 202
  factors improving, 203
Computed tomography
  in cerebrovascular ischemia/
      infarction, 77
  dual-energy quantitative, in
      osteoporosis, 178
  in pulmonary diseases, 122
  in subarachnoid hemorrhage, 79
Conduction disturbances, 103–105
Confidence interval, 269
Confounding, 251, 271–272
Congenital syphilis, 16
Congestive heart failure, 96–103
  classification of, 97*t*, 98
  clinical course of, 99–100
  clinical signs of, 97
  compensated, 96–97
  decompensated, 97
  diagnosis of, 98

Disseminated intravascular coagulation
   (intravascular coagulation and
   fibrinolysis), 135
Distribution, normal/gaussian, 263
Distributive shock, 231. *See also* Shock
Diuretics
   adverse effects of, 73*t*
   for cor pulmonale, 125
   drug interactions and, 239*t*
   guidelines for use on day of surgery
      and, 245
   for hypertension, 65, 66*t*, 70*t*, 73*t*
      combination medications, 70*t*, 71*t*
   interactions of, 67*t*
   for osteoporosis, 180
DKA. *See* Diabetic ketoacidosis
DNA gyrase, in quinolone mechanism of
   action, 38
DNA viruses, cancer association of,
   184–185
Dobutamine, for heart failure, 101
Dopamine
   antipsychotic mechanism of action
      and, 203–204
   for heart failure, 101
   for shock, 231
Doppler echocardiography
   color flow, in myocardial infarction, 89
   transesophageal, in cerebrovascular
      ischemia/infarction, 77
Double-blind (double-masked) study, 271
"Dowager's hump," 177
Doxazosin, for heart failure, 101
Doxorubicin, 190*t*, 193
Doxycycline, 56*t*
DPT vaccine, 223
Dressler syndrome, 92
DRS. *See* Diabetic Retinopathy Study
Drug dependence, 198, 199*t*
   physical, 198
   psychic, 198
Drug interactions, 236–237, 238–239*t*
Drug tolerance, 198
Dry eyes, in Sjögren syndrome, 145
Dual-energy quantitative computed
   tomography, in osteoporosis, 178
Dual-photon x-ray absorptiometry, in
   osteoporosis, 176, 178

Duplex ultrasonography
   in amaurosis fugax, 81
   in cerebrovascular ischemia/
      infarction, 77
DXA. *See* Dual-photon x-ray
   absorptiometry
Dyslipoproteinemia, 214
Dyspnea, 121

Early Treatment Diabetic Retinopathy
   Study, 261
EBV. *See* Epstein-Barr virus
Ecchymoses (purpura), 132
ECG. *See* Electrocardiography
Echocardiography
   in cerebrovascular ischemia/
      infarction, 77
   exercise (stress), 89
   in myocardial infarction, 89
   transesophageal Doppler, in
      cerebrovascular ischemia/
      infarction, 77
Echo-planar MR imaging, diffusion-
   weighted and hemodynamically
   weighted, in cerebrovascular
   ischemia/infarction, 77
Echothiophate, drug interactions and, 239*t*
Echothiophate iodide eye drops,
   succinylcholine and, 246
Edema, pulmonary, in congestive heart
   failure, 97
   management of, 102
Edrophonium, toxic reaction to, 236
EF. *See* Ejection fraction
Ehlers-Danlos syndrome, 132
Ejection fraction, in congestive heart
   failure, 98
Elderly. *See* Aging
Electrocardiography (ECG)
   in cerebrovascular ischemia/
      infarction, 77
   in congestive heart failure, 98
   exercise, 89
   in ischemic heart disease, 88
   preoperative, 240–241
Electrophysiologic testing, in ventricular
   arrhythmias, 108–109
ELISA. *See* Enzyme-linked immunosorbent
   assay

Gemfibrozil, for hypercholesterolemia, 116–118, 117t
Generalizability, of experimental study, 272
Generalizing estimating equations, 268
Genetic factors, in human carcinogenesis, 185
Genital ulcers, in Behçet syndrome, 150
Gentamicin, 57t
  for endocarditis prophylaxis, 13t
Gestational diabetes mellitus, 157
Giant cell (temporal) arteritis, 147, 147t, 149–150
Glaucoma, in diabetes, 167
Glipizide, 163t, 164
Glucocorticoids, 151–152
Glucose
  for medical emergencies, 228t
  plasma levels of
    in diabetes, 155, 158
      surgery and, 168, 245
      surveillance of, 164–165
    normal, 157
Glucose tolerance, abnormalities of, 157
  screening for, 218
Glucose tolerance test, 158–159, 218
Glutamate decarboxylase, in diabetes mellitus, 156
Glyburide, 163t, 164
Glycogen, in glucose homeostasis, 157–158
Glycosylated hemoglobin (fast hemoglobin/HbA₁/HbA₁C), in glucose-control surveillance, 164–165
Goiter, toxic nodular, 173
  diagnosis of, 171t
Gonococcus (Neisseria gonorrhoeae), 14–15
Goodness of fit (statistical), 264
Granulomas, conjunctival, in allergic granulomatosis, 148
Granulomatosis
  allergic (Churg-Strauss angiitis), 147–148
  Wegener, 147–149, 147t
Granulomatous colitis/ileocolitis (Crohn disease), 141
Granulomatous thyroiditis, subacute, 174

Graves disease, 172–173
  diagnosis of, 171t
  euthyroid, 173
Gray (unit of radiation), 184
Group A beta-hemolytic streptococci (Streptococcus pyogenes), 9
Guanabenz, 74t
Guanadrel, 75t
Guanethidine, 75t
Guanfacine, 74t
Gummas, syphilitic, 17
Gy. See Gray

Haemophilus influenzae, 13–14
  immunization against, 224
Hallucinations, 196
Halothane, drug interactions and, 238t
Hashimoto thyroiditis, 174–175
  hypothyroidism caused by, 174
HATTS (hemagglutination treponemal test for syphilis), 17
HbA₁. See Fast hemoglobin
HbA₁C. See Fast hemoglobin
HDL cholesterol. See High-density-lipoprotein cholesterol
Headache
  in hypertensive-arteriosclerotic intracerebral hemorrhages, 79
  in subarachnoid hemorrhage, 78
Head-tilt, chin-lift maneuver, for opening airway, 225, 226i
Heart block, 104–105
Heart disease, acquired, 85–111
  congestive failure, 96–103
  hypertension and, 61t
  ischemic, 85–96
  ophthalmologic considerations and, 111
  rhythm disturbances, 103–108, 110t
Heart failure. See Congestive heart failure
Heart transplantation, for heart failure, 102
Heart valves, replacement of, for heart failure, 102
Helper/inducer T lymphocytes, in HIV infection/AIDS, 27
Hemagglutination treponemal test for syphilis (HATTS), 17
Hemarthroses, 132
  in hemophilia, 134

Human leukocyte antigens
  in ankylosing spondylitis, 140
  in Hashimoto thyroiditis, 174
  in seronegative
      spondyloarthropathies, 140
  in systemic lupus erythematosus, 142
Human T-cell lymphotropic retrovirus type
    I (HTLV-I), 27
Human T-cell lymphotropic virus type III
    (HTLV-III), 27. *See also* Human
    immunodeficiency virus
Humoral immunity, 8
Hydralazine
  adverse effects of, 75*t*
  for heart failure, 101
  for hypertension, 66*t*, 75*t*
Hydrocortisone sodium succinate
  for medical emergencies, 228*t*
  for shock, 233
Hydroxychloroquine, retinal toxicity
    of, 139
3-Hydroxy-3-methyl glutaryl coenzyme-A
    (HMG-CoA) reductase inhibitors, for
    hypercholesterolemia, 116
Hydroxyprogesterone, in cancer
    chemotherapy, 192
Hydroxyurea, for sickle cell disease, 130
Hyperaldosteronism, hypertension in, 63
Hypercholesterolemia, 112–119
  diagnosis of, 113–114, 113*t*
  epidemiology of, 112
  treatment of, 114–118
    dietary, 114–115, 114*t*
    ophthalmologic considerations and,
        118–119
    pharmacologic, 114*t*, 115–118, 117*t*
Hyperglycemia, 158. *See also* Diabetes
    mellitus
Hypermetabolism, in hyperthyroidism,
    172–173
Hypersensitivity (allergic/leukocytoclastic)
    vasculitis, 147, 147*t*
Hypertension, 61–69
  classification of, 62–63, 62*t*
  definition of, 61
  drug therapy of, 65–69, 66–68*t*, 70–71*t*,
      72*t*, 73–75*t*. *See also*
      Antihypertensive drugs
  epidemiology of, 63

  screening for, 213–214
  secondary, 63
  treatment of, 63–69
  white coat, 63
Hypertensive-arteriosclerotic intracerebral
    hemorrhages, 79
Hyperthermia, malignant, 248, 249*t*
  preoperative evaluation of risk of, 242
Hyperthyroidism, 172–173
  secondary, diagnosis of, 171*t*
Hyphema, in sickle cell disease, 130
Hypnotic drugs, 204–206, 205*t*
  abuse of, 198–200
  drug interactions and, 239*t*
Hypochondriasis, 197
  in elderly, 201
Hypoglycemia
  insulin therapy causing, 161–162
  sulfonylurea-induced, 163
Hypoglycemic agents. *See also*
    specific type
  insulin, 159–163
  oral, 163–164, 163*t*
    drug interactions and, 239*t*
    surgery in diabetic patient and,
        168, 245
Hypometabolism, in hypothyroidism, 174
Hypothalamic-pituitary-adrenal axis (HPA
    axis), corticosteroids affecting, 152
Hypotheses
  alternative, 268
    sample size calculation and, 273
  null, 268
    types I and II errors and, 272–273
Hypothyroidism, 173–174
  diagnosis of, 171*t*
Hypovolemic shock, 231. *See also* Shock
"Hysterical blindness," 197

^{123}I, for thyroid scanning, 172
^{131}I, for Graves disease, 172
Ibuprofen, 153*t*, 154
Ibutilide, for atrial flutter, 107
ICF. *See* Intravascular coagulation
    and fibrinolysis
IDDM. *See* Insulin-dependent
    diabetes mellitus
Idiopathic thrombocytopenic purpura, 133
Idioventricular escape rhythm, 104

Psychotropic drugs, 203–208
  drug interactions and, 239t
PT. *See* Prothrombin time
PTCA. *See* Percutaneous transluminal
    coronary angioplasty
PTT. *See* Partial thromboplastin time
Pulmonary diseases, 121–125
  in allergic granulomatosis, 148
  evaluation of, 22–23
  obstructive, 121–122
    in ocular surgery candidate, 242
  postoperative considerations for patients
      with, 125
  preoperative considerations in patient
      with, 125, 242
  restrictive, 22
  treatment of, 23–25
Pulmonary edema, in congestive heart
    failure, 97
  management of, 102
Pulmonary function tests, 123
Pulseless disease (Takayasu arteritis),
    147t, 150
Purified protein derivative (PPD) test,
    23, 219
Purine antagonists, in cancer
    chemotherapy, 189t, 192
Purpura (ecchymoses), 132
  idiopathic thrombocytopenic, 133
  thrombotic thrombocytopenic, 133
PVCs. *See* Premature contractions,
    ventricular
Pyrimidine antagonists, in cancer
    chemotherapy, 189t, 192

Q wave infarction, 87
Q waves, in myocardial infarction, 88
QCT. *See* Dual-energy quantitative
    computed tomography
Quinidine, for arrhythmias, 110t
Quinolones, 38, 44–45, 57–58t. *See also*
    specific agent

Rad (unit of radiation), 184
Radiation, 186–188
  in cancer therapy, 186–188
  carcinogenic effects of, 183–184
  eye and adnexa affected by, 186–188
  tumors affected by, 186, 187t
Radiation optic neuropathy, 188

Radiation retinopathy, 187–188
Radioactive iodine
  for Graves disease, 173
  for thyroid scanning, 172
Radioactive iodine uptake, 172
Radionuclide scans
  blood-pool isotope, in ischemic heart
      disease, 89
  thallium-201, in ischemic heart disease,
      89–90
Radiosensitivity (tumor), 186, 187t. *See
    also* Radiation
RAIU. *See* Radioactive iodine uptake
Randomization, in clinical trials, 260, 271
Ranitidine, preoperative administration
    of, 243
Rapid plasma reagin test (RPR test), 17
  for screening, 219
Rauwolfia, 75t
Raynaud's phenomenon
  in scleroderma, 144
  in systemic lupus erythematosus, 142
RBBB. *See* Right bundle branch block
RBCs. *See* Red blood cells
Recall bias, 270
Red blood cells (erythrocytes), 127
  development of, 127–128
Regional enteritis (Crohn disease), 141
Regression analysis, 266
  multiple, 266
Regression line, 266
Reiter syndrome, 140
Relapsing polychondritis, 146–147
Relative risk, 213, 256
Rem (unit of radiation), 184
Renal disease
  hypertension and, 61t
  in scleroderma, 144
Renal failure, in diabetes, 166
Renovascular hypertension, 63
Rescue breathing, 225–226, 227i
Reserpine, 75t
Resistance, antibiotic, 39
Respiratory disorders. *See*
    Pulmonary diseases
Restriction, in clinical trials, 271–272
Resuscitation, cardiopulmonary, 225–229,
    226i, 227i, 229i, 230i
  medications used in, 228t

Sickle cell disease, 129
  ophthalmic manifestations of, 130
Sickle cell trait, 129
Sievert (unit of radiation), 184
Sigmoidoscopy, in cancer screening,
    216t, 217
Simvastatin, for hypercholesterolemia,
    116, 117t
Single-photon emission computed
    tomography, in ischemic heart
    disease, 90
Sinoatrial node, 103
Sinus arrest (sinus block/SA block),
    103–104
Sinus bradycardia, 103
Sjögren syndrome, 145–146, 146t
Skin tests, tuberculin, 23, 219
SLE. See Systemic lupus erythematosus
Slow-acting antirheumatic drugs, 139
Smoking
  hypertension and, 64
  in pulmonary diseases, 121
    cessation and, 123
Sodium, dietary, hypertension and, 64
Sodium bicarbonate
  for medical emergencies, 228t, 231
  for shock, 231
Sodium fluoride, for osteoporosis, 180
Somatization disorder, 197
Somatoform disorders, 197–198
Somatoform pain disorder, 197
Somogyi phenomenon, 161–162
Sorivudine, 25
Sotalol, for arrhythmias, 110t
Sparfloxacin, 45, 58t
Specificity, of diagnostic test, 213
SPECT. See Single-photon emission
    computed tomography
Spironolactone, 73t
Spondylitis, ankylosing, 140–141
Spondyloarthropathies, seronegative,
    139–141. See also specific type
Spore-forming intestinal protozoa,
    gastrointestinal infection in HIV
    infection/AIDS caused by, 35
ST segment elevation, in myocardial
    infarction, 88
Stable angina pectoris, 86
Standard deviation, 263–264
Standard error, 264, 269

Staphylococcus, 8–9
  aureus, 8–9
  epidermidis, 9
Statistical association, 268–272
  sample size and power and, 272–273
  validity/generalizability/consistency
    and, 272
Statistics
  analyses used in, 264–266
  data from follow-up studies and,
    266–267, 267i
    one vs. two eyes used in, 268
  terms used in, 262–264
Status epilepticus, 234
Stavudine, for HIV infection/AIDS, 31
Stem cells, lymphoid, 127
Stents, mechanical, in coronary artery
    disease, 93
Still disease, 141–142
Stokes-Adams syndrome, 104
Stool guaiac slide test, in cancer
    screening, 216t, 217
Stratification, in clinical trials, 272
Streptococcus, 9–10
  alpha-hemolytic, endocarditis caused
    by, prophylaxis for, 10–13t
  pneumoniae (pneumococcus), 9–10
    pneumonia caused by, 9
    immunization against, 223
  pyogenes (group A beta-hemolytic), 9
Streptokinase, 136
  for acute myocardial infarction,
    94–95, 136
  for thrombotic stroke, 136
Streptomycin, 57t
  drug interactions and, 239t
Stress echocardiograpy (exercise
    echocardiography), 89
Stroke, 76–78
  completed, 76
  incidence of, 76
  partial nonprogressive, 76
  treatment of, 77–78
Student's t-test, 264–265
Subacute thyroiditis, diagnosis of, 171t
Subarachnoid hemorrhage, 78–80
  aneurysmal, 78
Substance abuse, ocular trauma and, 208
Substance abuse disorders, 198–201. See
    also specific substance

Ventricular tachyarrhythmias, 108–109
Ventricular tachycardia, 106, 108–109
  treatment of, 108, 110t
Ventricular wall, rupture of, after
  myocardial infarction, 92
Ventriculography, 90–91
Verapamil
  adverse effects of, 74t
  for angina, 93
  for arrhythmias, 110t
  for hypertension, 66t, 74t
VF. See Ventricular septum
Vidarabine, for herpes simplex
  infection, 24
Vinblastine, 190t, 193
Vinca alkaloids, in cancer chemotherapy,
  190t, 193
Vincristine, 190t, 193
Virulence (microbial), mechanisms of, 7–8
Viruses
  agents for infection caused by,
    45–47, 60t
  cancer and, 184–185
Visual loss
  in elderly, psychopathology and,
    201–202
  functional, 197
Vitamin C (ascorbic acid)
  deficiency of (scurvy), 132
  drug interactions and, 238t
Vitamin D, for osteoporosis, 178–179
Vitamin K_1, administration of to
  newborns, 135
Vitamin K deficiency, coagulation
  disorders and, 134–135
VM-26. See Teniposide
Volume expansion, for shock, 231
Volume overload, 100
Von Willebrand disease, 134

Von Willebrand factor, 134
VP-16. See Etoposide
VT. See Ventricular tachycardia

Warfarin/warfarin derivatives, 136. See
  also Coumarin
  discontinuing before surgery, 246
Wegener granulomatosis, 147–149, 147t
Weight loss, unintended, as sign of
  diabetes mellitus, 155
Weight reduction
  blood pressure affected by, 64
  for diabetes mellitus, 158–159
Wenckebach type atrioventricular
  block, 104
Western blot analysis
  in HIV infection/AIDS, 30
  in Lyme disease, 20
White blood cells, 127
White coat hypertension, 63
Wisconsin Epidemiologic Study of
  Diabetic Retinopathy, 255–256
Wolff-Parkinson-White syndrome, 106
WPW syndrome. See Wolff-Parkinson-
  White syndrome

Xanthelasma, in dyslipoproteinemia, 214
Xanthine derivatives, for pulmonary
  diseases, 124t

Yeast infections, with *Candida albicans*,
  21–22

Zalcitabine, for HIV infection/AIDS, 31
Zidovudine, 46–47, 60t
  for HIV infection/AIDS, 30–31,
    46–47, 60t
  for postexposure prophylaxis,
    32–33, 34t